The Legacy of
JAMES BOWDOIN III

Edward Greene Malbone
Portrait of James Bowdoin III

The Legacy of
JAMES BOWDOIN III

INTRODUCTION BY
Katharine J. Watson

MFA objects: pp. 11, 18, 30, 31, 64, 81, 192, 213

ESSAYS BY
Kenneth E. Carpenter
Linda J. Docherty
Arthur M. Hussey II
Lillian B. Miller
Clifton C. Olds
Richard H. Saunders III
Susan E. Wegner

APPENDIX ESSAY BY
Laura Fecych Sprague

BOWDOIN COLLEGE MUSEUM OF ART
BRUNSWICK, MAINE 1994

The publication of *The Legacy of James Bowdoin III*
marks the Bicentennial of Bowdoin College, in
Brunswick, Maine, and the Centennial of the Walker
Art Building, today the location of the Bowdoin
College Museum of Art. This book accompanies
exhibitions of the same title at the Museum of Art
from October 15, 1993, to June 26, 1994.

Designed by Michael Mahan Graphics, Bath, Maine
Printed by Penmor Lithographers, Lewiston, Maine
All Bowdoin College Museum of Art photographs by
    Dennis Griggs unless otherwise noted
Cover photograph and frontispiece by
    Melville D. McLean, Fine Art Photography

Front and back covers: Attributed to Frans Francken III
    (Flemish, 1607—1667), *Achilles among the
    Daughters of Lycomedes* (detail) (painting in color on
    p. 152). Oil on panel.
    20 1/16 x 31 11/16 inches. Bequest of the
    Honorable James Bowdoin III. 1813. 2

Frontispiece: Edward Greene Malbone
    (American, 1777–1807), *Portrait of James Bowdoin III.*
    Watercolor on ivory, 3 1/4 x 2 1/2 inches. Gift
    of Mrs. Dorothy Hupper in honor of President
    Kenneth C. M. Sills '01 and Mrs. Sills h '52. 1951.7

ISBN: 0-916606-27-9

Library of Congress Catalog Card Number: 93-79512

For James Bowdoin III, Harriet Sarah Walker, and Mary Sophia Walker
on the occasion of Bowdoin College's Bicentennial and the
Walker Art Building's Centennial

The Legacy of James Bowdoin III is dedicated to the first major donor to
Bowdoin College, who in 1811 bequeathed works of art, scientific collections,
and a library to the College named for his father; it is also dedicated to
Harriet Sarah Walker and Mary Sophia Walker, whose gift in 1894
of the Walker Art Building, today the location of the
Bowdoin College Museum of Art, realized fully the promise implicit
in James Bowdoin III's bequest.

CONTENTS

PREFACE

*T*he Legacy of James Bowdoin III commemorates the founding of Bowdoin College, which was chartered by the General Court of the Commonwealth of Massachusetts on 24 June 1794, and the opening in February 1894 of the Walker Art Building, the gift of the sisters Harriet Sarah and Mary Sophia Walker in memory of their uncle, Theophilus Wheeler Walker. The title refers not only to this book of scholarly essays but also to the brochure and exhibitions, lectures, gallery talks, and performances that accompany it at the Bowdoin College Museum of Art through the academic year 1993–1994.

The chief goal of *The Legacy of James Bowdoin III* is to deepen knowledge and understanding of James Bowdoin, of the art, science, and library collections that he bequeathed, and of the role those collections have played in Bowdoin's and the nation's cultural history. In this centennial and bicentennial year, as the College and museum review their mission, it is critical that James Bowdoin III's enlightenment philosophy of education, as evidenced by his bequest, be remembered. By defining for the first time the significance of his legacy, the book and educational programs will be of assistance to that process of institutional self-evaluation.

A second goal of the *Legacy* project relates particularly to James Bowdoin III's gifts of art but can be applied to the other collections as well. By creating greater campus and public awareness of his donation of paintings, drawings, and a few prints, the book may encourage fuller assimilation of those collections and of the later gifts of art those collections stimulated into the life of the College. As the presence of art at Bowdoin from 1811 led to further donations and, by 1894, to the construction of the Museum of Art, so the combination of collections and the building to house them inspired in the twentieth century the teaching of art within the College's curriculum. Together these developments form one of the longest continuing traditions of the visual arts in the history of American culture.

A final goal of *The Legacy of James Bowdoin III* is to bring to appropriate conclusion the Walker Art Building's first century and at the same time to make way for the museum's increasingly vital role in the future of the College. The introspection of the project prepares a base from which the museum may develop, in the coming decades, a broader, more diverse perspective and an increasingly interdisciplinary intellectual ambition.

Katharine J. Watson
Director, Bowdoin College Museum of Art

ACKNOWLEDGMENTS

For the Bowdoin College Museum of Art, *The Legacy of James Bowdoin III* is a project that has taken a decade of preparation. It combines exhibitions from the permanent collections for which all of the museum's galleries have been reinstalled, a brochure for those exhibitions, a book of essays, and educational events scheduled throughout the academic year 1993–1994. The campus and community beyond have responded with generosity to the challenge of this bicentennial and centennial commemoration. In addition to the book's authors, professionals from other museums and libraries, scholars from within and outside the College, and Bowdoin students, graduates, parents, administrators, staff, museum volunteers, and bicentennial committees have assisted. With determination, skill, and grace, members of the Museum of Art staff realized the *Legacy* exhibitions, publications, and programming to a level of excellence especially deserving of recognition and appreciation.

The essays in the book *The Legacy of James Bowdoin III* comprise a new chapter in the history of American culture. This achievement is a collaborative venture to which the authors have given unstintingly of their time and expertise. Their work has been characterized by exceptional willingness to share intellectual methodology, research discoveries, technical information, and writing, editing, and exhibition curatorial responsibilities. The *Legacy* authors have received assistance not only from each other but from many individuals whose names are acknowledged in the essays and below.

Dianne M. Gutscher, curator, and Susan B. Ravdin '80, assistant curator, of Special Collections in the College's Hawthorne-Longfellow Library, responded to many questions and requests for aid, as did their colleagues at the Harvard University Archives, the Maine Historical Society, and the Massachusetts Historical Society. Charles C. Calhoun, author of the bicentennial history, *A Small College in Maine: Two Hundred Years of Bowdoin*, offered insight and information, including photographic references.

Sheila Rideout, a museum volunteer and docent, did extensive research on James Bowdoin III. She discovered the unpublished travel diary of Ward Nicholas Boylston at the Massachusetts Historical Society, which is referred to by several of the essayists. Her scholarship has served as a source for the museum's public education programs. Excerpts from the diary and unpublished documents in the society's collections are quoted with the permission of the Massachusetts Historical Society, Boston.

The work of three scholars provided a research base for discussion of the art building commission in a number of the *Legacy* essays. In 1972, Richard V. West, at that time director of the museum, published *The Walker Art Building Murals,* Occasional Papers I of the Bowdoin College Museum of Art. In 1985, Eileen Sinnott Pols '79 completed her art history master's thesis, *The Walker Art Building, 1894: Charles F. McKim's First Museum Design,* for the University of Texas at Austin. In 1990, Ann E. Robertson '90 wrote her art history undergraduate honors paper, *The Facade of the Walker Art Building: Indicator of the Architect's and Patrons' Intentions.* Ms. Pols was also helpful in advising two of the authors and the editor on material presented in her thesis.

Philip C. Beam, Henry Johnson Professor of Art and Archaeology Emeritus, and director of the museum from 1939 to 1964, provided valuable perspective on the history of the arts at Bowdoin College in his *Personal Recollections* of 1991. *The Legacy of James Bowdoin III* is in part shaped by his memories.

Susan L. Ransom, college publications editor, drafted initial descriptions of the whole project, established and monitored the publication schedule, and worked directly with each author on multiple text drafts. Ms. Ransom also wrote the exhibition brochure text.

Lucie G. Teegarden, director of publications for the College, oversaw the production of book and brochure. Ms. Teegarden and Ms. Ransom collaborated with Michael W. Mahan '73 of Mahan Graphics, who designed the publications. Dennis Griggs of Tannery Hill Studio took all the new photographs for the book and the brochure except the ones for the cover and the frontispiece, which were taken by Melville D. McLean, Fine Art Photography. Alice Steinhardt, slide curator of the College's Department of Art, unearthed photographic material for the book. Nick Humez compiled the book's index.

There are other contributors who joined in early discussions of *The Legacy of James Bowdoin III* to whom I wish to extend thanks. Martha G. Fales, a historian of American decorative arts, advised on archival, bibliographic, and collection research. Roger Howell, Jr. '58, William R. Kenan, Jr., Professor of Humanities, and president of Bowdoin College from 1969 to 1978, listened to early ideas about James Bowdoin III and John Smibert and guided research at the Public Records Office in London. Paul L. Nyhus, Frank Andrew Munsey Professor of History, encouraged *The Legacy of James Bowdoin III* from its inception, critiqued relevant lectures, and read drafts. Laurence B. Kantor, curator of the Robert Lehman Collection, Metropolitan Museum of Art, traveled to Brunswick to advise on the frames from the James Bowdoin III bequest of paintings. Dorothy Schwartz, executive director of the Maine Humanities Council, endorsed further study of James Bowdoin III, gave the first opportunity to present ideas publicly about the project, and informed the museum on outreach and education.

Ms. Schwartz, together with Henry Adams, then Samuel Sosland Curator of American Art, the Nelson-Atkins Museum of Art; Anne Palumbo, program coordinator, Art in Public Places for Prince George's County, Maryland; and Gary Kulik, assistant director for academic programs and editor of the *American Quarterly* at the National Museum of American History, Smithsonian Institution, assessed the project and gave support to the Museum of Art's funding requests.

Bowdoin undergraduates were crucial to research, transcribing and compiling archival documentation, gathering statistics, and checking text, footnotes, and bibliographies for the book. A number of students actually collaborat-

ed with the publication scholars; others discovered information through course assignments or honors papers which was subsequently used in essays. Jennifer S. Edwards '89 and Joanne E. Thompson '88 assisted Linda Docherty. Marie E. Bengtsson '81, Ms. Edwards, Cecile M. Green '88, Elizabeth H. Humphreys '93, Anita L. Kimball '90, Ann E. Robertson '90, and John R. Ward '83 provided material used by Susan Wegner. Shelley Langdale '85 and Julie McGee '82 compiled the inventory of James Bowdoin's paintings for Professor Wegner. Jo Kristin Johnson '94 and Jessica R. Skwire '94 aided Kenneth Carpenter. Ashley G. Wernher '93 catalogued the James Bowdoin III library on the computer for Mr. Carpenter. Christopher A. Row '94 and Meredith L. Sherter '93 checked footnotes, and Sara A. Pekow '95 worked on the bibliography for the whole book.

The exhibitions and educational programs for *The Legacy of James Bowdoin III* involved another cast of professionals outside of Bowdoin, the museum staff, volunteers, and students.

Gratitude must be expressed to those who facilitated the loans to the exhibition: Erik C. Jorgensen '87, director, Pejepscot Historical Society; Miss Susan L. Chandler; Louis L. Tucker, director, Massachusetts Historical Society; Dianne M. Gutscher and Susan B. Ravdin '80, Special Collections, Hawthorne-Longfellow Library; and Arthur M. Hussey II, Department of Geology, Bowdoin College.

For five years, works of art from James Bowdoin III's bequest were treated at the Williamstown Regional Art Conservation Laboratory in Williamstown, Massachusetts, in preparation for exhibition during *The Legacy of James Bowdoin III*. The contribution of Williamstown conservators was critical, especially that of Thomas Branchick, conservator of paintings and department head, who traveled to Bowdoin on several occasions to work on paintings and frames.

As principal installation designer, Robert Fuglestad advised on every aspect of presentation for the exhibitions, conferring with those essay authors who acted as curatorial consultants and with members of the museum staff. His commitment to the museum has been an important factor in realizing *The Legacy of James Bowdoin III*.

Many volunteers helped the professional staff as docents, office and mailing assistants, and receptionists during the installation of *The Legacy of James Bowdoin III*. Their loyalty and hard work are deeply appreciated. June Coffin, as both professional and volunteer, was particulary helpful to the staff, especially during the critical five months prior to the opening of *The Legacy*.

Without the unique circumstances of the centennial and bicentennial commemoration, *The Legacy of James Bowdoin III* would not have occurred. Essential support was given by the Bicentennial Committee, chaired by Trustee Emeritus Merton G. Henry '50 h '84 with the assistance of Vice-Chair Trustee Rosalyne S. Bernstein, and from the Museum Centennial Subcommittee members: Overseer Gordon F. Grimes '71, chair; Overseer Emeritus Timothy M. Warren '45, vice-chair; Peter C. Barnard '50, secretary emeritus, the President and Trustees, and Overseer Emeritus; Overseer David P. Becker '70; Overseer Emeritus Paul E. Gardent '39; Maria P. Gindhart '92; Barbara J. Kaster, Harrison King McCann Professor of Communication Emeritus; and James E. Ward, professor of mathematics and, in 1992–1993, dean of the College.

The funding for *The Legacy of James Bowdoin III* has come from many sources. Special gratitude is due Joanne and John W. Payson '63, Michael W. Mahan '73, Sheila and Michael Humphreys, parents of Elizabeth H. Humphreys '93, the Institute of Museum Services, a federal agency that offers support to the nation's museums, and the John Sloan Memorial Foundation, Inc. Additional support has come from the Bicentennial Observance Fund and the Museum of Art's endowments: the Class of 1976 Art Conservation Fund, the Stevens L. Frost Endowment Fund, the Elizabeth B. G. Hamlin Fund, the George Otis Hamlin Fund, the Halford and Parker Conservation Fund, the Lowell Innes Fund, and the Karl R. Philbrick Art Museum Fund.

The Association of Bowdoin Friends dedicated their annual gifts to the Museum of Art for 1991–1992 and 1992–1993 to the book *The Legacy of James Bowdoin III*. Their participation is particularly appreciated, as they represent the community beyond the campus served by the Museum of Art.

Final acknowledgments must be extended to the administration and Governing Boards of Bowdoin College, whose support of the Museum of Art and understanding of its purpose on the campus are fundamental to the achievement of every major project. In particular, I wish to thank Robert H. Edwards, president of the College, A. LeRoy Greason, former president of the College, Charles R. Beitz, dean for academic affairs, and Alfred H. Fuchs, former dean of the faculty, whose interest and commitment have been crucial to the completion of *The Legacy of James Bowdoin III*.

Katharine J. Watson

INTRODUCTION

Bowdoin College is named for James Bowdoin II (1726–1790), Boston merchant and governor of Massachusetts whose life encompassed financial and political success and intellectual achievement. His son, James Bowdoin III (1752–1811), donated land and money, art and scientific collections, and a library to endow the institution in his father's name. James III's accomplishments and reputation have been frequently confused with or overshadowed by those of his father. As a result, few people today, apart from scholars, can distinguish between the two James Bowdoins associated with the College. *The Legacy of James Bowdoin III* seeks to end this confusion, to accord the younger Bowdoin full recognition for his role in the early history of the College, and to define his place in American culture of the late eighteenth and early nineteenth centuries.

The *Legacy* also refers to the consequences of the acceptance by the College's Governing Boards of James Bowdoin III's donations. The existence of those objects at the College encouraged further, similar gifts and was an incentive for curriculum development, especially in the sciences during the nineteenth century and in the visual arts during the twentieth. The growing collections demanded new space; for example, the increasing need for an adequate facility for the art collection led eventually, between 1892 and 1894, to the construction of the Walker Art Building, the subject of the book's final essay.

Study of James Bowdoin III is long overdue. Anyone acquainted with the history of Bowdoin College feels a curious gap in information about him in view of his role as first benefactor of the school. Despite a number of scattered references to James Bowdoin III, there is no full biography. Among the most helpful published sources are the Bowdoin entries in Clifford K. Shipton's *Sibley's Harvard Graduates* and general histories of Bowdoin College, concluding with Charles C. Calhoun's *A Small College in Maine: Two Hundred Years of Bowdoin*, published in 1993 for the Bicentennial. Additional references are the series of college publications that began in 1966 with *Colonial and Federal Portraits at Bowdoin*

College by Marvin S. Sadik, then museum director. Mr. Sadik's biography of James Bowdoin in his discussion of the family portraits and his appendix essay, "James Bowdoin III as Art Collector," are the most perceptive and thorough treatment to that date. The *Colonial and Federal Portraits* catalogue encouraged Robert L. Volz's research for *Governor Bowdoin & His Family*, a Bowdoin College Hawthorne-Longfellow Library exhibition and catalogue of 1969, also a valuable source for information about James Bowdoin III.

Other information can be found in the writings of Gordon E. Kershaw, who concentrates on James Bowdoin II. In 1976, Kershaw contributed the essay *James Bowdoin: Patriot and Man of the Enlightenment* to the Museum of Art's catalogue for an exhibition of the same title organized by R. Peter Mooz, director from 1973 to 1976 of the Museum of Art. Mr. Kershaw's biography of James Bowdoin II was published in 1991 by the University Press of America.

Further testimony to James Bowdoin III's stature as collector is the catalogue *Old Master Drawings at Bowdoin College* of 1985 by David P. Becker '70, the greater part of which is devoted to an analysis of the drawings that were bequeathed along with Bowdoin's other collections in 1811. In his Introduction, Mr. Becker describes the history of the collection and surveys previous scholarship. His catalogue follows a tradition of study of the drawings which, as the oldest American collection of European drawings, have received considerable scholarly attention. In 1986, Susan E. Wegner wrote *Images of the Madonna and Child by Three Tuscan Artists of the Early Seicento: Vanni, Roncalli, and Manetti*, which was published as the Bowdoin College Museum of Art's Occasional Papers III. Both Mr. Becker's and Ms. Wegner's scholarly texts should be viewed as companion publications to the present book; because of their work, an essay on the drawings has not been included in *The Legacy of James Bowdoin III*.

Other sources of information about James Bowdoin III are the lectures I gave on his collecting with reference to John Smibert (1688–

1751). My ideas were first presented in 1982 at the symposium *Maine at Statehood: The Forgotten Years 1783–1820,* sponsored by the Maine Humanities Council, and in greater depth a year later as one of a series of campus lectures on the traditions of the College. The major achievement of that research was to demonstrate the need for some larger study of James Bowdoin III and to stimulate the interest of Bowdoin colleagues, particularly in the Department of Art, and of scholars outside the college faculty. Wherever helpful, my work has been absorbed, sometimes revised, into the texts of the *Legacy* essays.

The Legacy of James Bowdoin III was conceived by members of the Museum of Art staff and the Department of Art faculty in anticipation of the bicentennial and centennial year. Lillian B. Miller, historian of American culture and editor, the Peale Family Papers, National Portrait Gallery, Smithsonian Institution, has acted as an advisor to the project. The essay topics flow naturally from the presence of James Bowdoin III's collections and library on the campus; they also reflect, in part, the research interests of the contributing scholars.

The *Legacy* essays document and evaluate James Bowdoin's life; describe the collections he assembled and his patterns of giving; and analyze the results of his actions within the College's evolution. Particular emphasis is placed on his establishment of an art collection and the life of the collection on campus in the nineteenth and early twentieth centuries. Two essays set this focus in larger context: one examines the general history and intellectual foundations of the American college museum prior to 1894; another studies the commission of the Walker Art Building and its patrons, Harriet Sarah Walker and Mary Sophia Walker. An appendix essay summarizes the biographies of Theophilus Wheeler Walker, for whom the building is named, and of his nieces, who gave the building in his name after his death.

The cast of authors is heavily Bowdoin College-based; every author but two is either a graduate or currently a faculty member. But the issues they raise in their essays extend beyond a specific place, time, or established tradition and reflect their wide-ranging interests and larger world view. The fact that so many of the contributing scholars are part of the sponsoring institution is a deliberate and important decision. They are the closest to James Bowdoin III's collections, which some of them first knew as undergraduates, and others as teachers. They are most knowledgeable about these collections; and speaking, as they do, from inside the College, they are direct beneficiaries of James Bowdoin's bequests.

KEY

ABBREVIATIONS
BCMA is Bowdoin College Museum of Art.
BCSC is Special Collections, Hawthorne-Longfellow Library, Bowdoin College.

THE BOWDOINS
Neither James Bowdoin II nor James Bowdoin III used roman numerals in referring to himself. This designation is used as a convenience at the College and by historians.

CLASS YEARS
Holders of baccalaureate degrees from Bowdoin College are distinguished in the text with their class years after their names. Twentieth-century graduates always have the familiar apostophe and two digits (Elizabeth K. Glaser '81, for instance), while nineteenth-century graduates may have all four digits (Robert E. Peary 1877) or the more formal "Class of" designation (Alpheus Spring Packard, Class of 1816).

Holders of honorary degrees have an *h* between their names and the year the degree was awarded (Kate Douglas Wiggin Riggs h '04), and holders of degrees from the Medical School of Maine have a corresponding *m* (Henri Byron Haskell m 1855).

Holders of two or more degrees from Bowdoin have a string of numbers and letters after their names (Robert M. Cross '45 h '89).

DIMENSIONS
Height precedes width, which precedes depth.

ILLUSTRATIONS
Captions under the photographs have been kept as short as possible. Complete information on each object is in the List of Illustrations at the end of each chapter.

BOWDOIN AND WALDO
FAMILY TREE

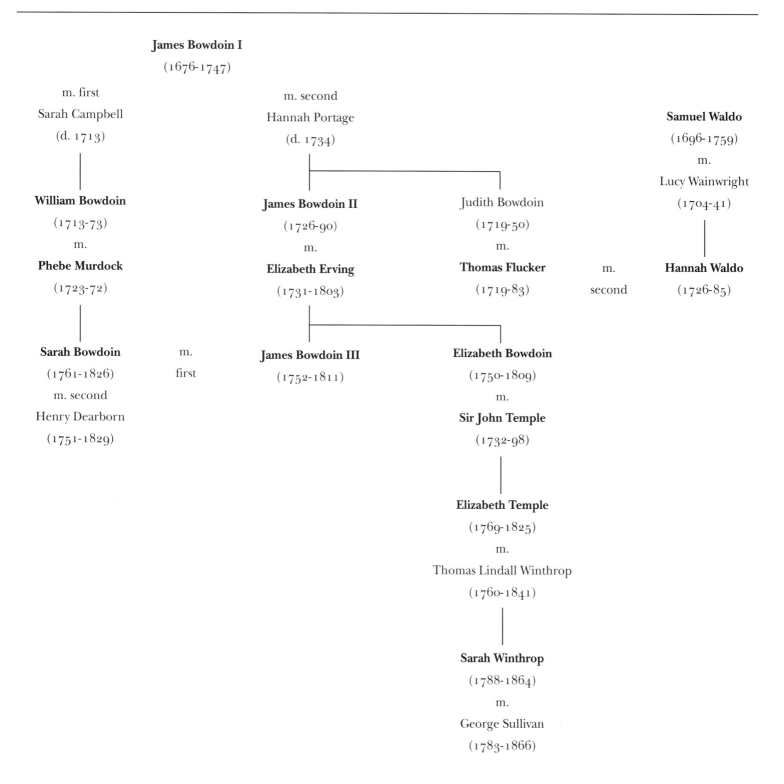

James Bowdoin I

(1676-1747)

m. first
Sarah Campbell
(d. 1713)

m. second
Hannah Portage
(d. 1734)

Samuel Waldo
(1696-1759)
m.
Lucy Wainwright
(1704-41)

William Bowdoin

(1713-73)

m.

Phebe Murdock

(1723-72)

James Bowdoin II

(1726-90)

m.

Elizabeth Erving

(1731-1803)

Judith Bowdoin

(1719-50)

m.

Thomas Flucker

(1719-83)

m.
second

Hannah Waldo

(1726-85)

Sarah Bowdoin

(1761-1826)

m. second
Henry Dearborn
(1751-1829)

m.

first

James Bowdoin III

(1752-1811)

Elizabeth Bowdoin

(1750-1809)

m.

Sir John Temple

(1732-98)

Elizabeth Temple

(1769-1825)

m.

Thomas Lindall Winthrop

(1760-1841)

Sarah Winthrop

(1788-1864)

m.

George Sullivan

(1783-1866)

Boldface indicates portrait(s) in *The Legacy of James Bowdoin III* exhibition, 1993–1994.

FIG. 1 Anonymous, *Portrait of James Bowdoin III*

JAMES BOWDOIN III
(1752–1811)

Richard H. Saunders III

On 3 January 1772, James Bowdoin II wrote a long and impassioned letter to his nineteen-year-old son, James Bowdoin III. His letter to "Jemmy," the moniker given his only male child, was prompted by the younger Bowdoin's departure for London. This first trip outside the colonies was taken primarily by the son to improve his precarious health,[1] although it also was becoming fashionable for wealthy colonial families to send their male children to London as a way to complete their education, to increase their community stature, and to enhance their job prospects. Like most fathers, Bowdoin relinquished parental control reluctantly and reminded his son that "a virtuous character, which necessarily includes self-government, a good intention of right action towards our fellow man, of a supreme regard to ye benevolent author of our Being, is ye perfection of human nature."[2] The tone of the letter (which implies that perhaps the father had reason to remind his son of the need for these qualities) expresses the heightened expectation that hovered over the younger Bowdoin throughout his adult life.

James Bowdoin III was heir to one of the largest mercantile and land fortunes in New England. His father (fig. 6), a graduate of Harvard (1745), was an ambitious and shrewd businessman who had made the Bowdoin family conspicuous in Boston society long before he was elected governor of Massachusetts in 1785. On 15 September 1748, he married Elizabeth Erving (1731-1803), the daughter of another of Boston's merchant princes, Captain John Erving, and the sister of his Harvard roommate of the same name. In succession this union produced two children, her namesake, born in 1750, and James Bowdoin III, born two years later, on 22 September 1752. The Bowdoins' commodious home (purchased from the elder Bowdoin's father-in-law in 1756)[3] was at the virtual summit of Beacon Hill in Boston at the northeast corner of what are now Beacon and Bowdoin Streets. The three-story house (torn down in 1843) was approached by a long flight of stone steps. It was adjacent to the equally substantial houses of Thomas Hancock, William Molineaux, and William Phillips—the latter being in-laws of the Ervings. Its conspicuous location was entirely fitting for a house that in the two succeeding decades became a cultural center as a result of the diverse Bowdoin family interests. Here could be found a personal library unrivaled in New England (which grew to 1,200 volumes by 1774) and a "Great upper Chamber" which contained numerous scientific instruments, including six telescopes, as well as "an Electrical machine & apparatus."[4] Throughout the house were displayed a dozen family portraits by Smibert, Badger, Blackburn, and others, as well as eight "large Paintings painted in Italy."[5] In addition, the stairhalls were decorated with about 100 prints—many presumably mezzotint portraits—and one fireplace mantel displayed plaster sculpture ornaments.[6]

The Bowdoin house was the center of a property with impressive gardens that stretched over the crest of Beacon Hill and down to what is now Ashburton Place. While no pictures of the house survive, J. G. Hales's 1814 map of Boston gives some sense of its footprint (fig. 2) in relation to surrounding properties. Here the Bowdoins cultivated grapes, pears, peaches, and apples that were the envy of Boston.[7]

At age five, when Jemmy sat with his sister for their double portrait by Blackburn (fig. 3) (color on p. 63), he probably had not yet sensed the privileged nature of his upbringing.[8] But such ideas may have come to mind soon after this date, as the elder Bowdoin imported French books for him—presumably to supplement his education at the Boston Latin School—and four years later thought of buying him a plantation in Grenada.[9]

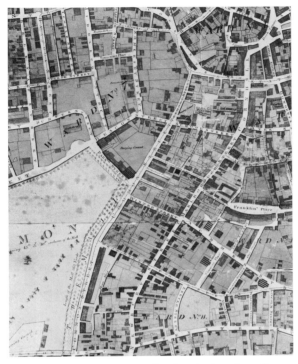

FIG. 2 1814 map of Boston, showing the location of James Bowdoin II's property

Everything about the Bowdoin household contributed to its cosmopolitan character. The exterior facade, although of wood, was rusticated to resemble stone and accented by an elaborate Georgian portico.[10] Elegantly furnished rooms were filled with high-style mahogany furniture. For entertaining, which happened with regularity, the drawing room was outfitted with six pairs of decanters, and the wine cellar was bursting with pipes of wine, a keg of brandy, and numerous other spirits.[11] Other elegant Boston homes were, like the Bowdoin house, equipped with Wilton carpets, carved card tables, and imported draperies. Few, however, had bird cages, soup tureens imported from Paris (fig. 5), hundreds of ounces of silver plate, and what was likely Boston's only French bidet. The Bowdoins were also one of only twenty-two Boston families in 1768 to possess their own carriage.[12] Clearly, this household was as well appointed as that of any aspiring London merchant of similar station.

The Bowdoins were pious without being inconvenienced by their religion. They worshipped, along with many others of their social station (including John Hancock, Joseph Warren, and John Singleton Copley) at the fashionable, affluent, and liberal Brattle Street Church, located only a few blocks below Beacon Hill. The elder Bowdoin contributed £200 in 1772 to its rebuilding and unsuccessfully offered land on Tremont Street to the church if it were resited.[13] Here, as in the political arena, the elder Bowdoin was outmaneuvered by John Hancock, his lifelong rival, who offered £1,000 and a 3,200 pound bell—the largest in Boston—if the church were to be rebuilt in the same location.[14]

By the time Jemmy was fourteen his father was importing fashionable attire for him—such as a beaver hat[15]—and negotiating a bride for him with the father's brother-in-law, Governor George Scott of Grenada:

The proposal you make about connecting honest Jemmy with the daughter of your Brother at Jamaica is very agreeable. There's no disparity of age and some other circumstances to make it unsuitable; she is eleven (you say) a pretty girl; now in London for her education, bids fair to be a fine woman. . . . He is fourteen; not ugly; will have the best education this Country affords; bids fair to be a clever fellow . . . To be Short, the boy is at your disposal.[16]

Like most other Boston patrician sons, James Bowdoin III went to Harvard (Class of 1771). For his first two years there he neglected his studies and later wrote that this lack of focus had caused him "more uneasiness than all the other circumstances of my life."[17] But he largely avoided the notorious student disorders of 1768 and youthful escapades that occupied some of his classmates (Winthrop Sargent, for example, entertained two prostitutes in his room one night in 1770).[18] During his last year at Harvard, however, Bowdoin's delicate health—probably due to tuberculosis[19]—necessitated that he withdraw from school prior to graduation. So on 26 December 1770, he sailed for London with the hope that the sea voyage and European air might restore him. His departure coincided with letters written by the elder Bowdoin on his behalf to Benjamin Franklin and Thomas Pownall, the former Massachusetts governor, among others.[20] While in England he was placed under the watchful eye of his uncle, Duncan Stewart (fig. 4), who monitored activities and expenses.

It probably was with some dismay that the elder Bowdoin—who had never traveled far from New England—found his parental authority severely compromised by the transatlantic distance. For example, in June 1771, he was initially pleased that his son had entered Christ Church, Oxford, as a gentleman commoner to study law.[21] But in response to his son's apparent intimation that he might remain in England for some time, Bowdoin cautioned "I intended you should see England again, but that I would have you return [to Boston] with him [George Erving, his mother's brother], and this I shall depend on."[22] He also informed his son that he would send him a copy of his Harvard diploma—received *in absentia*—which he thought would enable him to secure degrees from Oxford, Cambridge, and Edinburgh.[23]

The son's tenure as a law student was of short duration. By 6 November 1771, he reported that he had abandoned Oxford to enter the King's Riding School and reported almost gleefully "I have just begun to learn French, likewise Dancing and Fencing, all which I expect to be perfect master of before my return."[24] If only to

FIG. 3 Joseph Blackburn, *Portrait of Elizabeth Bowdoin and James Bowdoin III*

reassure his dumbfounded father of his seriousness of purpose, he added that he would write his next letter to him in French and that "for the future all my letters will be in that language. . . ."

Another parental shock was the speed with which his son spent money. Quickly, the father sounded the alarm of fiscal responsibility with the ominous reprimand: "you must have been very far from being a good oeconomist *and have spent it [money] very inconsiderately* [last part crossed out]."[25] Bowdoin also urged his son to read "An Essay on a Course of Liberal Education for Civil and Active Life" by Joseph Priestley, which was an attempt to make his classical curriculum more "useful."[26] One might guess, however, from the direction of the son's interests, that this advice fell on deaf ears.

In April 1772, James Bowdoin III returned to Boston, but stayed only briefly. One can imagine this twenty-year-old youth, fresh from England, most likely bored at being back in his family's Beacon Hill house. At least such a situation would help to explain why the elder Bowdoin was willing to allow his son to return to Europe in October 1773, this time to make the Grand Tour to Italy. Bowdoin traveled with Ward Nicholas Boylston, a fellow Bostonian and son of Benjamin Hallowell, one of the elder Bowdoin's business associates.[27]

The two travelers remained together until the following April. During their stay they visited numerous natural and historic sites and geologi-

FIG. 4 John Singleton Copley, *Portrait of Duncan Stewart*

FIG. 5 Charles-Louis Auguste Spriman, *Covered Tureen and Liner*

cal wonders. They attended social events and intermingled with the British community in both Naples and Rome. In Naples, where they stayed until 11 March, they viewed a number of churches at some length, including San Severino e Sossio, Santi Apostoli, and Santa Caterina a Formiello. They also traveled to see the museum at Herculaneum and the excavations at Pompeii. One evening they attended a masquerade ball hosted by the king of Naples, and other evenings they went to the opera. On several occasions they noted dining with Sir William Hamilton, the British envoy to Naples and an avid collector. A little over a year earlier Hamilton had sold his collection of more than 700 Greek vases, 175 terra cottas, 600 bronzes, and 6,000 coins to the trustees of the British Museum. It may have been in Naples that young Bowdoin contracted the same infectious enthusiasm with which Hamilton pursued collecting. Hamilton's residence was the social center for the British community, as noted by Bowdoin in a letter to his sister: "there are a great number of Englishmen here at present Lord Clive, Lord Moulton, Sir Thomas Clugers & c all these gentlemen I expect to meet at our Embassador's where it is customary for all Englishmen to resort almost every evening."[28]

While these two impressionable visitors were, according to Boylston's daily travel diary, awe-

struck by architectural and artistic wonders, the excursion that left the most vivid impression was an ascent of Vesuvius. Boylston recorded that "on our entering on the opposite side from where the Smoke issued the Smell of the Sulpher became very Disagreeable & increased upon our nearer approach to the chasms or fissures in the Rocks from such it issued attended with a noise not unlike a Blacksmiths forge, which emited a very strong wind & thick Smoke that instantly changed the colour of our shoe Buckles, & the metal buttons on our Coats to a dark copper cast . . ."[29] On 12 March Bowdoin and Boylston continued on to Rome, where they remained together for about a month. While there they benefited from the guidance of James Byers, a Scotsman, who served the British visitors as archaeologist, antiquary, and *cicerone*, possibly further nurturing Bowdoin's taste for collecting (although there is no material evidence that he made any purchases). Later that month he reported to his sister that he would be leaving Rome to visit Florence, Bologna, and Lyons.[30]

It was presumably in Italy that James Bowdoin III had his first adult portrait painted (fig. 1). In part this seems to celebrate his twenty-first birthday, which had occurred in September 1773. But it appears to be in response to pleading for such a portrait from his sister, whom he informed by a letter from Naples, "I shall improve the Hint given respecting my picture & get it taken according & send it you."[31]

During the course of the next year Bowdoin progressed to England, where he lived with his sister (fig. 7) and her husband, John Temple (fig. 8). Temple was a Boston native employed there by the British customs service until forced from office in 1770. The following year he was appointed surveyor general of customs in England, partly in an effort to bribe James Bowdoin II, his father-in-law, an ardent Whig, to stay in line on the Governor's Council.

In one sense, this was a curious time for the younger Bowdoin to be absent from Boston. Political hostilities verged on war, and by the time of his return, the first shots had been fired at Lexington and Concord. The most likely explanation is that the elder Bowdoin begrudgingly acceded to a headstrong son's instinct for wanderlust. In any event, by 12 September 1774, he wrote his son: "I have just recd yr letter of ye 12th of May dated at Lyons. . . . A winter voyage (as you say) will be disagreable, and therefore I would have you take passage for America by one of the first Spring Ships without fail . . . I absolutely depend upon seeing you in ye Spring."[32] As late as February 1775 the elder Bowdoin still had hopes that his son might go to Grenada to collect a large family debt owed by Governor Scott and set himself up as a planter.[33] By April the emerging conflict put an end to such thoughts.

The week following the battles of Lexington and Concord, a committee of Boston citizens led by James Bowdoin II requested a meeting with General Thomas Gage. Their purpose in approaching the commander of British forces in Boston was to reach accommodation so that Boston citizens might leave the town for the duration of the British blockade and occupation. The group reached an agreement, and the exodus was well under way by 30 April. Bowdoin's house was to be occupied by General John Burgoyne, while the neighboring Hancock house became the temporary residence of General Clinton. Bowdoin's destination was Middleborough, a rural town thirty-five miles south of Boston. There he had arranged to occupy the summer estate (fig. 9) of Judge Peter Oliver, a loyalist who fled the colonies for England. But initially they stayed at Braintree, where Bowdoin was observed to be in extremely poor health, as Abigail Adams commented to her husband:

He, poor gentleman, is so low that I apprehend he is hastening to a house not made with hands, he looks like a mere skeleton, speaks faint and low, is racked with a violent cough, and I think, far advanced in a consumption.[34]

On 29 November 1775, Bowdoin was cheered by his son's arrival at Middleborough. He had sailed in September from London to Philadelphia and then New York, and had made his way overland to Massachusetts.[35] If the elder Bowdoin harbored sentiments critical of his son's extravagances, they were momentarily set aside. He

FIG. 6 Robert Feke, *Portrait of James Bowdoin II*

must have been overcome with joy at the return of his only son, who might well have been expected to stay in England until hostilities ended. James Bowdoin III probably traveled home more lightly than planned, for he left with his sister a number of paintings, most likely the first he had ever purchased and about which she later observed:

I intend to get Mr. Christie [James Christie, the auctioneer] to see your pictures, that are here, and if he thinks they will fetch anything worth while to sell them, if not I fear the freight will be more than their worth to send to you.[36]

These he must have hoped would be sent to him when travel was not influenced by warfare.

After passing the winter with his family at Middleborough, James Bowdoin III undoubtedly welcomed the news that the British had evacuated Boston. He was given the distinction of riding into town with General Washington, presumably because the elder Bowdoin was bedridden much of the winter and his continued poor health prevented him from accepting this honor. The ride was also symbolic for the son. It signified his arrival in Boston as a figure of substance who over the next few years would represent his

FIG. 7 John Singleton Copley, *Mrs. John Temple*

father in business. James Bowdoin III, in a now well-known story, took Washington to the house of his grandfather Erving, where together they dined on salt beef—the best Boston had to offer.[37] Now that the British had departed, the Bowdoin family reoccupied its Beacon Hill house. The poor health of the elder Bowdoin, however, compelled him to retain his Middleborough retreat, where he spent a great deal of time through 1782.

Although many of his Harvard classmates served in the military, James Bowdoin III remained out of the range of gunfire. On one occasion he reported exuberantly to his father in Middleborough on the revolutionary fervor which was sweeping the population:

Every Body here at present seems to have a military Fever since the Rhode Island Expedition has begun. In Salem and Newbury the first people have turned out Volunteers . . . this has stirr'd up our Independant Company Light Infantry Company, & c. a number of other Volunteers to turn out. Mr Hancock goes, and takes the command of the Militia. Every thing seems to go on spiritedly and . . . promise Success.[38]

But despite such sentiments his own poor health may have made such a commitment

impractical for him. Years later it was said that the fond feelings of the Governor for his only son—rather than his son's health—prevented James Bowdoin III from joining the army.[39] Whatever the case, the younger Bowdoin focused on business.

Poor health and the war did, however, take their toll on the elder Bowdoin. At the very moment when he wished to establish his son in business, this seemed to be a daunting task. In more peaceful times, for example, he might have given his son the responsibility for management of Naushon, one of a small group of islands south of Cape Cod that the elder Bowdoin owned jointly with his half-brother, William. But the Elizabeth Islands, as they were called, were in a state of disarray, having been raided and pillaged by British and Rhode Island troops alike. War also made development of the family's extensive Kennebec Valley property impractical.[40] As a result, Bowdoin searched elsewhere for a source of new income and a means to develop his son's business acumen.

The most appealing opportunity the elder Bowdoin saw was increased direct trade with

FIG. 8 John Singleton Copley, *John Temple*

FIG. 9 House built by Chief Justice Peter Oliver in 1769 at Middleborough, MA. Occupied by James Bowdoin II and family, 1775–1782

Europe. The first venture along these lines to involve James Bowdoin III was the 1776 purchase of the brig *Flora*. Even more significant was a partnership between James Bowdoin III (whose investment, as his father noted, "although in his name, is on my own account and Risk") and Emanuel Michael Pliarne, a Frenchman. The three agreed that the Bowdoins would, under contract, ship goods to Nantes and once their value reached £80,000 Pliarne would dispatch military stores. Part of the plan required Pliarne and the younger Bowdoin to locate venture cargoes at various points along the East Coast. But even before the first cargo was sent, disaster struck. Two vessels, the *Alexandria* and the *Custis*, were captured, and James Bowdoin III and Pliarne journeyed to Virginia to settle accounts. The consequences of the visit were described by Martha Washington in a letter dated 7 March 1778:

I left Mr. Bowdoin in Alexandria, he was a good deal distressed on account of Mr. Pliarne, a french gentleman, his partner who was by accident drowned crossing the Potomack river, his Body was not found when I left home, his behavior and agreeable manner, rendered him a favourite with all that knew him, and caused his death to be much lamented.[41]

With these activities in ruins, the younger Bowdoin—again with his father's resources—turned his attentions to the potentially lucrative business of privateering. The results were equally disastrous. In 1779 the *Marlborough* and the *Hodshon*, two vessels the Bowdoins had financed, were captured before they had a chance to return any profit.

Throughout these trying times, Governor Bowdoin directed his son's advancement from Middleborough—albeit at arm's length. Their correspondence documents a loving relationship comprised of a dutiful and earnest son and a patient although demonstrative father determined to make his son successful.[42]

7

FIG. 10 Attributed to John Smibert, *The Continence of Scipio*

One pleasant diversion for the son was the return to Boston of the young aspiring artist John Trumbull, son of Connecticut's governor. Trumbull had overlapped with the younger Bowdoin for two years at Harvard, graduating in 1773. In September 1778 he settled into the studio formerly occupied by John Smibert and spent his days painting portraits and making copies of the paintings found there. During this period Trumbull's friendship with the Bowdoins and their in-laws intensified. James Bowdoin III's brother-in-law, John Temple, who himself had just arrived from London, and who would become a significant advocate for the artist, encouraged Trumbull to leave Boston for England so that he might study with Benjamin West.[43]

At the time that Trumbull was living in Smibert's studio, which occupied part of one-half of Smibert's double house, Susannah Sheaff(e), widow of William Sheaff(e), deputy surveyor of customs, occupied the other half of the house.[44] She was related to the Bowdoins by marriage (her daughter, Ann Sheaff[e], married James Bowdoin III's cousin, John Erving). It was also the time when the studio contents were being sold off by Belcher Noyes, the attorney for the studio's last owner, John Moffatt, John Smibert's nephew. Trumbull purchased eight paintings. This dispersal was also conceivably the catalyst for one or both of the Bowdoins to acquire over 140 drawings and a dozen paintings or more. The purchase, if made at this time, was most likely made with the elder Bowdoin's money, for as yet the son had no visible source of income.

Certainly, this was an opportune moment for the Bowdoin family to expand an art collection that was highly unusual, if not unique, in Boston.[45] An important influence was undoubtedly James Bowdoin III's recent Grand Tour.

FIG. 11 John Trumbull, *Sir John Temple and Family*

The vivid impressions of Naples and Rome conveyed by Ward Nicholas Boylston's travel diary make abundantly clear that the artistic treasures there made a substantial impression on the two travelers' sense of culture. They may also have whetted James Bowdoin III's appetite for the purchases he was forced to leave with his sister when he returned to Boston in 1775. His acquisitions were being added to a small collection that had been assembled by the Bowdoins at least by 1774. An inventory of the Beacon Hill house (wisely made by the elder Bowdoin before he turned his house over to General Burgoyne) makes clear that there were already over twenty paintings in the house. Some of the works, such as those described as being "painted in Italy," could conceivably have also come from Smibert's studio and been sold earlier by the aging John Moffatt as he needed money. This

suggests that the younger Bowdoin's later acquisitions may have been stimulated, in part, by his own father's interest in collecting (which until now has gone unrecognized). And while the presence of paintings in the Bowdoin College collection acquired by James Bowdoin III later in life makes it difficult to determine exactly which works came from Smibert's studio, such a transaction may have been the source for Smibert's copy of Nicholas Poussin's *Continence of Scipio* (fig. 10) (color on p. 165).[46] Its virtue, to Bowdoin as to Smibert, derived from the eighteenth-century belief that a good copy of an important painting was far superior to a lesser original.[47]

While these drawings and paintings may have had temporary quarters in the Bowdoins' Beacon Hill house, on 18 May 1780, James Bowdoin III married Sarah (Sally) Bowdoin (1761-1826), his orphaned first cousin, the

9

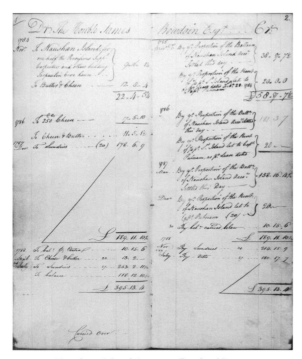

FIG. 12 Naushon Island Account Book of James Bowdoin II and James Bowdoin III, 1784–1802, pp. 1 and 2

daughter of his father's late half-brother, William Bowdoin, and William's late wife, Phebe Murdock Bowdoin. Soon thereafter the couple moved down the hill into the family home on Milk Street that Sally had inherited from her father. In July 1784, John Trumbull wrote his brother that he was painting a picture of Sir John Temple and Family (fig. 11) "which is to be a present to Mr. Bowdoin."[48] This gift was sent by Temple and his wife, James Bowdoin III's loving sister, Elizabeth, who urged her brother to hang it "over your best Parlor Chimne."[49]

On Milk Street the younger Bowdoin continued to live to a great degree in his father's shadow. For the most part, he avoided the political controversies that surrounded his more visible father. The one major exception occurred in 1782, when he suggested to James Sullivan, a Boston lawyer and sometime judge, that Benjamin Franklin had kept back money due the crews of Continental frigates and was using these funds to live the good life in Passy, France. Sullivan was outraged. He assumed (probably correctly) that Bowdoin had been told this by

John Temple, who was known to dislike Franklin. The episode erupted into a press battle that dominated the Boston papers for six months with the Bowdoin and Hancock factions trading salvos. The argument only ended when Temple dropped his request for Massachusetts citizenship and accepted appointment as consul general for Great Britain.[50]

On 31 March 1783, the younger Bowdoin returned from a business trip to New York with newspapers bringing Boston news of the peace.[51] For the next three years he lived in Boston and continued to manage his father's real estate holdings (particularly during the period his father was governor, 1785-1787). In 1786 he moved to Dorchester, where he lived at Mount Bowdoin, on the town's highest hill, with a panoramic view of Boston and the seacoast. His move there, as he noted in a letter to the Loyalist refugee Peter Oliver, was prompted by his "health requiring my residence in the country which has been for about a year. & not constrained from my private affairs to do business in the mercantile line I have hired a farm of about 70 acres of very good land in the town of

FIG. 13 Edward Greene Malbone, *Portrait of James Bowdoin III*

FIG. 14 French, *Court Suit (Coat, Waistcoat, and Trousers)* .
This suit is said to have been worn by Hon. James Bowdoin III to a ball given by Napoléon at the Tuileries.

01.110, 01.111, 01.112

11

FIG. 15 Gilbert Stuart, *Portrait of James Bowdoin III*

Dorchester."[52] James Bowdoin III was interested in corresponding with him about manufacturers and agriculture. In particular he sought advice on how best to develop Naushon Island (half of which he had acquired on his marriage to Sarah, the only child of his father's late half-brother), which he owned jointly with his father and which had suffered so badly during the war. Two years earlier the father and son had taken a renewed interest in the development of Naushon. Surviving accounts (fig. 12) indicate a steady increase in the profitability of the island from the sale of dairy products, produce, and livestock. James Bowdoin III may have taken a particular pride in Naushon because his ownership of it came from his marriage rather than from his father. This concern reflected both the primary, practical need to rehabilitate his financial resources, and on another level it reflected a family desire to see Massachusetts more fully develop its industries and agriculture.

Upon his father's death in 1790, James Bowdoin III inherited almost £10,000 in property, money, and personal belongings—one-third of his father's estate. His mother (who lived on until 1803) was given life occupancy of the

Beacon Street house while her son and his wife remained on Milk Street. The son's new wealth did not lead to extravagant expenditures. On the contrary, his father's admonitions about frugality had apparently taken root. For although he had the ability to build himself a stylish, Neoclassical house designed by the precocious architect Charles Bulfinch, he did not. This is particularly noteworthy since the Bulfinch family came from the same social circle as the Bowdoins. In 1785, for example, when Bulfinch made his only trip abroad, the governor wrote a letter introducing this "sensible well educated young gentleman" to Benjamin Franklin.[53] Further, two years later, just after Bowdoin finished his term as governor, Bulfinch submitted his first design for the Massachusetts State House, which was subsequently built about 100 yards from the Bowdoin house. By the mid-1790s, others of the son's social standing, such as James Swan, Harrison Gray Otis, and Perez Morton (James Bowdoin III's Harvard classmate), had turned to Bulfinch for new houses. James Bowdoin III, however, was apparently content to make minor improvements to Milk Street. In 1795, for example, he ordered looking glasses, girandoles,

FIG. 16 Gilbert Stuart, *Portrait of Mrs. James Bowdoin III*

chandeliers, and silk curtains for the drawing room.[54]

As one of the infant state's senior leaders, the elder Bowdoin had commanded tremendous respect, although he never captured the imagination of the populace as did Hancock. When George Washington visited Boston on his New England swing of 1789, however, it was Bowdoin (not Governor Hancock) with whom he ate dinner, and it was in the Bowdoin family pew at the Brattle Street Church that he sat on Sunday. Certainly, the profound symbolism of this was not lost on James Bowdoin III. While he would never outshine his father—and at age thirty-eight he must have sensed this—what he could do was to emulate his father's considerable service to Massachusetts.

James Bowdoin III's first venture into the political arena came in 1786, when he was elected to the Massachusetts House of Representatives. Two years later, he represented his new home of Dorchester at the Massachusetts convention to ratify the federal Constitution. There, along with his father, who sat for Boston, he joined the ranks of the Federalists, who favored the Constitution's acceptance. At one point, he defended Hancock who, by a previously agreed strategy, had proposed amendments in order to insure acceptance of the document.[55] Such Federalist sympathies, however, lasted only through the time of his election to the state Senate in 1793. By 1794 he abandoned the Federalists, who generally favored a strong, centralized government, the encouragement of industries, the needs of great merchants and landowners, and the British in foreign affairs. Their opponents, the Republicans, or Democratic Republicans, who James Bowdoin III chose to join, favored personal liberty, limits on federal powers, and the French. That year he joined the Democratic Club (called the Jacobin Club by some). With Hancock's death in 1793 the governor's race was wide open. James Bowdoin III, along with the arch-Republicans Francis Dana and Elbridge Gerry, was being named as a possible candidate. According to Abigail Adams, Bowdoin's defection to the Republicans was on the grounds that the Federalists had slighted him. This explanation of Bowdoin's actions, when presented to John Adams—soon to be the last Federalist President—brought the disparaging outburst that "Mr. Bowdoin's morality is the same with that of all . . . men who have more ambition than principle." He went on to say, "I have gone through a life of almost three score years, and how few have I found whose principles could hold against their passions, whose honors could contend with their interests."[56]

During his decade in Dorchester (1786-1796), James Bowdoin III's civic and philanthropic interests matured. While there he became an incorporator of the Massachusetts Charitable Fire Society, and in 1792 he was named a founding trustee of the Massachusetts Society for Promoting Agriculture, which distributed premiums for discoveries and innovations in agriculture and animal husbandry. That same year he was elected to the Harvard Corporation, where for the duration of the 1790s he was an active participant in meetings.[57] By 1796 Bowdoin moved his residence back to Boston. At the time of his departure he signaled his increasing interest in education with a parting gift to the town of ten acres of woodland, the income of which was to benefit the local schools.[58]

The 1790s also proved to be a decade of unprecedented growth in the number of American colleges. Between 1782 and 1802 nineteen colleges that are in existence today were chartered. This was more than twice the number of colleges founded in the preceding 150 years. Denominational rivalry, state loyalty, increasing wealth, and population growth were all contributing factors to this phenomenon.[59] It was precisely this combination of elements that stirred the residents of the District of Maine to lobby for a college. One of the advocates was Reverend Alfred Johnson, Sr., of Freeport. In 1792 he approached James Bowdoin III with the idea of endowing a college in Maine in Governor Bowdoin's memory. As recalled some years later by his son:

It occurred to my father & probably to others that the late learned Governor Bowdoin had left both a name & an estate that might be honorable and useful to the

13

FIG. 17 Gilbert Stuart, *Portrait of James Madison*

FIG. 18 Gilbert Stuart, *Portrait of Thomas Jefferson*

FIG. 19 Anonymous, *Ariadne,* sent by James Bowdoin III to Thomas Jefferson

College. He thereupon procured an introduction, made the suggestion to his son & heir, the late James Bowdoin [III], observing that Literature was poor & custom had connected patronage with the name. The thought took with him & he soon made proposals, but added that such were the vicissitudes of fortune, that he might never be able to do so much as might be anticipated from him.[60]

James Bowdoin III is said to have shrewdly pointed out that the act proposing such a college to the Massachusetts Legislature should leave out his father's name, since Governor Hancock's antipathy for his former rival might prevent him from approving any institution named Bowdoin College.[61] While it seems likely that Hancock would have given a cool reception to a legislative act authorizing the creation of Bowdoin College, the real reason for the delay may have been that legislators in the District of Maine "simply could not agree upon the location for the college or the composition of its boards."[62]

It is conceivable that many reasons influenced Bowdoin's interest in the college, but as he never explained them we are left to conjecture. At the most basic level, James Bowdoin III was, as a graduate of Harvard, the product of such an institution. His father—through numerous gifts to Harvard and his participation in the founding of the American Academy of Arts & Sciences in

1780—had himself expressed a life-long interest in the importance of education. He simultaneously provided his son with a model for acts of philanthropy. James Bowdoin III may have even embraced the belief so elegantly stated by Bowdoin's first president, Reverend Joseph McKeen that "every man who has been aided by a public institution to acquire an education and to qualify himself for usefulness, is under peculiar obligation to exert his talents for the public good."[63] Certainly, too, the District of Maine was inextricably linked to the fortunes of the Bowdoin family's source of wealth.

On a more personal level, James and Sarah Bowdoin had no heirs. He had passed forty, and his own infirmities may have caused him to reflect increasingly on the significance of having both himself and his father linked to an institution that would perpetuate the family name. He may also have been persuaded by the service he would be performing for the District of Maine, which with each year was growing dramatically in population (from just over 56,000 in 1784 to over 150,000 by 1800).[64] Lastly, he may have even found it curiously satisfying that although

FIG. 20 Rembrandt Peale, *Portrait of John Armstrong*

16

his father had surpassed him in almost every field of endeavor, he would do more to honor and perpetuate the family name by endowing a college in his memory.

Once his decision was made to support the creation of the College, Bowdoin took what has been best described as a "friendly but distant interest in its affairs."[65] He expressed views on the design of its first building (recommending a plan by Thomas Dawes, the architect of Harvard's Hollis Hall), contributed to the creation of a "Professorship of Mathematics & of natural & experimental Philosophy," and when efforts to get the school opened lagged, queried his friend Daniel Cony on such inaction. He took an active role in the selection of the Reverend Joseph McKeen as the school's first president, began soliciting equipment for its classrooms, and energetically sought books for its library. But, somewhat curiously, he never visited Brunswick to see the results of his generosity, even after Massachusetts Hall (1799-1802), the College's first building, was constructed and McKeen inaugurated.[66] Any curiosity he had about the school's appearance was outweighed (presumably) by his fragile health and his hesitance to make the boat trip necessary to see the College first-hand. His own thoughts about the educational goals sought by an institution such as this are mostly unknown, although on one occasion he wrote his sister regarding her son's educational interests in law, noting that "there is such a connexion between all the learned professions that success in any of them very much depends upon a well directed collegiate education in which the rudiments of science are deeply laid."[67]

Meanwhile, the profitability of James Bowdoin III's political maneuvering was far less apparent. In 1796, having moved back to Boston, he lost to Harrison Gray Otis in a race for the House of Representatives.[68] The following year he anonymously authored *Opinions Respecting the Commercial Intercourse Between the United States of America, and the Dominions of Great-Britain* (which was his assault on the Jay Treaty, by which Bowdoin felt Britain was given too much authority and France treated unfairly). During these same years Bowdoin held minor state offices (Governor's Council in 1794 and State Senate in 1801) and bided his time waiting for the political atmosphere (and his prospects) to improve. He thought he saw his opportunity in 1801 with the election of Jefferson as the first Republican president. Within weeks of the new president's inauguration, he wrote, offering, "I have no hesitance in tendering to you my Services without being able to point out in what way they can be particularly useful."[69] Although this offer apparently went unacknowledged, Bowdoin renewed an expression of interest the following year, when he learned that Rufus King was to retire as minister to England. This time, however, he was careful to express his interest through General Henry Dearborn, secretary of war, and a fellow landowner in the District of Maine, beseeching him to "mention my Name to President Jefferson as a successor to King."[70] By 19 November 1804, the interest had percolated through Jefferson's administration and Bowdoin was nominated, not for service in England, but to be "Minister Plenipotentiary to the Court of Spain." Although disappointed that he was not going to England, he accepted.

In preparation for his departure, Bowdoin wrote his uncle, George Erving, in London regarding what style of court dress Mrs. Bowdoin would be expected to wear in Madrid. He asked specifically to have a description that a *faiseur des robes* in Paris might use, "as she understands that hoops are worn in Court in Madrid, and that they are not here."[71] His impending departure may also have influenced him to have made a miniature of himself (fig. 13) (color frontispiece). It was painted by Edward Malbone, the leading miniaturist of his generation, who had recently come to Boston and opened a studio a few doors down Beacon Street. It is the most flattering and sensitive portrait of James Bowdoin III's adult life and apparently provided the source from which Gilbert Stuart's pendant (fig. 15) (color on p. 66) for his life portrait of Mrs. Bowdoin (fig. 16) (color on p. 71) was made.[72]

In March 1805, just prior to his departure for Spain, Bowdoin sent Jefferson the gift of a marble sculpture, now known to be *Ariadne* (fig. 19) but believed at the time to represent Cleopatra.

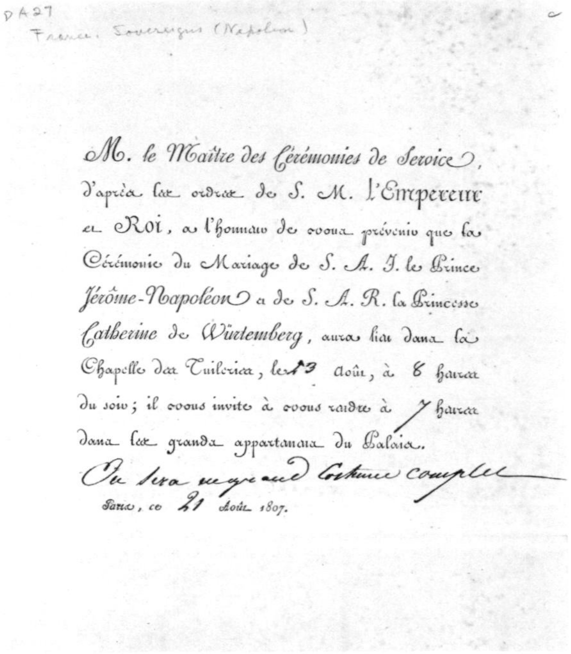

M. le Maître des Cérémonies de Service,
d'après les ordres de S. M. l'Empereur
et Roi, a l'honneur de vous prévenir que la
Cérémonie du Mariage de S. A. I. le Prince
Jérôme-Napoléon et de S. A. R. la Princesse
Catherine de Würtemberg, aura lieu dans la
Chapelle des Tuileries, le 23 Août, à 8 heures
du soir; il vous invite à vous rendre à 7 heures
dans les grands appartements du Palais.
On sera en grand Costume complet.
Paris, ce 21 Août 1807.

FIG. 21 Invitation from Napoléon to James Bowdoin III to attend the marriage of Prince Jérôme-Napoléon to Catherine de Würtemberg, 23 August 1807

The sculpture acted both as a token of respect and thanks for his appointment, but even more, it served to identify additional services he might perform:

Will you permit me to make a tender of my services in procuring for you any specimens of ye Arts, either in sculpture or painting; & although I am no adept, yet from having been in Italy & having viewed the works of ye best Masters, if you would entrust me with your Commissions, I would execute them in the best manner in my power. Accident having thrown in my way a handsome piece of Modern Sculpture, a Cleopatra copied & reduced from the ancient one now at Paris, which for many years lay at the Palace Belvidere at Rome: as I think it for the fineness of its Marble & the Neatness of its workmanship & finishing, among the best of ye Modern pieces of Sculpture, you will do me the favour to accept it & to place it in a Corner of your hall at Monticello: for which purpose I shall take the liberty of shipping it to you by ye first convenient opportunity. I was told it was purchased by a french Commissary in Italy, who wanted money: & that it had been taken from the apartments in ye Vatican, which were built by Pope Ganganelli Clement ye 14th, who was liberal as a Pope, & distinguished as a man of Taste & learning.[73]

Released from having to make the prerequisite trip to Washington to receive his send-off,

Bowdoin and his wife set out for Madrid in May. His orders were to settle the boundaries of Louisiana, to negotiate the purchase of the Floridas, and to obtain compensation for the spoilization of American commerce.[74] Bowdoin's health was so poor upon his arrival at Santander, on the north coast of Spain, that he immediately sought a passport to London in order to recuperate. By December he was sufficiently well to make his way to Paris, where he was instructed to remain until he was sure the American minister would be received by the court of Madrid.

Bowdoin's diplomatic frustrations were considerable. Foremost was his misfortune to be teamed in his deliberations with General John Armstrong (fig. 20), the minister to France. A Federalist, Armstrong held opposite attitudes about the international scene (Armstrong tilted towards England; Bowdoin tilted towards France) from those of his colleague. From the outset Madison, who described Bowdoin as "certainly respectable, altho' his talents are considered as moderate"[75] seems to have had far

FIG. 22 French, *Waistcoat*

FIG. 23 View of the Octagon Room at the Reuel Williams House, Augusta, Maine, with wallpaper depicting the *Sauvages de la mer Pacifique.*

greater confidence in Armstrong's ability to accomplish the nation's agenda. Bowdoin quickly made matters worse. His first error, considered by Washington to reflect a general naiveté and honest bungling—was to encourage Armstrong to inform France that its help was desired in settling the Spanish troubles. These consisted primarily of Spanish seizure of ships off Gibraltar and South America, border disputes over the Floridas, and desire of the United States to purchase the Floridas and Texas. Bowdoin thought Armstrong should hint that if these issues were resolved the United States might enter Napoléon's land war in Europe on the French-Spanish side against Russia, Prussia, and England. When Armstrong complained that he had no authority to make such a statement,

only intercession by a private American prevented Bowdoin from going to Germany to present this view to Napoléon. This situation, Jefferson observed to Madison, "changes considerably the idea we had formed of Bowdoin's caution and prudence."[76]

Bowdoin's diplomatic stock sank even lower when he endeavored to negotiate the purchase of the Floridas directly with Manuel Godoy, first minister of Charles IV of Spain, rather than through Napoléon and his minister, Talleyrand. Any legation clerk could have told Bowdoin that such a maneuver was impossible because Spain was a client state of France and all decisions with international implications were made in Paris. From this point in 1806, Armstrong (who was informed of Bowdoin's dealing by Talleyrand) ignored all personal contact with his colleague. Bowdoin was indignant that both Armstrong and the French had isolated him, and if he sensed why, only the bitterness of his reaction is communicated by his letters. Aside from invitations to the occasional social function, such as the wedding of Jérôme Bonaparte (fig. 21), Napoléon's brother, he was snubbed. His efforts to meet personally with Talleyrand and Napoléon were ignored on the technicality that he had not officially presented his papers in Madrid as Jefferson's minister to Spain.

Because Bowdoin's desire for direct and forthright negotiations ran counter to the prevailing pattern of subterfuge and intrigue, his tenure as diplomat was a failure. His frustrations led him to write Jefferson on 17 February 1808 that he planned to return home. The president thanked him and dutifully expressed an interest in having him stay on, but everyone involved must have breathed a collective sigh of relief when Bowdoin turned his attentions elsewhere.

While in Paris, Bowdoin diverted his mind with other pursuits. He seems particularly to have been determined to have the outspoken character of his political views matched by his aesthetic preferences. This sensibility led him to pursue the latest fashion in French taste. In Bowdoin's two years there he bought extensively. Not only were he and Mrs. Bowdoin attired in the latest French styles (figs. 14 and 22), but they purchased glassware, silver, and ceramics in vast quantities, as well as two expensive clocks. He considered his most important purchase to be a set of "French furniture made for our drawing room, consisting of sophas, chairs & window curtains"[77] which were valued at 6500 francs, approximately $1300. And while none of these furnishings are now located, they were most likely among the first in the French Empire style to be seen in Boston. As a consequence, Bowdoin can be credited with helping to inaugurate the craze for high-style furniture in the Empire style that swept through the eastern seaboard in the following decade.[78]

A recently discovered diary kept by Sarah Bowdoin during her stay in Paris details her considerable dedication to her husband's diplomatic mission. While she fervently desired to return to Boston, she was also captivated by Paris, awed by Napoléon, and charmed by French fashion. Her days consisted largely of letter writing, walks in the gardens of the Tuileries with her great niece, Sarah Bowdoin Winthrop, regular dinner parties for twenty or more French and American guests, lengthy evening conversations with her husband and friends over tea, and the occasional outing to the Louvre or shopping.

She emerges as a religious and caring person touched by her contact with others. In September 1807 she noted:

we observed with great regret and sorrow in a Portland paper of the 27 of July that the Doctor Red. M'Keen President of Bowdoin College was dead—he dyed on the 15 of July greatly regretted, beloved by *all* who knew him, particularly by those who were under his instruction and I fear it will be some time before they will find one that will supply his place, he was very amiable, & affable & added the mild, & agreeable compassion to the man of sense & letters.[79]

Sarah Bowdoin's activities enabled her to play an instrumental role in the selection of the French furnishings taken back to Boston. One purchase which apparently resulted from shopping excursions made during September 1807 is a set of panels of scenic wallpaper depicting *Sauvages de la mer Pacifique* (Natives of the Pacific) (fig. 23), now installed in the stairhall of the Asa Stebbins House, Deerfield, Massachusetts. Printed in 1804 after designs derived from Captain Cook's voyages, the paper became the talk of Paris after it was exhibited in 1806 at the Fourth Public Exhibition of Products of French Industry.[80]

The Bowdoins apparently sent the paper as a wedding gift to Sarah Lowell Cony. On 19 November 1807, she married Reuel Williams, the lawyer who oversaw Bowdoin College's Kennebec properties. Sarah, who had lived for extended periods of time with the Bowdoins in Boston, was the daughter of Daniel Cony of Augusta, Bowdoin's good friend and Kennebec land agent.[81] As with his purchase of furniture, Bowdoin's wallpaper was years ahead of its time in New England, and the same paper did not appear for sale in Boston until 1817.[82] If the wallpaper is a hint of the quality of Bowdoin's

FIG. 24 Gallery clock, given to the Brattle Square Church by James Bowdoin III

French purchases, his drawing room must have had a truly exotic character in a community such as Boston, where heretofore the prevailing taste had been for fashions derived predominantly from English models.[83]

James Bowdoin III's desire to acquire painting and sculpture with the same French flair seems muted by comparison. As unusual as it was for an American in the first decade of the nineteenth century to be collecting paintings, his tastes were largely conventional. It is unknown whether he devoted much time to looking at art while in Paris. But he may well have accompanied his wife to the Musée Napoléon in October 1806 to see the exhibition of 700 paintings installed there. Upon returning to their residence in the Hôtel de Rome, Sarah wrote:

went soon after Breakfast to the Louvre to see the exhibition of new paintings by French Artist[s]—the number supposed to be near 7 hundred pieces—many of them do great credit to the persons they were done by—there are many of the Emperor, & many of the battles wherein he has been engaged, such as Austerlitz, & those he was engaged in, in Egypt, also one of a milk woman, where the Emperor when a Boy had often been to get a drink of milk, when she discovers him coming in to her little Cotage she fell at his knees—he raised her, & made her a present of they say 500 livres—it took place when he was first Consul,—but the picture I think I was most pleased with, was a most beautiful infant Boy, laying asleep in a Basket cradle, quite naked, with a beautiful *widowed Mother*, very young leaning over it.[84]

The only contemporary French painting, other than family portraits,[85] that the Bowdoins are known to have acquired while in Paris was a portrait of the Comte de Mirabeau, the Revolutionary statesman and Physiocrat, whose philosophy was based on the belief that agriculture was the only truly productive occupation.

FIG. 25 Mansion House, Naushon Island, 1809. View from the south, 1992. The locust trees in the foreground are descendants of those laid out by James Bowdoin III.

While in Paris Bowdoin did purchase a group of thirteen pictures, but from his description of them as "good pictures, originals except in one or two instances"[86] it seems likely these were, with the exception of the Mirabeau portrait, Old Masters and/or copies after them.[87] These pictures are presumably among the group bequeathed to Bowdoin College, although there is no evidence they were bought with the College in mind, and the imprecise nature of the citation makes it impossible to tell which among the bequest they might be. His sculpture purchases were limited to six marble busts by "one of the principal sculptors of Florence." These he wanted as decorations for his library[88]

and were probably sought in emulation of Jefferson's sculpture-filled Hall at Monticello, to which Bowdoin had contributed his *Ariadne*. Whether these sculptures ever arrived is unknown, for they are not listed among the purchases he shipped from Paris.

In any event, upon Bowdoin's return to Boston in April 1808, his drawing room, outfitted with Stuart's portraits of Jefferson and Madison (figs. 17 and 18), which had been intended for his official quarters in Spain, was one of the most spectacular drawing rooms in the city. In fact, the furnishings probably retained their exotic character far longer than normal, because Jefferson's Embargo (on any

FIG. 26 Mansion House, Naushon Island, 1809. View toward Woods Hole, 1992

foreign trade), the subsequent Non-Intercourse Act, and the War of 1812 made trade uncertain until 1815.

The inability of James Bowdoin III to play a more prominent role in his official capacity as minister meant that he had time to turn his attentions elsewhere. One area of interest to which he had increasingly gravitated in the preceding two decades was agriculture. These interests had two levels of concern. The first was a personal satisfaction from the simple enjoyment he and Mrs. Bowdoin derived from their orchards and gardens. The second concern derived from his Jeffersonian-Republican sensibility and his political belief that the future of

America depended to a great degree on its ability to develop agriculture and animal husbandry in innovative and ambitious ways.

His primary vehicle for these attentions was Naushon Island. Bowdoin's letters from Paris to Thomas Winthrop are filled with instructions for improvements he desired there: he wanted locust trees (the descendants of which are standing today) planted adjacent to the stone enclosures to act as windbreaks; he asked that peach and cherry trees be planted; he mused that Louis Jean Marie Daubenton's *Instruction pour les bergers et pour les proprietaires de troupeaux* (Advice to Shepherds and Owners of Flocks) should be translated into English; and he tells of

FIG. 27 Mansion House, Naushon Island, 1809. View from the west, 1992

his plan to bring a German shepherd dog (for sheep herding) and a young French shepherd, Louis Guillaime Calot, back to Naushon.[89]

Most important, in 1806 he embarked on a plan to build a substantial summer house on the island. That house (fig. 25), the only one of the three primary dwellings in which he lived that is still extant, stands in glorious isolation, much as Bowdoin intended it. The site, which "commands the Bay & Harbor Nemmimesset [fig. 26] & gives almost a compleat horizon as far as ye eye can extend" was selected by Mrs. Bowdoin. The design, in a "plain substantial manner" (fig. 27) was drawn by George Sullivan, James Bowdoin III's secretary (who would later marry his great niece, Sarah Winthrop), and is a simply adorned Adamesque design with a hipped roof and a four-over-four room plan. To allow for its exposed site, Bowdoin requested that it have "no door in front [the east side] and only one principal one on the side wch shd be cover'd with a closed porch on acct of the N.E. wind to which it will be exposd."[90]

It was here, in the house completed in 1809, that James Bowdoin III spent the most satisfying moments of his last years. Traveling down from Boston early in the spring and remaining until the first cold winds of November, he concentrated on the issues that in his last years were the focus of his attentions. Here he penned the translation of Daubenton's advice to shepherds, oversaw the cultivation of crops, bred sheep, and ordered new strains of seeds.[91] His spiritual mentor, Jefferson, had also by 1809 retired to seclusion. Naushon was Bowdoin's Monticello. Here he could ignore the strident voices of

Massachusetts Federalists increasingly incensed by Federal policies. Like Jefferson, he was an experimental agriculturist. Like Jefferson, he made observations and adaptations of European crops, livestock, and methods of farming that put him in the vanguard of his contemporaries. Like Jefferson, he espoused the course of the common man, and at that time in our history the common man was the farmer. If Bowdoin differed with the Jeffersonian ideal, it was in choosing to emphasize farming's economic value rather than its value as a source of human virtue.[92]

The poor health that had plagued Bowdoin's entire life followed him to Naushon. By the spring of 1811 his health was shattered, and he retreated there for one final summer. At Naushon in July 1811, he penned his last letter, still preoccupied with issues of farming:

my health continues so feeble that I am unable to make such an appendix to the work [new edition of his translation of Daubenton] as I contemplated I think it however a useful work as it stands and ought to be in the possession of every farmer who owns or calculates upon keeping a flock of sheep.[93]

On 11 October 1811, James Bowdoin III died, seated in the easy chair of his bedroom (fig. 28) overlooking his estate at Naushon.[94] After a funeral service at Brattle Street Church, his remains were interred at the family tomb in the Granary Burying-Ground. As Bowdoin died without issue, he willed the College his art collection (seventy paintings and 141 sheets of drawings), his library, his scientific equipment, and his collection of minerals. The Boston newspaper obituaries—Federalist and Republican alike—were long and kind. *The Columbian Centinel* for 23 October 1811 made special mention of his activities at Naushon, which "were of consequence not so much to himself as to the agricultural and economical interests of his country." The most eloquent of the eulogies to him was read by Reverend J. S. Buckminster beneath the clock he had given to the Brattle Street Church.[95] This clock (fig. 24), perhaps symbolically, was a replacement for one given years earlier by his father.

Throughout his life, James Bowdoin III was never quite able to shake loose the mantle of his

FIG. 28 Federal easy chair, Boston area, c. 1790. This chair, in which James Bowdoin III is said to have died, is still in the Bowdoin Chamber in the Mansion House on Naushon Island.

father. In virtually every endeavor: student, philanthropist, statesman, he emulated the governor. The comparison, as he undoubtedly knew, was inevitable, and to a great degree it served him poorly. But by an odd quirk of fate, his failure to have children may have played an important role in his most significant gesture: to endow Bowdoin College in his father's name. For all his father's wealth, academic interests, intellectual rigor, and political accomplishments, he did not appeal to the makers of popular myths. The Bowdoin name, as a result, lives on today because of James Bowdoin III's decision to see his family's legacy perpetuated in this institution of higher learning.

NOTES

BCSC is Special Collections, Hawthorne-Longfellow Library, Bowdoin College.

I wish to thank Mr. Crosby Forbes, Mr. and Mrs. David C. Forbes, Mr. Roger Gregg of J. M. Forbes and Company, and photographer Erik Borg, for their help on the Naushon Island section of this essay.

1. James Bowdoin II [JB II] to Benjamin Franklin, 2 January 1771, Winthrop Papers [WP], Massachusetts Historical Society, Boston [MHS]. Quoted in Gordon E. Kershaw, *James Bowdoin II: Patriot and Man of the Enlightenment* (Lanham, MD: University Press of America,1991), 97. The Bowdoins did not sign themselves I or II or III. These numerals have been used for some time at Bowdoin College and by historians for convenience in telling the generations apart.

2. JB II to James Bowdoin III [JB III], 3 January 1772, WP.

3. Kershaw, 65.

4. Marvin S. Sadik, *Colonial and Federal Portraits at Bowdoin College* (Brunswick, ME: Bowdoin College Museum of Art, 1966), 40.

5. Kershaw, 87–8.

6. Inventory, 15 September 1774 [photocopy of MHS document in WP] Bowdoin Family Papers [BFP], BCSC.

7. Justin Winsor, *Memorial History of Boston* (1880), vol. 4, 612.

8. This double portrait, although unsigned, was probably painted at the same time Blackburn painted portraits of James Bowdoin III's maternal grandfather, John Erving, and his aunt, Elizabeth Bowdoin Pitts, and her husband, James Pitts (Detroit Institute of Arts). Both of the latter portraits are signed and dated 1757.

9. Clifford K. Shipton, *Sibley's Harvard Graduates* [Sibley], vol. 17 (1975), 48.

10. Kershaw, 100.

11. On one memorable occasion, as guests prepared to depart after an evening of revelry, they found the long flights of front steps covered with ice. Decorum set aside, they sat down and bumped their way to Beacon Street. Quoted in Winsor, II, 522, and Kershaw, 87.

12. "Names of Carriage Holders in Boston 1768," *Massachusetts Historical Society Proceedings*, 2nd Series, I, 225. Quoted in Kershaw, 105.

13. Kershaw, 91.

14. Charles W. Akers, *The Divine Politician* (1982), 130.

15. JB II Cashbook, 16 January 1767, WP.

16. JB II to George Scott, 8 May 1767, Governor James Bowdoin Letter Book, WP. Quoted in Sibley, vol. 17, 487.

17. JB III to Lady Temple, 31 October 1793, WP.

18. Sibley, vol. 17, 614.

19. Kershaw, 96.

20. JB II to Benjamin Franklin, 2 January 1771, WP. Quoted in Kershaw, 96–7.

21. At Oxford James Bowdoin III had the opportunity to see the collections of Elias Ashmole, left to Oxford in the form of the Ashmolean Museum. See Clifton Olds "The Intellectual Foundations of the College Museum," in this book, 33.

22. JB II to JB III, 12 June 1771, WP.

23. Kershaw, 98.

24. JB III to JB II, 6 November 1771, WP. Quoted in Sibley, vol. 17, 488.

25. JB II to JB III, 28 January 1772, WP.

26. Charles C. Calhoun, *A Small College in Maine: Two Hundred Years of Bowdoin* (Brunswick: Bowdoin College, 1993), 34.

27. Kershaw, 68.

28. JB II to Elizabeth Bowdoin Temple, 25 January 1774, WP.

29. Massachusetts Historical Society, Ward Nicholas Boylston, Travel Diary 1773–1775. I am indebted to Bowdoin College Museum of Art docent Sheila Rideout for bringing this unpublished travel diary to my attention.

30. JB III to Elizabeth Bowdoin Temple, 29 March 1774, WP.

31. Ibid.

32. JB II to JB III, 12 September 1774, WP. Quoted in Sadik, 138.

33. JB II to JB III, 15 February 1775, WP.

34. Kershaw, 209.

35. Kershaw, 211.

36. Elizabeth Bowdoin Temple to JB III, 24 March 1784, WP.

37. Sibley, vol. 17, 489.

38. JB III to JB II, 8 August 1778, WP. Quoted in Sibley, vol. 17, 489.

39. William Jenks, *An Eulogy Illustrative of the Life and Commemorative of the Beneficence of the Late Hon. James Bowdoin Esquire* (1812), 19.

40. Kershaw, 223.

41. Martha Washington to Mercy Otis Warren, 7 March 1778. *Warren-Adams Letters, II Massachusetts Historical Society Collections* 73 (Boston, 1905), 6.

42. See, for example, JB II to JB III, 8 August 1778, WP.

43. Theodore Sizer, ed., *The Autobiography of Colonel John Trumbull* (1953), 52.

44. Sizer, 65.

45. Aside from the isolated painting or paintings in Boston households (such as portraits attributed to Van Dyck and Rubens at Governor Hancock's, a Lely at Shrimpton Hutchinson's, and a few Old Masters owned by Peter Chardon) the Bowdoin house was a cultural oasis.

46. For a discussion of the chronological links between the two collections see David Becker, *Old Master Drawings at Bowdoin College* (Brunswick, ME: Bowdoin College Museum of Art, 1985), xiv-xv.

47. For a discussion of this view, and of the Bowdoin copies in particular, see Susan E. Wegner, "Copies and Education: James Bowdoin's Painting Collection in the Life of the College," in this book, 141. For Wegner on *The Continence of Scipio*, see 142 and 166.

48. Irma B. Jaffe, *John Trumbull: Patriot-Artist of the American Revolution* (1975), 311.

49. Elizabeth Bowdoin Temple to Mrs. JB III, 22 July 1784, in which she added "Mr T. takes no money yet and is happy to paint—I mention this lest my Friends think it extravagant," WP.

50. Sibley, vol. 15, 305.

51. Sibley, vol. 17, 489.

52. JB III to Peter Oliver [Dorchester, 1785?], BFP, BCSC.

53. Harold Kirker, *The Architecture of Charles Bulfinch*, 1969, 10.

54. JB III to George Erving, 23 June 1795, JB III Letterbook I, BCSC.

55. Merrill Jensen and Robert A. Becker, eds., *The Documentary History of the First Federal Elections 1788–1790*, vol. 1, 637. James Bowdoin III stated: "Your Excellency's propositions, are calculated to quiet the apprehensions of gentlemen, lest Congress should exercise an unreasonable control over the state legislatives, with regard to the times, places and manner of holding elections, which by the 4th section of the first article, are prescribed, etc. I have had my fears lest this control should infringe the freedom of elections, which ought ever to be held sacred."

56. Page Smith, *John Adams* (1962), vol. 2, 869.

57. Sibley, vol. 17, 491. It is suggested by Clifford Shipton that Bowdoin's Republican interests (on an increasingly Federalist board) may have precipitated his resignation in 1799.

58. Ibid.

59. Frederick Rudolph, *The American College and University* (1962), 56.

60. Recollections of Reverend Alfred Johnson, Jr., to A[lpheus] S[pring] Packard, 19 January 1835. "College History: Founding." BCSC.

61. Sibley, vol. 17, 491.

62. Calhoun, 18.

63. Calhoun, 31.

64. Calhoun, 33.

65. Calhoun, 19.

66. The General Catalogue of Bowdoin College (1894), xxv, states that "Mr. Bowdoin was urged to accept the position of President of the Board of Overseers, but declined owing to the difficulty of regularly attending the meetings in Brunswick."

67. JB III to Elizabeth Bowdoin Temple, 31 October 1793, WP.

68. Samuel Eliot Morrison, *Harrison Gray Otis* (1969), 86.

69. JB III to Thomas Jefferson, 24 February 1801, JBIII Letterbook I, BCSC.

70. *Collections of the Massachusetts Historical Society* (1907), Seventh Series, vol. 6, 235.

71. JB III to George Erving, 5 December 1804, JBIII Letterbook II, BCSC.

72. For a thorough discussion of the Stuart and Malbone portraits of JB III and Mrs. JB III see Sadik, 123–149. It is conceivable that the miniature of JB III was part of an exchange with his sister (who had been living in Boston since the death of her husband) for Malbone's portrait of her done at the same time.

73. JB III to Thomas Jefferson, 22 March 1805, JB III Letterbook II, BCSC. Quoted in Sadik, 208.

74. Sibley, vol. 17, 493.

75. *Letters and Other Writings of James Madison* (1865), vol. 2, 1794–1815. James Madison to James Monroe, Washington, 9 November 1804, 209.

76. Thomas Jefferson to James Madison, 11 May 1806, as quoted in Irving Brant, *James Madison Secretary of State, 1800–1809*, vol. 4 (1953), 363.

77. JB III to Thomas L. Winthrop, 9 May 1807, JB III Letterbook II, BCSC.

78. Bowdoin was so proud of these furnishings that he made a separate bequest of "furniture in the drawing room" to his nephew James Temple Bowdoin. See Temple Prime, *Some Account of the Bowdoin Family* (1894), 22.

79. Sarah Bowdoin Diary, 14 September [1807], BCSC.

80. Françoise Teynac, Pierre Nolot, and Jean-Denis Vivien, *Wallpaper: A History* (1981) trans. from the French, 112–113.

81. *Biographical Encyclopedia of Maine in the Nineteenth Century* (1885), 62.

82. Teynac, Nolot, and Vivien, 125.

83. Some Massachusetts travelers, such as John Adams, James Swan, and Richard Codman, had acquired French furniture prior to the time of Bowdoin's trip. All of their pieces, however, were in the earlier Louis XVI and Directoire styles, and many were pieces dispersed by the French Revolution. See F. J. B. Watson, "Americans and French Eighteenth-Century Furniture in the Age of Jefferson," in *Jefferson and the Arts: An Extended View* (1979), 274-293. Chancellor Robert R. Livingston (1746-1813), Jefferson's first minister to France (1801-1804), also returned to his house (on the Hudson River) with a number of pieces of French furniture. See "James Bowdoin and His Collection of Drawings," *Connoisseur* (December 1947), 120.

84. Sarah Bowdoin Diary, 24 October [1805], BCSC.

85. Portraits of JB III and Mrs. JB III were painted in Paris by Henri Van Gorp. See Sadik, 148.

86. JB III to [Thomas L. Winthrop, 13 May 1806], JB III Letterbook II, BCSC.

87. This pattern of collecting contrasts with that of Richard Codman, another Bostonian, who purchased over 100 pictures in Paris between 1794 and 1797. While some of his purchases were Old Masters and copies, he did acquire

more recent works, such as a night scene by Joseph Vernet. See Elizabeth Redmond, "The Codman Collection of Pictures," *Old-Time New England* 71 (1981), 103–106.

88. JB III to Sir Grenville Temple, 1 May 1807, JBIII Letterbook II, BCSC.

89. JB III to [Thomas L. Winthrop?], after 13 May 1806; JBII to Thomas L. Winthrop, 13 October 1807; Indenture of Louis Guillaime Calot, 17 August 1807; JBIII Letterbook II, BCSC. Daubenton's book was first published in 1782; the third edition came out in 1802. See also Kenneth E. Carpenter, "James Bowdoin as Library Builder," in this book, 107.

90. JB III to William Lee, 25 September 1806, JB III Letterbook II, BCSC.

91. These crops included turnips, for which the island became renowned. "Tarpaulin Turnips," so-called after the cove on the island where ships anchored, were known up and down the East Coast. See Amelia Emerson, *Early History of Naushon Island* (1935), 372.

92. A. Whitney Griswold, *Farming and Democracy* (1952), 22–25.

93. JB III to Joshua Belcher, 11 July 1811, JB III Letterbook II, BCSC.

94. Emerson, 409.

95. *Extract from A Disclosure By The Rev. J. S. Buckminster, Preached In The Church In Brattle Square, Boston, October, 1811, The Sabbath After the Interment Of Hon. James Bowdoin* (1848).

Starred works appear in color in this chapter. All works are the property of the Bowdoin College Museum of Art unless otherwise noted.

*1. Anonymous
     Portrait of James Bowdoin III, ca. 1771–1775
     oil on canvas
     30 1/4 x 25 1/2 inches
     Bequest of Mrs. Sarah Bowdoin Dearborn
     1826.1

2. 1814 map of Boston, surveyed by J. G. Hales, showing the location of James Bowdoin II's property
    Courtesy of the Trustees of the Boston Public Library

3. Joseph Blackburn
    active in America, 1754–1763
    Portrait of Elizabeth Bowdoin and James Bowdoin III, ca. 1760
    oil on canvas
    36 7/8 x 58 inches
    Bequest of Mrs. Sarah Bowdoin Dearborn
    1826.11

4. John Singleton Copley
    American, 1738–1815
    Portrait of Duncan Stewart, 1767
    oil on canvas
    50 x 40 inches
    Courtesy of the Scottish National Portrait Gallery

5. Charles-Louis Auguste Spriman
    French, active 1775–1781
    Covered Tureen and Liner and Tray, c. 1775
    silver
    Covered Tureen and Liner:
       10 1/4 x 15 1/4 x 8 3/8 inches
    Tray: 1 3/16 x 12 1/8 x 18 5/16 inches
    Gift of Miss Clara Bowdoin Winthrop in the name of the children of Mr. and Mrs. Robert C. Winthrop, Jr.
    1924.3.1

*6. Robert Feke
     American, 1707–1752
     Portrait of James Bowdoin II, 1748
     oil on canvas
     50 x 40 inches
     Bequest of Mrs. Sarah Bowdoin Dearborn
     1826.8

7. John Singleton Copley
    American, 1738–1815
    Mrs. John Temple (Elizabeth Bowdoin, Lady Temple), 1767
    pastel on paper
    23 1/4 x 15 3/4 inches
    Courtesy of Mrs. Irving Levitt

8. John Singleton Copley
    American, 1738–1815
    John Temple, 1765
    pastel on paper
    23 1/2 x 18 inches
    Courtesy of Mrs. Irving Levitt

9. House built by Chief Justice Peter Oliver in 1769 at Middleborough, Massachusetts
    Occupied by James Bowdoin II and family, 1775–1782
    Courtesy of the Society for the Preservation of New England Antiquities

10. Attributed to John Smibert
     b. Scotland 1688, active in America 1729–1751
     after Nicolas Poussin
     French, 1594–1665
     The Continence of Scipio
     oil on canvas
     46 x 62 inches
     Bequest of the Honorable James Bowdoin III
     1813.10

11. John Trumbull
     American, 1756–1843
     Sir John Temple and Family, 1784
     oil on canvas
     26 3/4 x 33 3/4 inches
     Courtesy of Mrs. Albert L. Key

12. Naushon Island Account Book of James
    Bowdoin II and James Bowdoin III,
    1784–1802, pp. 1 and 2
    Courtesy of the Trustees of Naushon Island

13. Edward Greene Malbone
    American, 1777–1807
    Portrait of James Bowdoin III, ca. 1804
    watercolor on ivory
    3 3/16 x 2 1/2 inches (oval)
    Gift of Mrs. Dorothy Hupper in honor of
    President Kenneth C. M. Sills '01 and
    Mrs. Sills h '52
    1951.7

*14. French
    Court Suit (Coat, Waistcoat, and Trousers)
    ca. 1805–1808
    Wool, silk, cotton linen; embroidered with
    silk and metallic thread, spangles and
    small pieces of glass
    Gift of Robert C. Winthrop
    Courtesy of the Museum of Fine Arts,
    Boston   *01.110, 01.111, 01.112*

15. Gilbert Stuart
    American, 1755–1828
    Portrait of James Bowdoin III
    oil on canvas
    28 1/2 x 24 inches
    Bequest of Mrs. Sarah Bowdoin Dearborn
    1870.6

16. Gilbert Stuart
    American, 1755–1828
    Portrait of Sarah Bowdoin (Mrs. James
    Bowdoin III, née Bowdoin; 2nd mar.
    Dearborn), before 1806
    oil on canvas
    30 x 25 1/8 inches
    Bequest of Mrs. Sarah Bowdoin Dearborn
    1870.7

*17. Gilbert Stuart
    American, 1755–1828
    Portrait of James Madison, 1805–1807
    oil on canvas
    48 1/4 x 39 3/4 inches
    Bequest of the Honorable James
    Bowdoin III
    1813.54

*18. Gilbert Stuart
    American, 1755–1828
    Portrait of Thomas Jefferson, 1805–1807
    oil on canvas
    48 3/8 x 39 3/4 inches
    Bequest of the Honorable James
    Bowdoin III
    1813.55

19. Anonymous
    Ariadne
    marble
    27 x 37 1/2 x 13 1/2 inches
    Monticello, Thomas Jefferson Memorial
    Foundation
    © 1992 Thomas Jefferson Memorial
    Foundation, Inc.
    Photographer: Edward Owen

20. Rembrandt Peale
    American, 1778–1860
    Portrait of John Armstrong, c. 1809
    oil on canvas
    29 x 23 3/4 inches
    Courtesy of the Independence National
    Historical Park

21. Invitation from Napoléon to James
    Bowdoin III to attend the marriage of
    Prince Jérôme-Napoléon to Catherine de
    Würtemberg, 23 August 1807
    Courtesy of the Massachusetts Historical
    Society, Boston

22. French
    Waistcoat, early nineteenth century
    (1800–1810)
    White satin with silk, gold thread, and
    spangles; lined with white cotton flannel
    Gift of Robert C. Winthrop
    Courtesy of the Museum of Fine Arts,
    Boston

    01.114

23. Anonymous
    View of the Octagon Room at the Ruel
    Williams House, Augusta, Maine
    Wallpaper depicting the *Savauges de la mer
    Pacifique*
    Designed by Jean-Gabriel Charvet and
    printed by Joseph Dufour, Paris, 1804
    Courtesy of Historic Deerfield, Inc.,
    Deerfield, Massachusetts

24. Gallery clock, given to the Brattle Square
    Church by James Bowdoin III
    Photography courtesy of the Massachusetts
    Historical Society, Boston

*25. Mansion House, Naushon Island, 1809
    View from the south, 1992
    Photograph by Erik Borg
    The locust trees in the foreground are
    descendants of those laid out by James
    Bowdoin III.

*26. Mansion House, Naushon Island, 1809
    View toward Woods Hole, 1992
    Photograph by Erik Borg

27. Mansion House, Naushon Island, 1809
    View from the north, 1992
    Photograph by Erik Borg

28. Federal easy chair, Boston area, c. 1790
    Mahogany with front legs inlaid
    Private collection

Walker Art Building, McKim, Mead & White, 1894

THE INTELLECTUAL
FOUNDATIONS OF THE
COLLEGE MUSEUM

Clifton C. Olds

If one were to survey the college and university museums of North America in 1993—examining their stated missions, their staffing, their acquisition and exhibition policies, and their role in the academic world of which they are a part—one would discover a relatively consistent pattern, a pattern not unrelated to the philosophical and organizational characteristics of the modern public museum. An investigation of the early history of academic museums or collections—those established before the close of the nineteenth century—reveals nothing like this homogeneity. Indeed, the eighteenth- and nineteenth-century foundations of American college museums are marked by such diversity in the nature of their collections, in their employment in the academic setting, and in the acquisition, care, and exhibition of materials, that no discernable pattern of creation and development would appear to exist. And yet there are some common factors, some shared attitudes and aspirations, that link the disparate chapters of this history, and in these one discovers the intellectual foundations of the modern college or university museum.[1] This essay will briefly examine some of these factors, not as part of a comprehensive review of the early history of American college museums, but as an investigation into the philosophical issues central to this development. It will focus on events leading up to the dedication of Bowdoin's Walker Art Building in 1894, not only because this book celebrates that event, but also because the middle years of the 1890s mark a point at which many of the ideas and aspirations inherent in the early development of the college museum either reach a conclusion or give way to a new conception of the institution.

The sources of many of the attitudes conditioning the early growth of American museums must be sought in the intellectual history of Europe, and much of this essay will deal with that relationship, but because its primary focus is the early history of the American college museum, a selective chronology of some major events in that history might be useful at the outset.[2]

1791 Dartmouth College establishes its museum of paintings, natural specimens, and ethnographic artifacts in Dartmouth Hall (there is a reference to a museum at Dartmouth as early as 1772, but its contents and location are unknown).

1811 James Bowdoin III bequeaths his art collection to Bowdoin College, establishing the earliest collegiate collection of European paintings, prints, and drawings. The collection would be supplemented in 1826 by the Bowdoin family collection of portraits.

1832 Yale University builds the Trumbull Gallery to house the paintings of John Trumbull, acquired from the artist in return for a life annuity. The university's collections would be transferred to Street Hall in 1868 and would be significantly enlarged in 1871 with the acquisition of James Jackson Jarves's collection of Italian paintings.

1855-65 Relief sculptures excavated from the palace of Assurnasirpal II are distributed to a number of American colleges.

1857 Harvard College acquires the Francis Calley Gray Collection of prints, which it would lend to the Boston Museum of Fine Arts in 1876. With the opening of the Fogg Museum in 1895, the collection would return to Cambridge.

1864 Vassar College Art Gallery is established with the acquisition of American and British paintings and prints from the collection of Elias Magoon.

1873 The University of Vermont constructs its Park Gallery in the school's library and expresses its intention to acquire works of art.

1874 Luigi Gregori, Notre Dame's first artist-in-residence, gives his collection of Italian paintings and drawings to the university (the paintings would be destroyed in a fire in 1879).

1876 Mount Holyoke Seminary (rechartered as Mount Holyoke College in 1888) establishes its Gallery for Science and Art in Lyman Williston Hall.

1882 Smith College dedicates its Hillyer Gallery, built to house a collection that already contains major works of American painting.

1888 Princeton University opens its Museum of Historic Art.

1894 Stanford University opens its Museum of Art. Bowdoin dedicates the Walker Art Building.

At the conclusion of his speech at the opening of the Walker Art Building in 1894, Martin Brimmer cited as the "essential elements of a more perfected life, Righteousness, Truth, and Beauty."[3] That all three of those ideals should be associated with art was a common belief in the nineteenth century, particularly among the American Transcendentalists. Emerson concludes his second essay on art by asserting that "beauty, truth, and goodness are not obsolete; they spring eternal in the breast of man; they are as indigenous in Massachusetts as in Tuscany or the Isles of Greece."[4] In this last decade of the twentieth century those exalted absolutes no longer have much currency in the thinking of those who deal with the arts, but in the nineteenth century they were both guiding principles and goals. The early history of the museum movement in America was a checkered one, but it is clear that those who concerned themselves with the collection and exhibition of material things did so in the belief that truth, righteousness, and beauty were an essential trinity. Without attempting to define the indefinable, and acknowledging the difficulties involved in separating any one of these ideas from the other two, I will use them as the categorical divisions of this essay.

TRUTH

Institutions of higher learning are by definition committed to the acquisition and communication of knowledge, and most of the functions of a college or university are directly or indirectly dedicated to that end. Museums are no exception, and although American schools would eventually come to appreciate the inspirational values of art, the early history of their collections is more intimately linked with their educational mission, at least as that mission was broadly defined. The actual coordination of the curriculum with the holdings of college museums is a more recent phenomenon, but there is every indication that early collections of natural and cultural objects were considered components of a scholarly apparatus. In this, they are the heirs to a European tradition that considered museums seats of learning, an attitude that explains the peculiar character of America's first college museums.[5]

THE *WUNDERKAMMER*

On 26 October 1772, in what may be the earliest recorded reference to a college museum in America, the Reverend David McClure wrote to the president of Dartmouth College to inform him that "I have collected a few curious Elephants Bones found about six hundred miles down the Ohio, for the young Museum at Dartmouth."[6] Whether this brief reference can be said to prove the existence of a museum in 1772 is open to question, but it is clear that soon after its founding, Dartmouth was beginning to acquire a collection of objects that eventually would constitute a museum as that term is now defined.[7] Over the course of the half-century following its dedication in 1770, Dartmouth acquired through gift or purchase a remarkable conglomeration of natural, mechanical, and ethnographic specimens, including fossils, minerals, stuffed birds and reptiles, Native American implements, artifacts acquired on Captain James Cook's expedition to the South Pacific, and such exotica as lava from Mt. Vesuvius, a stuffed zebra, and a "pinguin" from the Cape of Good Hope. Most of these items were the gifts of alumni and can hardly be considered components of a planned or structured collection, but there were a number of acquisitions that clearly reflected the college's desire to establish what was commonly known as "philosophical apparatus," i.e., a collection of natural and manufactured objects that would facilitate the study of what was then known as Natural Philosophy. At the commencement of 1772, Dr. John Phillips donated £175 for the purchase of this apparatus, and when President John Wheelock made a fund-raising trip to Europe in 1783, he used these and other monies to acquire the instruments considered central to scientific inquiry: an air pump, an orrery, telescopes, a thermometer, a barometer, and "electrical apparatus." In 1790, the trustees of the college voted to set aside a room in the middle of Dartmouth Hall as a repository for these instruments and for the collection of natural and ethnographic specimens, which once again earned the title "museum."

In the accumulation of these diverse and "curious rarities" (a phrase that appears often in the documents of the time), Dartmouth was essentially establishing what was known in England as a curiosity cabinet: a collection of natural and artificial objects—often unusual or exotic in form or provenance—that reflected not only the simple curiosity of its owner, but also and more significantly the intellectual concerns of the English Enlightenment. This fascination with the rare and the curious was a driving force behind the foundation of British and American museums. Dr. Johnson went so far as to define the word museum as "a Repository of learned Curiosities," a phrase echoed in Harvard College's description of its own collection as the "Repositerry of Curiosities."[8] The phenomenon

is much older than the eighteenth century, however, its roots having been nourished by the scientific revolution of the sixteenth and seventeenth centuries, and its growth promoted by contemporary developments in the areas of philosophy and education. Central to all of these developments is the concept of universalism.

The nominative Latin root of the term "university"—*universus*—can mean simply "the whole." Expanded, it can refer to the whole of existence, the universe itself. In that extended form, and in its incorporation in our word for an institution of higher learning, it refers to everything that can be known about the world: universal knowledge. Over the course of the last two centuries the concept has become quaint and archaic, made so by the explosive proliferation of scientific data and the attendant growth of philosophical doubt. But in the period in which the modern concept of the university was developing—most specifically the sixteenth and seventeenth centuries—universalism was a guiding principle in the establishment of scholarly and pedagogical goals. Beginning with the appearance of what has come to be called the "renaissance man"—a concept established and nurtured by humanists of the fifteenth century—the image of the learned individual soon became that of the polymath, the virtuoso, a person whose abilities and knowledge ranged so widely that the universe in its entirety could be said to be his study. The notion was stated most succinctly and beautifully in lines from an epitaph engraved upon the tomb of Carlo Marsuppini (d. 1453), chancellor of Florence and one of his city's leading scholars:

Stop and gaze upon the marbles that entomb a great sage, one for whose genius there was not world enough. Carlo, the great glory of his age, knew all that nature, the heavens, and humanity could produce.[9]

This conviction that the human mind could encompass all things knowable was both challenged and stimulated by the cosmographic and geographic discoveries of the sixteenth and early seventeenth centuries, discoveries that suddenly and dramatically expanded the sphere of human knowledge. The voyages to the New

World and the Far East, the Copernican reformation of the cosmos, and the development of the telescope and the microscope, all contributed to a new understanding of the world as a whole and a new awareness of the number and diversity of its components. This early chapter in the "information explosion," promoted and disseminated by the printed book, would bring about revolutionary changes not only in the sphere of science, but also in that of philosophy, since radical shifts in our understanding of the world inevitably call for radical shifts in the analysis of our understanding. The revolution of the sixteenth and seventeenth centuries was not only scientific but epistemological.

Like most revolutionary events, however, this development was colored and complicated by vestigial convictions, superstitions, and prejudices, so that the early decades of the scientific revolution were marked not by the appearance of formal and logically structured disciplines based upon purely empirical observation, but instead by an almost chaotic tangle of fact and fiction resulting from the blending of new observations and old beliefs. The results of new discoveries in the areas of zoology, botany, and what we would now call anthropology were frequently distorted by classical and medieval conceptions of nature, so that the strange plants, animals, and human beings of the New World or Africa were often described in terms reflecting the fanciful images of Pliny the Elder or the medieval bestiary. Astronomy was obliged to accommodate both astrology and the fears of the Church. The pseudoscience of alchemy, while actually establishing certain principles and techniques that would find a place in the genuine science of chemistry, led scientists in directions that were more mystical than clinical. It was an age in which an emerging rationalism was forced to contend with the stubborn traditions of hermetic philosophy. Typical of this ambivalence is the career of Paracelsus, who as a chemist and physician championed the cause of empirical observation, but as a mystic and neo-Platonist sought truth in the arcane theories of alchemy; or that of scientists like Johannes Kepler or Thomas Hariot, whose fame as brilliant mathematicians and astronomers was equaled by their reputation for astrological prognostication.

This strange wedding of new science and old mysteries produced a peculiar breed of scholars: men whose curiosity and intellectual ambition knew no bounds, but who demonstrated an almost childlike fascination with everything strange, bizarre, fanciful, exotic, miraculous, or grotesque. Taking their cue from Aristotle, who in his treatises on Poetics and Rhetoric had emphasized the dramatic value of the extraordinary and unexpected, the humanists of the sixteenth century found the miraculous and the monstrous more stimulating than the normal and the commonplace, and so the goals of human curiosity became the curiosities of nature.[10] The phenomenon has often been related to mannerist tendencies in art and literature, and the comparison is probably apt, but it tends to obscure its intellectual facet, for in the quest for a comprehensive knowledge of the world, scholars considered the rare and "abnormal" products of nature and humanity as sources of enlightenment. As Joy Kenseth has pointed out:

If one wanted to comprehend and fully appreciate the creative capacities and ingenuity of human beings, then it stood to reason that the exceptional, rather than the ordinary, object should be collected. Similarly, nature's rarities were to be preferred to her commonplaces. By studying the unusual performances of nature or her "errors," one could gain insight into her variability and ultimately discover her hidden truths.[11]

One of the principal manifestations of this attitude is the chamber of wonders, or *Wunderkammer*, as it was known in the German-speaking world, a collection of natural specimens and cultural artifacts characterized by an almost encyclopaedic range and by a decided emphasis on the unusual. A typical chamber might contain a mineral collection, stuffed fauna of particularly exotic provenance (crocodiles were particularly popular), freakish malformations of nature, rare botanical specimens (often those thought to have magical or curative properties), sea shells and corals, birds' eggs, ethnographic curiosities from the New World, Africa, and Asia, scientific apparatus (especially astronomical instruments), automata, holy relics and objects of historical significance, mummies, and legendary "marvels" (embalmed mermaids, unicorn horns, etc.). Because it often included books and manuscripts, gems and cameos, precious objects of gold and silver, antique sculpture, and contemporary painting, prints, and drawings, the *Wunderkammer* also functioned as a library, a treasury, and an art gallery.[12] The passion for such heterogeneous collections was international, leading to the appearance of *chambres des merveilles* in France, *musei naturali* in Italy, and curiosity cabinets, or gentlemen's cabinets, in England and America. The German term *Wunderkammer* remains the most popular reference to the phenomenon, however, and with good reason, for in its nominative form the word "wonder" effectively describes the rare and surprising items found in these sixteenth-century cabinets, while the verb speaks to an active sense of wonder which Descartes described as the first step toward knowledge. As William Schupbach points out in his informative essay on the origins of cabinets of curiosities, "wonder was a proper reaction for the learned as well as for the uninstructed: wonder, paraphrased perhaps as inquisitive delight in novelty, mingled with awe and gratitude, was part of the natural history and natural philosophy of the time."[13]

As will be apparent to the reader, a description of the typical *Wunderkammer* of the sixteenth century suggests that the Dartmouth Museum was an eighteenth-century version of this European phenomenon, and to an extent it was. But to understand fully the early development of American college museums, it is also necessary to consider the evolving character of the *Wunderkammer* and its gradual transformation into an institution of intellectual and pedagogical stature.

The most ambitious collections of the sixteenth and early seventeenth centuries were understandably those of European princes: the Medici grand dukes, the monarchs of France, Duke Albrecht V of Bavaria, Archduke Ferdinand II, and most notably Emperor Rudolf II, archduke of Austria and king of Hungary and Bohemia. This passion for collecting was not confined to the nobility, however; cabinets of curiosities could be found in monasteries, the private studies of learned men, and eventually schools, for the didactic value of these collections was apparent to everyone who believed that knowledge was gained through the observation of nature and human achievement—*naturalia et artificialia*.[14] The scholar's devotion to the *Wunderkammer* was not without its difficulties, however, for the very glory of the thing—its encyclopaedic nature—posed serious problems for anyone who believed that knowledge must be submitted to a process of logical categorization. No one doubted the value of a "universal" collection; Francis Bacon, in proposing an ideal scholarly apparatus that would include a library, garden, zoo, and cabinet of natural and artificial specimens, hoped that in such an establishment one would have "in a small compass, a Model of Universal Nature."[15] The statement was echoed in the words of the great Bolognese naturalist Ulisse Aldrovandi, who described his own formidable collection as "a universal forest of knowledge."[16] But the principle of plenitude made sense only if tamed by the principles of logic, and as the *Wunderkammer* entered the era of Rationalism and Enlightenment, it underwent a scholarly transformation that reached its climax in England in the establishment of the Royal Society and the founding of the Ashmolean Museum at the University of Oxford.

Since Francis Bacon, in urging James I to establish an institute for the study of science, laid the groundwork for the founding of the Royal Society, he might be said to be its spiritual and intellectual forefather. As a champion of inductive reasoning whose proposed system of empirical observation or "experimental philosophy" would lead directly to the growth of British empiricism, Bacon was understandably devoted to the direct study of the material world. His dream of a kind of intellectual estate, within which the scholar would have access to extensive collections of fauna, flora, and the works of man, testifies to his conviction. At the same time that he proposed a collection of "universal nature," however, Bacon also proposed a corpus of knowledge subdivided into the history of creatures, the history of marvels, and the history of arts.[17] For Bacon, knowledge and the means to knowledge implied structured categories and systematic method, and this approach was his great legacy to the scientists of the later seventeenth century. When the Royal Society was founded in 1660 it was founded on the principles Bacon had formulated, and although its early history was often marked more by the enthusiasm of its scientists than by systematic methods of investigation—a rigorous methodology would have to await Newton—its devotion to experiment and observation was passionate.[18] True to its chartered title, the Royal Society for the Promotion of Natural Knowledge, it immediately began to form its own version of the *Wunderkammer*, or "Repository." With the addition of the private cabinet of Robert Hubert in 1666, the society could claim one of the world's largest collections of natural specimens, and one of the few that was open to the public. This sudden elevation of the curiosity cabinet to the stature of a scientific laboratory-museum was not unique in the seventeenth century: only six years after the founding of the Royal Society, France founded its Académie Royale des Sciences, with Christian Huygens its first secretary. Competing with these royal establishments were a number of museums associated with major universities, most notably those of Pisa, Leiden, Basel, Bologna, and Oxford.[19]

As was to be the case with American college museums, the foundations and growth of these European university collections often depended upon private donors, although sometimes indirectly. In 1661, the University of Basel acquired the cabinet of the Amerbachs, the remarkable family of printers, legalists, and humanists who had been prominent in the intellectual life of Basel since the time of Erasmus (whose own cabinet was inherited by Bonifacius Amerbach). In an admirable instance of cooperation between town and gown, this gigantic collection of art and artifacts was purchased by the city of Basel and installed on university property as one of the first public museums. The collections of individual faculty members also became the bases of university collections, as happened with the cabi-

net of Ulisse Aldrovandi, professor of natural history at the University of Bologna, or that of the seventh-century Danish naturalist Ole Worm, whose collection was a pedagogical tool of the University of Copenhagen.[20]

The most immediate prototype of the American college museum, however, was that of the University of Oxford. Elias Ashmole had acquired the remarkable cabinet of the insatiable traveler and collector John Tradescant the Elder, who earlier had established his own museum, known as Tradescant's Ark.[21] Ashmole bequeathed the Tradescant cabinet to Oxford in 1677, adding his own collection of antiquities and requiring the university to house the lot in an appropriate building. The Ashmolean Museum—perhaps the first museum to consider itself a public institution—opened in 1683. While there had been earlier collections of natural and artificial "rarities" at Oxford, most notably the natural specimens of the Anatomy School, it is symptomatic of the confluence of art and science in early academic museums that no clear distinction was made between what belonged in the Anatomy School and what constituted the proper holdings of the Ashmolean.

Nothing so dramatic as Ashmole's bequest marks the origins of the American collegiate museum, but the intellectual ambience is a common bond. Five years before Ashmole acquired Tradescant's Ark, Harvard had acquired its first telescope as a gift of Governor John Winthrop.[22] It was a modest beginning to the history of American college collections, but the gift implied that the American student deserved the same philosophical apparatus that his European counterpart enjoyed, and it anticipated America's willing acceptance of its intellectual heritage. The notion that an educated man should be educated in all things was clearly a European legacy enthusiastically accepted by American intellectuals of the colonial era, whose universalist sympathies marked every aspect of their public and private lives. Benjamin Franklin and Thomas Jefferson, both of whom owned cabinets of curiosities and philosophical apparatus, are certainly the most famous examples of such American virtuosi, but there were many others, including James Bowdoin II. Having studied natural philosophy with John Winthrop IV at Harvard, Bowdoin became an admirable representative of the American Enlightenment, and in the process acquired all the paraphernalia of learning. His own philosophical apparatus included the requisite telescopes and globes, a microscope, an orrery, "electrical machines," and a library containing the writings of Berkeley, Hutcheson, Hume, Locke, Newton, Descartes, Rousseau, and Voltaire. He was also a collector of paintings, a subject addressed by other essays in this catalogue.[23]

The biographies of these statesmen-scholars show that the physical means to universal knowledge—the diverse collections of books, natural specimens, and scientific apparatus that formed the basis of inductive learning—were as important for the American scholar as they were for his European counterpart. It is not surprising, therefore, that such collections became the nuclei of many academic collections, their appearance and growth within the scholarly community explaining much about the nature and the philosophical goals of the American college museum.[24] We have already seen the degree to which the Dartmouth cabinet resembled the *Wunderkammern* of Europe, but Dartmouth was not alone in its acquisition of such materials. When Thomas Hollis endowed a professorial chair in mathematics and natural philosophy at Harvard in 1727, he included a large collection of "philosophical apparatus" for the instruction of Harvard students, a collection destroyed in the fire that struck Harvard Hall in 1764. The rebuilding of the Harvard cabinet between the year of the fire and 1800 was spurred by donations of specimens of natural history and important mineral collections, including one given by James Bowdoin II.[25] His son, James Bowdoin III, bequeathed to Bowdoin College his own collection of philosophical apparatus, which was installed in the College's Massachusetts Hall. The University of Vermont began assembling a cabinet of curiosities in the early nineteenth century, and in 1885 found it necessary to convert its library into a museum that would accommodate its collections of art, ethnographic objects,

and zoological and geological specimens.[26] At Mount Holyoke, where the college collection was given its own quarters in Lyman Williston Hall in 1876, American paintings and copies of the Old Masters coexisted with a "missionary cabinet" containing ethnographic materials from Asia, Africa, the Americas, and the South Seas.[27] The same is true of Yale, where Trumbull's collection of paintings shared the Gallery of Fine Arts with native American and Polynesian artifacts.

While these collegiate *Wunderkammern* were not always as encyclopaedic as their European predecessors (there is no evidence that Holyoke's contained natural specimens), they reflect a universalist attitude that has persisted well into our own day and still conditions the American liberal arts curriculum and its distribution requirements. As late as the 1950s, Ivy League schools were still promoting the image of the "well-rounded man," America's equivalent of the Elizabethan "compleat gentleman" and an idea rooted in the European concept of the *virtuoso* and his comprehensive collection of *naturalia et artificialia*. In the twentieth century the lines of disciplinary demarcation have become much more defined, as has the concept of a museum. Natural specimens and ethnographic collections may occupy the same building, but the idea of exhibiting works of art beside the wonders of nature is no longer current, in part because the philosophical and theological foundations of the idea have crumbled. In the nineteenth century, however, those foundations were firm, and their stability reflected the notion that art and science were essentially inseparable.

ART AND SCIENCE

In late medieval attempts to reconcile Aristotelian thought and its nominalist implications with the neo-Platonic idealism of orthodox Christian dogma, theologians took refuge in the notion that every material thing is in some way possessed by the Holy Spirit, that all of nature is alive with meaning. In the age of the *Wunderkammer* this notion achieved a status bordering on pantheism, to such a degree that nothing—not even the most freakish or malformed products of nature—could be considered alien to the Divine Plan. Allied with this attitude toward nature was the idea that the artist was God's tool, a co-creator whose talents were God-given and whose achievements were divinely inspired. Thus every object—natural or artificial—was worthy of attention and capable of leading the mind to God. The theological implications of this concept were often modified or even ignored by the empiricists of the Enlightenment, for whom sensation and association were the only certain paths to truth, but their emphasis on inductive cognition simply reinforced the encyclopaedic tendencies of sixteenth-century thought, since empirically-acquired knowledge was considered directly proportionate to the number of things observed. And in the nineteenth century, the deistic element reemerged in the transcendentalist movements of European and American thought, as nature in its full panoply became the valid object of both scientific and theological speculation. Art had a place in this scheme, in part because it was the product of human nature, in part because the visual arts were valued as much for their ability to reproduce nature as they were for their aesthetic value. Thus it was that art and science continued to be as intimately linked as they had been in the early *Wunderkammern.* American museums founded around the time of the Revolution—institutions like the Columbian Museum in Boston and the Tammany American Museum in New York—routinely combined natural specimens, ethnographic items, and paintings. Indeed, a broadside issued by the Tammany Society at the time of the founding of its museum (1791) stated that it was ready to accept "everything and from whatever clime."[28]

Even though the full-fledged *Wunderkammer* eventually disappeared from the American campus, the same linkage of art and science can be observed in the later history of American college museums, at least where language is concerned. It is somehow appropriate that the art collection of Mount Holyoke was first housed in the Lyman Williston Hall for Science and Art, or that the first director of the Trumbull Gallery at Yale was a professor of chemistry who edited the *American Journal of Science and Art.*[29] In fact, Yale is a good example of the concordance—if not to say confusion—of art and science in nineteenth-century academia. When the Yale art collection was moved to Street Hall in 1868, it shared those quarters with artifacts from the South Pacific, while Yale's Peabody Museum of Archaeology and Ethnography (founded in 1867) housed a number of objects that could have been defined as "fine art."[30] To the degree that science included archaeology and anthropology, the union of art and science was celebrated poetically in lines recited at the dedication of the Yale Gallery:

City of Elms, rejoice! for thou
Thy crowning grace receiveth now
And Yale, exalt thy honored head;
Proclaim, Science and Art are wed.[31]

To understand the persistence of this notion, one that had outlasted a somewhat naive fascination with "curiosities" and now resided in the more sober realm of academic research, one must consider the didactic values attributed to art and artifacts. Before art became "fine" in the sense of aesthetic refinement, assuming a qualitative superiority that would justify its exclusive position in a world of lesser objects, it served as a pedagogical instrument for historical and moral instruction, or, in other words, as one component of the familiar philosophical apparatus.

Typical of the attitude is a letter sent by Matthew Vassar to the Reverend Elias Magoon, chair of the Committee of the Art Gallery of Vassar Female College, in 1864, the year in which the Vassar Gallery was established. In stating his hopes for the new museum, Vassar noted that "it was specially the wish of the Founder that its walls and portfolios should be adorned with the most significant instructive educating forces of those materials, as I have always believed that if man delight in the material works of his maker they will greatly aid his moral and spiritual culture."[32] This "educating force" of a museum was to become a standard justification for the establishment of public museums in the late nineteenth century and often was seen as far more significant than the collecting of objets d'art. James Jackson Jarves, whose collection of Italian paintings will be discussed later in this essay, emphasized the didactic value of museums, stating that "It is requisite that our public should have free access to galleries in which shall be exhibited in chronological series specimens of the art of all nations and schools, arranged according to their motives and the special influences that attended their development."[33]

This remarkably liberal, democratic, and scholarly approach—so clearly an echo of the Enlightenment—resulted in three significant characteristics of the nineteenth-century art museum: the chronological and art-historical arrangement of its exhibits, its willingness to expand the traditional definition of art, and its tolerance of copies and reproductions.

ART AS HISTORY

While art history as an academic discipline came relatively late to American academia, works of art have always been considered valid documents of history. The collections of portraits that constituted the earliest art collections of many colleges and universities were appreciated less for their aesthetic merits than for their references to the founding and development of the institutions that housed them. This attitude was as deeply rooted in European tradition as was the cabinet of curiosities, and takes us back once again to the Renaissance. Inspired in part by Petrarch's *De viris illustribus*, series of paintings and prints representing famous men and/or women became widely popular in the later fourteenth and fifteenth centuries, establishing a tradition that would undergo a typically encyclopaedic expansion in the sixteenth. The Italian humanist Paolo Giovio, for example, collected scores of portraits of famous persons, living and dead, a practice that Germain Bazin correctly compared to Vasari's biographical approach to art history.[34] In the seventeenth century an increasingly scholarly and objective approach to history reinforced this obsession with persons of note, especially in France and England, and American colleges and universities were clearly heirs to this tradition. While it is true that a large number of the portraits ac-

quired by the schools were those of founders, administrators, faculty, and alumni, there is good evidence that portraits of historical significance were highly valued. Portraits of the early presidents of the Republic were not only acquired by gift, but were actively sought, as exemplified by Princeton's commissioning of Charles Willson Peale's *Washington at the Battle of Princeton*.[35] Before fire destroyed Nassau Hall in 1802, Princeton's gallery of portraits included portraits of the kings and queens of England as well as those of American patriots. Other notable collections of portraits were those of Yale and Bowdoin, both of which contained, and still contain, works by painters of the stature of Feke, Smibert, Copley, and Stuart. Although many of these early portraits were distributed among the halls and offices of their institutions, they eventually became the nucleus of genuine art collections, in part because of their historical relevancy. The early college museums did not ignore questions of aesthetic merit (the words "elegant" and "grand" were often used to describe portraits), but the emphasis was on the educational value of works of art. The Reverend Elias Magoon, chair of Vassar's Committee on the Art Gallery, made this clear in his report to Vassar when he claimed that works of art "constitute the true history of humanity," a statement echoed by the artist and critic Eugene Benson, who maintained that "museums of art are the best means of fostering and cultivating the historic sense."[36] James Jackson Jarves, whose conception of historical sequence, quoted above, was influenced by the writings of French philosopher-historian Alexis Francois Rio, and whose own collection of Italian "primitives" was prodigiously art-historical, proposed museums that would educate their public, advocating didactic exhibitions organized chronologically.[37] In a letter to Charles Eliot Norton, who had tried in vain to obtain Jarves's collection of Italian paintings for Harvard, Jarves wrote:

Besides illustrating the progress of painting in Italy, my object has been also to show the development of the Christian idea in art, getting together for that purpose, as great a variety of pictures as possible. Thus besides its artistic and esthetic value, the gallery should possess an historical and religious one. Hence not the least of its importance is its consecutiveness in these several aspects.[38]

Jarves's statement was echoed in countless declarations of the mission of the college museum. Long after civic museums had made aesthetic responses to the object the principal thrust of their philosophy, college museums were maintaining that "the desideratum for us, as for any institution of higher learning, is to be able to illustrate the history of civilization through works of art."[39]

While Jarves's own collection was narrow in its focus, both in terms of medium and chronology, his willingness to collect works of art that were not currently in vogue is symptomatic of a growing tolerance and objectivity where art was concerned. In this area, however, Jarves was anticipated by Ralph Waldo Emerson and the sculptor Horatio Greenough, both of whom championed a broadening of the definition of art.[40] Januslike, Emerson and Greenough looked back to the universality of the *Wunderkammer* and forward to the day when the art historian and the anthropologist would begin to share their concerns.

ART AS MATERIAL CULTURE

In his important study of the history of museums, Germain Bazin observed that:

the nineteenth century was the Century of History. Museums were flooded to the point of overflowing with products created by all kinds of human endeavor, by all peoples of all periods. Thus was initiated a great idolatry of the past, a counterbalance to a certain complaisance toward the present that passed like a moment in the accelerated race toward the future, the perspectives of which were nightmarish.[41]

The pessimistic note in Bazin's appraisal echoes an American attitude to which we will return at the close of this essay, but the reference to diversity is equally applicable to the development of American college museums.

Although the nineteenth-century definition of "civilization" was often shamefully restricted, some of the early college museums and their supporters were remarkably enlightened in their promotion of a broad, comprehensive coverage of human endeavors in the arts. It is true that their natural sympathy for the classical world and its Christian sequel conditioned their thinking and led to the collections of plaster casts and Old Master copies that provided indirect access to the great Western tradition, but American academia was also heir to the Enlightenment, and this legacy was consequential. The impassioned dedication of earlier humanists to the cultures of Greece and Rome had been tempered by the relativistic spirit of British empiricism, a spirit that seems to pervade the statements of many of those involved with the early college museums. James Jackson Jarves held that "Art is universal. It unites mankind in common brotherhood."[42] In discussing the proper role of a museum, Jarves asserted:

A modern museum aims to present an entire epitome of the art phase of human life. Hence every object, even of homeliest use, in which exists complete or partial idealism. . .finds its proper place in it. . . .

The war clubs, tapas and gourds of the Polynesians are no longer rude curiosities but instructive specimens in their ornamental designs.[43]

As both a refutation of the cultural condescension inherent in the curiosity cabinet and a plea for the continuation of its universality, Jarves's statement reflects an egalitarian sentiment expressed by a number of writers of his generation. Ralph Waldo Emerson's definition of art was broad enough to encompass everything from "the tattooing of the Owhyhees to the Vatican Gallery," and included the simplest of utilitarian objects.[44] In what might be considered an early advocacy of the study of "material culture," Emerson maintained that America "must come back to the useful arts, and the distinction between Fine and useful arts be forgotten." It is in statements like these, or in Emerson's assertion that the "useful arts" include navigation, chemistry, and "all the grand and delicate tools and instruments by which man serves himself," that the spirit of the *Wunderkammer* and its philosophical apparatus endured.[45]

This egalitarian attitude toward the products of human culture, although related to a number of socially-conscious and reform-minded movements in the Anglo-American art world of the late nineteenth century, suffered something of an eclipse when the first great public museums began to appear in New York, Boston, and the other cities of the eastern seaboard. For these institutions, art was still to be defined as the old academies had defined it, and their collections were generally focused upon the Old Masters and the antiquities of the Western World. As we shall see, many college museums followed the same narrow course, in part because their patrons were often the same individuals who supported the new civic museums. But in the academic environment the universalist character of the curiosity cabinet died a slower death, and in some instances managed to survive. The University of Vermont, for example, still exhibits art and ethnographic materials in the Robert Hull Fleming Museum, and its natural specimens were not separated from these until the middle of the twentieth century. It seems improbable that American schools will ever return to exhibiting art and natural specimens side by side, and yet the potential exists for just such a resurrection of the *Wunderkammer*, as the Hood Museum at Dartmouth demonstrated in its recent exhibition dedicated to that phenomenon.[46] One could imagine the approbation Dartmouth might have received from Jarves, who maintained that "both Science and Art are essential to the complete existence of man."[47]

ART IN REPRODUCTION

What Jarves did not approve of was a reliance on anything but original works of art. In his critical writings, he rails against copies of Old Masters, which he considered no better than caricatures of the originals.[48] He was not alone in this opinion, but there was no consensus on this issue. The collecting of copies of works of art has a long history, of course. The Romans collected copies of Greek art as a matter of course, and even the most discriminating of Renaissance patrons—Isabella d'Este is a prime example—included copies in their collections. Both the Romans and their Renaissance successors had access to original works of art, however, and America was not so blessed, at least not as far as

the Old Masters were concerned. George Fisk Comfort, dean of the School of Fine Arts at Syracuse University, in advocating the acquisition of casts and photographic reproductions, lamented that "it is impossible now to get good original works of any historic artist of past periods."[49] It was a statement lacking in prescience, particularly since it was made just three years before Yale acquired the Jarves collection of Italian primitives, but it mirrored a general pessimism concerning America's ability to compete with the great museums of Europe. Charles Perkins, a collector in his own right and a prolific if conservative writer about art (he was one of the many who opposed Yale's acquisition of the Jarves collection), echoed Comfort's lament, but tempered his pessimism with a hint of egalitarian idealism. In advocating the use of reproductions, copies, and plaster casts, Perkins asserted that the goal of a museum should be the exhibition of "material for the education of a nation in art, not at making collections of objects of art," a statement anticipating twentieth-century attacks on the elitism of museums.[50]

Some educators were less than enthusiastic about this trend. Dr. Magoon, in his report on the Vassar Gallery, advocated the acquisition of engraved copies of masterpieces in European museums, but later in the same report he made an impassioned plea for the collection of originals rather than "sterile copies" or "a mass of dead engravings."[51] Martin Brimmer, in his address given at the opening of Bowdoin's Walker Art Building, recommended the acquisition of casts and reproductions, but admitted their limitations.[52] Whatever their ambivalence, the directors of the early college museums depended heavily on copies and reproductions. The University of Michigan had a museum of art as early as 1855, but there is no evidence that it contained anything but plaster casts of famous works of sculpture. Most of the eastern museums housed some original works of art, and some could boast of many, but photographs of early installations inevitably show a fair sampling of casts and reproductions. As late as 1900, Yale was still exhibiting 150 casts of sculpture, and with the exception of the Gray and

Randall collections, Harvard was similarly dependent on reproductions of one form or another.

One might have expected that the greater availability and lower cost of native productions would have been considered an acceptable alternative to European Old Masters, and certainly preferable to reproductions, but American critics were of two minds on this score. In his report to Vassar, Dr. Magoon urged the new Art Gallery to acquire one hundred original oil paintings, of which twenty could be European, "but at least sixty must be first-rate transcripts of American landscape, mainly along the Hudson, Lake George, New Hampshire, and Vermont." He also advocated the acquisition of "at least another hundred water-color pictures. . .because, out of America, that is the best art intrinsically, and, for female culture, it is the best everywhere."[53] Perkins, on the other hand, considered examples of American art, "whatever their merits. . . not fit implements for the instruction of the nation in art."[54] These two conflicting attitudes mirror a larger conflict between those who championed national values while promoting a kind of cultural xenophobia, and those who saw in the art of Europe a means of elevating the taste of the young republic, a subject to which I will turn at the close of this essay.

THE PROMOTION OF RIGHTEOUSNESS

While American scholars recognized the purely documentary value of art, their concerns usually went far beyond the narrow bounds of art history. Many of the academics who first turned their attention to the arts were ministers and missionaries, and they shared with Emerson the conviction that "there is higher work for Art than the arts."[55] In this they often parted company with the British empiricists and French *philosophes* whom they otherwise admired. The idea that British empiricism links the rationale of the *Wunderkammer* with the philosophical foundations of the American college museum is hardly debatable, considering the common emphasis on inductive reasoning and the easily documented relationship between the intellectual history of England and that of its colony. In its purest form, however, British empiricism either had no time for metaphysical or theological speculation, or resorted to a kind of dispassionate deism. As attractive as this stance may have been to certain of the Founding Fathers, it ran counter to the precepts of those early American schools in which Christian orthodoxy ruled the day, and to that extent the intellectual context and pedagogical goals of the early college museums were more closely associated with certain attitudes of the sixteenth century than with those of the Enlightenment. Typical of the former is a remarkable treatise published by Samuel Quiccheberg in 1565, in which this Flemish physician proposed a comprehensive museum— he called it a *universo teatro*—that would seek to embrace all aspects of the natural and artificial worlds, and would arrange its universal collections according to a logical system based indirectly on Pliny's *Naturalis historia*, and directly on Quiccheberg's familiarity with the collections of Duke Albrecht V of Bavaria.[56] Throughout his treatise, Quiccheberg emphasizes the degree to which universal knowledge will lead the mind to God, and although his hypothetical museum was never actually built, this theistic orientation would characterize much of late sixteenth- and seventeenth-century thinking about the nature of museums. Perhaps the most scholarly *Wunderkammer* of its day, the Jesuit *Musaeum Kircherianum*, was described by its curator as dedicated to "the Glory of God."[57]

In America, where higher education has often had strong religious affiliations, this tendency to see spiritual value in the collection of material things has had a long history. Many of the earliest college collections of natural and ethnographic wonders were donated by alumni who had served as missionaries in the New World, Africa, and Asia, and their gifts were seen as contributions to the education of Christian men and women. The Reverend David McClure, whose gift of mastodon bones anticipated the Dartmouth *Wunderkammer*, referred to the animal as "this greatest of the works of the Creator," an observation typical of pre-

Darwinian paleontology, and of the tendency to view natural phenomena as the language of God. The theological aspect of early collecting is exemplified by the fact that Mount Holyoke's collection of exotica from three continents—the equivalent of an English gentleman's cabinet—was known as the "Missionary Cabinet," and was first catalogued by a professor of "Theism and Christian Evidences."[58]

No less religious in its motivation was the collection of European and American art. When the Reverend Magoon sold his collection of oil paintings, watercolors, and prints to Vassar in 1864, the college acquired what Magoon had considered a guide to "Christianity Illustrated by its Monuments."[59] In his report to Vassar, made earlier in that same year, Dr. Magoon spoke of natural forms as "God's works of art, his original thoughts, his music, his poems," and held that "man's delight in God's work is the mightiest means of moral culture."[60] In Matthew Vassar's letter to Magoon, in which he first discusses the educational value of the gallery, he goes on to say that "if man delight in the material works of his maker they will greatly aid his moral and spiritual culture."[61] It is clear that in the minds of Magoon and Vassar, art shares this revelatory power, and they were hardly alone in this belief. Jarves had stated the idea in typically blunt terms when he wrote, "The rules of Art are absolute. They are moral laws implanted by God in the heart of Nature, and are independent of human frailty or invention."[62]

The degree to which art was considered inspirational in the literal sense of the word—i.e., capable of effecting spiritual renewal in the hearts and minds of its audience—is reflected in many statements calling for the creation of museums. Eugene Benson, a painter and writer whom contemporaries considered America's leading art critic, believed that art museums not only fostered and cultivated "the historic sense," but also "nurse the sentiment of reverence," a statement echoing Emerson's assertion that "the contemplation of a work of great art draws us into a state of mind which may be called religious."[63] This emphasis on the spiritual nature of art sometimes acquired a mystical intensity

comparable to both the Transcendentalists' worship of nature and the Renaissance conviction that artists were divinely inspired. In his report to Vassar, the Reverend Magoon spoke rapturously about the impact of "Original Art," asserting that "a beauty-haunted mind not only tends most directly towards the fountain of creation—the mind of God—but it therein both sees the wisdom and shares the power of divinity itself."[64] Martin Brimmer, in the closing moments of his address marking the opening of Bowdoin's new museum, noted that to understand the inspiration behind a work of art, one "must look back again into the artist's heart, and there see with him his new vision of the Divine."[65]

The old notion that the artist was in some sense an agent of the Creator explains in part the admiration for, or at least the tolerance of, the art of non-Western cultures, as expressed in the writings of Emerson and Jarves. Emerson summarized the attitude and placed it in the context of nineteenth-century historicism when he wrote:

Now that which is inevitable in the work has a higher charm than individual talent can ever give, inasmuch as the artist's pen or chisel seems to have been held and guided by a gigantic hand to inscribe a line in the history of the human race. This circumstance gives a value to the Egyptian hieroglyphs, to the Indian, Chinese and Mexican idols, however gross and shapeless. They denote the height of the human soul in that hour, and were not fantastic, but sprung from a necessity as deep as the world. Shall I now add that the whole extant product of the plastic arts has herein its highest value, as history; as a stroke drawn in the portrait of that fate, perfect and beautiful, according to whose ordinations all beings advance to their beatitude?[66]

It is within the context of Christian pedagogy that one can understand the spirit in which a number of eastern schools acquired their most monumental works of art: a series of low-relief sculptures of Assyrian kings and deities from the palace of Assurnasirpal II at Kalhu, near modern Nimrud. Excavated in 1845 by the young British archaeologist Austen Layard, over fifty slabs were shipped to the United States and eventually distributed among American museums, most of them going to colleges and universities.[67] Usually it was alumni—often missionaries to Iraq—who negotiated these acquisitions, and it is clear that their value to these men and their alma maters lay in their relationship to Biblical history and their use in moral instruction. In a letter of 7 August 1855, the Reverend Dwight Marsh offered five of the slabs to Williams College and informed President Mark Hopkins that "my great desire & prayer is that students who look upon the relics of the past may think wisely of time & be led to take a deeper interest in the efforts to rescue the degraded from the beastliness of their present life, & the eternal dangers impending. . . . May they remember that God is older than the ages—that the glorious future of America is not eternity."[68] Bowdoin's slabs were consigned to the art gallery built as part of the college chapel, as was much of Bowdoin's art collection before 1894, but the location was appropriate given the degree to which art was considered illustrative of the history of religion.

The historical and moral lessons to be learned from art depended largely upon its subject matter, of course, but questions of aesthetics were by no means ignored. Those questions were asked not in the context of dispassionate formal analysis, however, at least not in England and America, where the moralistic approach of John Ruskin was the predominant method of appraising the value of art. For most of the artists and critics of the late nineteenth century, aesthetic excellence was both an end in itself and a means to an end, having as its goals the elevation of public taste and the promotion of what was loosely termed "culture."

THE UTILITY OF BEAUTY

As noted above, the realms of art and science—once juxtaposed if not actually combined in the *Wunderkammer*—would eventually separate and become independent, both physically and intellectually. In 1893 the ethnographic specimens that shared Street Hall with Yale's art collection were moved to the Peabody. One year later, Bowdoin College dedicated a museum committed *solely* to the fine arts, the same year in which Oxford opened a new Ashmolean Museum

now stripped of its natural and ethnographic specimens. While thirty years earlier Yale could speak of the wedding of art and science, Martin Brimmer described the new Bowdoin museum as a "building devoted not to religion, nor to letters, nor to science, but to art."[69]

This sudden narrowing of the focus of the college museum followed three decades of impassioned calls for public art museums. Early in the nation's history, those who supported the arts were forced to contend with almost iconoclastic opposition on the part of those who equated art with decadence, an opposition encapsulated in John Adams's widely-quoted assertion that "from the dawn of history [the arts] have been prostituted to the service of superstition and despotism."[70] As the nineteenth century progressed, however, the passion for culture grew. Enthusiasm for the arts covered a broad spectrum of positions ranging from jingoistic insistence on the superior character of American art to an obsequious worship of the European Old Masters, but both camps held that Americans needed to become cultured and that museums were one means to that end. European critics agreed. When Jarves exhibited his collection of Italian primitives in Paris in 1859, Thomas Adolphus Trollope wrote that "they have furnished forth galleries for the delight and art instruction of every nation of Europe, and now they are called on to perform a similar civilizing office on the other side of the Atlantic."[71] Jarves entertained the same hope, and although his collection was eventually consigned to a college museum, he continually advocated the establishment of public museums for the education and edification of the American people. He shared this attitude with men like Comfort, Benson, and Perkins, all of whom subscribed to the view that art had the power to raise both the moral tone and the aesthetic sensibilities of its audience. Perkins maintained that museums could "raise the standards of taste, furnish materials for study to artists and archaeologists, affect industry, and provide places of resort for the general public where amusement and unconscious instruction will be combined."[72]

It was an idea whose time had come. In 1870, the same year in which Perkins issued that statement and one year before the Jarves collection found a permanent home at Yale, New York's Metropolitan Museum of Art and Boston's Museum of Fine Arts were chartered, and the following decade saw the establishment of the Corcoran Gallery, the Pennsylvania Museum (now the Philadelphia Museum of Art), and the Chicago Art Institute.[73] Behind the founding of these civic institutions lay a clearly populist sentiment: the idea that art should be accessible to everyone, and that the general populace would experience a degree of intellectual and spiritual uplift from exposure to great art (or to reproductions of great art, which was more often the case in these early years). Drawing inspiration from the writings of Joshua Reynolds and John Ruskin, many American critics moved beyond the realm of "good taste" to envision a society in which art would counteract the pernicious effects of industrialization and the attendant deterioration of design.[74] America, however, was assumed to be a classless society; while the leaders of the British Enlightenment held that the aristocracy should assume responsibility for the welfare of society, America counted upon its institutions of higher learning to train a cultural elite capable of guiding the country in matters of taste, to counter what many saw as the roughness, vulgarity, and naivete of its people. Art education was considered a means to that end.

The challenge was met, although slowly and somewhat haphazardly. In the same period in which the educational role of the civic museum was being defined, a few American schools—most of them women's colleges—acknowledged the educational value of art, often with enthusiasm. Vassar's commitment to the "educating force" of its collection has already been cited, and when Smith College was founded in 1871, its prospectus stated that "more time will be devoted than in other colleges. . .to the examination of the great models of painting and statuary."[75] Smith immediately took steps to fulfill this prophecy: in its first years it bought only a few casts and photographs, but by 1881, when the Hillyer Gallery was dedicated, the collection already contained works by Inness, Wyant, Homer, William Morris Hunt, and other promi-

nent American painters of the period. The central figure in this development was the president of Smith, L. Clarke Seelye, who in his inaugural address in 1875 asserted that the college "should have its gallery of art, where students may be made directly familiar with the famous masterpieces."[76] Instead of waiting for alumni to donate works of art, Seelye made personal visits to the studios of contemporary artists and convinced them to sell one or more of their paintings to the college at a price the college could afford.

But the coordination of collegiate collections and the teaching of art history was sporadic at best, and nonexistent at worst. Lectures on the fine arts were being delivered at American colleges as early as 1800, and in the second half of the nineteenth century courses in art history began to appear in the curricula of a number of schools, but these were usually taught by professors of painting, classics, history, literature, or religion.[77] As a legitimate discipline taught by someone eminently qualified to do so, art history in America essentially had its beginning with Harvard's appointment of Charles Eliot Norton in 1873.[78] Norton's ideas about the place of the fine arts in a college curriculum mirror those of John Stuart Mill, who in 1867, in his inaugural address as honorary president of the University of St. Andrews, had made an impassioned defense of the educational value of the fine arts. Norton also corresponded with John Ruskin, who described to the former his proposal for the study of the fine arts at Oxford. In 1865 Norton had tried to persuade the city of Boston to acquire the Jarves Collection of Italian paintings, and he was familiar with some of his era's most prominent collectors of art, but until 1896, when lantern slides became available, Norton's famous lectures were delivered without reference to visual images, and there is no evidence that he ever made use of the art collections of Boston. Like many historians of his day, he believed in the cyclical theory of cultural evolution, and considered the art of his own time decadent and debased, unworthy of attention except as an illustration of the corruption of modern society and its slavish dependence on industrialization.[79] Harvard's Fogg Museum was opened in 1895, two years before Norton retired from teaching, but its collection of original works was minimal at that time, and there is no evidence that Norton ever considered it part of his own "philosophical apparatus."

Of far greater significance for the interaction of the art museum and the art historian was the appointment of Allan Marquand to the faculty of Princeton in 1881. For all of his knowledge of the history of art, Norton's approach to the subject was that of the social philosopher, while Marquand was a true art historian, a scholar whose studies of the della Robbia are art-historical in every sense. And unlike Norton, Marquand understood the potential of a college collection. The son of the founder and president of the Metropolitan Museum, Marquand helped to establish Princeton's Museum of Historic Art and became its first director in 1893. With that appointment, the history of the college museum in America entered a new phase, one in which its role in the pedagogical activities of the institution gradually acquired a permanence and a definition it could not achieve in its first century.

The years 1893-1895 mark a watershed in many ways. In addition to the appointment of Marquand as director of the Princeton Museum, 1893 saw Oberlin acquire its first work of art, an event that initiated that college's distinguished history of collecting. In 1894, Bowdoin dedicated the Walker Art Building and installed a collection of American and European paintings and drawings that anticipated the comprehensive collections of the next century. In that same year, Stanford opened the first university museum on the West Coast, Leland Stanford declaring that its collections would compare favorably with "the most famous of European museums."[80] And one year later, Harvard dedicated the Fogg Museum, the institution that would train many of the directors and curators of America's museums.

With these events, the American college museum entered a new phase, one in which professionally trained directors and curators—men and women whose qualifications often included advanced degrees in art history—shaped an institution that was more clearly defined, more narrowly focused, more structured in its organization, more aggressively acquisitive, and more public in its orientation. In the process, it lost much of its universalist character, and with it something of the sense of wonder with which the early collectors compiled their cabinets of curiosities. That character does survive in the small, local historical museums of America, and on a grand scale in the Smithsonian Institution, which in many ways is the greatest of all *Wunderkammern*. As recently as 1968, a participant in a Smithsonian Institution Conference on Museums and Education commented that the conferees had "gathered together for a week in Vermont in the name of STUFF— the goods of the universe, things: old or new, typical or unique, essential or optional, etc."[81] That sentiment is worthy of the humanist collectors of the sixteenth and seventeenth centuries, but it seems strangely old-fashioned in the second half of the twentieth. Whether current trends in art-historical scholarship, many of which have placed an increasingly greater emphasis upon objects and materials that have traditionally been considered something other than "fine art," will lead the modern museum back to its universalist roots remains to be seen. Even more problematic is whether museums will ever return to the sweeping philosophical and spiritual concerns that Martin Brimmer touched upon in his dedication of Bowdoin's Museum of Art. Truth, Righteousness, and Beauty are no longer the certainties they were in the nineteenth century, and the college museum—bound as it is to the attitudes of academia as a whole—may find it difficult to preserve even the echo of its early idealism.

NOTES

1. For the remainder of this essay, the phrase "college museum" will signify both college and university collections.

2. Among the most important studies of the history of museums and collecting are the following (listed in chronological order): Julius von Schlosser, *Die Kunst- und Wunderkammern der Spätrenaissance: Ein Beitrag zur Geschichte des Sammelwessens* (Leipzig, 1908); Germain Bazin, *The Museum Age*, trans. Jane van Nuis Cahill (New York: Universe Books, 1967); *The Origins of Museums*, ed. Oliver Impey and Arthur MacGregor (Oxford: Clarendon Press, 1985); *The Age of the Marvelous*, ed. Joy Kenseth (Hanover, NH: Hood Museum of Art, Dartmouth College, 1991).

A comprehensive history of the American college museum has yet to be written, but a fine survey of the earliest collections can be found in the catalogue of an exhibition held at Mount Holyoke College in 1976 (Jean Harris, *Collegiate Collections 1776-1886* [South Hadley, MA: Mount Holyoke College, 1976]). I am indebted to Professor Harris for her invaluable references to sources central to this essay. I also wish to acknowledge the good advice and assistance of Linda J. Docherty, Judy Hurd, Lillian B. Miller, Susan L. Ransom, Katharine J. Watson, and Susan E. Wegner.

3. Martin Brimmer, *An Address Delivered at Bowdoin College Upon the Opening of the Walker Art Building* (Boston: Houghton, Mifflin and Co., 1894), 31.

4. Ralph Waldo Emerson, *The Complete Works of Ralph Waldo Emerson*, ed. E. W. Emerson, vol. 7, Art (Boston: Houghton, Mifflin and Co., 1904), 57.

5. A number of writers on this topic have stated that the earliest collections of art held no place in the pedagogical systems of their institutions. It is true that the teaching of art history as that discipline is now defined would not become commonplace in American colleges and universities until the late nineteenth century (see below), but there is much evidence to suggest that works of art were considered legitimate components of the "philosophical apparatus" central to both European and American learning. There is certainly reason to believe that James Bowdoin III saw his art collection and his scientific instruments in that light.

6. The letter is in the McClure collection of Baker Library at Dartmouth. See W. Wedgwood Bowen, *A Pioneer Museum in the Wilderness* (Hanover, NH: Dartmouth College Museum, 1958), 1. Detailed information on the history of the Dartmouth Museum can be found in Bowen's publication and in Jacquelynn Baas, "A History of the Dartmouth College Museum," in *Treasures of the Hood Museum of Art, Dartmouth College* (New York: Hudson Hills Press in association with the Hood Museum of Art, Dartmouth College, 1985), 10-20.

7. The Charleston Museum, founded in 1773, was probably the earliest American institution to be so designated. Its collections consisted primarily of natural specimens, and it eventually became the property of the College of Charleston. See Joel Orosz, *Curators and Culture: The Museum Movement in America, 1740-1870* (Tuscaloosa: University of Alabama Press, 1990), 22. The earliest American collection that might have met the definition of a museum was apparently the Library Company of Philadelphia, founded in 1731.

8. See Lawrence W. Levine, *Highbrow/Lowbrow: The Emergence of Cultural Hierarchy in America* (Cambridge, MA: Harvard University Press, 1988), 147. The term "curiosity" has a long and protean history. In a French lexicon edited by Robert Estienne in 1538, *curieux* described a person who was knowledgeable about *"choses antiques,"* and in the second half of the sixteenth century, a *cabinet de curiositez* was added to the collections of Francis I to house rarities from the New World (see Bazin, 67, 70). The etymology of "museum" is complex and elusive. As the word itself indicates, *musaeum* originally implied a place sacred to the muses, although it eventually came to designate more specifically the library at Alexandria, and in its earliest usage in English it often referred simply to a library or study. In the period under discussion here, however, it had begun to be associated with universal knowledge. Paula Findlen has pointed out that "the proliferation of museums in the sixteenth and seventeenth centuries can be seen as a logical outcome of the desire to gather materials for a text. The pursuit and revival of classical language, literature, and philosophy that have most commonly been identified as the core of the humanists' programmes could not have arisen without the recognition that the piles of information, scattered throughout the world, might be shown to mean something were they to be brought into the study and compared: collecting was about the confrontation of ideas and objects, as old cosmologies met new ways of perceiving, that fueled the learned and curious discourses of early modern Europe" (Paula Findlen, "The Museum: Its Classical Etymology and Renaissance Genealogy," *Journal of the History of Collections 1*, no. 1, 1989, 61-62.)

9. SISTE VIDES MAGNUM QUAE SERVANT MARMORA VATEM I INGENIO CUIUS NON SATIS ORBIS ERAT QUAE NATURA POLUS QUAE MOS FERAT OMNIA NOVIT KAROLUS AETATIS GLORIA MAGNA SUAE. The epitaph is by Desiderio da Settignano, and the tomb is in the church of Santa Croce.

10. For the popularity of Aristotle's treatises in the sixteenth century see Rensselaer Lee, "Ut Pictura Poesis: The Humanistic Theory of Painting," *Art Bulletin 22* (1940), 230.

11. Kenseth, 88. Kenseth's monumental catalogue to an equally ambitious exhibition must be considered the definitive study of the *Wunderkammer* and its cultural context.

12. Strictly speaking, a collection of art was housed in a *Kunstkammer*, a collection of precious objects in a *Schatzkammer*, but the heterogeneous nature of these collections often defied such categories. For a discussion of these terms and their evolution, see Ernst Gombrich,

"The Museum: Past, Present, and Future," in *The Idea of the Museum: Philosophical, Artistic, and Political Questions,* Problems in Contemporary Philosophy, ed. Lars Aagaard-Mogensen, vol. 6 (Lewiston, NY: Edwin Mellen Press, 1988), 99126.

13. William Schupbach, "Some Cabinets of Curiosities in European Academic Institutions," in *The Origins of Museums,* ed. Oliver Impey and Arthur MacGregor (Oxford: Clarendon Press, 1985), 170.

14. A number of writers on the early history of museums have tended to ignore or underestimate the intellectual character of the pre-Enlightenment *Wunderkammern,* many of which were either established or supervised by scholars of the order of Paolo Giovio and Athanasius Kircher. Established within the Jesuit College at Rome, Kircher's collection—the *Musaeum Kircherianum*—attempted to encompass new knowledge in a structured system compatible with theological orthodoxy (see Findlen, 66-67).

15. Francis Bacon, *Gesta Grayorum,* English Reprint Series, no. 22 (Liverpool: Liverpool University Press, 1968), 47.

16. Cited in Findlen, 65.

17. See Kenseth, 132.

18. The Society received its charter from Charles II in 1662, although it did not announce the establishment of its collections until 1666. For its founding and character, see Michael Hunter, "The Cabinet Institutionalized: The Royal Society's 'Repository' and Its Background," in *Origins of Museums,* 159-168.

19. In the case of Pisa and Leiden, the formation of collections was an outgrowth of instruction in medicine. At the University of Pisa, the "physic garden" or *hortus medicus,* established in 1543, eventually developed into a full-fledged *Wunderkammer,* complete with marvels and exotica as wondrous as those of the great Hapsburg cabinets. The University of Leiden also possessed a physic garden, but its own *Wunderkammer* was an adjunct of its anatomy theater, initiated in the late sixteenth century as a collection dedicated to comparative anatomy, but evolving into a cabinet of curiosities as rich as that of any princely treasure house.

20. See Kenseth, 86.

21. See Bazin, 144; and Arthur MacGregor, "The Cabinet of Curiosities in Seventeenth-Century Britain," in *Origins of Museums,* 147-158. The Cambridge equivalent of the Ashmolean—the Fitzwilliam Museum—was established by the bequest of Richard, Viscount Fitzwilliam, in 1816.

22. For a discussion of early American cabinets of philosophical apparatus, see Orosz, 11-25.

23. A good introduction to James Bowdoin II is Gordon Kershaw, *James Bowdoin: Patriot and Man of the Enlightenment* (Brunswick, ME: Bowdoin College Museum of Art, 1976). That the collections of these learned Americans were eventually absorbed by museums is more a matter of circumstance than design, but occasionally collecting and exhibiting were synonymous. One of the most interesting and well-documented examples of an American *Wunderkammer* is that of the painter Charles Willson Peale, whose museum, founded in 1786, combined natural specimens, ethnographic materials, and portraits of the heroes of the Revolution. See Edgar Richardson, Brooke Hindle, and Lillian B. Miller, *Charles Willson Peale and His World* (New York: Harry N. Abrams, Inc., 1983).

24. Although this essay deals primarily with collegiate collections, it should be noted that various institutions of learning have played a role in the history of museums. In the eighteenth century, European academies and art schools often collected paintings and sculptures for the instruction of their students, and these collections sometimes evolved into public museums. Among the American equivalents of this phenomenon are the Pennsylvania Academy of the Fine Arts, founded in 1805, and the American Academy of the Fine Arts in New York, founded in 1802. Emulating European academies, learned foundations like Philadelphia's American Philosophical Society and the Boston Athenaeum also collected art.

25. Orosz, 17-20.

26. *Checklist of the Paintings, Prints and Drawings in the Collection of the Robert Hull Fleming Museum,* comp. Nina G. Parris (Burlington, VT: University of Vermont, 1977), 7.

27. Harris, 49-54.

28. Cited in Winifred Howe, *A History of the Metropolitan Museum of Art* (New York: The Metropolitan Museum of Art, 1913), 6. The linking of science and art is personified by a number of early American collectors, including Charles Willson Peale (see note 23) and Francis Calley Gray. The latter, a wealthy Salem ship owner, was an amateur scientist and a collector of both natural specimens and art. His collection of engravings was left to Harvard, which also benefited from his endowment of its Museum of Comparative Zoology (see Marjorie Cohn, *Francis Calley Gray and Art Collecting for America* [Cambridge, MA: Harvard University Press, 1986]).

29. It is true that Benjamin Silliman, the first director of Yale's gallery, was the nephew of Trumbull, but it was not uncommon for a professor of science to direct a college museum. As late as 1856, Dartmouth's museum as well as its library were directed by Oliver Payson Hubbard, professor of chemistry, mineralogy, and geology.

30. See Harris, 41-42.

31. *Handbook of the Gallery of Fine Arts* (New Haven: The Associates in Fine Arts at Yale University, 1931), 5.

32. Cited in *Vassar College Art Gallery Catalogue* (Poughkeepsie: Vassar College, 1939), 11.

33. James J. Jarves, "On the Formation of Galleries of Art," *Atlantic Monthly*, July 1860, 106.

34. Bazin, 56. Paolo's "Museum Jovianum" inspired a number of galleries of portraits—including one established by Catherine de' Medici—and was often reproduced in printed editions.

35. See Donald Egbert, *Princeton Portraits* (Princeton: Princeton University Press, 1947), 4.

36. Magoon's report is reprinted in its entirety in the *Vassar College Art Gallery Catalogue* (Poughkeepsie: Vassar College, 1939), 17-24; and in *Vassar College Art Gallery: Selections from the Permanent Collection* (Poughkeepsie: Vassar College, 1967), xi-xiii. Benson's comments appear in his article, "Museums of Art as a Means of Instruction," *Appleton's Journal*, 15 January 1870, 80.

37. Jarves, "On the Formation of Galleries," 106. For the influence of Alexis Francois Rio on American conceptions of historical sequence, see: W. G. Constable, *Art Collecting in the United States of America: An Outline of a History* (London: Thomas Nelson and Sons, 1964), 32.

38. Cited in Francis Steegmuller, "James Jackson Jarves: Thumb-nail Sketch of a Collector," *Magazine of Art* 41 (April 1948): 135. For a complete biography of Jarves, see Francis Steegmuller, *The Two Lives of James Jackson Jarves* (New Haven: Yale University Press, 1951). For the collection itself, see Richard Offner, *Italian Primitives at Yale University* (New Haven: Yale University Press, 1927).

39. From the *Bulletin of Smith College Hillyer Art Gallery*, May 1920.

40. Emerson's essays on art are well known and will be quoted below. For the writings of Greenough, see *Form and Function; Remarks on Art*, ed. Harold A. Small (Berkeley: University of California Press, 1947).

41. Bazin, 7.

42. James J. Jarves, *Art Hints: Architecture, Sculpture, and Painting* (New York: Harper & Bros., 1855), x.

43. James J. Jarves, "American Museums of Art," *Scribner's Monthly*, July 1879, 406.

44. From Emerson's second essay on art: *The Complete Works of Ralph Waldo Emerson*, ed. E. W. Emerson, vol. 7, Art (Boston: Houghton, Mifflin and Co., 1904), 38. For the influence of European cultural relativism on American thought, see Lillian Miller, *Patrons and Patriotism: The Encouragement of the Fine Arts in the United States, 1790-1860* (Chicago: University of Chicago Press, 1966), 16-32.

45. Ibid., 39-40.

46. See Kenseth. In reconstructing a typical *Wunderkammer* of the sixteenth century, Kenseth and the curators of Dartmouth's Hood Museum were able to draw upon many of the natural, ethnographic, and mechanical specimens that still exist in the collections of the college.

47. Jarves, *Art Hints*, 6.

48. See Steegmuller, 177. The issue of copies is covered more extensively in Susan E. Wegner's essay for this book.

49. George Fisk Comfort, "Esthetics in Collegiate Education," *The Methodist Quarterly Review* (October 1867), 589.

50. Charles Perkins, "American Art Museums," *North American Review*, CXI, no. ccxxviii, (July 1870), 9. As president of the Boston Art Club, Perkins was energetic in his promotion of art education in the Boston area.

51. *Vassar Catalogue*, 1939, 21-22.

52. Brimmer, 26.

53. *Vassar Catalogue*, 1939, 25-26.

54. Perkins, 6.

55. Emerson, *Complete Works*, vol. 2, Art, 363.

56. For Quiccheburg, see Kenseth, 84-85. The full title of Quiccheberg's treatise is *Inscriptiones vel tituti theatri amplissimi*.

57. See note 14.

58. Professor Anna Edwards. See Harris, 49n.

59. Ibid., 36.

60. *Vassar Catalogue*, 1939, 20-21.

61. Ibid., 11.

62. Jarves, *Art Hints*, 66.

63. For Benson, see his "Museums of Art as a Means of Instruction," *Appleton's Journal*, 15 January 1870, 80. Benson's reputation as a critic is made clear in Mantel Fielding's *Dictionary of American Painters, Sculptors and Engravers*, ed. Glenn B. Opitz (Philadelphia: Lancaster Press, 1926), 26 or (Poughkeepsie, N.Y.: Apollo, 1983). Emerson's statement is found in *Complete Works*, vol. 7, 51.

64. *Vassar Catalogue*, 1967, xi.

65. Brimmer, 30. Goran Schildt has commented on the pervasiveness of this attitude in both Europe and America: "It is hard to deny that there is a religious element, a substitute for religion, in the 19th century's attitude to art—it has its roots in Kant's and Hegel's theological speculations about the reflection of the divine consciousness in human intellect." (Goran Schildt, "The Idea of the Museum," in *The Idea of the Museum: Philosophical, Artistic, and Political Questions,* ed. Lars Aagaard-Mogensen, Problems in Contemporary Philosophy, vol. 6 [Lewiston, NY: Edwin Mellen Press, 1988], 89.)

66. Emerson, *Complete Works,* vol. 2, 353-4.

67. Yale acquired four in 1854, Amherst six in 1855, Dartmouth six in 1856, Bowdoin five in 1860. Among other institutions that received at least one slab were Auburn, Union College, the University of Vermont, and Williams. See: John Stearns and Donald Hansen, *The Assyrian Reliefs at Dartmouth* (Hanover, NH: Dartmouth College Museum, 1953), and Barbara N. Porter, *Assyrian Bas-Reliefs at the Bowdoin College Museum of Art* (Brunswick, ME: Bowdoin College Museum of Art, 1989).

68. Cited in S. Lane Faison, Jr., *Handbook of the Collection: Williams College Museum of Art* (Williamstown, MA: Williams College Museum of Art, 1979), unpaginated, entry no. 2.

69. Brimmer, 32.

70. *Familiar Letters of John Adams and His Wife, Abigail Adams, During the Revolution,* ed. Charles Francis Adams (New York: Hurd and Houghton, 1876), 334. For a fuller discussion of this resistance, see Constable, 11; and Miller, *Patrons and Patriots,* 12-14. Supporters of the arts as both social goods and means of enlightenment included Thomas Jefferson, who proposed the study of the fine arts as part of the curriculum of the University of Virginia. Katharine Watson has called to my attention that James Bowdoin III owned a copy of the *Sketches of History* by Henry Home, Lord Kames (London: A. Strahan and T. Cadell, 1788), in which Bowdoin marked the following passage:

Beauty was studied in objects of sight; and men of taste attached themselves to the fine arts, which multiplied their enjoyment and improved benevolence [I:219].

71. *From the London Athenaeum* of 12 February 1859, cited in Helen Comstock, "The Yale Collection of Italian Paintings," *The Connoisseur,* vol. 118 (September 1946): 45.

72. Perkins, 5. There was some resistance to this notion: Benjamin Ives Gilman, appointed secretary of the Museum of Fine Arts Boston in 1893, wrote that the museum was "primarily an institution of culture and only

secondarily a seat of learning . . . not didactic but aesthetic in primary purpose." (Benjamin Gilman, *Museum Ideals of Purpose and Method* [Boston: Boston Museum of Fine Arts, 1918], xi, 98.)

73. The first American institution to meet the modern definition of an art museum was probably the Wadsworth Athenaeum, founded in 1842. For this and the early growth of public museums, see Edward Alexander, *Museums in Motion: An Introduction to the History and Function of Museums* (Nashville: American Association for State and Local History, 1979), 31-34.

74. For a good review of this aspect of American art criticism, see Miller, *Patrons and Patriots*, 16.

75. Cited in *The Smith College Museum of Art Catalogue* (Northampton, MA: Smith College, 1937), v.

76. Cited in Charles Chetham, "Why the College 'Should Have its Gallery of Art,'" *Smith Alumnae Quarterly*, February 1980, 3.

77. John Witherspoon, president of Princeton from 1766 to 1794, was noted for his lectures on the fine arts, and William and Mary added the fine arts to its curriculum at the urging of Thomas Jefferson. For other instances of early art education see Harris, 11-16 and 51.

78. For Norton, see Kermit Vanderbilt, *Charles Eliot Norton: Apostle of Culture in a Democracy* (Cambridge, MA: Belknap Press, 1959). Norton's name figures prominently in the history of American institutions involved with the arts. When the Archaeological Institute of America was founded in 1879, Norton was named its first president, Martin Brimmer its vice president. A number of Norton's students—most notably Paul Sachs and Alfred Barr—were to become dominant figures in the development of the twentieth-century American art museum.

79. For the theories of Norton, Ruskin, and Emerson, see Miller, *Patrons and Patriotism*, 24-32. Among the figures who shared Norton's pessimistic view of contemporary art was Charles Perkins, who advocated the chronological arrangement of museum exhibits so that they would "illustrate the rise and progress of the arts and their gradual decadence" [Perkins, 9].

80. Cited in Carol Osborne, *Museum Builders in the West: The Stanfords as Collectors and Patrons of Art, 1870-1906* (Palo Alto: Stanford University Museum of Art, 1986), 17.

81. M. Thurman, "Museums and Education: The Role of the Art Object," in *Museums and Education,* ed. Eric Larabee (Washington, D.C.: Smithsonian Institution Press, 1968), 139.

FIG. 1 John Smibert, *Portrait of James Bowdoin II as a Boy*

PRESERVING OUR ANCESTORS: THE BOWDOIN PORTRAIT COLLECTION

Linda J. Docherty

Before Sarah Bowdoin married Henry Dearborn in 1813, she signed a contract with her future husband.[1] In this document, the widow of James Bowdoin III exempted all property owned by her at the time of her re-marriage from claims by either Dearborn or his heirs. Mrs. Bowdoin's fortune was substantial; it consisted of real estate, stocks, bonds, mortgages, and miscellaneous personal property. The latter category included "household furniture, plate, pictures, carriages, horses," and other appurtenances attached to her Milk Street house.[2]

Sarah Bowdoin's prenuptial agreement presages contemporary desires to protect wealth accrued during a first marriage for the children of that union. Although she and James Bowdoin III had produced no offspring, arrangements had been made prior to his death for descendants of his sister (and her cousin), Lady Temple, to become their official heirs. When Sarah Bowdoin Dearborn died in 1826, her estate was divided among nephews, nieces, and their progeny with one noteworthy exception: the Bowdoin family portraits.

The specific mention of pictures in her wedding contract indicates that Sarah Bowdoin recognized the monetary value of her ancestral gallery. Her bequest of the paintings to Bowdoin College suggests, however, that she herself estimated their worth by different standards. Sarah's calculated attempt to preserve intact the image of the Bowdoin family draws attention to a fundamental dichotomy in viewer response to portraiture: individuals with personal attachment to sitters see portraits as equivalents of nature, while those with no such ties regard them solely as works of art.

Both attitudes have shaped the history of the Bowdoin portrait collection. Formed in a spirit of dynastic pride, it is for modern viewers an exemplary display of American art in the colonial and federal periods. In this bicentennial year, Bowdoin College may, and indeed should, continue to take pride in its distinguished holdings of early American paintings. The occasion also invites us to reacquaint ourselves with the individuals whose likenesses grace our museum walls. A study of the creation and bequest of the present collection reveals that, as patrons of portraiture, the Bowdoins were consistently motivated by familial ideals and bonds. By absorbing these portraits into its art gallery, Bowdoin College has highlighted their aesthetic value rather than the family history they embody.[3]

Since Marvin Sadik published his comprehensive catalogue of portraits at Bowdoin College in 1966,[4] scholarship on American art has been enriched by both social history and literary theory. Whereas early histories of portraiture, including Sadik's book, were primarily concerned with questions of biography and attribution, recent studies have focused on issues of contextualization and interpretation. More than objective records, American portraits of the colonial and federal periods are now viewed as examples of "self-fashioning" on the part of aspiring subjects. Artists who collaborated with sitters in this image-making process are seen not only as skilled craftsmen, but also as shrewd business-people and/or political ideologues.

Much has been written about the artful intentions underlying the creation of colonial and federal portraits, yet the response of viewers to these images remains more elusive. To some extent, lack of knowledge reflects lack of information; given the paucity of documentary evidence, it is difficult to determine whether ideals of character were successfully communicated in paint.[5] A study of response to portraiture is further complicated by the ineluctable association

FIG. 2 Anonymous, *Portrait of James Bowdoin I*

of painted likenesses with living people. In the words of Richard Brilliant:

Private portraits elicit a great variety of emotional responses from the members of their audience, especially because the psychological space is so narrow and the personal attention so focused. This is very much the case with family portraits, or, more properly, portraits of the viewer's family, when the strength of the emotional attachment renders the artistic component of the image nearly invisible.[6]

Uniting, as it does, nature and art, portraiture may be looked at from either side.

Nature and art have long vied for preeminence in Western aesthetic thought. Among the ancients, conflicting views of their proper relationship existed side by side. For some writers, art was an imitation of nature, and the best art was that which succeeded in deceiving the spectator entirely. For others, art had the power to improve upon nature and could therefore claim superiority.[7]

By the eighteenth century, the latter view prevailed among academic theorists. In his third *Discourse* (1770), Sir Joshua Reynolds told students of the Royal Academy:

There are excellencies in the art of painting beyond what is commonly called the imitation of nature . . . a

mere copier of nature can never produce any thing great; can never raise and enlarge the conceptions, or warm the heart of the spectator.[8]

Reynolds encouraged young painters to approach their models in a spirit of rivalry. According to his teachings, invention, the source of genius, consisted of combining material from diverse sources in an original way.

Although Reynolds himself had earned his reputation as a portraitist, he viewed history painting as the highest form of art. History painting exemplified the "great style," in which nature appeared in its ideal or general form, uncorrupted by specific details. Portraiture, by contrast, had an unshakable obligation to real nature that limited its power to stimulate the viewer's moral (as opposed to material) sense. Reynolds noted that portrait-painters could give their subjects an aura of grandeur and timelessness by smoothing out faces and eschewing fashionable dress, yet he cautioned in *Discourse* IV (1771):

If an exact resemblance of an individual be considered as the sole object to be aimed at, the portrait-painter will be apt to lose more than he gains by the acquired dignity taken from general nature. It is very

FIG. 3 Anonymous, *Portrait of William Bowdoin as a Boy*

difficult to ennoble the character of a countenance but at the expense of the likeness, which is what is most generally required by such as sit to the painter.[9]

To make their images live in the future, portraitists risked jeopardizing their success in the present.[10]

Of course, no American portrait of the eighteenth or early nineteenth century was entirely artless. The veristic "plain style" used by Charles Willson Peale signified the moral virtue of his republican worthies as clearly as the European grand manner appropriated by colonial artists had highlighted the material values of their predecessors.[11] Even before the Revolution, naturalism was equated with seriousness. When John Greenwood commissioned John Singleton Copley to paint a portrait of his mother, Mrs. Humphrey Devereux, in 1770, he stipulated:

I am very desirous of seeing the good Lady's Face as she now appears, with old age creeping upon her. I shoud chuse her painted on a small half length or a size a little broader than Kitt Katt, sitting in as natural a posture as possible. I leave the pictoresque disposition intirely to your self and I shall only observe that gravity is my choice of Dress.[12]

Throughout this period, Americans understood the implications of both accuracy and idealization and often made specifications accordingly.

Colonial and federal viewers were also capable of judging aesthetic quality in portraiture. Writing to his mother in Charleston in 1751, Peter Manigault called his picture by Allan Ramsay "not only an exceeding good Likeness, but a very good Piece of Painting." Emphasizing the fact that he was depicted in his own clothes, the young man explained that he had chosen the more expensive Ramsay over William Keble because the latter's technique "looked more like Plaistering than Painting."[13]

While early Americans appreciated portrait-painting as an art, the responses that survive suggest that they associated the finished products more with nature. In his 1715 *Essay on the Theory of Painting*, the English portraitist Jonathan Richardson wrote:

The picture of an absent Relation, or Friend, helps to keep up those Sentiments which frequently languish by Absence and may be instrumental to maintain, and sometimes to augment Friendship, and Paternal, Filial, and Conjugal Love, and Duty.[14]

FIG. 4 English, after Kneller, *Portrait of Charles Montagu*

Richardson's theory is borne out by William Byrd's response to a portrait of the Earl of Egmont, sent to him as a gift in 1736.

I had the honour of your Lordships commands of the 9th of September, and since that have the pleasure of conversing a great deal with your picture. It is incomparably well done & and the painter has not only hit your ayr, but some of the vertues too which use to soften and enliven your features. . . . It is no wonder perhaps that I could discern so many good things in the portrait, when I knew them so well in the original.[15]

Although Byrd obviously did not confuse the painting with the man, it served as a reminder of character and a means of keeping alive a friendship.

In the eyes of eighteenth- and early nineteenth-century viewers, the human subject of portraiture was the true "original." A portraitist's originality resided less in power of invention per se, than in ability to capture the essential nature—physical, social, and/or moral—of a sitter. Painted likenesses functioned as enduring signs of living, or once living, indi-

FIG. 5 Joseph Badger, *Portrait of James Bowdoin I*

viduals. When Charles Pinckney's widow sent a copy of her late husband's portrait to their sons in London, she wrote their guardian:

Mr. Raven has been so good to take charge of my dear Mr. Pinckneys picture which I sent to his children that the Idea of his person may not wear out of their Infant minds. I make no doubt they will venerate even his shadow and I dare say you will be so good to give it a place in your parlour for the present if 'tis not very inconvenient.[16]

Motivated by similar desires, Abigail Adams lamented Gilbert Stuart's slowness in completing paintings of her husband and herself. "I know not what to do with that strange man Stewart," she said in a letter to her son:

The likeness is said to be good, both of your Father and me, that I shall regret very much if he cannot be prevaild upon to finish them as our Children may like to look upon our Likeness when the originals are no more seen.[17]

Both of these women valued portraits as a means of preserving the memory of life.

With the above points in mind, that portraits embody a dialectic between nature and art and that Americans of the colonial and federal periods viewed them as both, let us turn to the Bowdoin portrait gallery. The core of the museum's present collection consists of fourteen family pictures bequeathed to the College in 1826 by Sarah Bowdoin Dearborn, formerly Mrs. James Bowdoin III.[18] Three of these works, the Gilbert Stuart paintings of Mr. and Mrs. James Bowdoin III and a Christian Gullager portrait of James Bowdoin II, remained with Mrs. Dearborn's heirs until their deaths at the end of the century. In the decades that followed her bequest, more images of the Bowdoins came as gifts to the College; these included a second version of Gullager's painting, companion miniatures of James Bowdoin III and his sister Elizabeth, Lady Temple, and pictures of Lady Temple and her granddaughter, Sarah Winthrop Sullivan, by Stuart. Today the collection of Bowdoin portraits spans a hundred years from 1725 to 1825. It represents one of the richest and most influential families in early New England and the most accomplished artists, save one, working in America at that time.[19]

FIG. 6 John Faber, Jr., after Vanderbank, *Portrait of Sir Isaac Newton*

As a group, the pictures of the Bowdoin family exemplify a self-conscious tradition of artistic patronage. The oldest of the portraits are two anonymous paintings of James Bowdoin I (1676-1747) (fig. 2) and his eldest son, William (1713-73) (fig. 3), dated around 1725.[20] Although executed by different hands, the poses of father and son are similar in both works. Turned three-quarters from the viewer with face frontal and right arm akimbo, they mimic the English court style of Sir Godfrey Kneller, which was known to colonial artists through mezzotint engravings (fig. 4).

While expressing the aristocratic aspirations of the Bowdoins, this pair of images also exemplifies the early eighteenth-century attitude toward childhood. William's costume is virtually identical to that of his father; except for his unpowdered hair and the bird he holds, he looks like a miniature adult. Writing of children's portraits in this period, Karin Calvert notes:

FIG. 7 Robert Feke, *Portrait of James Bowdoin II*

cers hastily twisted their cravats through their coats when summoned to arms without warning.

As a patron of portraiture, James I clearly saw himself as the father of a dynasty. The image of William, his only surviving son by his first wife, Sarah Campbell (d. 1713), was commissioned at a time when pictures of children were comparatively rare in the New World.[22] In 1736, the elder Bowdoin ordered yet another painting of another son, James Bowdoin II (1726-90) (fig. 1), the child of his second marriage, to Hannah Portage (d. 1734).[23] For this work, he had available a far more sophisticated artist, John Smibert, who had come to America with Bishop Berkeley's "Bermuda Group" in 1729 and subsequently settled in Boston.

The freshness and animation of Smibert's portrait of James II reflects the artist's early training in England and Italy. Like his half-brother, William, the boy wears adult costume, but rather than being rigidly posed within the picture space, he seems to be momentarily arrested as he strides across it. Smibert represents James II as a youthful hunter, charming and, at the same time, commanding and self-assured.[24] The bow

Childhood had no positive attributes of its own considered worthy of expression. A child was merely an adult in the making and childhood, as a period of physical and spiritual vulnerability, was a deficiency to be overcome.[21]

By the time a boy was six or seven, he had cast off the petticoat worn by women and infants and assumed, like William, the appearance of his father.

When James Bowdoin I was a child, he could only have dreamed of the social status implicit in these portraits. The son of Pierre Baudouin (d. 1706), a French Huguenot refugee, he had emigrated to the New World with his family by way of Ireland, finally arriving in Massachusetts in 1686 at the age of ten. Religious persecution, financial insecurity, and Indian raids had marked his boyhood, and the memory of these experiences must have kindled in James I both a sense of pride and a concern for survival. In this early portrait, the unusual style of the cravat may allude not only to the sitter's French ancestry, but also to his ability to combat vicissitudes. Worn in a fashion called "Steinkerque," it commemorates a 1692 battle in which French offi-

FIG. 8 Robert Feke, *Portrait of Elizabeth Bowdoin*

60

and arrow he carries are attributes not only of the aristocratic sportsman, but also of Cupid, the god of love. Derived from emblem books, such iconography testifies to the emotional bonds that existed between parents and children in colonial America.[25]

Five of James I's children lived to adulthood, yet only the two sons survive in portraiture. Such apparent neglect does not reflect lack of affection, but rather the fact that daughters lacked the power to carry on the family name. While the Bowdoin patriarch seems to have desired portraits of his male children as signs of dynastic continuation, his progeny of both sexes were similarly anxious to preserve the image of their father. At the end of James I's life, Joseph Badger painted a second portrait of him in two versions. James Bowdoin II owned the picture now at Bowdoin College (fig. 5), while his sister Elizabeth Bowdoin (Mrs. James Pitts) owned what may have been the original, now in the Detroit Institute of Arts.[26]

When Badger painted these portraits, James I was one of the most powerful men in New England. While amassing a fortune in shipping and real estate, the elder Bowdoin had also held appointive judiciary offices and been a member of the elite Governor's Council. The choice of a self-taught house and sign painter to portray such a personage reflects the paucity of artistic talent in Boston after Smibert abandoned painting and before the arrival of Robert Feke. It also suggests a sense of urgency about the commission, which is dated the year of the sitter's death. Assuming that William Bowdoin had first claim to the anonymous picture of James I, which constituted a companion to his own portrait as a boy, it seems probable that the idea for the second likeness originated with James II.

As a model for his painting of James I, Badger turned to a 1726 mezzotint of Sir Isaac Newton, engraved by Faber after a painting by Vanderbank (fig. 6). This prototype was frequently used by colonial artists for both male and female sitters, particularly those who had achieved a venerable old age.[27] In the Bowdoin portrait, Badger replaced the classical column with a ship and added a table with paper, pen, and inkwell.[28]

FIG. 9 Robert Feke, *Portrait of William Bowdoin*

FIG. 10 Robert Feke, *Portrait of Phebe Bowdoin*

While these changes signify the mercantile activities of James I, the choice of the Newton prototype bespeaks the interests of his younger son.

FIG. 11 Beckett, after Wissing, *Portrait of the Princess Ann*

FIG. 12 John Smith, after Kneller, *Portrait of Her Royal Highness Princess Ann of Denmark*

Unlike his father, who was primarily a man of business, James II had a passion for intellectual pursuits. As a student at Harvard, he had studied Newtonian science with the celebrated professor of mathematics and natural philosophy John Winthrop IV. The library of James II contained a 1714 edition of the *Principia*, which may have been a college text, along with several semipopular versions of this influential but recondite work.[29] James II graduated from Harvard in 1745. Painted shortly thereafter, Badger's portrait of James I may have been conceived by the young man as a tribute to both his literal and intellectual fathers.

In 1748, James Bowdoin II again sat for his portrait, this time to Robert Feke, whose elegant brush recorded the coming-of-age of a second generation of the Bowdoin family. Feke's companion portraits of the future governor and his wife, Elizabeth (née Erving, 1731-1803) (figs. 7 and 8) (color on p. 5), have traditionally been assumed to commemorate their marriage of that date. Colonial portraits were frequently commissioned

to honor a change in social status. For James II, 1748 was not only the year of his wedding, but also, and perhaps more importantly, the year after he became heir to James I's estate.[30] James II and his half-brother, William, each received two-sevenths of their father's vast wealth.[31] The fact that Feke also painted companion portraits of William Bowdoin and his wife, Phebe (née Murdock, 1723-72) (figs. 9 and 10) suggests that money, more than matrimony, may have prompted this explosion of Bowdoin patronage.

To appreciate their subtle differences, it is useful to compare Feke's Bowdoin portraits along gender as well as matrimonial lines. Of the two male figures, William is the most impressive; he occupies more picture space, wears a more elaborate waistcoat, and holds a gold-tipped walking stick that enhances his aura of authority. While James II is also elegantly attired, he is a less assertive figure. Feke shows him with hand tucked into his waistcoat in a pose of rhetorical modesty.[32] When these portraits were painted, the future reputations of the Bowdoin half-brothers

FIG. 13 Joseph Blackburn, *Portrait of Elizabeth Bowdoin and James Bowdoin III*

remained to be determined. William's penchant for cards and dice at Harvard did, however, present a suggestive contrast to James II's serious attention to his studies.

As represented by Feke, William Bowdoin displays the self-importance of an eldest son. His right hand hangs vertically over a massive stone plinth while the forefinger of the left hand makes a strong horizontal gesture toward the center. Head, arms, and hands form a broad triangle that secures William's literal and symbolic position. In Feke's portrait of James II, the upper body again forms a triangle, but the base is narrower and the figure as a whole is not anchored to the setting.

For his paintings of Elizabeth Erving Bowdoin and Phebe Murdock Bowdoin, Feke looked to print sources, most notably to late seventeenth-century images of Princess Anne. Phebe's portrait can be traced to a 1692 mezzotint by Smith after Kneller (fig. 12), while Elizabeth's is based on a 1683 mezzotint by Beckett after Wissing

(fig. 11).[33] In both cases, Feke borrowed selectively, copying the hands, but changing the poses, settings, and attributes.[34] While the Bowdoin men appear standing, their wives are shown seated by their sides.

Each of Feke's female portraits complements its male companion. Like William, Phebe rests her right arm on a massive stone plinth. Although husband and wife do not face each other, they balance each other. His walking stick suggests that he belongs to the world of action, while her book connotes a more contemplative personality.

Although superficially similar to his portrait of Phebe, Feke's representation of her sister-in-law, Elizabeth, shows the sitter with body and head turned in opposite directions in a more lively pose. Dressed in bright blue, the younger woman holds an emblem of love, roses, which like love contain both sensory pleasure and the power to inflict pain.[35] In this pair of paintings, the greater animation of Elizabeth's likeness bal-

FIG. 14 Joseph Blackburn, *Portrait of the Isaac Winslow Family* 42.684

ances the comparatively modest characterization of her husband.

As portrayed by Feke in 1748, these two handsome young couples must have seemed to presage a long and healthy life for the Bowdoin line. Such was not to be the case, however. Only one of William and Phebe Bowdoin's offspring, a daughter, Sarah (1761-1826), lived past infancy. James II and Elizabeth had just two children, Elizabeth (1750-1809) and James III (1752-1811). James Bowdoin III married his cousin Sarah Bowdoin in 1780, but the union was without issue. By the end of the century, the responsibility for carrying on the family name had fallen to the heirs of James II's daughter, Elizabeth, Lady Temple.

In hindsight, Joseph Blackburn's double portrait of Elizabeth and James Bowdoin III as children is both engaging and sadly ironic (fig. 13). Painted around 1760, it shows brother and sister facing each other in poses that recall companion portraits of married couples. Elizabeth appears

as an elegant woman in satin, lace, pearls, and feathers. James III, on the other hand, is dressed in a modified version of adult costume. Instead of a full cravat, the boy wears a black ribbon tied around the ruffle of his shirt. Compared to Smibert's portrait of James II, this image reflects the later eighteenth-century recognition of an intermediate stage between childhood and adulthood.[36]

Blackburn's representation of Elizabeth and James III is replete with signs of new life. Elizabeth's lap is laden with fruit, a familiar symbol of abundance, and in her raised left hand, she displays a pear. Her brother holds a bird that appears to be a sibling of the two babies in his tricorn hat. Unlike the stiff creature in the anonymous portrait of his uncle William, James III's captives are chirping almost audibly for food. The background of the picture is somber in tone. The sun is setting over a vast landscape and, partially concealed behind Elizabeth, an urn serves as a subtle reminder of death.

FIG. 15 Christian Gullager, *Portrait of James Bowdoin II*

Arrayed resplendently before it, the children and their attributes embody the promise of growth and rebirth.

While it heralds the coming of another Bowdoin generation, Blackburn's painting also signals changes in eighteenth-century society. By the 1760s, the family had begun to be conceived less exclusively in terms of lineage and more as a nuclear unit. Fundamental to this transition was a new attitude toward the child.[37] Through the writings of Enlightenment philosophers, most notably Jean-Jacques Rousseau, childhood entered Western consciousness as a condition different from, and even superior to, adulthood. No longer seen as depraved beings tainted with original sin, children now appeared as innocent by nature and capable of being shaped by proper nurture. Under these circumstances, women assumed unprecedented importance as wives and mothers, and portraiture on both sides of the Atlantic became more matricentric.[38]

Blackburn's picture of the Isaac Winslow family (fig. 14), in which Lucy Waldo Winslow (1724-1757) occupies the center of the compo-

sition, is an early example of this new social and pictorial organization. Although the father, Isaac Winslow (1709-1777), retains authority through his standing pose, he is positioned to one side of the group with his left hand gesturing toward his wife. The baby on her lap, Hannah (1755-1819), reaches playfully toward her elder sister, Lucy (1749-1770), whose fruit-laden skirt leads the eye back toward the figure of her mother. This work is closely related to the slightly later image of the Bowdoin children, most notably in the treatment of the young girls.

The Bowdoin and Winslow families belonged to the same wealthy Boston society. James Bowdoin II and Isaac Winslow were both graduates of Harvard College, leading members of the Kennebec Proprietorship, and on more than one occasion, patrons of the same artists.[39] The fact that James II and his wife do not appear in Blackburn's picture is surprising, given these circumstances, and seems to reflect an inherited view of the purpose of family portraits. When James II commissioned this painting of his children, he was following a precedent set by James I. Although the inclusion of Elizabeth reflects changing attitudes toward women and children

FIG. 16 Christian Gullager, *Portrait of James Bowdoin II*

FIG. 17 Gilbert Stuart, *Portrait of James Bowdoin III*

FIG. 18 Anonymous, *Portrait of James Bowdoin III*

dressed figure is surrounded by books, a globe, papers and inkwell, and a portrait bust.

Gullager's portrait of James Bowdoin II is a small picture with the trappings of a much larger work. In design as well as detail, it is similar to John Singleton Copley's full-length portrait of John Adams (fig. 19), painted in London in 1783.[41] The Bowdoin image is notably different in effect, however, not only because of the artist's inferior ability, but also because of its source in miniature painting. With his head turned to the side, James II becomes an object for contemplation, rather than a subject who actively projects his personality onto the observer. The empty clawfoot chair, which directs the eye to the center of the composition, adds a hint of domesticity to the scene. It seems to invite one to sit and ponder the "distinguished,

in this period, Blackburn's representation of her and James III serves primarily to celebrate continuation of the Bowdoin line.

Having already been painted as a boy and as a young man, James II apparently thought it unnecessary to pay for another image of himself. Despite his importance as a political and intellectual leader in the decades surrounding the Revolution, this modest and serious man never again sat for a major portrait. After his death in 1790, the lack of a definitive likeness of the former governor seems to have prompted invention of a small full-length image that survives in two painted versions (figs. 15 and 16) and an 1835 wood engraving.

Many questions surround this unusual representation, which has been attributed to the Danish immigrant artist Christian Gullager. Far more ambitious than most Gullager portraits, the head is copied from a miniature of James II in his later years.[40] While adhering faithfully to this likeness, the work as a whole represents the sitter as a philosopher-statesman. Standing in an impressive architectural space with classical columns and a baroque curtain, his elegantly

FIG. 19 John Singleton Copley, *Portrait of John Adams*

FIG. 20 Gilbert Stuart, *Portrait of James Madison*

learned, and virtuous character"[42] of the late governor.

While Copley's painting of Adams directs the viewer's response with the sitter's glance and gesture, Gullager's work preserves both the appearance and the idea of James II in a manner that encourages individual engagement. More than a reduction of an official portrait,[43] it looks like an expanded miniature, a private image of a public man.[44] Gullager's son later recalled that the likeness of James II "was so correct that it was immediately purchased by his family and several copies were taken for friends."[45] The two oil panels were, in fact, once owned by Elizabeth (fig. 16) and James III (fig. 15), and, as we shall see, this peculiar picture was prized by subsequent generations.[46]

The third chapter in the history of Bowdoin family portraits begins with an anonymous painting of James Bowdoin III as a young man (fig. 18) (color on p. xx). Little is known about this work, which came to the College as part of Sarah

Bowdoin Dearborn's original bequest. With his high forehead, upturned mouth, and cleft chin, James III is clearly recognizable from Blackburn's portrait of him as a boy. While the expression is alert, the sitter's frail frame testifies to the ill health from which he suffered for most of his adult life.

Family pressure, more than personal pride, seems to have prompted James III to sit for his portrait at this time. Writing to his sister from Naples in January 1774, he promised, "I shall prove the Hint given respecting my picture and get it taken accordingly and send it to you."[47] Whether or not this particular likeness was the outcome of that pledge, it appears to have been painted either in England or on the Continent, where the sitter toured for several years after completing his studies at Harvard.

The choice of artist was clearly an inferior one, which suggests that James III took little personal interest in his picture. Awkwardness of execution is particularly evident in the oversized right hand. Although the book he holds alludes appropriately to the young man's character as a bibliophile, the frilled shirt and braided buttonholes are far more noticeable aspects of his appearance. In its ornamental delicacy, this portrait of James III bespeaks the effects of European travel and presents a striking contrast to Feke's weighty representation of his father at the same age.

As a patron of portraiture, James III's most important legacy is the companion pictures of Thomas Jefferson and James Madison that he commissioned from Gilbert Stuart (figs. 20 and 21) (color on pp. 14 and 15).[48] Painted between 1805 and 1807, these sober and dignified likenesses of the president and his secretary of state were originally intended to hang in the official residence in Madrid. For the governor's son, the appointment as Jefferson's minister to Spain marked the high point of his public career. Although his diplomatic mission proved unsuccessful, the Stuart commission provides ample evidence that he understood and respected the power of portraiture in the public sphere.

In private life, both James I and James II had commissioned paintings of their children, but

James III had no heirs to boast of. This fact may account for both his apparent indifference to family portraiture and the fact that companion pictures of him and his wife were painted only after he received the assignment to Madrid (figs. 17 and 23).[49] In this case, too, Gilbert Stuart was the artist of choice. Although the circumstances remain unclear, we know that Sarah Bowdoin sat for Stuart before the couple sailed for Spain in 1805. On 29 November 1806, Elizabeth Temple Winthrop (1769-1825), whose own portrait was in process, wrote to her aunt in Paris, "I asked [Stuart] if he could alter the drapery of the one which he took of you, which he can with much ease when he returns."[50] The same letter from Mrs. Winthrop suggests that Stuart's painting of James III was planned, but not executed prior to departure. She commented, "[Stuart] is a very pleasant companion, and promises himself much pleasure in conversing with my uncle when he returns."[51]

Although intended to be a pair, Stuart's representations of Mr. and Mrs. James Bowdoin III are uneven in treatment and detail. Whereas she appears before a classical column and an open sky, he is depicted against a plain background which contains the hint of an interior oval. Sarah Bowdoin's face is clearly defined and warm in tone; her red shawl highlights the pink in her cheeks and lips. Her husband's visage, by contrast, is more tentatively handled, and its overall sallowness is underscored by the ochre strip of his vest.

The mantilla Mrs. Bowdoin wears is an unusual element of costume that may be a specific allusion to Spain. Stuart's portrait of Elizabeth Temple Winthrop (fig. 22) also shows the sitter in a mantilla and suggests that her uncle's ministry accrued to the glory of the entire family.[52] If the appointment to Madrid occasioned the Stuart commission, however, the painting of James III gives no sign of it. Although he sent Stuart pencils and colors from Paris through Elizabeth's husband, Thomas L. Winthrop,[53] James Bowdoin III may never have met the artist. Stuart's unusually bland representation of the Spanish minister seems more likely to be a copy of Edward Malbone's miniature (fig. 24) (color frontispiece) than the result of a life sitting.

FIG. 21 Gilbert Stuart, *Portrait of Thomas Jefferson*

Whatever its history, this likeness remains the enduring image of the first patron of Bowdoin College.[54]

If James III contributed little to the collection of Bowdoin family portraits, his sister, Elizabeth, more than made up the difference. At the age of seventeen, the governor's eldest child married John Temple, who became the eighth baronet of Stowe in 1786. Lady Temple spent most of her married life in London and New York, but she returned to Boston after her husband's death in 1798. The couple had four children, Elizabeth (Mrs. Thomas L. Winthrop), Grenville, Augusta, and James, who later changed his surname to Bowdoin.

A miniature of Lady Temple in later life (fig. 25) seems to have been a companion to that of James Bowdoin III. Like Blackburn's double portrait, these pendant likenesses represent brother and sister in a format that calls to mind traditional representations of husbands and wives. By the time these miniatures were painted, such allusions could not have been wholly unintentional. Apart from their close personal relationship, Elizabeth and James III shared the heavy responsibility for carrying on the Bowdoin line.

In contrast to her brother, Lady Temple evinced an interest in and desire for family portraits at an early age. Her own likeness as an adult was first recorded in pastel by Copley on the occasion of her marriage to John Temple (1732-1798) in 1767 (figs. 26 and 27).[55] Living, as she subsequently did, on the opposite side of the Atlantic, Elizabeth not only longed for pictures of her relatives, but also expressed that longing in writing. In a 1775 letter to her mother, she lamented, "I often wish I had some resemblance of you and my father, but I now despair of it since you let Mr. Copley go, without having them taken."[56] When James III wrote to his sister from Naples that he would have his portrait painted and send it to her, he was presumably responding to a similar plea.

Lady Temple was equally concerned to have her own image remain vivid in the eyes of her family. The above-mentioned letter to her mother states, "I have given Jemmy [James III] our profiles which I beg may be hung on each side your glass in your bed room that you may think often of the originals."[57] In 1785, John Trumbull painted a group portrait of Sir John, Lady Temple, and two of their children (fig. 28), which was apparently planned as a gift to her brother and sister-in-law. On 27 July 1785, Elizabeth wrote to Sarah Bowdoin:

Mr. Trumbull is now painting Mr. Temple. He has finished Grenville, Augusta and myself. When it is done we mean to send it to you and my brother to hang over your best parlour Chimne. It will be about the size of the picture that is now hanging there.[58]

In both these instances, Lady Temple conceived family portraits for a specific location. We are left to wonder what Trumbull's picture of the Temple family was intended to replace and what this representation of familial affection would have meant to the childless couple.

During the last years of her life, Lady Temple became an avid patron of Gilbert Stuart. She commissioned a bust-length portrait of herself (fig. 29) and a copy of Trumbull's portrait of her husband as a companion (fig. 30); she then had Stuart copy her portrait in an expanded format as a mate to Trumbull's original painting of Sir John (Canajoharie Library and Art Gallery).

FIG. 22 Gilbert Stuart, *Portrait of Elizabeth Winthrop*

In her 1806 letter to her aunt in Paris, Elizabeth Temple Winthrop reported on her mother's activities:

Stuart has just finished her picture, which is an excellent likeness. He is also copying my father's and my mother gives them to me to take the place of those done by Copley. I have sat three times for mine, as my mother is determined to have all her children taken by him.[59]

Unlike her father, who had apparently bequeathed the Feke paintings to his son as part of the Beacon Street household,[60] Lady Temple intended the portraits of Sir John and herself specifically for their daughters. The Trumbull-Stuart pair went to Augusta Temple Palmer (who had herself been painted by Trumbull), while the Stuarts were given to Elizabeth Temple Winthrop.

In 1966, Stuart's original painting of Lady Temple came to Bowdoin College, along with another Stuart portrait of her granddaughter, Sarah Winthrop Sullivan (1788-1864) (fig. 31). The second child of Elizabeth Temple Winthrop, Sarah had accompanied her great-uncle and his wife on his ministry to Spain. She apparently sat for Stuart shortly after the party returned to Boston in 1808, since her mother's 1806 letter

FIG. 23 Gilbert Stuart, *Portrait of Sarah Bowdoin*

FIG. 24 Edward Greene Malbone, *Portrait of James Bowdoin III*

Because James III and Sarah were cousins, their collection of family pictures was both rich and comprehensive. It included two representations of their grandfather, James I, the portraits of William and James II as children, the four Feke paintings of their parents, Blackburn's picture of Elizabeth and James III, Gullager's posthumous *James Bowdoin II,* the youthful image of James III, and their own likenesses by Stuart. As the last of her generation (Lady Temple had died in 1809), Sarah Bowdoin took care to preserve the Bowdoin family from neglect and/or separation by others less personally involved in its memory.[64]

Before his death, James III had approached his sister's youngest son, James Bowdoin Temple, about becoming his official legatee. In an 1803 letter, he referred to "requirements & promises I made my late father, that in case I did continue without children, I should sellect some one of his Relations, a young man of worth and good reputation, to bear up his name."[65] James III went on to stipulate that his nephew must take the name of Bowdoin, become a citizen of

indicates that the artist knew nothing of her at that date.[61] This likeness may have been painted to celebrate her 1809 marriage to George Sullivan, who had served as James III's secretary in Europe. Sarah Sullivan is the last of five generations of Bowdoins represented in the museum's collection of family portraits. In her homely features and kindly expression, we can see shades of both her grandmother, Lady Temple, and her great-uncle, James III, whose name and whose portrait her great-aunt Sarah entrusted to her care.

When James Bowdoin III died in 1811, he left all his pictures "excepting family pictures" to Bowdoin College.[62] This group of seventy paintings included the Stuart portraits of Jefferson and Madison, which would have had educational value as representations of American worthies. James III's bequest contained eight additional portraits that he distinguished from family pictures as works of art.[63] The portraits of the Bowdoins went to his wife, Sarah, with no stipulation as to how they should eventually be disposed of.

FIG. 25 Edward Greene Malbone, *Portrait of Elizabeth Bowdoin, Lady Temple*

the United States, and form a matrimonial connection, all of which he ultimately did. Efforts to perpetuate the Bowdoin legacy did not end here, however. Two sons of Elizabeth Temple Winthrop, James and John, and two sons of Sarah Winthrop Sullivan, George and James, also changed their names to Bowdoin in the ensuing years.

While these newly-named Temples, Winthrops, and Sullivans inherited James III's estate, they did not gain custody of the family portraits. Rather than deliver her ancestors into the keeping of a human namesake, Sarah Bowdoin entrusted them to the institution her husband had named in honor of his father. Her will of 1812 states, "My Family Pictures I give to the College named Bowdoin in Brunswick, except my late Husband's & my own shall be retained during the life of Mrs. Sarah B-Sullivan, and Mrs. Eliza B-Winthrop."[66] Sarah Bowdoin's qualification of her bequest to Bowdoin College suggests that the Stuart portraits had personal significance to her niece and great-niece. Since Elizabeth Temple Winthrop predeceased her aunt in 1825, the pictures of James III and Sarah passed directly to Sarah Sullivan.

Sarah Bowdoin's special fondness for her great-niece is everywhere apparent in her will. In leaving her the Milk Street estate, she referred to the young woman as "my beloved, affectionate, worthy Neice." Beyond this bequest of real property, Sarah Bowdoin left twenty thousand dollars in trust for Sarah Sullivan and her children, explaining, "It is not for want of regard, or attachment to George Sullivan Esquire, Husband to my said Neice, that I give the said twenty Thousand Dollars in trust for her during her marriage State, but only on account of the uncertainty of all human events." Upon Mrs. Sullivan's death, her trust was assigned to her second son, James, provided he took and retained the name of Bowdoin and, if he should die without children, to his elder brother, George Richard, on the same conditions.[67]

Through her disposition of the family portraits and her efforts to perpetuate the Bowdoin name, Sarah Bowdoin displayed profound allegiance to the family that was hers both by birth

FIG. 26 John Singleton Copley, *Portrait of John Temple*

FIG. 27 John Singleton Copley, *Portrait of Mrs. John Temple (Elizabeth Bowdoin, Lady Temple)*

FIG. 28 John Trumbull, *Sir John Temple and Family*

and by marriage. Although her union with her cousin had produced no children, it seems to have been characterized by loyalty and affection. Her will begins with the following request:

It is my first desire that wherever I may die, I may be deposited in the same Tomb with my worthy, affectionate, deceased Husband—it being not only a wish of my own, but a promise I made to him a long time previous to his Death, that Wherever he was laid, I would be laid also.

While honoring a personal promise to James III, Sarah Bowdoin's will also reflects her determination to ensure her husband's legacy in this world. She achieved this aim by protecting the images and the individuals most closely associated with him.

When Sarah Bowdoin Dearborn died in 1826, Stuart's paintings of her and James III went, as stipulated, to Sarah Sullivan. While complementing her own portrait by Stuart, these pictures

must have reminded her of her great-uncle's ministry and the trip they had made to Europe together with her future husband. Before the other Bowdoin paintings were delivered to the College, Sarah Sullivan asked the Governing Boards for permission to retain, for a few years, the picture of Governor Bowdoin now attributed to Gullager. On 5 September 1826, the Trustees voted to deny her request on the grounds that it conflicted with her great-aunt's intentions. The following day, the Overseers voted against the Trustees.[68]

Although Gullager's small portrait of James II was the least prepossessing image in the Bowdoin collection, it was the only one that stressed achievement as much as appearance. For Bowdoin College, the picture represented the philosopher-statesman in whose honor the institution had been named; for the governor's descendants, it depicted the most illustrious figure in the family's history. Both sides had reason to desire the painting, and both continued to do so as long as they equated portraiture with nature more than art.

Sarah Sullivan died in 1864, at which time her sons, James Bowdoin and George Richard James Bowdoin, petitioned the College to keep, for their lifetimes, the pictures that had been temporarily retained by their mother. Although the Boards denied their request on 1 August 1865,[69] no works changed hands until George R. J. Bowdoin died in 1870. In that year, the two remaining Stuarts were accessioned, and the Boards, reversing their earlier decision, granted Mrs. George Bowdoin permission to keep the Gullager during her life.[70] The last painting in Sarah Bowdoin Dearborn's original bequest came to the College in 1894, the year the Walker Art Building was dedicated.

When the Bowdoin portraits were transferred from family to college their character as images changed. From their arrival in 1826, these paintings were displayed together with the art collection given by James III in 1811 (fig. 32). In

FIG. 29 Gilbert Stuart, *Portrait of Elizabeth Bowdoin, Lady Temple*

their 1882 *History of Bowdoin College,* Nehemiah Cleaveland and Alpheus Spring Packard made no mention of Sarah Bowdoin Dearborn's separate donation of family pictures. Writing of James I, they noted, "His portrait, as well as those of son and grandson, now adorns the college gallery of paintings."[71] Although the names of the family members were not forgotten, the memory of them as living individuals faded with the passing of generations. As art acquired an aesthetic as well as a moral and educational value in American culture, the original Bowdoins became hidden behind the men who had portrayed them.

George Thomas Little's "Historical Sketch" in the Bowdoin catalogue of 1894 exemplifies this transmutation of family portraits from nature into art. Writing of paintings at the College, he noted:

Portraits of Thomas Jefferson and James Madison, painted by Gilbert Stuart at Mr. Bowdoin's special request, are admirable specimens of American art. The Bowdoin family portraits which were received at later date include good examples of the work of Robert Feke, John Singleton Copley, and possibly of John Smibert.[72]

FIG. 30 Gilbert Stuart, *Portrait of John Temple*

When Gilbert Stuart's portraits of Lady Temple and Sarah Sullivan were given to the museum in 1966, the College News Service similarly emphasized artistic over human significance. The advance release read, "President Coles noted that the two gifts bring Bowdoin's collection of Stuart paintings to nine." It went on, "Marvin S. Sadik, Director and Curator of the Bowdoin Museum, described the two oils as 'exceptionally vivid examples of Stuart's work, painted at the top of his form.'"[73] Although both Coles and Sadik remarked on the historical importance of the Stuart paintings, neither speculated on their meaning to the Bowdoin family.

When thirty-six portraits from Bowdoin College traveled to New York in 1966, they elicited a similar response. *New York Times* critic John Canaday claimed that James III had "thought of the portraits as historical records rather than as works of art" and, consequently, left no list of the painters' names. By way of correction, he continued:

But the names [of the artists] are an admirable roster . . . . Now taking precedence over the names of the subjects they portrayed, the artists in their various styles range from a provincial awkwardness that is appealing largely only because it is touching in its impotent effort to be something more than it is, to an adequate presentation of the formula developed by the fashionable portrait painters in England.[74]

Looking at the Bowdoin portrait collection from outside the College, Canaday located its importance exclusively in its makers. His review seems to confirm Walter Benjamin's remark that "the portrait becomes after a few generations no more than a testimony to the art of the person who painted it."[75]

To view the Bowdoin portraits solely as works of art, however, is to miss their original significance as equivalents of nature. As a group, these

FIG. 31 Gilbert Stuart, *Portrait of Sarah Sullivan*

pictures represent a proud and loyal family, whose hold on the future was tenuous at best and never far from their minds. Richard Brilliant might have been speaking for the Bowdoins when he wrote, "Portraiture challenges the transiency or irrelevancy of human existence and the portrait artist must respond to the demands formulated by the individual's wish to endure."[76] By commissioning paintings of their children, duplicating likenesses of their parents, sending pictures to one another, and ultimately bequeathing all these images to the institution that bore the family name, the Bowdoins strove not only to celebrate their success, but also to guarantee their survival. In their portraits, Bowdoin College can see vividly preserved the family history of its ancestors.

FIG. 32 Bowdoin Gallery, Bowdoin College Museum of Art

NOTES

BCSC is Special Collections, Hawthorne-Longfellow Library, Bowdoin College. BCMA is Bowdoin College Museum of Art.

1. I would like to thank Joanne E. Thompson '88 and Jennifer S. Edwards '89, who provided both research assistance and insights of their own on the Bowdoin portrait collection while I was preparing this essay. I am also indebted to Clifton C. Olds, Susan E. Wegner, Katharine J. Watson, and Susan L. Ransom, whose helpful suggestions and judicious criticism enabled me better to know and understand the Bowdoin family.

2. Bowdoin-Temple Papers, Massachusetts Historical Society, Boston.

3. Marvin S. Sadik, *Colonial and Federal Portraits at Bowdoin College* (Brunswick, ME: Bowdoin College Museum of Art, 1966).

4. Ibid.

5. On viewer response to colonial and federal portraiture, see Jessie Poesch, "'In just Lines to trace'—The Colonial Artist, 1700-1776," in *The Portrait in Eighteenth-Century America,* edited by Ellen G. Miles (Newark, DE: University of Delaware Press, 1993).

6. Richard Brilliant, *Portraiture* (London: Reaktion Books, 1991), 19.

7. See Erwin Panofsky, *Idea: A Concept in Art Theory,* translated by Joseph J. S. Peake (New York: Harper & Row, Icon Editions, 1968), 14-15.

8. Sir Joshua Reynolds, *Discourses on Art,* edited by Robert W. Wark (New Haven: Yale University Press, 1975), 41.

9. Ibid., 72.

10. Taking their cue from Reynolds, American art writers also distinguished between "historical" or "poetic" and "common" portraits. See, for example, Daniel Fanshaw's 1827 review of the second National Academy of Design exhibition, discussed in William H. Gerdts, "Natural Aristocrats in a Democracy, 1810-1870," in *American Portraiture in the Grand Manner: 1720-1920,* by Michael Quick, exh. cat. (Los Angeles: Los Angeles County Museum of Art, 1981), 28-29.

11. See Brandon Brame Fortune, "Charles Willson Peale's Portrait Gallery: Persuasion and the Plain Style," *Word and*

Image 6 (October-December 1990):308-24; and T. H. Breen, "The Meaning of 'Likeness': American Portrait Painting in an Eighteenth-Century Consumer Society," *Word and Image* 6 (October-December 1990):325-50.

12. Quoted in Richard H. Saunders and Ellen G. Miles, *American Colonial Portraits, 1700-1776,* exh. cat. (Washington D.C.: Smithsonian Institution Press for the National Portrait Gallery, 1987), 49-50.

13. Ibid., 48.

14. Ibid., 45.

15. Ibid., 17.

16. Ibid., 49.

17. Quoted in Eleanor Pearson DeLorme, "Gilbert Stuart: Portrait of an Artist," *Winterthur Portfolio* 14 (Winter 1979):340.

18. In this essay, I have limited my discussion to portraits whose subjects can be identified with relative certainty. Excluded from this category is a portrait of an unknown woman whom Sadik identifies as Elizabeth Bowdoin, Lady Temple, and attributes to Samuel King.

19. John Singleton Copley is the exception. On other colonial and federal portraits in the BCMA, see Sadik.

20. Unless otherwise indicated, information on the Bowdoins and their portraits is taken from Sadik. For additional information on the family, see Gordon E. Kershaw, *James Bowdoin: Patriot and Man of the Enlightenment,* exh. cat. (Brunswick, ME: Bowdoin College Museum of Art, 1976); Gordon E. Kershaw, *James Bowdoin II: Patriot and Man of the Enlightenment* (Lanham, MD: University Press of America, 1991); and Robert L. Volz, *Governor Bowdoin & His Family: A Guide to an Exhibition and Catalogue,* exh. cat. (Brunswick, ME: Bowdoin College, 1969).

21. Karin Calvert, "Children in American Family Portraiture, 1670 to 1810," *William and Mary Quarterly* 39 (January 1982):97.

22. See Calvert, 89.

23. Since the youthful portraits of William and James II were painted after the deaths of their respective mothers, we can assume that the idea for both commissions originated with James I. On Smibert and Bishop Berkeley, see Susan Wegner's essay in this book.

24. On this painting, see Saunders and Miles, 124-25.

25. See Roland E. Fleischer, "Emblems and Colonial American Painting," *American Art Journal* 20 (1988):3-35.

26. A second sister, Judith Bowdoin, died in 1750 without children and, as far as we know, without a portrait of her father.

27. See Waldron Phoenix Belknap, Jr., *American Colonial Painting: Materials for a History* (Cambridge: Belknap Press of Harvard University Press, 1959), 280. On Badger's use of this prototype, see Saunders and Miles, 190-91.

28. We know that John Smibert used mezzotints of ships for backgrounds in his merchant portraits, and Badger may well have done the same. See Saunders and Miles, 24.

29. Kershaw 1976, 35-36. Kershaw describes James II as a "Newtonian," who "thought of God as the 'prime mover' who had established the universe as a marvelous clockwork mechanism and had then left man to work out his own destiny." Ibid., 32.

30. It was also the year in which he received his master's degree from Harvard.

31. The remaining three-sevenths was divided among his three daughters, Mary Bowdoin (Mrs. Balthasar Bayard), Judith Bowdoin (Mrs. Thomas Flucker), and Elizabeth Bowdoin (Mrs. James Pitts).

32. This interpretation of the "hand-in" gesture is based on research presented by Arlene Meyer at an NEH Summer Seminar for College Teachers on "Portraiture," Houghton Library, Harvard University, 1990. For alternative explanations, see Robin Simon, *The Portrait in Britain and America* (Oxford: Phaidon, 1987), 73-75.

33. See Belknap, Plates XX and XXI. As a prototype for his portrait of Phebe Bowdoin, Feke may also have used a 1705-10 mezzotint by Simon after Richardson's painting of the actress Anne Oldfield. This variation of Kneller's *Princess Anne* shows the female sitter with a book. See Belknap, 292 and Plate XXIII.

34. On the selective use of mezzotint sources, see Trevor J. Fairbrother, "John Singleton Copley's Use of British Mezzotints for His American Portraits: A Reappraisal Prompted by New Discoveries," *Arts* 55 (March 1981):122-30. On the importance of mezzotints for female portraits, see Martha R. Severens, "Jeremiah Theus of Charleston: Plagiarist or Pundit?" *Southern Quarterly* 24 (Fall-Winter 1985):56-70.

35. See Fleischer, 3.

36. See Calvert, 100-101.

37. See Philippe Ariès, *Centuries of Childhood: A Social History of Family Life,* translated by Robert Baldick (New York: Vintage Books, 1962), 365-404.

38. See Margaretta M. Lovell, "Reading Eighteenth-Century American Family Portraits," *Winterthur Portfolio* 22 (Winter 1987):243-64. For information on eighteenth-century French art and society, see Carol Duncan, "Happy Mothers and Other New Ideas in Eighteenth-Century French Art," in *Feminism and Art History: Questioning the Litany,* edited by Norma Broude and Mary D. Garrard (New York: Harper & Row, Icon Editions, 1982), 201-19.

39. On Winslow family portraits, see *The Winslows: Pilgrims, Patrons and Portraits,* exh. cat. (Brunswick, ME: Bowdoin College Museum of Art, 1974).

40. On Gullager, see Louisa Dresser, "Christian Gullager, an Introduction to His Life and Some Representative Examples of His Work," *Art in America* 37 (July 1949):103-79. The miniature of James II was at one time attributed to John Singleton Copley and is currently in private hands. A painted copy of it, formerly owned by the governor's descendants, is in the Massachusetts Historical Society.

41. On this painting, see Jules Prown, *John Singleton Copley,* 2 vols. (Washington, D.C.: National Gallery of Art, 1966; Cambridge: Harvard University Press, 1966), 2:300; and Andrew Oliver, *Portraits of John and Abigail Adams* (Cambridge: Harvard University Press, 1967), 40.

42. Notice of the portrait in the *Columbian Centinel,* 16 November 1791, quoted in Sadik, 96.

43. This possibility was suggested by Louisa Dresser. See Sadik, 92. Large public commissions account for only a small percentage of portraits painted in colonial and federal America, and no record of such a painting of James II has come to light. Prints, on the other hand, were extremely popular in the early years of the Republic as a means of bringing images of notable Americans into ordinary homes. Gullager may have conceived this picture as a model for an engraving.

44. Although there is no indication that the governor's descendants commissioned the original painting, they may have allowed the artist access to the miniature. The miniature itself was subsequently engraved by Samuel Hill.

45. Quoted in Sadik, 93.

46. It is possible that Mrs. James Bowdoin II retained one of these two paintings until her death in 1803.

47. Quoted in Sadik, 87. James III's Harvard biography quotes a similar letter to James II dated the same day. See Clifford K. Shipton, *Sibley's Harvard Graduates,* vol. 17 (Boston: Massachusetts Historical Society, 1975).

48. On the Stuart portraits of Jefferson and Madison, see my forthcoming article entitled "Public Portraits/Private Lives: Gilbert Stuart's Portraits of Thomas Jefferson and James Madison for James Bowdoin III."

49. Although James III sent portraits of Sarah Bowdoin, Sarah Winthrop, and George Sullivan from Paris to the family in Boston in 1806, he included no likeness of himself. On 29 April 1807, Elizabeth Temple Winthrop wrote to her aunt, "Do persuade my Uncle to have his done like the ones of yours and Sarah's and give it to me." Quoted in Sadik, 147-48. Elizabeth Temple Winthrop was the eldest daughter of Elizabeth Bowdoin, Lady Temple. Sarah Winthrop was Elizabeth Temple Winthrop's daughter.

50. Quoted in Sadik, 146. Bowdoin-Temple Papers, Massachusetts Historical Society, Boston.

51. From the same letter as above, note 50. Bowdoin-Temple Papers, Massachusetts Historical Society, Boston.

52. A mantilla also figures in Stuart's unfinished portrait of Mrs. Perez Morton (Worcester Art Museum), a close friend of both the artist and the Bowdoin family. Lace veils worn without hats became fashionable for women at this time. See Katherine Morris Lester and Bess Viola Oerke, *Accessories of Dress* (Peoria, IL: Manual Arts Press, 1940), 68. I would like to thank Laura K. Mills '93 for this reference.

53. See letter in Sadik, 146.

54. In 1812, the portrait was engraved by J. R. Smith for *Polyanthos.*

55. Elizabeth's portrait was painted two years after that of her husband as a companion to it. See Prown, 1:230.

56. Quoted in Sadik, 98. Transcript in object file 1924.1, BCMA. Bowdoin-Temple Papers, Massachusetts Historical Society, Boston.

57. Ibid. A silhouette of John Temple by John Meirs is currently in the Massachusetts Historical Society. See *Witness to America's Past: Two Centuries of Collecting by the Massachusetts Historical Society,* exh. cat. (Boston: Massachusetts Historical Society and Museum of Fine Arts, Boston, 1991), 143. The society also owns a companion silhouette of James Bowdoin II.

58. Object file 1924.1, BCMA.

59. Quoted in George C. Mason, *The Life and Works of Gilbert Stuart, 1820-1894* (New York: B. Franklin Reprints, 1972), 265. It is unclear what happened to the Copley por-

traits at this time, but they were subsequently owned by Mrs. Winthrop's oldest daughter, Elizabeth Winthrop Tappan (1787-1860), who lived with her grandparents, Sir John and Lady Temple, until they died. Letter from Augusta Temple Tappan, BCSC.

60. See Volz, 9. The will of James II makes no specific mention of pictures.

61. See letter in Sadik, 154.

62. Bowdoin Papers, Documents File, Last Will and Testament of James Bowdoin III, BCSC.

63. One of these works is listed as "Portrait Painter."

64. Sarah Bowdoin's early life is shrouded in mystery. Born in the twenty-second year of her parents' marriage, the only child of William and Phebe Bowdoin was orphaned in 1774 at the age of thirteen. What happened to her after that date is uncertain, but it is possible that she spent the Revolutionary years in her uncle James II's household. (See the reference to a "Sally Bowdoin" in Kershaw 1976, 81.) Sarah's relationship with her cousin may have developed at this time, after James III returned from his European sojourn.

Since this essay was written, a diary that Sarah Bowdoin kept from October 1806 to February 1808, during the couple's diplomatic sojourn in Paris and London, has been acquired by BCSC.

65. Quoted in Sadik, 140.

66. Maine Historical Society, Portland, Maine.

67. If neither of the sons produced an heir, the Milk Street property was to pass to Mrs. Sullivan's daughters in succeeding order of birth. Sarah Bowdoin's will expresses dissatisfaction with the fact that James Temple Bowdoin had not fixed his residence permanently in America.

68. Vote of the Governing Boards, 5 September 1826, BCSC.

69. Vote of the Governing Boards, 1 August 1865, BCSC.

70. Vote of the Governing Boards, 12 July 1870, BCSC.

71. Nehemiah Cleaveland and Alpheus Spring Packard, *History of Bowdoin College* (Boston: James Ripley Osgood & Company, 1882), 31.

72. George Thomas Little, "Historical Sketch," in *General Catalogue of Bowdoin College and the Medical School of Maine 1794-1894* (Brunswick, ME: Bowdoin College, 1894), 29. This text was copied verbatim in Louis C. Hatch, *The History of Bowdoin College* (Portland, ME: Loring, Short & Harmon, 1927), 448. The Gullager portrait was once thought to be by Copley.

73. Object file 1966.89, BCMA. Bowdoin College News Service, 16 December 1966.

74. John Canaday, "With Special Reference to Robert Feke," *New York Times* (Sunday, 18 September 1966), D:33. Canaday erroneously assumed that James III had bequeathed the portraits to the College.

75. Quoted in Brilliant, 151.

76. Ibid., 14.

Starred works are reproduced in color in this chapter. All works are the property of the Bowdoin College Museum of Art unless otherwise noted.

*1. John Smibert
   b. Scotland 1688,
   active in America 1729–1751
   Portrait of James Bowdoin II as a Boy, 1736
   oil on canvas
   34 7/8 x 26 7/8 inches
   Bequest of Mrs. Sarah Bowdoin Dearborn
   1826.5

2. Anonymous
   American, eighteenth century
   Portrait of James Bowdoin I, ca. 1725
   oil on canvas
   36 1/4 x 29 3/4 inches
   Bequest of Mrs. Sarah Bowdoin Dearborn
   1826.4

3. Anonymous
   American, eighteenth century
   Portrait of William Bowdoin as a Boy, ca. 1725
   oil on canvas
   30 1/4 x 25 inches
   Bequest of Mrs. Sarah Bowdoin Dearborn
   1826.3

4. English
   after Kneller
   Portrait of Charles Montagu, 1715–1725
   mezzotint
   13 1/4 x 9 7/8 inches
   Courtesy of the Winterthur Museum

*5. Joseph Badger
   American, 1708–1765
   Portrait of James Bowdoin I, ca. 1747
   oil on canvas
   50 1/4 x 40 1/4 inches
   Bequest of Mrs. Sarah Bowdoin Dearborn
   1826.6

6. John Faber, Jr.
   English
   after Vanderbank
   Portrait of Sir Isaac Newton, 1726
   mezzotint
   13 3/4 x 9 1/8 inches
   Courtesy of the Winterthur Museum

7. Robert Feke
   American, 1707–1752
   Portrait of James Bowdoin II, 1748
   oil on canvas
   50 x 40 inches
   Bequest of Mrs. Sarah Bowdoin Dearborn
   1826.8

8. Robert Feke
   American, 1707–1752
   Portrait of Elizabeth Bowdoin (Mrs. James
      Bowdoin II, née Erving), 1748
   oil on canvas
   50 1/8 x 40 1/8 inches
   Bequest of Mrs. Sarah Bowdoin Dearborn
   1826.7

9. Robert Feke
   American, 1707–1752
   Portrait of William Bowdoin, 1748
   oil on canvas
   50 1/4 x 40 1/4 inches
   Bequest of Mrs. Sarah Bowdoin Dearborn
   1826.10

10. Robert Feke
American, 1707–1752
Portrait of Phebe Bowdoin (Mrs. William
Bowdoin, née Murdock), 1748
oil on canvas
50 1/4 x 40 3/8 inches
Bequest of Mrs. Sarah Bowdoin Dearborn
1826.9

11. Beckett
English
after Wissing
Portrait of the Princess Ann
mezzotint
13 1/16 x 9 7/8 inches
Courtesy of the Winterthur Museum

12. John Smith
English
after Kneller
*Portrait of Her Royal Highness Princess Ann of
Denmark 1692*
mezzotint
14 5/16 x 10 7/16 inches
Courtesy of the Winterthur Museum

*13. Joseph Blackburn
active in America, 1754–1763
*Portrait of Elizabeth Bowdoin and James
Bowdoin III*, ca. 1760
oil on canvas
36 7/8 x 58 inches
Bequest of Mrs. Sarah Bowdoin Dearborn
1826.11

14. Joseph Blackburn
active in America, 1754–1763
Portrait of Isaac Winslow and His Family, 1755
oil on canvas
54 1/2 x 79 1/2 inches
Abraham Shuman Fund
Courtesy of the Museum of Fine Arts,
Boston
42.684

15. Christian Gullager
American, 1759–1826
Portrait of Governor James Bowdoin II, ca.
1791
oil on panel
10 3/4 x 8 5/8 inches
Bequest of Mrs. Sarah Bowdoin Dearborn
1894.2

16. Christian Gullager
American, 1759–1826
Portrait of Governor James Bowdoin II, ca.
1791
oil on panel
10 3/4 x 8 5/8 inches
Gift of Miss Clara Bowdoin Winthrop
1924.1

*17. Gilbert Stuart
American, 1755–1828
Portrait of James Bowdoin III
oil on canvas
28 1/2 x 24 inches
Bequest of Mrs. Sarah Dearborn Bowdoin
1870.6

18. Anonymous
Portrait of James Bowdoin III, ca. 1771–1775
oil on canvas
30 1/4 x 25 1/2 inches
Bequest of Mrs. Sarah Bowdoin Dearborn
1826.1

19. John Singleton Copley
American, 1738–1815
Portrait of John Adams, 1783
oil on canvas
93 3/4 x 58 inches
Bequest of Ward Nicholas Boylston to
Harvard College, 1828
Harvard University Art Museums
Courtesy of the Harvard University Portrait
Collection

20. Gilbert Stuart
American, 1755–1828
Portrait of James Madison, 1805–1807
oil on canvas
48 1/4 x 39 3/4 inches
Bequest of the Honorable James
   Bowdoin III
1813.54

21. Gilbert Stuart
American, 1755–1828
Portrait of Thomas Jefferson, 1805–1807
oil on canvas
48 3/8 x 39 3/4 inches
Bequest of the Honorable James
   Bowdoin III
1813.55

22. Gilbert Stuart
American, 1755–1828
Portrait of Elizabeth Winthrop (Mrs. Thomas
   Lindall Winthrop, née Temple), 1806
oil on canvas
73.8 x 61.2 cm
Courtesy of the Massachusetts Historical
   Society, Boston

*23. Gilbert Stuart
American, 1755–1828
Portrait of Sarah Bowdoin (Mrs. James
   Bowdoin III, née Bowdoin, 2d mar.
   Dearborn), before 1806
oil on canvas
30 x 25 1/8 inches
Bequest of Mrs. Sarah Bowdoin Dearborn
1870.7

24. Edward Greene Malbone
American, 1777–1807
Portrait of James Bowdoin III, ca. 1804
watercolor on ivory
3 3/16 x 2 1/2 inches (oval)
Gift of Dorothy Hupper in honor of
   President Kenneth C. M. Sills '01 and
   Mrs. Sills h'52
1951.7

25. Edward Greene Malbone
American, 1777–1807
Portrait of Elizabeth Bowdoin, Lady Temple, ca.
   1804
watercolor on ivory
3 3/16 x 2 7/16 inches (oval)
Gift of Dorothy Hupper in honor of
   President Kenneth C. M. Sills '01 and
   Mrs. Sills h'52
1951.8

26. John Singleton Copley
American, 1738–1815
Portrait of John Temple, 1765
pastel on paper
23 1/2 x 18
Courtesy of Mrs. Irving Levitt

27. John Singleton Copley
American, 1738–1815
Portrait of Mrs. John Temple (Elizabeth
   Bowdoin, Lady Temple), ca. 1767
pastel on paper
23 1/4 x 15 3/4 inches
Courtesy of Mrs. Irving Levitt

28. John Trumbull
American, 1756–1843
Sir John Temple and Family, 1784
oil on canvas
26 3/4 x 33 3/4 inches
Courtesy of Mrs. Albert L. Key

29. Gilbert Stuart
American, 1755–1828
Portrait of Elizabeth Bowdoin, Lady Temple
oil on panel
28 x 23 inches
Gift of Robert Winthrop
1966.89

30. Gilbert Stuart
American, 1755–1828
Portrait of John Temple
oil on panel
74.5 x 61.2 cm.
Courtesy of the Massachusetts Historical
Society, Boston

31. Gilbert Stuart
American, 1755–1828
Portrait of Sarah Sullivan (Mrs. George
Sullivan, née Winthrop)
oil on panel
28 x 23 inches
Gift of Robert Winthrop
1966.90

32. Bowdoin Gallery, Bowdoin College
Museum of Art, ca. 1900

LE BOLET TUBEREUX

Boletus tuberosus. *on le trouve en août et septembre dans les bois. son* **CHAPEAU** *a quelquefois jusqu'a 18 pouces de diamètre, sa chair est très epaisse, continue avec celle du pédicule, changeant de couleur presqu'aussitôt qu'on l'entame, ses* **TUYAUX** *sont très longs, très menus, contigus avec la chair sur laquelle ils ne sont qu'appliqués et de laquelle on les sépare facillement sans qu'il y ait de déchirement sensible, dans l'etat de jeunesse, son* **CHAPEAU** *est convexe en dessus et concave en dessous, sa super-ficie est sèche, sa chair ferme, cassante et d'un jaune paille: dans l'etat de vieillesse, il est convexe en dessus et en dessous, sa su-perficie est humide, sa chair est moins ferme, d'un jaune plus clair et parsemée d'un nombre prodigieux de piqûres de vers.* **PEDICULE** *plein, continu avec le chapeau, très renflé à sa base et peu evasé à son extremité supérieure.*

N.B. Les fig. A et B representent ce **CHAMPIGNON** *dans differents âges. La fig. C démontre une partie du chapeau coupée verticalement, il y a une varieté dont les tuyaux sont blancs.*

Quand il est jeune il a un goût exquis sitôt qu'il est un peu avancé en âge, il devient d'une amertume insuportable. la chair de la varieté est amère dans l'etat de jeunesse, comme dans l'etat de vieillesse.

Fɪɢ. 1 Bulliard's sumptuous *Herbier de la France* (1780-93) is one of the many scientific and agricultural books in James Bowdoin's library.

JAMES BOWDOIN III
AS LIBRARY BUILDER

Kenneth E. Carpenter

In 1811, James Bowdoin III bequeathed to Bowdoin College a library of about 780 titles in 2,050 volumes and "131 bundles of Pamphlets, in number about 2,117."[1] The bequest probably at least tripled the number of books already at the College,[2] and gave Bowdoin one of the largest libraries in the United States, perhaps third among the colleges of New England.[3] That was the judgment of contemporaries, and it is borne out by statistical information available today, even if the numbers are by no means precisely comparable. Harvard College's library, clearly the largest in the country at that time, had 9,296 titles in its 1790 catalog. In 1791, Yale had 1,582 titles, and Brown had 1,220 in 1793.[4] The figures in 1811 would, almost certainly, not have been markedly different, for library growth was generally slow. Only half a page was required to record Harvard's acquisitions of 1806-07.[5]

In 1811, it was still possible for an individual to have library holdings comparable to, or greater than, those of institutions. When Thomas Jefferson sold his library to the United States in 1815, he had 6,707 volumes. In 1819, the library of the polymath clergyman William Bentley of Salem comprised more than 4,000 volumes. Most remarkable was the library of Benjamin Vaughan of Hallowell, which is said to have numbered more than 10,000 volumes in 1797. Such figures show that some individuals owned more books than James Bowdoin did, but the number was few.[6]

The library of James Bowdoin III was his own creation, not a family collection, for his father's library had been bequeathed to the American Academy of Arts and Sciences.[7] Only two books from the Bowdoin College bequest, it seems, had been owned by the father, and only a few others had belonged to James Bowdoin's mother, Elizabeth Erving Bowdoin. Almost all of the books were collected by James Bowdoin III himself. From inscriptions on the pamphlets, however, it is clear that they had been gathered by three generations of Bowdoin men, by James Bowdoin III's mother, and also by Sarah Bowdoin Bowdoin, his wife (and first cousin). Unlike many collectors, no Bowdoin ancestor, not his uncle (and father-in-law) William Bowdoin or James Bowdoin II, customarily bound groups of pamphlets in volumes. The pamphlets were stored, it seems, in a cabinet rather than on the shelves, and James Bowdoin III followed the example of his ancestors.[8]

The pamphlets are an important resource for scholars, but it was the books that James Bowdoin valued, and it was their bequest that earned him the gratitude of the College's authorities. The books were the fulfillment of an unstated promise, and they justified naming the College after the father of James Bowdoin III. In a letter to Jesse Appleton of 6 November 1811, Benjamin Vaughan expressed the idea that expectations existed of James Bowdoin and that they had been realized: "Mr. Bowdoin always appeared to me an honorable man; & I conceived that he would realize all the expectations he had raised. He has done so; & merits our thanks to a high degree." Vaughan, an even greater collector, indulged in the sense of superiority of the man with more books when a week later, on 12 November 1811, he wrote again to Appleton, "You have now the rudiments of a good library, & I hope you will soon begin to have pupils." At the same time, though, his sentence suggests part of the importance of the bequest to Bowdoin College: it gave the fledgling institution more of the status that has always been important in attracting students (fig. 2).

The importance of the bequest can also be measured monetarily. The books were valued at $5,362.26 (fig. 3); two globes at $75; the mineralogical, chemical, and electrical apparatus and instruments at $904.37 1/2; and the art at

Hon.le JAMES BOWDOIN, Esq.r

FIG. 2

$7,035, for a total of $13,376.63 1/2. This came to several times the salary of the president, who was at that time paid $1,000 per year. There were only two professors and a tutor at the College, so James Bowdoin's bequest exceeded several times over the entire instructional outlay of the institution.

For James Bowdoin, though, such benefits or measurements were not the important ones. To him books were central to education, and education was vital in fostering the public good. The form of his gift was thus, to him, the most appropriate and the most important, more significant than money, or than land that could be transformed into money. Evidence indicates that he long planned it this way and that he to a considerable extent collected books—and perhaps other objects—for the College. This gives him a claim to being the first American to collect, in large part, for an educational institution.

In grand gestures the complexity of human motivation can always be seen, and it is possible to find in Bowdoin's gifts more, or rather less, than philanthropy. Support for Bowdoin College can thus be viewed also as an effort to memorialize a father who was deeply concerned about continuing the family name,[9] or as a self-interested attempt to increase the value of Bowdoin's vast land holdings in the District of Maine. Yet, despite the inherent difficulty of sorting out calculation from emotion, or gauging the power of an emotion, it is clear that among the factors behind his philanthropy was a deep caring for young people and their education. In this he was not alone among the "young men of 1776." To mention but one example: Jefferson founded a university; and even though the younger Bowdoin was not a leader in the Revolution, the support of the college in Maine can be seen as another instance of a member of that generation trying to pass on its ideals through education.[10] More specific evidence from his correspondence shows that he greatly valued education, particularly collegiate education. Here is an extract from a letter of 31 October 1793 to his sister, Elizabeth Bowdoin Temple, written in response to a request for financial assistance for her son James:[11]

His Education, if he attends to it, ought to qualify him for one of y.e learned Professions, w.ch if his Inclination favours it, his Habits Manners & Studies sh.d be directed to it. But there is such a Connexion between all y.e learned Professions, that Success in any of them, very much depends upon a well directed collegiate Education, in w.ch the Rudiments of the Sciences are to be deeply laid, in order to the making a distinguished Figure in any of them. . . . Young Men who go to College, should have before them y.e Expectation of a learned Profession, and not be suffered to justify their Inattention to Study, by thinking they will take to other Pursuits.

The specific reference to "collegiate Education" in this letter of 1793 indicates that Bowdoin's gift of money and lands in 1794 had behind it a true concern for education. "Young Men" in general, however, were to be the beneficiaries, not the nephew in question. The letter's moralizing tone must have prepared its reader for that outcome (James Bowdoin stated that he did not have sufficient ready cash). Although the nephew had incurred his uncle's disapproval, such aloofness was not typical of James Bowdoin. Other letters contain repeated queries or observations about individual young people, expressions of concern, bits of advice, and indications of concrete assistance in furthering their education.

The most detailed letter of advice to a young person is a letter of 16 April 1799 to James, the nephew about whom Bowdoin wrote in 1793. This letter is notable for its detail (no aloofness here), and it is also an instance in which James Bowdoin concretely related education and books.[12]

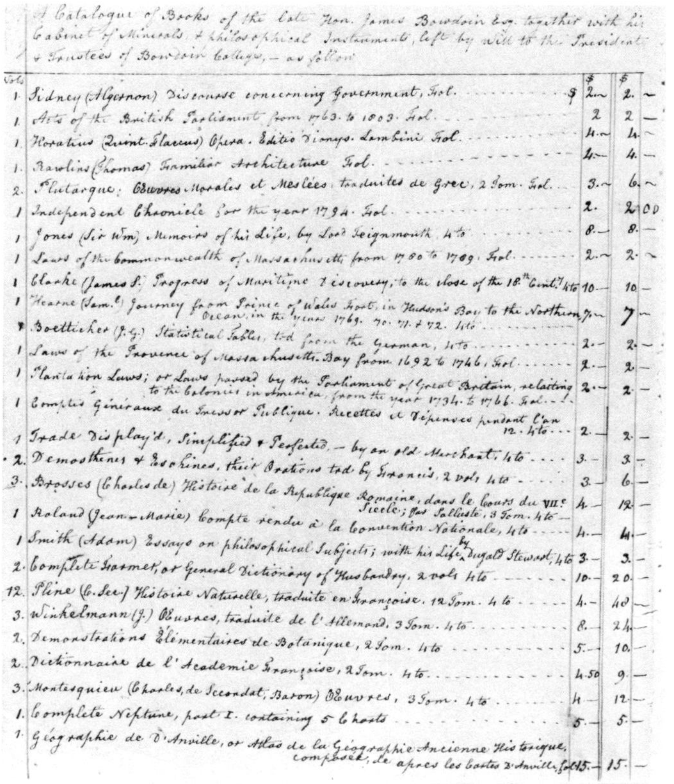

A Catalogue of Books of the late Hon. James Bowdoin Esq. together with his Cabinet of Minerals & Philosophical Instruments, left by will to the President & Trustees of Bowdoin College, — as follow

Vols		$	$
1	Sidney (Algernon) Discourse concerning Government, Fol.	2.–	2.–
1	Acts of the British Parliament from 1763. to 1803. Fol.	2	2 –
1	Horatius (Quint. Flaccus) Opera. Editio Dionys. Lambini Fol.	4.–	4.–
1	Rawlins (Thomas) Familiar Architecture Fol.	4.–	4.–
2	Plutarque; Œuvres Morales et Meslées traduites de Grec, 2 Tom. Fol.	3.–	6.–
1	Independent Chronicle for the year 1794. Fol.	2.	2.00
1	Jones (Sir Wm) Memoirs of his Life, by Lord Teignmouth. 4to	8.–	8.–
1	Laws of the Commonwealth of Massachusetts from 1780 to 1789. Fol.	2.–	2.–
1	Clarke (James S.) Progress of Maritime Discovery, to the close of the 18th Centy. 4to	10.–	10.–
1	Hearne (Saml.) Journey from Prince of Wales Fort, in Hudson's Bay to the Northern Ocean, in the years 1769. 70. 71. & 72. 4to	7.–	7.–
1	Boetticher (J. G.) Statistical Tables, trd from the German, 4to	2.–	2.–
1	Laws of the Province of Massachusetts Bay from 1692 to 1746, Fol.	2.–	2.–
1	Plantation Laws; or Laws passed by the Parliament of Great Britain, relating to the Colonies in America, from the year 1734. to 1766. Fol.	2.–	2.–
1	Comptes Généraux du Tresor Publique. Recettes et Dépenses pendant l'an 12. 4to		
1	Trade Display'd, Simplified & Perfected, — by an old Merchant, 4to	2.–	2.–
2	Demosthenes & Eschines, their Orations trd by Francis, 2 vols 4to	3.–	3.–
3	Brosses (Charles de) Histoire de la Republique Romaine, dans le Cours du VII.e Siecle; par Salluste, 3 Tom. 4to	3.–	6.–
1	Roland (Jean-Marie) Compte rendu à la Convention Nationale, 4to	4.–	12.–
1	Smith (Adam) Essays on philosophical Subjects; with his Life by Dugald Stewart, 4to	4.–	4.–
2	Complete Farmer, or General Dictionary of Husbandry. 2 vols 4to	3.–	3.–
12	Pline (C. Sec.) Histoire Naturelle, traduite en Françoise. 12 Tom. 4to	10.–	20.–
3	Winkelmann (J.) Œuvres, traduite de l'Allemand. 3 Tom. 4to	4.–	40.–
2	Demonstrations Élémentaires de Botanique, 2 Tom. 4to	8.–	24.–
2	Dictionnaire de l'Academie Françoise, 2 Tom. 4to	5.–	10.–
3	Montesquieu (Charles, de Secondat, Baron) Œuvres, 3 Tom. 4to	4.50	9.–
1	Complete Neptune, part I. containing 5 Charts	4	12.–
1	Géographie de D'Anville, or Atlas de la Géographie Ancienne Historique, composée, de apres les Cartes D'Anville, fol.	15.–	15.–

FIG. 3 The first page of the catalog of the bequest of James Bowdoin III. The entries contain the appraised value of each volume and work.

I have recd. several Letters from you, since your engaging in ye. british army; . . . I believe by this time, you begin to see that there are no great Sports to be found in traversing ye. ocean in all directions, enduring ye. dangers of Disease Slavery & Death, in a Service where ye rewards are too small to compensate such hazards. . . . In ye. midst of these discouragements, you ought to endeavour to connect with your professional information, ye small recompence w.ch your situation does or may afford you: w.ch is a clear & determinate knowledge of ye. geographical situation, climate, Government, Laws, manners, habits, commerce, & productions of ye. countries & places, to w.ch your military duty may call you. These ought to be arranged under distinct heads & connected with your Journal of occurrences w.ch you ought to keep, and wherein ye. Business, observations & duties of each day ought to be particularly & handsomely stated, and in order that you may have competent means to fullfill your enquires it sh.d. be your aim to connect yourself in ye. best societies in every place, to w.ch you may be called & to make these enquires ye. subject of conversation: the best histories & travel writers ought to be sought for & if possible procured, that your own observations may be compared therewith & if necessary corrected. . . . Consult with some merchant, wherever you may be, in regard to a voyage say to ye. cape of good Hope, Bombay, Madrass or Calcutta as ye. case may be: acquaint them with ye. prices of articles commonly shiped to & from this country: if you are in India acquaint yourself with ye. trade to & from Indostan to ye. red sea to moka & Suez, and up [?] ye. persian Gulf to Bussova: acquaint yourself also with ye. trade from Surat up ye. Indus to astrachan into ye. Russian empire & ye north of europe by ye. Wolga-know ye. State of this trade wether it is prosperous or not & by what people it is at present carried on whether by arminian or chines Merchants or by ye. Banyans of India or Jews of Turkia. It is said by voltaire that ye. arminians command ye. Trade at astrachan as ye. Banyans did in India & ye. Jewes in Turky. there were quarters in astrachan appropriated to ye. people India. Peter ye. Great cut a canal between ye. Wolga & Dniper for ye. accommodation of this Trade. know whether it passes principally by that rout to Petersburg. Before ye. discovery of ye. Cape of good Hope it was as common for ye. people of india to be trading in ye. north of europe as for Romans to pass into india by arabia. The east indians went into persia & embark upon ye. Styreanian or caspian sea ascended ye. Wolga & Kama rivers to great

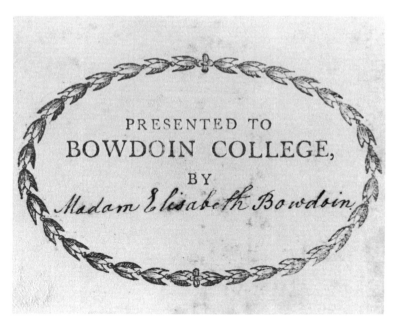

Permia & from thence embarked for y^e. North Sea or y^e. Baltic. . . . Dont thro^h false pride allow yourself to suppose that these enquiries are unworthy of your notice. . . . Commerce as I understand is not beneath y^e. enquiry or pursuit of y^e. first men in England, many of y^e. nobility are indeed ably concerned in it: therefore dont deceive yourself upon this point thro^h Juvenile ideas that commercial enquiries cannot be consistently made by British officers. you will find voltaire's History of Peter y^e. Great & y^e. abbé Raynal's History of the two indias will assist you in these enquires and also D^r. Robeson's & Lt Dow's Histories of Indostan: y^e. last I have not seen but I have heard a great character of it: your observations ought also to extend to y^e. animals & productions y^e. arts & manufactures of India how they open y^e. earth whether they use y^e. Plough what its constructions & generaly what machines they are for giving force to Labour? how do they spin & weave & whence is it they are enabled to dispose of manufactures so much cheaper than europeans is it owing to y^e. superiority of their instrument of Labour y^e. cheapness of living or to both? These subjects classed under distinct heads as has been before suggested may be made a source of information to yourself & of plesure & utility to your friends & be a means of filling up many hours of idle time wch must otherwise hang heavily upon your hands or be unprofitably spent in listlessness & lounging or in drinking & debauchery.

A young person who especially touched James Bowdoin was Sarah Lowell Cony, daughter of Daniel Cony, his agent in Maine.[13] She actually stayed with the Bowdoins, as is clear from a letter of 7 September 1801 to Daniel Cony, in which Bowdoin refers to her as an "amiable girl & well deserving all the little attentions we paid her." Bowdoin also sent apologies for not writing sooner to Sarah and adds, "I hope however she continues studying her French, & devotes a short time in each day thereto."

The letter to Sarah herself, dated 4 September 1801, becomes even somewhat playful. After first detailing the virtues that Sarah should continue to practice, Bowdoin adds:

Let me then ask you, how goes your french? do you read & study it as much, as when you were in Boston? do you read the newspapers, particularly that dreadful vehicle of sedition the Aurora? Or are your Fathers eyes so much better than mine that he has no need of your friendly assistance in this respect?

The distinguished gentleman of nearly fifty years went on to challenge her to a contest to see who will write most frequently and whose English will be "the most pure" and whose French "the most correct."

Several years later, during Bowdoin's stay in France, he entered into an even more unusual relationship with a young person, as attested by the indenture in the letterbooks in the Bowdoin College Library. Bowdoin did not, however, gain just an employee, as is shown by a letter to William Barnet from Naushon Island on 25 August 1810:

Enclosed you will find a letter for Mr John Noel Calot, father to the lad whom I sent to America from Paris, his name is Louis William Calot & is likely to make a very likely man, he conducts much to my satisfaction, I have given him schooling & mean again to do it next winter. I shall be obliged to you to have the letter sent to his father & so rece. & forward to me any letter he may see fit to write to his son.[14]

While abroad in the years 1805-1807 Bowdoin also remembered young people at home. He wrote to Thomas L. Winthrop, the husband of his niece Elizabeth Temple Winthrop, on 20

December 1805, "I have bôt a number of School Books, w^hich I shall send to you for the use of y^our Boys by the first opp^ty." He also remembered from Paris the children of employees. Thus, James Bowdoin's repeated and concrete expressions of concern about young people and their education shows that powerful emotions were at work in the childless man.

What is more, books are often linked with education. Of Bowdoin, it could be said, as it has been of Jefferson, that he "was dependent on books, tended to take his knowledge from them rather than from direct experience, and approached the world with studied eyes."[15] James Bowdoin, though he had himself traveled, did not advocate travel and experience as the pathway to knowledge. (The letter to his nephew of 16 April 1799, quoted more extensively above, states: "there are no great Sports to be found in traversing y^e. ocean in all directions.") Instead, Bowdoin urged the young people of his acquaintance to learn from books. It is not surprising that James Bowdoin, once he had done his duty in making available "unrestricted funds," should then turn to what intensely mattered to him, ultimately leaving to the College in 1811 not money, but, rather, tangible objects—art works, mineralogical specimens, scientific instruments, and books.

James Bowdoin's concern for books for the College had been demonstrated well before 1811. On 2 November 1804, he wrote to the English scientist Dr. John Coakley Lettsom to thank him for the gift of some "scientific apparatus." He then went on to write about the connection between commerce and the arts and to point out that England would procure benefit from flourishing manufactures in this country, and that manufactures would be stimulated by educational institutions.[16] All of that, written at length, was only a preamble to a specific concern, the library of Bowdoin College:

Having been in England and a member of Christ Church College, Oxford, & having been formerly acquainted with some respectable gentlemen there, &

ENCYCLOPÆDIA BRITANNICA.

FIG. 5 The frontispiece to the first volume of the *Encyclopaedia Britannica* (Edinburgh, 1797), showing the various sources of knowledge. The encyclopedia was acquired by the College with an 1802 gift from Madam Elizabeth Bowdoin. In giving instructions for its expenditure, James Bowdoin noted the probability that he himself would later make a "donation of Books."

knowing what I had occasion to observe, that there were many private Libraries in England, some of w.ch were of little use to their possessors: I have had the Idea, that if a Gentleman of known Talents, information & influence, which I am well persuaded befits you as a just character, would undertake to make known the situation of a respectable & promising infant literary institution, that is wanted an addition to its Library, & additional articles to its apparatus for Philosophical Experiments, I conceive there are many respectable English Gentlemen, who would be glad of ye opportunity to contribute a few Books to ye institution, & some articles, perhaps of Little Value to themselves which would prove of y.^e greatest advantage. Be assured Sir, that your friendly aid and patronage upon this subject would be gratefully rec.^d & honorably noticed.

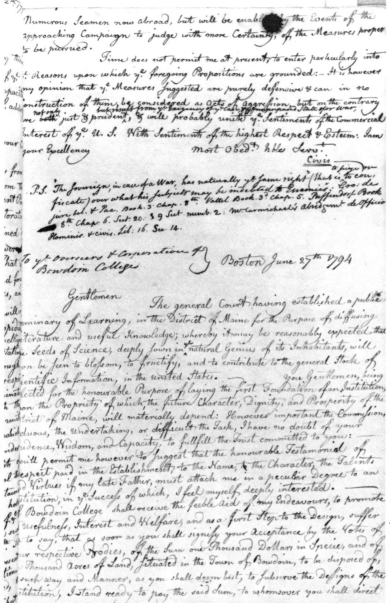

FIG. 6 James Bowdoin's letter of 27 June 1794 to the Overseers and Corporation of Bowdoin College, announcing his intention to make a gift of money and lands. Reproduced from the first of two bound volumes of outgoing correspondence.

James Bowdoin had reason to hope for success. On the same page of the publication recording his 1794 gift to the Massachusetts Society for Promoting Agriculture, it is noted that the society received a donation of ten guineas from "Dr. Lettsom, London."[17]

Moreover, Bowdoin, with his long ties to Harvard College, is likely to have known that gifts of books from the British Isles had greatly strengthened the Harvard Library. He may even have known that Harvard had hopes for Lettsom.[18] After the Harvard Library catalog of 1791 was printed, the Harvard Corporation decided on 19 January 1791 to send a copy to Lettsom, one of eight donors or potential donors to receive a copy.[19] Harvard's hopes met with disappointment, for Lettsom gave only sixteen books.[20] So did James Bowdoin's hopes. American institutions could no longer, as they had before the Revolution, inspire munificent beneficence from Englishmen. Although the letter did not succeed in its purpose, it remains as testimony to James Bowdoin's concern for the library of the institution that in 1806 would graduate its first class.

Four years earlier, in 1802, when that class enrolled at the College, there had also been a concrete expression of the tie in James Bowdoin's mind between young people, education, and books—and Bowdoin College. As if to mark that the College was now a functioning reality, an institution carrying out its purpose of educating the young, James Bowdoin wrote to President McKeen with an offer of a gift. The letter is dated 16 August 1802, scarcely more than two weeks before the College opened. The pertinent passage reads:

My mother has requested me to communicate to you & thro[h] you to y.[e] trustees of y.[e] college, that it is her intention to order £100 ster.[g] to be laid out in engl.[d] by her Brother Geo. Erving Esq.[r] in Books for the use of y.[e] college. M[r]. Erving is a man of Letters & learning, & is well calculated to execute a Commission of y.[e] kind proposed; she therefore wishes you or the trustees to forward to her as soon as may be a catalogue of such Books as you or they shall deem suitable, & she w.^d transmit it to her Brother, who will take ye earliest opp.^{ty} of purchasing & shipping them.

After receiving the list of desired books from President McKeen, Bowdoin sent it off to his uncle George Erving, resident in London, with a letter, dated 14 November 1802. Its pertinent passage reads:

[It] w.^d probably require £500 to purchase them. I notwithstanding enclose it unaltered. I have selected a few Books from it, wch are contained in ye mem.^o, wch I herewith send; as it is probable at some future time I may make Bowdoin College a donation of Books: and as there is ample room to invest my mother's donation without including those, wch are taken into my mem.^o, I sh.^d wish that her Books may not include any of ye works contained in my mem.^o. She wishes ye nett value of ye Books sh.^d amount to £100 sterling, independent of any charges, wch she desires me to request you to advance, & that she will refund you therefor, by paying their am.^t to M^r. Winthrop on your acc.^t, or by remitting you a Bill therefor, if you shall prefer it. . . .

The funds of Elizabeth Bowdoin permitted the purchase of 104 volumes, among them the third edition of the *Encyclopaedia Britannica* (Edinburgh, 1797), 18v., with supplement of 1801 (figs. 4 and 5). (In that same year the Harvard College Library acquired 42 volumes.)[21]

Although the monetary gift was from James Bowdoin's widowed mother, it is possible, at the very least, that its form—money to be spent on books—was inspired by the son. Certainly, the gift was in line with the statement of the son that "it is probable at some future time I may make Bowdoin College a donation of Books."

That possibility may even have been earlier in James Bowdoin's mind when he referred to "a first step" in his letter of 27 June 1794 (fig. 6), the one in which he offered to the Overseers & Corporation of Bowdoin College a gift of money and lands. It would have been natural for him to think of bequeathing a library, for two relatives had recently done so. One was his uncle (mother's brother) William Erving, who had in 1790 bequeathed books to Harvard and to the American Academy of Arts and Sciences.[22]

Even more important was the closest possible example: James Bowdoin's father, upon his death on 6 November 1790, had bequeathed his library. Its 1,200 volumes went in 1790 to the American Academy of Arts and Sciences, which was granted "liberty to sell such books as the Academy may direct, the proceeds to be applied to the purchase of new books."[23]

The father's bequest must have had an impact, perhaps even a painful one, on the son. Not to inherit those books was to suffer a significant financial loss. The library was valued at 540 pounds, at a time when the mansion on Beacon Street, together with its land, stables, and other outbuildings, was valued at 2,500 pounds.[24] Since James Bowdoin received the Beacon Street house as part of his inheritance, he obtained many feet of bookshelves, empty of their former riches.[25]

In order to understand fully the loss to the son, it is necessary to consider the utility of the father's library, and that requires laying aside the modern view of books. For us, the general collection of a parent would hold few books of interest, perhaps the works of a few canonical authors, but almost certainly not earlier encyclopedias (the 11th Britannica did not exist), rarely a history or travel account, probably not the parent's gardening manual, and, of course, not the scientific or mathematical text. The books of one generation now look stale to another—for the purpose of general reading as opposed to scholarship. Not so in the eighteenth century. New books did not so much supersede as add to the older, which were often valued for the information in them decades after publication. As shown by a letter quoted above, Voltaire's life of Peter the Great retained for James Bowdoin value as a source of information on commerce. So, too, would much in the library of James Bowdoin II have retained value for James Bowdoin III.

Only if the library of the elder Bowdoin had been largely theological would the son have failed to regret its loss. Such was not the case. The father had Aesop, Anacreon, Cicero, Demosthenes, Horace, Juvenal, Longinus, Lucretius, Sallust, Seneca, Sophocles, Tacitus, Virgil, Xenophon; many grammars and dictionaries of ongoing utility; the modern historians

FIG. 7 James Bowdoin's library was rich in multi-volume sets in beautiful bindings, as is shown by his copies of the collected works of Mably, Rousseau, Voltaire, and Bulliard, among others.

FIG. 8 The *Gazette nationale, ou le Moniteur universel* was the semi-official newspaper of the French Revolution, and the varied styles of bindings show that Bowdoin purchased volumes at various times in his special efforts to acquire a complete set from 1789 up through 1807, the year of his departure from Paris. His 36-volume file of this research source was probably for decades the only one in this country. The three volumes in red leather on the top shelf are the sumptuous *Collection complète des Tableaux historiques de la Révolution française.*

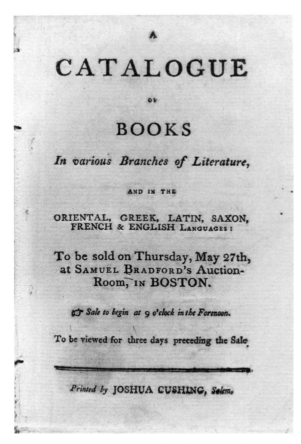

A

CATALOGUE

OF

BOOKS

In various Branches of Literature,

AND IN THE

ORIENTAL, GREEK, LATIN, SAXON,
FRENCH & ENGLISH Languages:

To be sold on Thursday, May 27th,
at SAMUEL BRADFORD'S Auction-
Room, IN BOSTON.

☞ *Sale to begin at* 9 *o'clock in the Forenoon.*

To be viewed for three days preceding the Sale

Printed by JOSHUA CUSHING, *Salem.*

FIG. 9 In Boston, James Bowdoin was able to buy books, both old and new, in several languages, as shown by this auction catalog of 1802. He thoroughly read and marked it, and in the entry for "Moeridis Atticistæ Lexicon Attic. by Pierson" indicated his intention to buy for the "College." He failed to do so. Very concerned about price, he may have thought the book fetched too much.

Burnet, Clarendon, Dalrymple, Douglass, Minot, Vertot; works of Hume, Hutcheson, Locke, Montesquieu, Rousseau, Voltaire; scientific treatises of Buffon, Linnaeus, Newton, Whiston; law treatises such as the Frederician code of 1761, Pufendorf; economic treatises by Butel-Dumont, Lord Sheffield, Postlethwayt's commercial dictionary; and much, much more. Many of these the son subsequently purchased and put back on those once-empty shelves.

James Bowdoin III did, of course, have some books of his own in 1790. A few books are inscribed as being the property of James Bowdoin junior: *Tristram Shandy* (London, 1765); Pierre Restaut, *Traité de l'orthographe*

françoise (1770); Joseph Marshall's *Travels through Holland, Flanders, Germany, Denmark, Sweden, Lapland, Russia, the Ukraine, and Poland* (London, 1773), 3v.; Nathaniel Kent, *Hints to Gentlemen of Landed Property* (London, 1775); Hugh Blair's *Sermons* (Dublin, 1779); *Perpetual Laws of the Commonwealth of Massachusetts* (Boston, 1789); Mercy Warren's *Poems, Dramatic and Miscellaneous* (Boston, 1790).[26] James Bowdoin must have had other books in addition to these, but the father's bequest faced him with the task of building a library to replace that of his father. In the end, he outdid his father.[27]

That the library of James Bowdoin III was essentially a creation of the 1790s and the first decade of the nineteenth century is clear. The majority of the titles and volumes were published after 1789. The title percentages are: pre-1790 titles: 37.9 percent; post-1789 titles: 58 percent; uncertain, 4.1 percent. The volume percentages are: pre-1790 volumes: 45.3 percent; post-1789 volumes: 52.6 percent; uncertain: 2.1 percent. The situation becomes even clearer when one takes into consideration in the calculations pre-1790 titles and volumes that were definitely acquired after 1789. It is clear that 66 percent of the titles and 62.7 percent of the volumes were definitely acquired after 1789. If the hypothesis is correct that James Bowdoin purchased from the Boston bookseller Nancrede most of the French books not acquired in Paris, the percentage of post-1790 acquisitions would rise. Moreover, the publication dates of James Bowdoin's United States imprints show very little buying before 1790. Of the titles 81.4 percent were published later than 1789; 87.1 percent of the volumes.

Books were added by a variety of means. A few were gifts; at least two were acquired by advance subscription; some books were definitely purchased at auction; many were supplied by an uncle in London, at Bowdoin's expense but partially at the uncle's choosing; and some were acquired, it seems, by an American ship captain who bought books as one of the services he performed for Bowdoin. Large numbers were also purchased from local booksellers; and, in addition, Bowdoin acquired about 400 volumes, nearly a fifth of his library, while he was in Paris.

Only three books were gifts with personal inscriptions.[28] Some of the pamphlets were also gifts.

Advance subscription was, like gifts, not an important means of acquisition. Bernardin de Saint-Pierre's *Studies of Nature* (Worcester: Printed for J. Nancrede, Boston, 1797) stands out. The three-volume work was priced at $7 in boards and $9.50 in gilt calf; James Bowdoin acquired his in boards.

James Bowdoin also bought at auction. One of the catalogs among his pamphlets is *A Catalogue of Books in Various Branches of Literature, and in the Oriental, Greek, Latin, Saxon, French & English Languages: To be Sold on Thursday, May 27th, at Samuel Bradford's Auction-Room, in Boston* (Salem: Printed by Joshua Cushing) (fig. 9). The auction took place in 1802.[29] In this catalog many books are marked, some only by a line next to the entry; some have the word "cheap"; others have "if cheap," or "if very cheap." A few have "if not" or "if" or "if very."[30] One Euripides, *Opera omnia, ex edit. Barnesii* (Leipzig, 1778-88; 5v.) is described in the catalog as "the best edit. splendidly bound, in Russia leather & marbled leaves." The annotation next to it, is "if very cheap indeed." Bowdoin was drawn to the book, but he did not let himself become a bibliophile who loved books as beautiful objects. Some books have prices, with, in a couple of instances, what appear to be names of purchasers. Next to one entry is a price of $2.10 and the word "College." The book is: "Moeridis Atticistæ Lexicon Attic by Pierson, best edit. scarce, 8vo. L. Bat. 1759." This work by Moeris, edited by Johannes Pierson, seems not to have been acquired. Three works, however, have a "B" next to the entry. One is "Ward's Treatise on Neutral Rights" (1801), with the entry annotated "if not excessive." Bowdoin did, indeed, own a copy of Robert Ward's *A Treatise of the Relative Rights and*

FIG. 10 Michael Symes, *An Account of an Embassy to the Kingdom of Ava* (London, 1800), is one of the books purchased, shipped—and even selected—for Bowdoin by his uncle George Erving, a Loyalist who lived in London. Bowdoin wrote to his uncle that he read it with "much pleasure," and the book contains a characteristic form of marking by Bowdoin: a vertical pencil line in the margin. Bowdoin's book buying through Erving began in 1799.

Duties of Belligerent and Neutral Powers, in Maritime Affairs (London, 1801). The other book, with only a straight line next to the entry, in addition to the "B," is "Bynkershoek Traité des Ambassadeurs, 4to." Bowdoin's 1811 bequest to the College included Cornelis van Bijnkershoek,

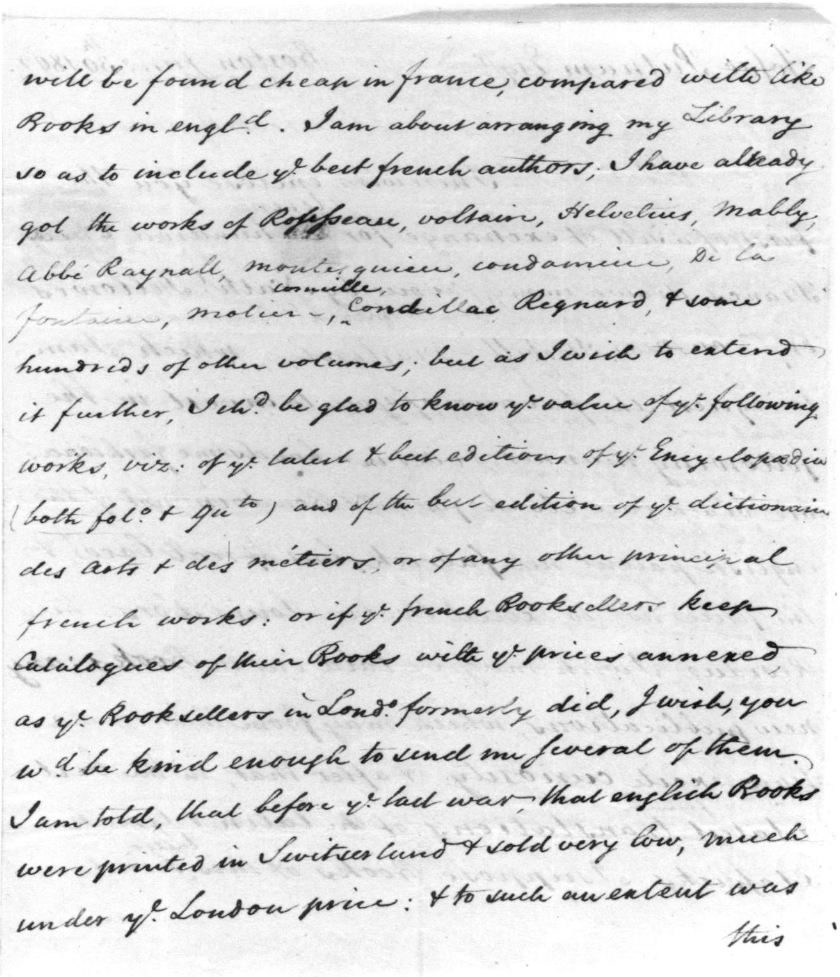

will be found cheap in france, compared with like
Books in engld. I am about arranging my Library
so as to include ye best french authors; I have already
got the works of Rosseau, voltaire, Helvetius, Mably,
abbé Raynall, montesquieu, condamine, De la
fontaine, molier, corneille, Condillac Regnard, & some
hundreds of other volumes; but as I wish to extend
it further, I shd be glad to know ye value of ye following
works, viz: of ye latest & best editions of ye Encyclopædia
(both folo & quto) and of the best edition of ye dictionaire
des arts & des métiers, or of any other principal
french works: or if ye french Booksellers keep
Catalogues of their Books with ye prices annexed
as ye Booksellers in Londo formerly did, I wish, you
wd be kind enough to send me several of them.
I am told, that before ye last war, that english Books
were printed in Switzerland & sold very low, much
under ye London price: & to such an extent was
this

FIG. 11 In this letter to the ship captain Jesse Putnam of 30 June 1802, Bowdoin asked for help in acquiring French books, including Diderot's *Encyclopédie*, but he noted that he already had the best French authors: Rousseau, Voltaire, Helvetius, Mably, abbé Raynal, Montesquieu, Comdamine, La Fontaine, Molière, Corneille, Condillac, and Regnard. He had been able to purchase them in Boston.

Traité du juge competent des ambassadeurs, tant pour le civil, que pour le criminel, traduit du Latin de Mr. de Bynkershoek (La Haye, 1723). The other is "Schlegel's Examination of Sir Wm. Scott's Judgment on the Swedish Convoy, 1801" (almost certainly Johan Frederik Vilhelm Schlegel, *Upon the Visitation of Neutral Vessels under Convoy; or, An Important Examination of a Judgment Pronounced by the English Court of Admiralty*, London, 1801, 187 pp.), a work that was not part of James Bowdoin's library at the time of his death.[31]

Bowdoin read the Bradford catalog from the first page to the last. He marked nearly ninety entries out of the 1,227. Anyone who did that surely bought at other auctions, though little direct evidence exists. One auction purchase was Edward Wortley Montagu, *Reflections on the Rise and Fall of the Ancient Republicks* (London, 1778), for it is inscribed on the flyleaf: "Bowdoin's. Bôt at auction. 5p." Another auction purchase was [William Douglas], *A Summary, Historical and Political of the First Planting, Progressive Improvements and Present State of the British Settlements in North-America . . . by W.D.* (Boston, 1747-1750), which is inscribed, "Bowdoin's 1/2 bot at auction."

Although Bowdoin had only one additional auction catalog among his pamphlets, another Bradford catalog, this one for a sale on 14 October 1802, there were many sales in Boston at which James Bowdoin could have acquired books published earlier.[32] Booksellers also had stocks of earlier books, including imports from England and France; see, for example, catalogs of Joseph Nancrede. Thus, unless specific information is present, it is impossible to determine whether books were purchased new at the time of publication, at auctions, or from booksellers' stocks.

Probably more important than auctions to James Bowdoin's collecting were individuals abroad who acquired books on Bowdoin's account, sometimes at their own choosing. One person who did so was his uncle George Erving, a Loyalist who had become a merchant in London. Erving had supplied Governor Bowdoin with books, and it was natural that he should perform that service as well for his nephew.[33] The earliest such request was in 1799. In a letter dated 2 November of that year,

1. *Corvus cristatus*, Blue Jay. — 2. *Fringilla Tristis*, Yellow Bird or Goldfinch.
3. *Oriolus Baltimorus*, Baltimore Bird.

FIG. 12 One of the few works purchased by James Bowdoin in the years 1808 to 1811 were three volumes of Alexander Wilson's magnificent *American Ornithology*, the first of the notable studies of American birds.

THÉOPHILE BARROIS, fils,

Libraire

pour les Livres Étrangers,

Quai Voltaire, N5.

à Paris.

FIG. 13

Bowdoin enclosed a "sett of exch.^{a} for £125" and asked that £100 be paid to James Bowdoin Temple (he was not such a hard uncle after all), and that the residue:

be appropriated to y^e. payment of what I stand indebted to you & for y^e. purchase of a few Books, wch I shall request y^e. favor of you to procure for me & for y^e. mem.^{o} of wch pleased to be referred to y^e. postscript. . . .[34]

For some reason, it was necessary for Bowdoin to send a bill of exchange for the same purpose on 1 July 1800, in which he asks that the remainder—after paying £100 to James Bowdoin Temple and discharging the debt to Erving, be spent in "procuring for me such new publications, including Chauchard's Map of Germany &c.^{a} &c.^{a} wch you have had ye politeness to subscribe to for me) as you may think worth perusal."

The request for the map led to some difficulties for Erving. Bowdoin wrote to him on 13 December 1800:

I am sorry that M^r. Stockdale's refusal to fullfill y^e. conditions of y^e. subscriptions for publishing Chauchard's map of Germany, to wch you had been polite eno^u to place y.^{r} name on my acc^t. & sh.^{d} have been y^e. occasion of so much uneasiness to you, as to lay y^e. foundation of a misunderstanding between you & m^r. Stockdale: altho^u I wish much to have procured y^e. map, I am still sorry that you ever contemplated y^e. obtaining it for me.

Some other books did, however, finally arrive in Boston, and they were much appreciated (fig. 10). On 31 January 1801, Bowdoin started off his letter by expressing his thanks:

I have rec.^{d} y.^{r} much esteemed favour of y^e. 10th of Oct.^{o} together with y^e. Books, wch you have been so obliging as to procure me. The embassy to Ava [Michael Symes, *Account of an Embassy to the Kingdom of Ava*, London, 1800] I have read wth much pleasure: it describes a people respectable for wealth, population & improvem.^{ts}, who were scarcely known either to y^e. antients or moderns; & fills up an important gap in Geography, wch may possibly be a means of opening a new & convenient channel of commerce, to ye interior of china, through y^e. Irrawaddy & Keen-duem rivers. Sonnini [C. N. S. Sonnini de Manoncourt, *Travels in Upper and Lower Egypt*, the one-volume edition of London, 1800], I have in part read & expect both pleasure & information from its further perusal. The other Books equally meet my approbation, & I am to thank you for ye trouble I have given you.

Again to Erving, on 12 May 1801:

The Picture of Buonaparte, ye three pamphlets together with the Books by the Minerva I have duly rec.^{d} & in good order, for which I am much obliged to you. The Books I have not Read, but have no doubt, I shall be much pleased with them. I am more particularly to thank you for ye Pamphlets not merely as your present, but for ye important information they contain. That written by M^r. Boyd points to a very threatening evil arising from ye stopping ye issues of specie in payment of Bank Bills. . . .

Bowdoin went on to say much more about Boyd's pamphlet. Again on 14 November 1802 he wrote to Erving to thank him for books and pamphlets and for his trouble in "procuring & transmitting them." In the same letter he asked Erving for the following:

Russell hist.^{y} antient Europe [he perhaps acquired at this time William Russell's *History of Modern Europe*, London, 1794]; Stuart view of Society during ye dark ages [probably Gilbert Stuart, *View of Society in Europe*, 1792; never acquired by Bowdoin]; "Thompson's spirit of gen.^{l} his.^{ty} from ye 8.th to ye 18th century in lectures on ye progress of Society in manners, Legislation &c.^{a} [George Thomson, *The Spirit of General History, in a Series of Lectures, from the Eighth to the Eighteenth Century, Wherein Is Given a View of the Progress of Society in Manners and Legislation during That Period*, London, 1791, was not acquired by Bowdoin]; The his.^{ty} of France from ye earliest times to ye present important era. 5 vol.^{s} [apparently never acquired by Bowdoin]; The his.^{ty} of Spain by John Gifford. 3 vol.^{s} [apparently never acquired by Bowdoin]; Thompson's translation of Suetonius's 12 Caesars. 1 vol 8vo [Bowdoin had London, 1796]; Description of Greece by Pausanias translated by Taylor. 3 vol.^{s} 8vo [Bowdoin had a 1794 3-volume edition]; Potter's

Translation of Euripides [not acquired by Bowdoin]; ditto of Aeschylus. 2 vol. [Bowdoin had the London, 1779 edition]; Franklin's translation of Sophocles [Bowdoin had the 1793 edition]; Thucydides by Sanetti. 2 vol.[s] [not acquired by Bowdoin]; Dissertations by Sir W.[m] Jones & others on y.[e] antiquities, arts, sciences & Literature of Asia. 2 vol.[s] [Bowdoin had *Dissertations and Miscellaneous Pieces Relating to the History and Antiquities, the Arts, Sciences, and Literatures of Asia*, by Sir W. Jones and others, London, 1792]; Roman Conversations by the late Jos.[h] Wilcox. 2 vol. [Bowdoin owned the 2d ed., London, 1797, 2v.]; D[r]. Reid's essays on y.[e] intellectual & active powers of man. 3 vol. [not acquired by Bowdoin]; A Latin & english diction.[ary], large & clear print [Bowdoin had many dictionaries]; Ferguson's Lectures on mechanics, Hydrostatics, &c.[a] last ed.[n] [Bowdoin had James Ferguson's *Lectures on Select Subjects in Mechanics, Hydrostatics, Hydraulics, Pneumatics and Optics. With the Use of Globes, the Art of Dialing, and the Calculation of the Mean Times of New and Full Moons and Eclipses*, 8th ed., London, 1793]; Franklin's Tour from Bengal to Persia" [Bowdoin had William Francklin's *Observations Made on a Tour from Bengal to Persia, in the Years 1786-7*, 2d ed., London, 1790]; Rawlins familiar architecture. Plates [Bowdoin owned a 1768 edition]; Williams view of y.[e] constitution, commerce, & Revenues of Holland, Denmark, Russia and Poland. 2 vol. [not acquired by Bowdoin]; any new publications: if there be funds left sufficient therefor. I sh.[d] like to have handsome editions of y.[e] works of Cicero, Virgil & Horace in Latin.

Bowdoin did not get all that he requested, but he may have obtained more from Erving.

No more shipments from Erving are recorded in 1803, but, after expressing to Erving on 14 May 1804 that a shipment on the *Minerva* had been lost, he wrote again on 8 November 1804 to say that the shipment had arrived. It contained John Barrow, *Travels in China* (London, 1804) as well as Lord Teignmouth's *Memoirs of the Life, Writings, and Correspondence of Sir William Jones* (London, 1804). In the same letter he indicates

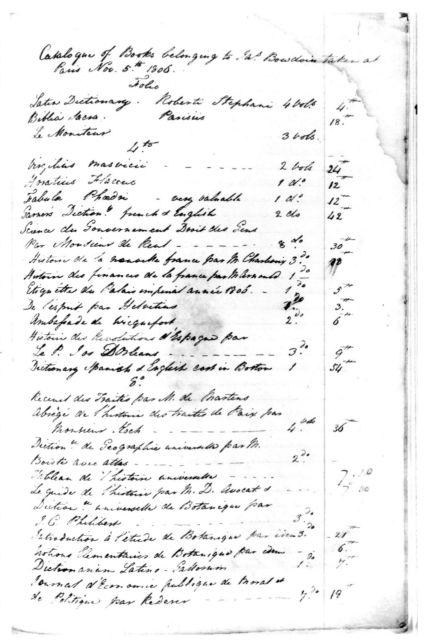

FIG. 14 The first page of the list of approximately 400 volumes that Bowdoin purchased in Paris. The list was prepared, with prices, before the books were shipped home. Their arrival in Boston necessitated building more bookshelves in the second floor library on Beacon Hill in Boston.

that he received Sir George Staunton's *An Authentic Account of an Embassy from the King of Great Britain to the Emperor of China*, but that he already has a copy. It seems that he owned the Philadelphia, 1799 edition, which made superfluous the London, 1798 second edition. Bowdoin in reply asked for other of Teignmouth's books, specifically the *Digest of the Laws of Hindus* begun by Teignmouth and finished by Colebrooke. Clearly, Erving was continuing to select books for James Bowdoin, and he was good at judging his interests.

By this time George Erving was in the last years of his life and perhaps no longer active (he died early in 1806), and Bowdoin turned to the two sons of his sister, Elizabeth, to help him buy books abroad (figs. 7 and 8). On 10 May 1804, he wrote to James Bowdoin Temple that James's brother, Grenville Temple, had sent him a copy of Volney's *Travels in the United States*, though it had been lost. On 17 May 1804, Bowdoin wrote

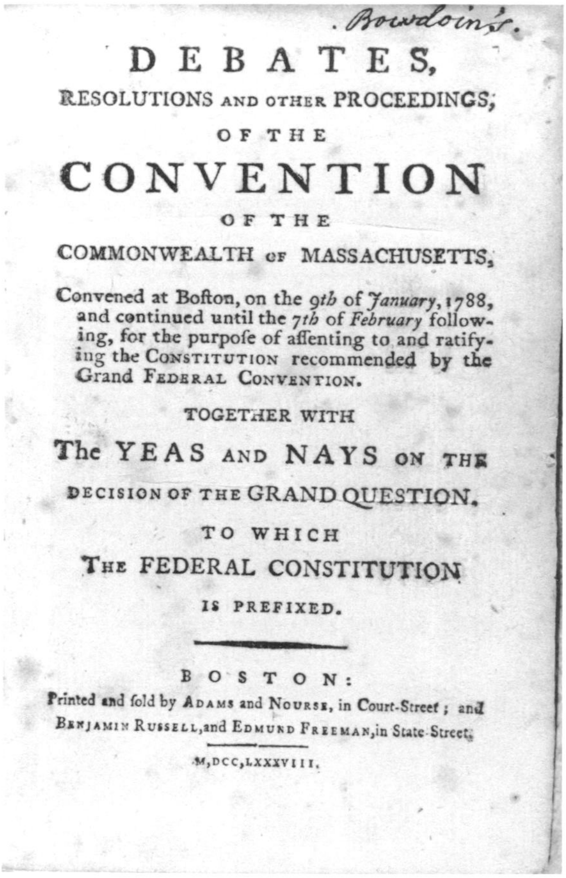

DEBATES,
RESOLUTIONS and other PROCEEDINGS;
OF THE
CONVENTION
OF THE
COMMONWEALTH of MASSACHUSETTS,

Convened at Boston, on the 9th of January, 1788, and continued until the 7th of February following, for the purpose of assenting to and ratifying the CONSTITUTION recommended by the Grand FEDERAL CONVENTION.

TOGETHER WITH
The YEAS and NAYS on the
DECISION OF THE GRAND QUESTION.
TO WHICH
The FEDERAL CONSTITUTION
IS PREFIXED.

———

BOSTON:
Printed and sold by ADAMS and NOURSE, in Court-Street; and BENJAMIN RUSSELL, and EDMUND FREEMAN, in State-Street;

M,DCC,LXXXVIII.

FIG. 15 James Bowdoin III and his father, then governor of Massachusetts, were delegates to the Massachusetts constitutional convention of 1788. In the 1780s and 1790s he customarily wrote his name in books. His ending that practice may be a sign that he had decided to give his library to the College.

to Grenville, and after reporting that his bookseller had put a copy of Volney into his hands, the only copy as yet received in Boston, he went on:

As you have been obliging enough to offer me your friendly service to procure me anything I might want in france or Italy, I shall take it as a favour if you would procure me ye Moniteur from ye 8.th year exclusive to the time of your quitting France: I have ye first years complete in 16 folio Vols. I wish to have put together in sheets, so as to secure them & forwarded, & I will have them bound so as to match those I have.

Bowdoin had earlier sought to get books from France. On 30 June 1802 he wrote to Jesse Putnam, whose brother William was for a time superintendent of Naushon Island, and after giving him instructions about buying some lace, he directed (fig. 11) that the residue of a "sett of exchange"

be laid out in Books: any new publications, which may from their reputation excite Curiosity; & after that, in the best, & latest french translations of the latin & Greek Classicks: I suppose, Books of this latter kind will be found cheap in france, compared with like Books in engl.^{d}: I am about arranging my Library so as to include ye best french authors; I have already got the works of Rousseau, Voltaire, Helvetius, Mably, abbé Raynall, Montesquieu, Condamine, De la fontaine, Moliere, Corneille, Condillac, Regnard & several hundred other volumes;[35] but as I wish to extend it further, I sh^d be glad to know ye value of ye following works, viz.: of ye latest & best edit^{ions} of ye Encyclopaedia, (both fol.^{o} & q^{to}) & of the best edition of ye dictionaire des arts & des métiers, or of any other principal french works: or if ye french Booksellers keep Catalogues of their Books with ye prices annexed, as ye Booksellers in Lond.^{n} formerly did, I wish you w^{od} be kind enough to send me several of them.[36] I am told before ye last war, that english Books were printed in Switserland & sold very low, much under ye Lond.^{n} price: & to such an extent was this business carried on, that all ye best english literary works could be readily procured there. Please to advise me on this subject, and to acquaint me whether you shall be able and willing to procure me such Books, as I may from time to time want from france & from Switserland. The french System of Commerce, whatever it may prove, will be very important to ye world generally & in particular to ye U. St. and I shall be much obliged to you to favour me with your opinion upon the subject: & to send me any new publications, wch may from time to time be offered to ye public in regard to it. I have a valuable work published in 1790 entitled De la balance du Commerce &c^a. par M. Arnould.

A letter to Putnam on 12 March 1803 is ambiguous as to whether Putnam had earlier supplied French books. It is likely that he had, for Bowdoin had a copy of Diderot's *Encyclopédie*, one of the works earlier requested in the 1802 letter. The letter of 1803 reads:

As soon as I shall receive ye Books requested, I will then make up my mind in regard to ye purchase, wch I proposed of french books. I wish however you w.^d send me a Latin & french dictionary to be well printed & not unwieldy in size: you must recollect that I am fifty y.^rs old, & that as we advance, the print ought to be of a good size & clear: please to let it be by the most approved author & ye latest edition: I wish also you w.^d send me ye latest tarriff of duties on the importations & exportations to & from france: if you c.^d procure for me those of Spain & holland, it w.^d much oblige me. . . . Sh.^d there be any acts of ye french, spanish or dutch governm.^ts wch shall have a tendency to affect our commerce, & you can procure & transmit them to me without too great an expence, I shall be obliged to you, to furnish me with them from time to time, as they may be published.

The above letters to Jesse Putnam and to Sir Grenville Temple provide almost the only available information on James Bowdoin's buying from local booksellers. That of 17 May 1804 to Sir Grenville refers to "my Bookseller" (the one who had placed into his hands the only copy of Volney yet received in Boston). It would seem that James Bowdoin did not make shopping expeditions to the various booksellers in Boston. Instead, one bookseller, whose identity is not known, took care to supply—and flatter—this valued customer.

Bowdoin did, it seems, buy older books from Boston booksellers when the opportunity arose. Among his pamphlets is *A Catalogue of Books, Consisting of a Large Collection of the Various Branches of Literature Alphabetically Disposed under Several Heads. . . for Sale, Wholesale or Retail, at James White's Book and Stationary-Store, Franklin's Head, opposite the Prison, Court-Street, Boston.* The catalog is undated, but was issued in the late 1790s.[37] It is likely that he also purchased French books locally, from the French emigré bookseller Joseph Nancrede. Among James Bowdoin's pamphlets is a catalog published in

1798 by Nancrede, which lists many multi-volume French works of the sort that Bowdoin listed in his letter of 1802 to Putnam: "Rousseau, Voltaire, Helvetius, Mably, abbe Raynal, Montesquieu, Condillac, De la fontaine, Regnard, Moliere, Corneille, & several hundred other volumes."[38] Nancrede also dealt in English books, and, of course, American. He would be a logical candidate for the bookseller referred to proprietarily on 17 May 1804 as "my bookseller," but he was by then out of business, the remainder of his stock having been auctioned in February 1804.[39]

In Paris, where James Bowdoin was from November 1805 to the fall of 1807, it is clear that a bookseller from whom he bought much was Théophile Barrois, for at least fifteen books have Barrois book labels inserted. Barrois was an international bookseller who issued catalogs (Bowdoin had two copies of one from 1806) offering books in Dutch, English, German, Italian, Portuguese, and Spanish (fig. 13). He clearly also sold French books. Bowdoin must have done considerable shopping to judge by the various catalogs among his pamphlets. There is an 1807 catalog of military books for sale by Magimel; a catalog of "cartes et ouvrages géographiques" for sale by G. Delisle & Philippe Buache (Paris, [n.d.]); a *Catalogue général de livres sur l'agriculture* (Paris, Chez Meurant, 1801), an unpriced listing of all books on agriculture, so it claimed; a catalog of scientific instruments for sale by Lerebours; and *Premier extrait du catalogue des livres français qui se trouvent à la librairie polyglotte circulaire de Parsons, Galignani et comp.* (Paris, 1805), this last with many entries annotated "vid." If he actually saw, he did not buy, with one possible exception.

By no means did Bowdoin acquire only current books in Paris. Even in buying from Barrois he could have acquired older books (the first edition, 1776, of Adam Smith's *Wealth of Nations* was, for instance, available from Barrois). There exists in his letterbooks in the Bowdoin College Library a "Catalogue of Books belonging to Jas. Bowdoin taken at Paris Nov. 5th 1806," the date being the time it was begun (fig. 14). According to this catalog of more than 400 volumes,

Bowdoin bought in Paris most of the books he owned concerning Louisiana and Florida, as well as most of those concerning international negotiations. As usual he acquired dictionaries, a Latin dictionary of Stephanus (1511), Garner's French and English dictionary, a pocket dictionary of the principal languages of Europe (which perhaps did not come to the College), some important works of political and economic thought: Filangieri, *Science de la legislation* (1799), 7v.; Ganilh, *Essai politique sur le revenu publique* (1806), 2v.; Nicolo Donato, *L'homme d'état* (1767), 2v; Playfair's edition of Boetticher's *Statistical Tables . . . of All the States of Europe* (1800), one of the few English acquisitions; Grotius, *Le droit de la guerre* (1724), 2v. During this stay in Paris Bowdoin also bought a copy of Helvetius, *De l'esprit* (1758). Much science was among the purchases, including three introductions to botany and a "dictionnaire universelle" of botany; a dictionary of chemical pharmacy and a treatise on pharmacology; a work on irrigation; one of the only two Spanish works in his library, *Instruction para pastores* (Bowdoin also had an elegant edition of *Don Quixote* and claimed in a letter of 30 January 1805 to Henry Dearborn that he had "made some proficiency in acquiring the Spanish Language"); a 6-volume, 1761, edition of the great eighteenth-century French agriculturist Duhamel du Monceau; *Manuel vétérinaire des plantes* by Buc'hoz (1799); *Nouvelle découverte sur le flux et le reflux des mers*, by Deslaurières (1806); a chemical work of Chaptal (1807), 4v.; three works on mineralogy, including l'abbé Haüy's *Traité de minéralogie* (1801), 5v.[40] and his *Traité élémentaire de physique* (1806), 2v.; the *Systeme sexuel des végétaux* of Linnaeus; a French work on forests, and several on mineral waters (fig. 1).

Covering various fields (mathematics, literature and the fine arts, the physical sciences, and the "sciences morales et politiques," with a volume as well on the decimal system) was one of the most important sets in his library, the nineteen volumes of the *Memoires* of the Institut national des sciences et des arts (1798-1806). Bowdoin also acquired some editions of the classics, and the purchase of four copies of the 1806

Didot edition of *Les bucoliques de Virgile* perhaps presaged the next phase of his life; after his return, Bowdoin devoted himself to building a house on Naushon Island and to fostering economic activities there, especially sheep-raising. As he wrote on 26 August 1809, "My wish is retirement & to avoid political squabbles."[41]

Bowdoin largely even stopped adding to his library after his return from France. He did arrange for the subscription to the *Moniteur* to be continued through the end of 1807. The bound volume subsequently arrived, as did a few other books sent on from Paris. In an undated letter, apparently written between 19 and 23 January 1809, Bowdoin thanked Isaac Cox Barnet for letters and for some books, "among which I observe Winkelmanns Histoire des Arts &c. for which I am much obliged to you."[42]

Among the handful of American books, which because of their date of publication had to have been acquired after returning from Paris, are Alexander Wilson's *American Ornithology* (Philadelphia, 1808-11) in 3v. (fig. 12); Bristed's *Hints on the National Bankruptcy of Britain* (New York, 1809); John Pinkerton's *General Collection of Voyages* (Philadelphia, 1809), in 16 parts; Robert Ker Porter, *Travelling Sketches in Russia and Sweden* (Philadelphia, 1809); Robert Livingston's *Essay on Sheep* (New York, 1809); Barlow's *Columbiad* (Philadelphia, 1809), 2v.; an incomplete copy of William Paley's *Works* (Boston, 1810-12), 4 vols. out of 5. The only imprint of those years from Britain is, predictably, George Mackenzie's *Treatise on the Diseases and Management of Sheep* (Edinburgh, 1809). There are, of course, a few pamphlets from 1808 to 1811, some of which came to him simply because of his being a donor to a society. But after James Bowdoin returned from France with the approximately 400 books he bought there, he does not seem to have added significantly to the collection.

The heavy French purchases in Paris, when added to the numerous large sets acquired in Boston, mean that a major portion of Bowdoin's library was in French. He seems to have read French so well that he was indifferent whether a book was in English or French. In the letter of

30 June 1802 to Jesse Putnam, Bowdoin asked for "best & latest french translations of the latin & Greek classicks," and added, "I suppose Books of this latter kind will be found cheap in france, compared with like Books in engl.[d]." He also had in French translation books that he could easily have acquired in the original English, above all Catherine Macaulay's *Histoire d'Angleterre* (1791-92), 5v.

The statistics of place of origin of the books in James Bowdoin's library show the French dominance:

Table 1: Statistics of Place of Origin in James Bowdoin's Library

United States
Titles: 129   Volumes: 249

(Boston: 52 titles, 89 volumes; New York: 20 titles, 24 volumes; Philadelphia: 37 titles, 103 volumes; other U.S.: 20 titles, 33 volumes)[a]

Great Britain
Titles: 296   Volumes: 595

France[b]
Titles: 326   Volumes: 1156

Latin (misc. imprints)
Titles: 17   Volumes: 27

Miscellaneous (Italy, Spain, unidentified, and non-books)
Titles: 15   Volumes: 21

Total:
Titles: 783   Volumes: 2048

A count of titles alone would make it seem that James Bowdoin's library is an English-language collection, with 54.3 percent in English (Great Britain, 37.8 percent; U.S., 16.5 percent), as opposed to 41.6 percent in French. The volume count gives a markedly different perspective on the library. It shows that the majority of the volumes are in French, 56.4 percent, as opposed to 29.1 percent British, and 12.2 percent U.S. (total of 41.3 percent).[c]

The statistics are one way of getting at the nature of the library and the motivation of the man who formed it. Another way of looking at the same issues is to note instances in which the contents of the library intersect with other aspects of the life of James Bowdoin.

When in England in 1771, Jemmy, as the younger Bowdoin was known, began "to learn French, likewise Dancing and Fencing, all of which I expect to be perfect master of before my return."[43] In the library is G. A. B. Gallini's *A*

---

[a] The Boston figures include ten copies of *Constitutional Republicanism, in Opposition to Fallacious Federalism* (Boston, 1803), by Benjamin Austin.

[b] Includes French books with imprints outside France.

[c] These statistics represent an attempt to analyze the record of the library as given in Abbot's 1811 catalog. The totals do not, however, quite match Abbot. The numbers are off by about half a percent of the books. The discrepancy could, of course, be rectified, but the investment of time and money would not bring with it a corresponding benefit. For instance, Abbot sometimes records a supplement, or an atlas, with the entry for the main work, sometimes not. Similarly, Abbot records multiple copies of works when they are present. He notes only a few pamphlets. Inevitably, there are also unidentified works, including some with imprint or date not known, since a few of the books seem no longer to be present at Bowdoin. Thus, reconciling the statistics would not really give a clearer picture of the library.

The basis for detailed work on the library was initially a catalog prepared on cards by Dr. Neils Sonne and Father Pawel M. Dawley in the 1970s. It is in the Bowdoin College Library and, despite some omissions, has been indispensable. I am also grateful to Ashley G. Wernher '93, who entered the cards into the computer, for her work provided a subsequent step toward the statistics that are given here.

FIG. 16 After being appointed minister plenipotentiary to Spain, charged by President Jefferson with settling the limits of the Louisiana Territory and with purchasing Florida, James Bowdoin prepared himself by forming a collection of books on those areas, as well as on the art of negotiating. Reproduced here is the engraved title page to Louis Hennepin, *Nouvelle decouverte d'un tres grand pays situé dans l'Amerique entre le nouveau Mexique, et la mer glaciale* (Amsterdam, 1698).

Treatise on the Art of Dancing (London, 1765), an early sign of the intimate connection in James Bowdoin's mind between education and books. Because he was a student at Oxford, the *New Oxford Guide*, 5th edition [1767?], which is among his pamphlets, must have been useful.

In October 1773, Bowdoin set out on the ship *The King of Naples*, and from Naples went to

Rome, Florence, Bologna, Lyons, and London.[44] Two books, at least, were very likely souvenirs of that trip, appropriate ones for a wealthy young man. They are two magnificent plate books, Pietro Santi Bartoli's *Colonna Traiana* (Rome [1576]) and Pietro Ferrerio's *Palazzi* (Rome, ca. 1575]). Filippo Titi, *Nuovo studio di pittura, scoltura, et architettura nelle chiese di Roma* (Rome, 1708) is also likely to have been an acquisition from that trip. Yet another book had to have a particular appeal to Bowdoin, J. J. Le Français de Lalande's anonymously issued *Voyage d'un François en Italie, fait dans les années 1765 & 1766* (Venice, 1769), 8v., whether acquired in the 1770s or later.

In James Bowdoin's later life, public service led to the acquisition of certain books. He was a member of the Massachusetts Constitutional Convention of 1788, and, naturally, its proceedings, *Debates, Resolutions and Other Proceedings of the Convention of the Commonwealth of Massachusetts* (Boston, 1788) are in his library, actually inscribed "James Bowdoin junrs" (fig. 15).

James Bowdoin's appointment as minister plenipotentiary to Spain, charged by President Jefferson with settling the limits of the Louisiana Territory and purchasing Florida, led him to acquire books. Among those on Florida and Louisiana are: P. F. X. de Charlevoix, *Histoire et description generale de la nouvelle France* (1744), editions in both 6 vols. and 3 vols.; Baudry des Lozières, *Voyage à la Louisiane fait dans les années 1794 à 1798* (1802), along with a *Second Voyage* (1803); *Vue de la colonie espagnole du Mississippi* (1803), edited by Berquin Duvallon; LePage du Pratz, *Histoire de la Louisiane* (1758), 3v.; Joutel, *Journal historique du dernier voyage de m. de la Salle; Memoires des commissaires du roi et de ceux de sa majesté brittanique sur les possessions & les droits respectifs des deux courronnes en Amerique* (1755-57), 5v.; Louis Hennepin, *Nouvelle decouverte d'un tres grand pays situé dans l'Amerique entre le nouveau Mexique, et la mer glaciale* (1698) (fig. 16); *Histoire de la conqueste de la Floride, par les espagnols sous Ferdinand de Soto* (1685), present in two copies; Dumont, *Mémoires historiques sur la Louisiane* (1753). James Bowdoin, of course, had abbé Raynal's *Histoire philosophique et politique des etab-*

lissemens et du commerce des Europeens dans les Deux Indes (1778), 7v. (one volume was missing at the time of the inventory).

Collections of treaties and works on diplomacy were also purchased, mainly while Bowdoin was in Paris as a diplomat: these include Wicquefort, *L'ambassadeur et ses fonctions* (1715), 2v.; *Mémoires touchant les ambassadeurs et les ministres publics, par L. M. P.* (n.d.), also by Wicquefort; Martens, *Recueil des principaux traites d'alliance, de paix . . . depuis 1761* (1791), 2v.; Koch, *Abrégé de l'histoire des traités de paix . . . depuis la paix de Westphalie* (1796-97), 4v.; Bougeant, *Histoire des guerres et des négociations qui precederent le traité de Westphalie* (1751), 6v.; [François de Callières], *De la maniere de negocier avec les souverains*; [Antoine Pecquet], *Discours sur l'art de negocier* (1737); *Memoires et instructions pour les ambassadeurs ou lettres et negotiations de Walsingham* (1700); Pierre Jeannin, *Les Negotiations de monsieur le president Ieannin* (1659), 2v.; *Histoire des négociations et du traité des Pyrénées* (1750), 2v.; *Mémoire historique sur la négociation de la France & de l'Angleterre, depuis le 26 mars 1761 jusqu'au 20 Septembre de la même année* (1761); William Burck, *Histoire des colonies européennes dans l'Amérique* (1767).

Although certain areas of emphasis in the library can be related to particular aspects of Bowdoin's life or to the happenstances of his opportunities for book buying, it is necessary as well to look at James Bowdoin's library in a broader cultural context, with the aim of seeing, not what was specific to him, but rather the ways in which he was representative, or, as the case may be, intellectually divergent from his contemporaries.

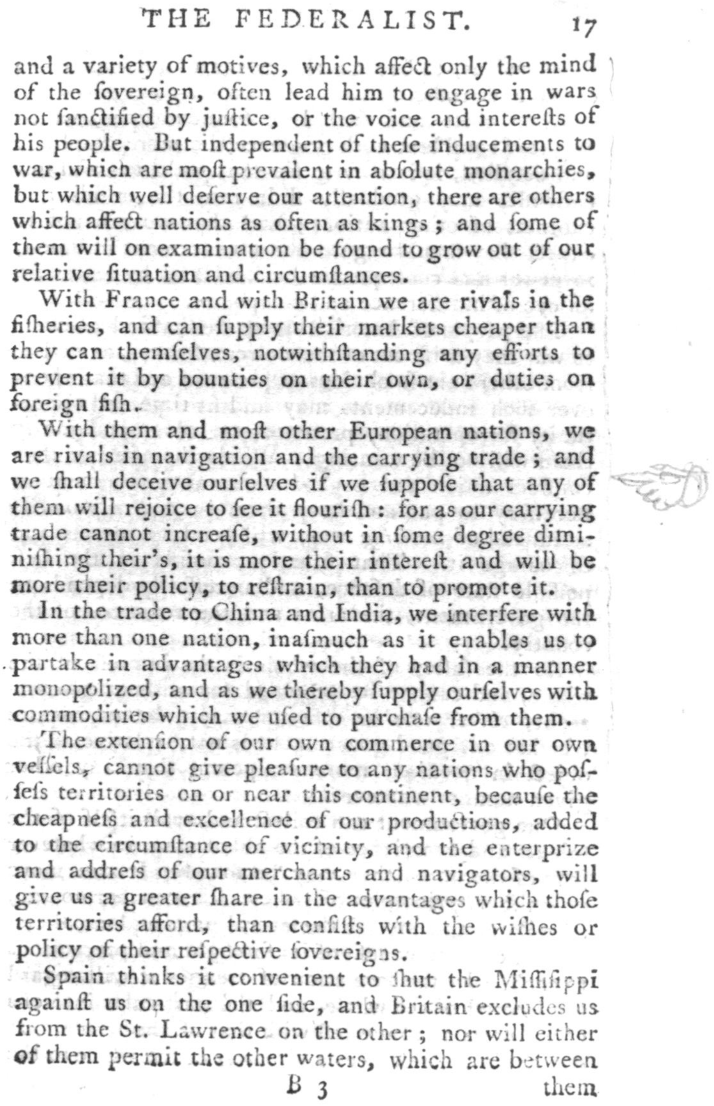

THE FEDERALIST. 17

and a variety of motives, which affect only the mind of the ſovereign, often lead him to engage in wars not ſanctified by juſtice, or the voice and intereſts of his people. But independent of theſe inducements to war, which are moſt prevalent in abſolute monarchies, but which well deſerve our attention, there are others which affect nations as often as kings; and ſome of them will on examination be found to grow out of our relative ſituation and circumſtances.

With France and with Britain we are rivals in the fiſheries, and can ſupply their markets cheaper than they can themſelves, notwithſtanding any efforts to prevent it by bounties on their own, or duties on foreign fiſh.

With them and moſt other European nations, we are rivals in navigation and the carrying trade; and we ſhall deceive ourſelves if we ſuppoſe that any of them will rejoice to ſee it flouriſh: for as our carrying trade cannot increaſe, without in ſome degree diminiſhing their's, it is more their intereſt and will be more their policy, to reſtrain, than to promote it.

In the trade to China and India, we interfere with more than one nation, inaſmuch as it enables us to partake in advantages which they had in a manner monopolized, and as we thereby ſupply ourſelves with commodities which we uſed to purchaſe from them.

The extenſion of our own commerce in our own veſſels, cannot give pleaſure to any nations who poſſeſs territories on or near this continent, becauſe the cheapneſs and excellence of our productions, added to the circumſtance of vicinity, and the enterprize and addreſs of our merchants and navigators, will give us a greater ſhare in the advantages which thoſe territories afford, than conſiſts with the wiſhes or policy of their reſpective ſovereigns.

Spain thinks it convenient to ſhut the Miſſiſippi againſt us on the one ſide, and Britain excludes us from the St. Lawrence on the other; nor will either of them permit the other waters, which are between

B 3 them

FIG. 17 The first edition of the *Federalist Papers* is one of the many books showing that James Bowdoin, who inherited great wealth and status, saw himself as a man of affairs. He read as well as owned books appropriate to that role, and the pointing finger in the margin is a sign that a passage particularly interested him.

Unusual is only the strength of the holdings on diplomacy, not that Bowdoin had some such works. The presence of some is to be expected in the library of a man of affairs of the late eighteenth and early nineteenth centuries.[45] Despite his "rather retired manner in society,"[46] James Bowdoin was a member of the General Court from 1786 to 1790, twice a member of the Massachusetts Senate (1794 and 1801), a member of the Governor's Council in 1796, a fellow of the Harvard Corporation during much of the 1790s, and a trustee of the Massachusetts Society

Superent quibus hoc Neptune dedisti.

Virg: Æn: V.

FIG. 18 The Bowdoin family wealth derived partially from commerce, and to James Bowdoin, who himself engaged in trading ventures, neither commerce nor books about commerce were unworthy of a gentleman. Reproduced here is the frontispiece to Richard Rolt's *New Dictionary of Trade and Commerce* (London, 1756). Its anonymous preface is by Samuel Johnson.

for Promoting Agriculture for two years. He published a closely reasoned work on trade policy. Bowdoin played a public role and had aspirations: he would have preferred being minister to the Court of St. James's rather than minister to Spain.

James Bowdoin, in addition to works on diplomacy, needed books on various parts of this country, collections of laws and treaties, geographical works, treatises on law and politics (Machiavelli, Montesquieu, the *Federalist Papers* [fig. 17], Filangieri, federal laws as well as collections of the laws of the states, Blackstone's *Commentaries*, Puffendorf, etc.), plus economic works (Smith's *Wealth of Nations*, Sheffield on the commerce of the American states, Necker on French finance, dictionaries of trade and commerce [including the major ones by Postlethwayt and Rolt (fig. 18)], Malthus, Gallatin on the finances of the United States, to name only some of the better known). Many of these books were actually ones that Madison in 1783 believed should be accessible to members of the Continental Congress.[47]

It is only from our vantage point that such books seem more appropriate for the study of the philosopher. James Bowdoin used these materials. He wrote long letters about political and commercial matters, and recently received works are sometimes analyzed at length. In his one published work on commerce, *Opinions Respecting the Commercial Intercourse between the United States of America, and the Dominions of Great-Britain* (Boston, 1797) (fig. 19), Bowdoin quotes works by Adam Anderson, Josiah Child, David Hume, Blackstone, Montesquieu, Adam Smith, Brian Edwards, Gallatin, Chalmers, Tench Coxe, Joseph Nourse, and Postlethwayt, plus many governmental acts.

Bowdoin was not creating a library that could be called a scholar's paradise. He was forming a useful tool,[48] one that had to be honed. Thus, he sought from Henry Dearborn, Jefferson's secretary of war, copies of acts and government reports. George Erving earned Bowdoin's gratitude for the interesting pamphlets as well as the beautifully printed travel accounts. For the man of affairs, such works were especially useful.

To eighteenth-century Americans the phrase "useful knowledge" came trippingly from the tongue or pen. Americans formed societies to promote and propagate "useful knowledge." They gave addresses on "useful knowledge," as did Ebenezer Fitch of Williams College, the president of an institution not unlike Bowdoin College, in his *Useful Knowledge and Religion, Recommended to the Pursuits and Improvement of the Young* (Pittsfield, 1799). Indeed, a variant expression, "useful Learning," rather than "useful knowledge," stands out, as when, in the late 1740s the directors of the Redwood Library in Newport, Rhode Island, drew up a list of books suitable for propagating "Virtue, Knowledge & useful Learning." At that point "useful knowledge" had not yet become the cliché. From about 1760, however, "the quest for useful knowledge . . . was in full swing in America."[49]

Bowdoin's own father put the case for the connection between learning and usefulness in his 1780 inaugural address before the American Academy of Arts and Sciences. There he expressed the hope that such societies would "aid and invigorate the individual: benefitting by their production not only the communities in which they are respectively instituted, but America and the world in general."[50] Governor Bowdoin did not, however, narrowly define usefulness. For him, the study of the "antiquities of America," that is the history of the European colonists, also constituted "political and other useful knowledge."[51] Useful was thus not limited to the practical. All of the arts and sciences were "useful," and only gradually were the practical ones split away to form the focus of more limited societies. That process began in the eighteenth century with, for example, the formation of the Philadelphia Society for Promoting Agriculture (1785) and the Massachusetts Society for Promoting Agriculture (1792), but only after the War of 1812 did societies devoted to medicine, applied science, and the mechanical arts come to be founded in large numbers. The founding of those societies is a sign of a growing

split between the "pure" and the "useful." Thus, by mid-century the concept of "useful knowledge" had become narrowly defined as the practical, in contrast to the late eighteenth and early nineteenth centuries, when the useful was much broader.[52]

Gentlemen such as James Bowdoin did not neglect the practical. In fact, they embraced it. In 1793, Bowdoin was recorded as a trustee of the Massachusetts Society for Promoting Agriculture, and he was, at least in the society's early years, a major donor, if by no means the largest.[53] His interest in the society continued even from France. On 20 December 1805, he wrote from Paris to Thomas L. Winthrop:

I shall send you a work concerning ye treatment & management of sheep by M. d'Aubenton, wch I find is extremely well rec.^{d} in Spain, & ought to be translated under ye direction of ye Mass.^{a} agricultural society. I send you two of them with ye desire that you will present one of them to ye society in my name with my Respects & assure them that it will give me great pleasure to fullfill any commission they may wish for in Europe if my situation shall allow it.

His willingness to "fullfill any commission" shows his general support of the society. At the same time, as later events showed, he was indirectly expressing in this letter his own desire to translate Louis Jean Marie Daubenton's *Instruction pour les bergers et pour les propriétaires de troupeaux, avec d'autres ouvrages sur les moutons et sur les laines*, 3d ed. (Paris [1802]). The translation first appeared in 1810 in an edition of thirty copies, which James Bowdoin, ever cautious, sent out to see whether it would be approved. It was, and he had another edition printed for wider distribution.[54]

James Bowdoin was a man of property, with vast wooded areas, under which there might be minerals. He owned sheep, made cheese, and engaged in other agricultural activities. He built a house on Naushon Island. All of these led him especially to be concerned with the practical and account for the description of him in his obituary as "a man of letters, and particularly fond of those studies which contributed to the improvements in which he was engaged,"[55] referring to changes being made at Naushon. Among the books in his library reflecting such interests were

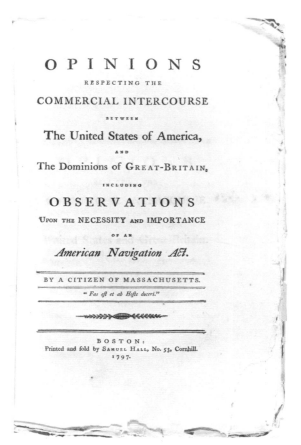

OPINIONS

RESPECTING THE

COMMERCIAL INTERCOURSE

BETWEEN

The United States of America,

AND

The Dominions of GREAT-BRITAIN,

INCLUDING

OBSERVATIONS

UPON THE NECESSITY AND IMPORTANCE

OF AN

American Navigation Act.

BY A CITIZEN OF MASSACHUSETTS.

" *Fas eft et ab Hofte doceri.*"

BOSTON:
Printed and fold by SAMUEL HALL, No. 53, Cornhill.
1797.

FIG. 19 James Bowdoin used his political and economic works in writing this attack on British commercial policy. In fact, he marked in his copy of Adam Smith's *Wealth of Nations* (Philadelphia, 1789) the passage that he quoted in *Opinions*.

The Complete Farmer; or, a General Dictionary of Husbandry in All Its Branches (London, n.d.); William Taplin, *Gentleman's Stable Directory*, 10th ed. (London, n.d.); Thomas Miles, *Concise Practical Measurer; or, a Plain Guide to Gentlemen and Builders* (London, 1740); Duhamel du Monceau's *Traité de la culture des terres* (1753-61), 6v., and the abbé Rozier's *Cours complet d'agriculture . . . ou dictionnaire universel d'agriculture* (1781-1805), 12v., a work now little known but at one time so valued that it went through translations, despite being so voluminous.

It is probable that James Bowdoin had a greater percentage of practical works than did collectors of an earlier generation, but he certainly did not equate the useful with the practical. In fact he was accustomed to linking "useful knowledge" and "literature." In his letter of 27 June 1794 offering support to the College, he noted its "purpose of diffusing Literature and useful Knowledge; whereby it may be reasonably expected, that the seeds of Science, deeply sown in ye natural Genius of its Inhabitants, will soon be seen to blossom, to fructify, and to contribute to the general Stock of Scientific Information in the united States." The linkage suggests more than a narrow definition of the useful, as does the continuation of the letter: "You, Gentlemen, being selected for the honourable Purpose of laying the first Foundation of an Institution, upon the Propriety of which, the future Character, Dignity, and Prosperity of the District of Maine, will materially depend. . . ." Thus, "literature" and "useful knowledge" leads to "character" and "dignity," as well as "prosperity."

The same pattern—that virtue ultimately rests on "literature" and "the sciences"—occurs in a letter to his land agent and longtime friend, Daniel Cony, on 17 August 1795: "Literature & the Sciences give force to Population and Improvement. On them depend your Constitution, Laws, Religion, Morals, which pursued in all their Ramifications, determine the fate of a Country; whether it shall be Virtuous, prosperous & happy; or vicious, unfortunate & wretched."

Since "literature" did not mean to James Bowdoin imaginative writing but rather all kinds of writings, including the erudite of various types,[56] it is clear that in his mind education, in addition to promoting prosperity, was also useful because it fostered a moral citizenry and a just polity. The set of evils ("vicious, unfortunate & wretched") and the set of goods ("Virtuous, prosperous & happy") are each made up of related components. One could no more be vicious and prosperous than suffer from the twentieth-century malaise of being prosperous and wretched.

More than the practical furthered the "Virtuous, prosperous & happy." The classics also did so. Reading them "served effectively as an agent of individual and social progress, directed as it was toward the inculcation of virtue and moral duties, the development of taste, and toward social utility, particularly in the political sphere, for the promotion of freedom and the prosperity of the country."[57] The classics were able to have such an effect because they were a repository of models of private and civic virtue.[58]

James Bowdoin's library was rich in the historical and political writings of the classical authors: Aristotle's *Ethics and Politics* (London, 1797), 2v.; Cicero's *Select Orations* (London, 1777), 2v.; histories of Herodotus (London, 1791), 4v., and Polybius (London, 1772), 4v.; Suetonius, *Lives of the First Twelve Caesars* (London, 1796); various editions of Tacitus in English, French, and Latin; plus many other authors in French: *Lettres de Ciceron a Atticus* (1787), 4v.; *Tusculanes de Cicéron* (1776), 2v.; Plutarch, *Oeuvres* (1665), 2v., and *Vies des hommes illustres* (1778), 12v.; Sallust in Latin (*C. Crispi Sallustii Belli Catilinarii & Jugurthini Historiae*, Edinburgh, 1733). He also, however, had a sufficient number of other classics to demonstrate affection for classical poetry and drama: Aeschylus (in English, 1779); Horace (two editions in Latin, 1567 and 1713; a French edition of 1763, and an English of 1790); Juvenal, *Satires* (1802); Martial, *Epigrammes* (n.d., but apparently 1807), 3v.; Ovid (two editions, in Latin, 1660, and French, undated but probably 1767); Terence (in Latin, 1751); complete works of Virgil in Latin (1717), and in French (1783, 3v.; 1802, 4v.), the *Bucoliques* (1806) and the *Georgics* in Latin and English (1800). Homer was not present.[59]

Bowdoin did not just come by his classical works by accident; he took steps to get them. As noted above, he asked Jesse Putnam in the letter of 30 June 1802 for editions of the classics in French. Later the same year, on 14 November, he wrote, as quoted above, to George Erving in London and asked for, among other books English translations of various classical works by Suetonius, Pausanias, Euripides, Aeschylus, Sophocles, and Thucydides, in each case asking for a specific translation. Then he added, more generally, "I sh.^d like to have handsome editions of ye works of Cicero, Virgil & Horace in Latin." It has been said that most Americans read their classics (Jefferson, Samuel Adams, John Adams, and James Wilson among the Revolutionary gen-

eration being exceptions) in translation, or else derived what they needed by way of parallels and examples from recent works on ancient history and political theory.[60] Bowdoin had copies of several such works on ancient history, among them Millot's *Elements of General History* (1796), 5v., and his *Elémens de l'histoire d'Angleterre, depuis son origine sous les romains jusqu'au regne de George II* (1769), 3v.; Vertot, *Histoire des révolutions de la république romaine* (An quatrième), 3v.; Adam Ferguson, *History of the Progress and Termination of the Roman Republic* (1799), 5v.; Middleton's *Life of Marcus Tullius Cicero* (1801), 3v.; and Montagu, *Reflections on the Rise and Fall of the Ancient Republicks* (1778). Whatever the motives behind his buying some books in Latin, he acquired them mainly while in Paris in the last decade of his life.

Classical histories were not the only ones from which "useful knowledge" was drawn. History of all sorts could, as Benjamin Franklin put it, "fix in the Minds of Youth deep Impressions of the Beauty and Usefulness of Virtue of all kinds."[61]

James Bowdoin's coverage of history was so extensive—one earlier commentator on his library counts 115 historical titles[62]—that he clearly shared the contemporary view of the importance of history. The number of works that can be considered historical rises if one includes many works that we would today consider political, and especially if law is included.

At the same time that the number of historical works in Bowdoin's library indicates his belief that historical reading would promote a country "Virtuous, prosperous & happy," Bowdoin did not have the strong collection of Whig history that could be expected of a member, chronologically, of the generation of Jefferson and Madison. A comparison with Jefferson makes this clear; its point of departure is H. Trevor Colburn's account of Jefferson's historical reading in *Lamp of Experience* (p. 159), with "not JBIII" or "JBIII" noted in brackets after each work:

By 1771, when he advised young Robert Skipwith on his book buying, Jefferson was able to include Sidney's *Discourses* [JBIII], Bolingbroke's *Political Works* [not JBIII], Rollin's *Ancient History* [not JBIII], Stanyan's

Grecian History [not JBIII], the Gordon translations of Tacitus [not JBIII the Gordon translation] and Sallust [not JBIII], as well as works by Clarendon [not JBIII], Hume [JBIII], and Robertson [JBIII]. Into his Commonplace Book went passages from Dalrymple's *Essay on Feudal Property* [not JBIII], Spelman's *De Terminis Juridicis* [not JBIII], Kames' *Historical Law Tracts* [JBIII], Sullivan's *Feudal Laws* [not JBIII], Blackstone's *Commentaries* [JBIII], Molesworth's *Account of Denmark* [not JBIII], and the [to Jefferson] anonymously written *Historical Essay on the English Constitution* [not JBIII]. He had his own copies of William Petyt's *Ius Parliamentum* [not JBIII], Thornhagh Gurdon's *History of Parliament* [not JBIII], and Anthony Ellis' *Tracts on Liberty* [not JBIII]. Later he acquired copies of Henry Care's *English Liberties* [not JBIII], Rushworth's *Historical Collections* [not JBIII], Acherley's *Britannic Constitution* [not JBIII], Atkyn's *Power of Parliament* [not JBIII], Catherine Macaulay's popular *History of England* [JBIII, in French], Trenchard and Gordon's *Cato's Letters* [not JBIII], and—of course—Burgh's *Political Disquisitions* [JBIII]. The list is not quite endless. But it is extraordinary for the representation Jefferson accorded the "True Whigs." These were books Jefferson bought not once, but twice, or three times, books he found essential to his political existence, books which served him beyond the realm of his practice of law.

Just as Jefferson's representation of the "True Whigs" was extraordinary, so was James Bowdoin's lack of these historical works. Out of twenty-four books listed above, Bowdoin had but six, plus one in French. Bowdoin had a large number of other historical works, which indicates that he saw history as useful in instilling virtue, but, for him, Whig history lacked certain uses that it had for others. Born in 1752, Bowdoin was nine years younger than Jefferson (b. 1743), but he was old enough to be a member of the cohort of the "younger of the 'young men of the Revolution'" (Joel Barlow, b. 1754; Timothy Dwight, b. 1752; Philip Freneau, b. 1752; Alexander Hamilton, b. 1757; James Madison, b. 1751; John Marshall, b. 1755; Gouverneur Morris, b. 1752; David Ramsay, b. 1749; Edmund Randolph, b. 1753; Noah Webster, b. 1758).[63] The members of that generation who were active in politics drew strength especially from the Whig historians, who supported Parliamentary claims against royal prerogatives. The works of Sir Henry Spelman, Sir Robert Molesworth, Thomas Gordon, Walter Moyle, John Trenchard, James Burgh, Catherine Macaulay, and John Cartwright enabled the young men of the Revolution to see themselves as inheritors of English liberties.[64]

Bowdoin, though chronologically a member of the revolutionary generation, was not collecting during those years; and, in the last decade of the eighteenth century and the first of the nineteenth—when he was collecting—the need to find justification for separation no longer existed. Neither did Americans, on the analogy of universal physical laws, need to find in history universal laws that governed human affairs, certainly not the lesson of history that growth inevitably was followed by decline and decay. The revolutionary generation, instead, increasingly rejected in the 1780s that view of the utility of history, in favor of a belief in the incomparability of American history.[65] Although by the 1790s history was no longer needed to support separation and to serve as a guide to the future, history did continue to be a source from which, by example, virtue and morality might be inculcated.

History seems to have been that for James Bowdoin, but also something more: the record of the on-going striving for liberty. To the Jeffersonian Republicans, of which Bowdoin was one, the American Revolution was part of a process of change, one that would be ongoing, since, as Jefferson wrote to Madison in September 1789, "the earth belongs in usufruct to the living."[66] Although James Bowdoin III would not have seen those words, the son of James Bowdoin II (the governor, member of the Royal Society, friend of Franklin, founding member of the American Academy of Arts and Sciences, member of the Harvard Corporation) was powerfully drawn to a set of beliefs that were undergirded by support for change at the hands of the living. He never did escape from his father's injunctions (see fn. 67) but it seems likely that the desire to do so led James Bowdoin III, a great landowner, a person who might have been expected to support order over liberty, to become instead a Jeffersonian Republican in the midst of Federalist New England.

In James Bowdoin's mature adulthood the most powerful symbol of the human striving for liberty was the French Revolution, whose signalling event, the fall of the Bastille, took place just about a year and a half before the death of his father, on 6 November 1790. The revolution in Paris and the revolution in the younger Bowdoin's life were very close together in time, and he remained fascinated throughout the remaining two decades of his life with the revolution that preceded his no longer being "Junior."[67] To be sure, Americans initially greeted the French Revolution with "universal delight,"[68] so much so that, as noted by the Salem clergyman and diarist William Bentley, Bostonians were being urged to address each other as Citizen.[69] The year 1793 marks, however, the point at which the upper classes, especially in New England, turned away from France. Not so James Bowdoin.

Bowdoin documented the events in France. He obtained a file of the *Gazette nationale, ou le Moniteur universel*, a folio-sized newspaper that has been described as the "semiofficial newspaper of record." It contained transcripts of proceedings in the Assembly, whereas other papers reported only the essence.[70] Bowdoin did not just, opportunistically, buy a file; he purchased a file while in this country and then took pains to add to it by subsequently acquiring additional volumes, the last by subscription while in Paris. Ultimately he had thirty-four, virtually complete from the start of publication up through 1807. His desire for the fullness of record provided by these volumes demonstrates that Bowdoin's attraction to France had roots much deeper than his family's Huguenot background or the lure of the French Enlightenment. Equally so do the three magnificent volumes, *Collection complète des Tableaux historiques de la Révolution française* (1802-04) (fig. 20). What the *Moniteur* did in words, these did in pictures, and volume-by-volume they represent by far his major investment in books. Each of the three volumes was appraised in 1811 at $100.

FIG. 20 As part of an effort to bring together a thorough documentation of the French Revolution, Bowdoin acquired a pictorial history, *Collection complète des Tableaux historiques de la Révolution française* (Paris, 1802-04). At the time it was the most valuable work in his library, appraised at $300.

James Bowdoin's collecting of history had, therefore, a twist that was perhaps unique to him among Americans of that time: the collecting of fundamental material for the study of France during the revolutionary era. Even Harvard had no volume of the *Moniteur* before 1840, and there is still recorded in America but one other copy of the *Tableaux*.

In two other areas of collecting, he was, however, quite conventional: travel books, and language grammars and dictionaries. The eighteenth century was a period in which travel literature particularly flourished, and James Bowdoin owned a good deal of it. Quite apart from travels to Louisiana and Florida, which were relevant to his service as minister plenipotentiary to Spain (and other works already mentioned), he had Samuel Hearne, *Journey from Prince of Wales's Fort, in Hudson's Bay to the Northern Ocean, in the years 1769, 1770, 1771, & 1772* (1795); C. A. Fischer, *Voyage en Espagne, aux années 1797 et 1798* (1801), 2v., plus several accounts of journeys through Spain; baron de Lahontan's *Nouveaux voyages . . . dans l'Amerique Septentrionale* (1715), 2v.; George Forster, *Journey from Bengal to England* (1798); Eyles Irwin, *Series of Adventures in the Course of a Voyage up the Red-Sea* (1780); J. B. Le Chevalier, *Voyage de la Propontide, et Du Pont-Euxin* (1800), 2v.; Volney's *Voyage en Syrie et en Égypte* (1787, 2v.; also 1799, 2v.), also present in English (1798); Charpentier Cossigny, *Voyage au Bengale* (1798-99), 2v.; A. E. Van Braam, *Authentic Account of the Embassy of the Dutch East-India Company to the Court of the Emperor of China, in the years 1794 and 1795* (1798), 2v.; William Francklin, *Observations on a Tour from Bengal to Persia* (1790); J. F. G. de la Perouse, *Voyage round the World in the Years 1785, 1786, 1787, and 1788* (1798), 3v.; Antonio de Ulloa and Jorgé Juan's *Voyage to South America* (Dublin, 1765), 2v.; Barthelemy, *Voyage du jeune Anacharsis en Grèce* (1790), 7v.; Le Vaillant, *Voyage . . . dans l'intérieur de l'Afrique* (1790), 2v.; Thaddeus Mason Harris, *Journal of a Tour into the Territory Northwest of the Alleghany Mountains Made in the Spring of the Year 1803* (Boston, 1805); John Quincy Adams's *Letters on Silesia, Written During a Tour through that Country in 1800, 1801* (1804); Vivant Denon's *Travels in Upper and Lower Egypt During the Campaigns of General Bonaparte* (New York, 1803), 2v.; C. F. Damberger, *Travels through the Interior of Africa* (1801); Mungo Park's *Travels in the Interior of Africa in the Years 1795, 1796, & 1797 . . . Abridged* (1799); James Bruce, *An Interesting Narrative of the Travels of James Bruce, Esq. into Abyssinia to Discover the Source of the Nile, Abridged* (Boston, 1798); Aeneas Anderson, *Narrative of the British Embassy to China, in the Years 1792, 1793, and 1794* (New York, 1795). There was a clear emphasis on recent travels. James Bowdoin also had histories and descriptive works on Paraguay, Poland, Portugal, Mexico, and the Turkish empire, as well as many of less exotic areas.

Grammars and language dictionaries formed an important part of James Bowdoin's library,

and in this respect he seems to have been representative of his era as well. For example, James Madison on 24 January 1783 presented to the Continental Congress "a list of books proper for the use of Congress," and one of the entries was "the best Latin Dictionary with the best grammar & dictionary of each of the modern languages."[71] Bowdoin had forty-odd grammars and dictionaries, in English, French, Greek, Hebrew, Italian, Latin, and Spanish. Jefferson, in a library more than three times as large, had 155.[72]

Bowdoin did not buy theology extensively. To be sure, he had Bibles and parts of the Bible in English, French, and Latin. He also owned some sermons and other theological works by such notables as Joseph Butler, Richard Hooker, William Paley, William Blair, and Samuel Clarke, plus three copies of Job Orton's *Exposition of the Old Testament* (Charlestown, 1805). (There must be a story there.) Not only was the quantity of theological literature modest, some were, as Benjamin Vaughan pointed out in a letter to Jesse Appleton of 6 November 1811, "free on the score of religion, particularly a work of Dupuis's."[73] Fitting into that category was Helvetius, *De l'esprit* (1758), his *Oeuvres complettes,* (1774), 4v., and the more modern *Introduction to the New Testament* (1801-02), 4v., by Michaelis, one of the founders of modern Biblical criticism.

English literature (in contrast to French) is another area, like medicine and theology, in which James Bowdoin had few books. He owned Gray, Milton, Pope, Shakespeare, Sterne, and a few others, but he had more books on Louisiana.

Art is similar, though one would have expected more. Besides a few works on architecture, including some plate books, Bowdoin had *Elements of Criticism* (Edinburgh, 1763), 3v., by Henry Home, Lord Kames; *Anecdotes des beaux arts* (Paris, 1776), 3v.; Lacombe's *Dictionnaire des beaux-arts* (Paris, 1759); and Winckelmann's *Histoire de l'art* (Paris, 1794-95), 3v. (fig. 21). The set of Winckelmann was received from Paris in 1809. It was apparently not something bought by Bowdoin himself, but a special desideratum that he had someone else acquire for him. Whether it should be seen as a rounding off of the library, or a belated effort to collect in a new area, the circumstances of its acquisition show particular intentionality.

In whatever subject field, James Bowdoin did not, however, devote to his collecting the attention of a scholar or the love of a bibliophile. That he asked George Erving to acquire for him Thompson's translation of Suetonius or Taylor's of Pausanias stands out. Bowdoin was tempted by the Euripides in the 1802 Bradford auction that was described as "the best edit. splendidly bound, in Russia leather & marbled leaves," but he did not buy it. The plate books that he presumably bought on his trip as a youth to Italy constitute a sign of incipient bibliophily, but he was generally successful in holding down that part of himself and, instead, in emphasizing price over other qualities.

A sign that Bowdoin did not lavish on his collection the attention of a bibliophilic scholar is his failure to arrange his books in any particular order.[74] Not only was there no subject order, the books were not even arranged alphabetically, as was commonly done in American private libraries.[75] This can be determined from the inventory prepared after his death. Housed in the Massachusetts Historical Society, the inventory is signed by Joseph Peirce, S. Blagge, and William Bradford, who identify themselves as "Appraisers." At the end of the inventory is a statement that at the Probate Court held at Boston on 9 March 1812, the executors presented "this Inventory and made oath it contained all the Estate of said deceased, in said County of Suffolk."[76]

Although the inventory has a date of 1812, it was prepared before "A Catalogue of Books of the late Hon. James Bowdoin Esq. together with his Cabinet of Minerals, & philosophical Instruments, left by Will to the President & Trustees of Bowdoin College," dated 3 December 1811, which is in the Bowdoin College Library. It is by the College's agent, John Abbot, who at that time served as librarian and professor of ancient languages, as well as an Overseer and secretary of the Boards. The catalog lists the books on twenty-five pages, with the lower half of the twenty-fifth page also recording engravings, maps, the collection of minerals, two

globes, a refracting telescope, electrical apparatus, etc. Page twenty-six notes several more items, including a "convex mirror, left for Mrs Bowdoin" and "one Air Pump, of peculiar construction, left with Mrs Bowdoin in Boston, for y^e. use of y^e. Surgeons," which are followed by the statement:

Receiv'd of Thomas L. Winthrop and Richard Sullivan Esquires, Executors to the last Will & Testament of the Hon. James Bowdoin Esq. lately deceased, his Library of books, his Cabinet of minerals, and his philosophical instruments, bequeathed in said Will to the President & Trustees of Bowdoin College; — agreeably to the foregoing correct catalogue, & as valued by the Appraisers employed by the said Executors.

Boston Decr 3.^{d} 1811. John Abbot Agent authorized by the said President & Trustees of Bowd. College

The inventory gives the number of volumes making up each title, the format of the work, the value per volume, and the total value of the work.[77] The inventory contains one element of information not in the catalog, that is, the style of binding, but it has a far more abbreviated record of authors and titles. The appraisers' inventory does often give the author's last name and title ("Humes Essays"), but never the first name and usually only the title ("Treatise on Cattle"; "Wealth of Nations"), in English, even if the book is in French. The inventory was prepared so hastily that a number of volumes were omitted.[78]

The Bowdoin College Library needed a fuller bibliographical record than the inventory provided. It needed a "catalogue," as Abbot termed his work. Thus, after the books arrived in Brunswick, they were checked against the inventory but then listed anew in more sophisticated fashion. The Abbot Catalogue is not, therefore, a list of the books as they appeared on the shelves of James Bowdoin's house in Boston. The inventory seems, however, at least initially to be such a record, for it begins by recording the books shelved in case 1, on the first shelf. It proceeds through shelf 10.

The only ordering of the books in case 1 is by size, since, for reasons of space, the folio-sized books are grouped together. Case 1 had 10 shelves, with shelf 1 being the top shelf in the

FIG. 21 Winckelmann's great history of art (Paris, 1794-95) was shipped to Bowdoin in 1809, after his return from Paris. He must have especially sought it, perhaps to complement the collection of art that he had formed.

following list (see the footnote for an explanation of the terms relating to size).[79]

    Shelf 1: 92 volumes (12° & 8°)
          2: 58 volumes (12° & 8°)
          3: 81 volumes (8° & 12°)
          4: 89 volumes (8°)
          5: 105 volumes (8° & 12°)
          6: 128 volumes (8° & 12°)
          7: 64 volumes (4°)
          8: 54 volumes (2^O)
          9: 61 volumes (4° & 8°)
        10: 253 volumes (8° & 4°) (Was the
          bottom shelf subdivided to make two?)
    Total number of volumes in case 1: 985

It could be that all the shelves were of the same depth, but it may be that shelves 8, 9, and 10 were deeper than the others in order to accommodate the larger books. That would have meant that books could be rested on the part of the 7th shelf that projected out into the room.

The listing of the books in case 1 is followed by an indication of case 2, shelf 5, and the number of volumes noted is 205.

There is then an indication where case 3 begins, but the listing simply records 741 volumes without shelf designation. The very first item consists of the three very large volumes of the *Tableaux.* Also among the first books listed are the thirty-four volumes of the *Moniteur.* These folios are followed by quartos, then octavos and duodecimos, in alternation, then quartos and octavos in alternation. If the order is, in fact, shelf order, it is very unusual. The common pattern is for folios to be on the lower shelves, and only one picture of a library has been found with folio volumes higher than ones of smaller size. It is of the Bibliothèque Nationale's manuscript reading room.[80] In a reading room that contains frequently cited reference works, it makes sense to have the largest books sufficiently high that older knees do not have to cope with the strain of heavy books. Such could account for larger books being higher than smaller ones in case 3 in the Bowdoin mansion, for a new bookcase had been built in the "Library Room" to accommodate the three trunks of books that arrived from France.[81] Case 3 in the inventory did, in fact, consist largely, though not exclusively, of books purchased in Paris (some of the Parisian books were also shelved elsewhere).

Since the inventory shows that case 3 was special, any efforts by James Bowdoin to arrange books in a logical order would have to appear in case 1.[82] Even though duplicates are not side by side, there are hints of an effort at logical arrangement. For instance, on shelf 3 are fifty-one volumes of law, but they are by no means all that Bowdoin owned. On shelf 4 are "Adams New England," "Belknaps American Biography," "Belknaps Newhampshire," "Williams History of Vermont," "Minot's History of Massachusetts," "Insurrection & Rebellion by R'd Minot," "History of Virginia by Robertson," but the "History of the District of Maine" (by James Sullivan) is separated from those by twenty-six books. The laws of Massachusetts, New Hampshire, and New York are on the same shelf but separated from each other. "Mackenzie on Merino Sheep," "Care of Sheep," and "Advice to Shepherds" are together, but not the other works on sheep that Bowdoin owned.

Although Bowdoin did not relate to his books as would a bibliophile or scholar, he did read them, for he cited them in published writings, referred to them in private correspondence, and placed in many of them his characteristic marks. Moreover, Bowdoin actually uses the word "pleasure" with respect to reading (see the letter, cited earlier, of 31 January 1801 to Erving).

Bowdoin's library was not, however, formed solely for the pleasure of reading or for its utility to a man of affairs. Neither was it a mere accumulation of a wealthy man. James Bowdoin's book buying was to some extent motivated by a philanthropic goal. He may have been the first American to form a library to give away.

In the letter of 14 November 1802 quoted above, James Bowdoin noted the probability that he would one day make "a donation of books." It is only a short step from that to the proposition that he in part formed the library with the intention of donating it to the College.[83] The belief in "collegiate education," the close link in his mind between education and books, the emotional power of the desire to help young people obtain an education, and the example of others who also donated libraries—all of these themes in James Bowdoin's life make it plausible that at some point he consciously began to buy books with Bowdoin College in mind.

Other kinds of concrete evidence exist. In addition to annotating an entry in the Bradford auction catalog of 1802 with the word "College," Bowdoin changed in a telling way his practice with respect to ownership inscriptions. A few books acquired before his father's death in 1790 are inscribed with a signature such as "Bowdoin junr's." Others dated 1791 or later drop, of course, the "junr's." They are instead inscribed "Bowdoin's," or occasionally "Jas. Bowdoin" or "James Bowdoin's." Some books published before 1791 are so inscribed, but books published after 1801 (or definitely acquired after that date) do not have his name written in, in any form, with two exceptions. It is as if the books were not permanently "Bowdoin's," but rather "Bowdoin College's," and the exceptions strengthen this supposition. One of them is his copy of Daubenton's *Instruction pour les bergers* [1802], which he purchased in Paris and subsequently translated. The other with his name written in is his copy of Haüy's *Traité de minéralogie* (1801), also acquired in Paris, and particularly meaningful to Bowdoin because he also purchased Haüy's collection of minerals.

The motive of enriching an institution with one's collection has stimulated many to form libraries. The history of American libraries is rich with examples, though none so early. Such collections typically have an obvious focus, for example an author (Cervantes), a historical figure (Lincoln), a type of book (incunabula), a printer (Aldus Manutius), or a subject (Americana).

The library of James Bowdoin seems, in contrast, to be heterogeneous and unfocused. Yet, underlying emphases can be perceived in terms

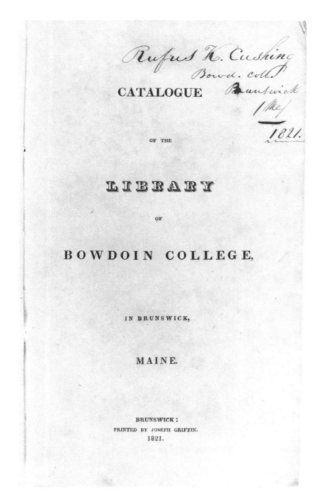

CATALOGUE

OF THE

LIBRARY

OF

BOWDOIN COLLEGE,

IN BRUNSWICK,

MAINE.

BRUNSWICK:
PRINTED BY JOSEPH GRIFFIN.
1821.

FIG. 22 Through this printed catalog, arranged by subject, the College made accessible its library, one of the largest in the country. To a considerable extent James Bowdoin's bequest made it so.

of types of material, rather than subject, and these relate to a major activity of his during the 1790s.

James Bowdoin was chosen a fellow of the Harvard Corporation on 10 September 1792. The Corporation was then and still is one of the two governing boards of Harvard. It is the one with a small membership that regularly meets with the Harvard president. Bowdoin was a member for almost seven years, until his resignation effective 10 June 1799.[84] During those years he was frequently in attendance at meetings, some of which concerned the Harvard College Library. Annually the Corporation joined a committee of the Overseers "to examine" or "to inspect" "the Library, Museum, and Philosophical and Chymical Apparatus." "Examine" and "inspect" convey to late twentieth-century ears general oversight. We would have to add adverbs to those terms ("closely," "minutely," "in detail") to make them fit what the members of the Corporation and Overseers actually did. The committee of the Overseers and the members of the Corporation took an inventory of the library, book by book, and they reported whether any books were missing. James Bowdoin would have learned exactly what was in the Harvard Library.

Bowdoin also participated as a member of the Corporation in decisions about what to buy for the library. "Purchased by the Corporation" appears in the most complete list of acquisitions of the period, and that expression was not a formality.[85] The purchases during that period were of three main types: 1) major reference works; 2) periodicals; and 3) multi-volume sets. A list follows of purchases in those categories. (Two works purchased in multiple copies, obviously for classroom use, and three other single-volume works have been omitted.)

Books Purchased by the Harvard Corporation, 1793-1799

1793
    Bryant's Mythology. 3v.
    Encyclopedia, American ed. vols. 9 and 10
1794
    No record of purchases, but there must have been volumes of the Encyclopedia.
1795 (since Commencement)
    Encyclopedia, American ed. vol. 14
1796 (July)
    Nicholson's Chemical Dictionary. vols. 1 and 2 (not identified as a purchase, but no donor is noted, as was otherwise customary)

    Encyclopedia, American ed. vol. 15

    Journal des mines. 8 vols. (not identified as a purchase, but no donor is noted) (The number of vols. is unclear.)
1797 (9 May)
    Encyclopedia, American ed. vol. 16

    Journal des mines, vol. 5, 6, 7 (6 is repeated, presumably an error) (These two are not actually identified as purchases, but there is no donor listed, and we know that the Corporation was purchasing the Encyclopedia Americana.)

1797 (before commencement)
Goldsmith, O., History of the earth and animated nature. 4v. 2 sets

Hume's History of England. 8v. 2 sets

Encyclopedia, American ed. vol. 17

1797 (since commencement)
Gillies's History of ancient Greece, 4v.

1798
Mackintosh Grammar French & English. 2 v. (not identified as a purchase, but no donor is noted)

1799
John Nicholson's Philosophical journal. 2v.

Gregory, G. Oeconomy of nature. (a 3-vol. work)

Hume's History of England.

Nichol's Philosophical journal (5 nos.)

These purchases, though few in number, were logical choices. The Corporation had to buy major reference works, because the standard method of library growth at the time—gifts of materials—would not work for reference books. Even though individuals bought such works, the individuals also did not give them up, at least not in timely fashion.[86] It must also have been clear then, as now, that a library cannot rely on private persons for periodicals: too many missing issues and volumes, and delay in receipt. The reason for purchasing the multi-volume sets is less clear. Indeed, the acquisition of duplicates suggests particular reasons. Yet, it is reasonable to argue that an institution should invest in multi-volume sets other than reference works, and for the same reason: the lessened likelihood of their being received as gifts.

In James Bowdoin's library the holdings of reference works, periodicals, and multi-volume sets are so extensive that they constitute collecting categories. Moreover, since those particular categories were ones that James Bowdoin observed Harvard buying institutionally, it is arguable that he was buying institutionally—for a college that bore the family name in the District of Maine.[87]

Here are the multi-volume reference works in James Bowdoin's library:

Chambers' *Cyclopaedia: or, an universal dictionary of arts and sciences* (London, 1786), 5v.; the Encyclopedia Americana, *Encyclopaedia; or, a Dictionary of Arts, Sciences, and Miscellaneous Literature* (Philadelphia, 1798), 18v., with a 3-vol. supplement (1803); the great Diderot encyclopedia, *Encyclopédie, ou Dictionnaire raisonné des sciences, des arts et des métiers . . . Nouvelle édition* (Geneve, 1777), 35v., plus 4 vols. of plates, 1778-79; Thaddeus Mason Harris, *The Minor Encyclopedia, or Cabinet of General Knowledge: Being a Dictionary of Arts, Sciences, and Polite Literature* (Boston, 1803), 4v.; J. B. Jaubert, *Dictionnaire raisonné universel des arts et métiers, contenant l'histoire, la description, la police des fabriques et manufactures de France et des pays étrangers . . . Nouvelle édition* (Lyon, 1801), 5v.; A. F. M. Willich, *The Domestic Encyclopaedia; or, a Dictionary of Facts, and Useful Knowledge,* (Philadelphia, 1804), 5v. (The *Encyclopaedia Britannica; or, a Dictionary of Arts, Sciences and Miscellaneous Literature,* 3d ed., Edinburgh, 1797, 18v., with a 2-volume supplement of 1801, is not among this number; Bowdoin arranged for his mother to buy it, but he did not purchase this multi-volume reference work for himself.)

Further evidence that James Bowdoin was buying for an institution comes from comparing his holdings with those of Jefferson, his contemporary. In 1815, when Jefferson sold his library to the United States, he had 6,700 volumes, nearly three times as many as James Bowdoin; but his library contained, instead of six encyclopedias, only five. Three of those, Chambers, Diderot and d'Alembert, and the American edition of the Britannica were also owned by Bowdoin, though Bowdoin had the supplement to the last-named, which Jefferson did not. Two other encyclopedias were not owned by Bowdoin, the *Encyclopédie méthodique,* in 136 and a half volumes, and Oven's *Dictionary of arts and sciences,* 4v. It is even possible that Bowdoin did not buy the *Encyclopédie méthodique* because he knew that Benjamin Vaughan of Hallowell had a copy that the College might (in fact, did) one day receive.[88]

The comparison indicates that James Bowdoin's considerably smaller library had gone beyond the collection of a gentleman/man of affairs; Bowdoin was buying a category—the category that Jefferson in the manuscript catalog of his library called Polygraphical.[89]

The presence of other large, polygraphical works supports the assertion that Bowdoin was collecting a category. Others in his library are the *Mémoires* of the Institut national des sciences et arts (Paris, 1798-1806), in 19 volumes; the *Histoire de l'Academie royale des inscriptions et belles lettres* (1717-1786), 43v., and Bruzen la Martiniere, *Le grand dictionnaire géographique et critique* (La Haye, 1725-1739), 9v. in 10.

There were also some important periodicals, apart from the 34-volume *Gazette nationale, ou Moniteur universel:* the *Journal d'économie publique,*
7v.; and, especially interesting in light of Harvard's buying, 21 volumes of the *Journal des mines* (1795-1807).

Yet other multi-volume works were present in James Bowdoin's library in abundance. Counting only works with five volumes or more, there were 73 titles, with 870 volumes (fig. 22).

Thus an even greater book collector, Benjamin Vaughan[90] of Hallowell, did not have it quite right when, after Bowdoin's death, he wrote to President Jesse Appleton: "Mr. Bowdoin was not a great scholar; less so than his father perhaps; but still he kept good company and read good authors, and you will have the library of a gentleman, if not of a high scholar."[91] James Bowdoin's library was, indeed, that of a gentleman, but a gentleman who seems to have formed it to give away.

NOTES

BCSC is Special Collections, Hawthorne-Longfellow Library, Bowdoin College.

I am grateful to Dianne M. Gutscher and Susan B. Ravdin of Special Collections in the Bowdoin College Library. Ms. Ravdin especially provided time-consuming assistance in identifying works in the Abbot catalog that were not among James Bowdoin's library. Ms. Gutscher and student assistants spent many hours checking the quotations and book titles. Staff at the Massachusetts Historical Society and the Harvard University Archives provided their customary professional and cheerful assistance. Charles C. Calhoun of Bowdoin College and Thomas J. Siegel, tutor in history and literature at Harvard, kindly read the paper, and their comments led to improvements. Susan L. Ransom and Katharine J. Watson, especially, made numerous helpful suggestions.

1. The number of titles and volumes depends in part on how one counts, which means that the figures are not precise. The number of pamphlets is recorded in the inventory prepared by John Abbot, the agent of the Bowdoin Overseers who went to Boston to carry out the wishes of legatee. Many of the pamphlets, actually issues of periodicals, were bound into 128 volumes at a cost of $43.20 in 1827. They were subsequently disbound.

2. Roger Michener, "The Bowdoin College Library: From Its Beginnings to the Present Day," Master's thesis, University of Chicago Graduate Library School, 1972, citing (p. 7) George T. Little, *General Catalogue of Bowdoin College 1794-1894* (Brunswick, ME., 1894), 34, says that there were some five hundred books in the library at the opening of the College in 1802; it is not clear whether that figure includes the 104 volumes bought with the gift of £100 from Madam Elizabeth Bowdoin in 1802. Michener also notes that on 6 September 1803, the College authori-

ties appropriated $1,000 for books. That sum could have brought in from 100 to 1,000 volumes. Among the letters received by Bowdoin President Joseph McKeen is one from Benjamin Vaughan, 2 October 1804, recording that he was sending *Antient Universal History,* 21v., and *Modern Universal History,* 44v. Unfortunately, the manuscript catalog prepared by John Abbot in 1808 (referred to by Michener, p. 8) is not in existence, so one can only speculate that in 1811 the Bowdoin College Library contained fewer than 1,000 volumes.

3. See the Reverend William Jenks, *An Eulogy, Illustrative of the Life, and Commemorative of the Beneficence of the Late Hon. James Bowdoin, Esquire, with the Notices of his Family; Pronounced in Brunswick, (Maine) at the Request of the Trustees and Overseers of Bowdoin College, on the Annual Commencement, Sept. 2d, 1812* (Boston, 1812), in which he notes that the College's library, "though still considerably deficient in classical and biblical literature, probably ranks now the third among those, which supply the Colleges of New England with employment."

4. For the statistics of college libraries, see Joe W. Kraus, "The Book Collections of Early American College Libraries," *Library Quarterly* 43 (1973): 144.

5. See Kenneth E. Carpenter, *The First Hundred Years of the Harvard University Library* (Cambridge, MA: Harvard University Library, 1986), 44-45.

6. Louise Chipley, "The Enlightenment Library of William Bentley," *Essex Institute Historical Collections* 122 (1986): 3 provides data on Bentley's library. On the Vaughan library, see Emma Huntington Nason, *Old Hallowell on the Kennebec* (Augusta, Maine, 1909), 86. Craig C. Murray, *Benjamin Vaughan (1751-1835): The Life of an Anglo-American Intellectual* (New York: Arno Press, 1982), 500, gives a figure of between 10,000 and 12,000 volumes at Vaughan's death; his source is an article by J. S. C. Abbott in the *Christian Weekly* (1876), 466. Other

notable post-colonial early libraries recorded by Edwin Wolf, 2nd, in "Great American Book Collectors to 1800," *Gazette of the Grolier Club,* no. 16 (June 1971): 3-25, are: Mather Byles, Jr., 2,730 volumes in 1790, sold at auction; Benjamin Franklin, also in 1790, 4,276 volumes, scattered by sale; John Adams, 3,019 surviving volumes from the collection given to the town of Quincy in 1822, with some, perhaps, from other members of the Adams family; the Harvard scientist John Winthrop, in excess of 3,100 volumes in 1820, which went to Allegheny College; Isaac Norris II, 1,636 surviving volumes from the 1784 gift to Dickinson College; William Mackenzie, 7,051 volumes, acquired through gift and purchase by the Loganian Library and the Library Company of Philadelphia; Edward Lloyd IV of Wye House, Maryland, 2,550 volumes in 1796. Another major early library, that of Thomas Wallcut, part of which is at Bowdoin College, was described by Earl R. Taylor, "Thomas Wallcut, 1758-1840: Portrait of a Bibliophile," *The Book Collector* 32 (1983): 155-70; it contained the extraordinary number of ten thousand pamphlets. The number of books that Wallcut collected is not known; but even after gifts to the Massachusetts Historical Society and the American Antiquarian Society, he was still able to make a gift of 558 to Bowdoin College in 1819.

7. Both of the individuals who wrote to Jesse Appleton about James Bowdoin's library (letters in Appleton correspondence, BCSC) believed that Governor Bowdoin, James Bowdoin III's father, had formed the nucleus of the collection. George Thacher of Biddeford, who also gave books to the College, wrote on 14 May 1812: "It gives me much pleasure to hear of the increase of the Library at Bowdoin College; I have always felt an interest in that institution, & nothing that has a tendency to raise its reputation can be indifferent to me. I had heard that Mr. Bowdoin had left a Legacy of Books to it, but their number I did not know. Presuming Mr. Bowdoins Legacy was made of of [*sic*] Books from his late fathers Library as well as his own I think there must be among them many rare & valuable ones." Benjamin Vaughan was equally wrong, when he wrote on 6 November 1811 about Bowdoin III increasing "the French books, which he probably rec^d. from his father."

8. Douglas L. Wilson, "Jefferson's Library," in Merrill D. Peterson, ed., *Thomas Jefferson: A Reference Biography* (New York: Charles Scribner's Sons, 1986), 170, noted, for example, that Jefferson organized and bound hundreds of pamphlets. Counted as among James Bowdoin's 2,100 pamphlets were large numbers of issues of periodicals. Library lore has it that many pamphlet volumes were stolen by a ring of book thieves in the 1930s. The fact that the pamphlets came from various sources, losses from among the pamphlets, plus the absence of an inventory of them are all factors that make it difficult to write about the pamphlets in detail.

9. See the letter of James Bowdoin III to James Bowdoin Temple, 11 September 1803, quoted in Marvin Sadik, *Colonial and Federal Portraits at Bowdoin College* (Brunswick, ME: Bowdoin College Museum of Art, 1966), 140.

10. Peter Charles Hoffer, *Revolution and Regeneration: Life Cycle and the Historical Vision of the Generation of 1776*

(Athens: University of Georgia Press, 1983), 70-73. Bowdoin also owned a copy of Daniel Alexandre Chavannes, *Exposé de la méthode élémentaire de H. Pestalozzi* (1805).

11. Bowdoin-Temple Papers in the Winthrop Papers, Massachusetts Historical Society, microfilm reel 50. Quotations are by permission of the Massachusetts Historical Society, Boston, Massachusetts.

12. This letter is transcribed from two folio letterbooks, 1791-1811, BCSC. Other letters whose location is not otherwise identified are also from those letterbooks.

13. Sarah Cony married Reuel Williams on 19 November 1807. The groom went on to serve Maine in the U.S. Senate from 1837 to 1843, during which time his wife is reputed to have been a prominent hostess. See Nason, 31, 278-79. Daniel Cony represented Hallowell in the General Court of Massachusetts and was for a time a member of the Executive Council. He was a judge in Kennebec County, "an Overseer of Bowdoin College, and the founder and endower of Cony Female Academy"; see Nason, 30.

14. Amelia Forbes Emerson, *Early History of Naushon Island,* 2d ed. (Boston: Howland and Company, 1981), 389; the location of the original letter is not identified.

15. Merrill D. Peterson, "The American Scholar: Emerson and Jefferson," in *Thomas Jefferson and the World of Books: A Symposium Held at the Library of Congress September 21, 1976* (Washington, D.C.: Library of Congress, 1977), 29.

16. This statement about the broad effect of educational institutions echoes that made in 1780 by James Bowdoin II before the American Academy of Arts and Sciences about the effect of Harvard College. See note 23.

17. *Rules and Regulations of the Massachusetts Society for Promoting Agriculture* (Boston, 1796), 77.

18. Governor Bowdoin had also been in touch with Lettsom, and possibly the son had been aware of that. See the letter of 25 January 1790 in the Massachusetts Historical Society.

19. Harvard University, Corporation Records, VIII, 307.

20. Josiah Quincy, *The History of Harvard University* (Cambridge: John Owen, 1840) 2: 577.

21. The number of Harvard acquisitions comes from a record book in the Harvard University Archives, UA III.50.15.70.2 (folder 2). The books acquired with Madam Elizabeth Bowdoin's gift are listed in the invoice of George Erving in the Bowdoin College Library Records. They are a disparate lot, on history, botany, and scientific instruments, along with the tragedies of Euripides and much theology, notably prophecy and chronology. The significant proportion of theological works contrasts with James Bowdoin's library, which contains few.

22. The bequest to Harvard read: "Whereas I have never been married and so of course have not benifeted [*sic*] Society by adding to their Number and being unwilling to pass thro' an Existance without proffiting Communitey it is my will and Pleasure that a Sum of Money not less than One Thousand Pounds be paid as soon as it conveniently can be after my Decease into the Hands of the Overseers & Corporation of Harvard Colledge for the

sole use and purpose of enlarging the Salary of the Professor upon Chymistry who is to rec. the Annual Interest of Item. I give unto Harvard Colledge all my Books upon Astronomy, Mathematics and Geometry together with my Books upon Gunnery and Fortification and Mensuration and as there is maney easey [sic] Treatesis in them, I am in hopes that it will induce the Young there to study the Mathematics more than they have done of late Years." The portion of the will relating to the American Academy reads: "I give unto the American Academey of Arts and Sciences all my Books upon Agriculture also one great Volume upon Mill Work printed in Dutch with Two Quarto Dictionaries, the one in English & Dutch the Other Dutch and English." The will was dated 8 December 1790. (See Bowdoin/Temple Papers, Massachusetts Historical Society, microfilm reel 50).

23. The terms of the will were reported in the *Memoirs of the Academy of Arts and Sciences,* vol. 2, pt. 2, p. 149. When the academy was established in 1780, James Bowdoin II was its first president. His inaugural address contained a statement about the importance of educational institutions, their ripple effect if you will, that may have inspired the son to support the new college in Maine: "To have said thus much on the subject of the college [Harvard], will not, on this occasion, be deemed impertinent, as the instituting of it was, not merely consistent with the forming such a society as ours, but necessary to precede it." (See *A Philosophical Discourse, Addressed to the American Academy of Arts and Sciences . . . in Boston, on the eighth of November M, DCC, LXXX, after the Inauguration of the President into Office* [1780], 16. The Academy deposited on indefinite loan at Bowdoin College in 1949 all of the remaining 565 volumes; they are now shelved with the books of the son. The son subsequently became a member of the American Academy of Arts and Sciences, but he was never recorded among the lists of donors of books and money to the academy.

24. Gordon E. Kershaw, *James Bowdoin II: Patriot and Man of the Enlightenment* (Lanham, MD: University Press of America, 1991), 291. The will was signed on 23 March 1789, and there is no way of knowing whether there was an earlier version or versions and their content.

25. James Bowdoin III did not move from his house in Dorchester to the Beacon Street mansion until 1802, at some point between February and early May. It is tempting to speculate that he did not do so until he had enough books to fill the bookshelves in a significant way.

26. A volume of poetry by a woman so stands out in James Bowdoin's library that it is perhaps worth noting an earlier exchange that may have had something to do with the book's acquisition. In late June, Mercy Warren sent the manuscript of her work to Governor Bowdoin, and he immediately returned it with a letter saying that he had to go to Connecticut and to his regret could not read the poems. See *Collections of the Massachusetts Historical Society,* 7th series, vol. 6 (1907), 197-98.

27. No unusual similarities between the father and the son have been discerned, with respect to either the content of the collections or the collecting methodology. In décor of the library, however, there exists a curious similarity. In a letter of 9 May 1807 to Thomas L. Winthrop, Bowdoin noted that he had ordered "six marble Busts with their pedestals to be shipt from Leghorn to be put in my Library." The father also had busts, presumably in the library; on 10 August 1770 he recorded in his Cash Book paying Joseph Riboud 16s. for busts of Addison and of Shakespeare. He also paid an additional 1s.2d. for mending an "Image."

28. Poivre's *Travels of a Philosopher,* printed in Augusta, Maine, in 1797, is inscribed: "Hon. James Bowdoin from his friend D Cony"; and Benjamin Dearborn's *The Columbian Grammar: Or, an Essay for Reducing a Grammatical Knowledge of the English Language to a Degree of Simplicity* (Boston: Printed for the author, 1795), is inscribed very formally: "The Honorable James Bowdoin Esqr from his hble serv^t The Author." One Frenchman, a monsieur Fleuret, presented Bowdoin with *L'art de composer des pierres factices aussi dures que le caillou, et recherches sur la manière de bâtir des anciens, sur la préparation, l'emploi et les causes du durcissement de leurs mortiers* (1807); it was apparently sent by mail after Bowdoin had left Paris.

29. Thursday and 27 May coincided in 1802, making it the only possible date during the relevant time span.

30. It is not clear whether these were casual variations or codes.

31. James Bowdoin did lend from his library. Thus, in an undated letter to Henry Dearborn, clearly from April 1802, he expressly noted that he was sending a particular pamphlet. (He did ask for it back.)

32. Robert Winans, in his *A Descriptive Checklist of Book Catalogues Separately Printed in America 1693-1800* (Worcester: American Antiquarian Society, 1981), records eleven auctions held in Boston in 1800. That was a high point, and there were far fewer earlier, or later, but the rarity of these catalogs may well mean that we have an insufficient picture of this method of book distribution. For instance, James Bowdoin's Bradford auction catalog of 14 October 1802 is not recorded in George L. McKay, *American Book Auction Catalogues from 1713 to 1934* (New York, 1937).

33. In May 1789, Governor Bowdoin asked Erving to send him the Transactions of the Royal Society; Kershaw, *James Bowdoin II,* 272.

34. Quoted from the letterbooks, BCSC.

35. Bowdoin was exaggerating in saying that he had a set of Corneille. He did, however, have Rousseau, 24v.; Voltaire, 70v.; Helvetius, 4v.; Mably, 22v.; Raynal, 7v.; Montesquieu (only *Oeuvres posthumes* in 1v.); Condillac, 3v.; La Fontaine, 2v.; Regnard, 4v.; and Molière, 6v. He did, indeed, have "several hundred other [French] volumes." Among them may have been Pierre Bulliard's splendid *Herbier de la France, ou Collection complète des plantes indigènes de cet empire* (Paris, 1780-93), 6v., though it is possible that this set is one that Putnam subsequently acquired for Bowdoin.

36. Bowdoin is perhaps here recalling the catalogs he had of the London firm of G. G. J. and J. Robinson. Present among his pamphlets are copies issued in 1790, 1791, and 1792, all, however, unmarked. He also had *A catalogue of optical, mathematical, and philosophical instruments, made and sold by W. and S. Jones* (London, 1795), which also contained some books, again without annotations. There is no evidence that Bowdoin purchased directly from Britain.

37. Winans, entry 247, dated [1797?].

38. The text of the letter as reproduced here is from that in BCSC. Other versions of the letter exist in the letterbooks and in the Boston Public Library. In order to increase the chances that a letter would get to its intended recipient, more than one copy was sometimes sent. The wording of the versions and the order of names vary slightly in the list of authors. The editions Nancrede offered are different from those Bowdoin owned, in most cases, but, of course, Nancrede might well have had editions other than those listed in his catalogs.

39. Madeleine B. Stern, "Joseph Nancrede, Franco-American Bookseller-Publisher, 1761-1841," *Papers of the Bibliographical Society of America* 70 (1976): 1-88, esp. 56-57. The one instance noted of Bowdoin subscribing in advance to a work was one published by Nancrede; see above. The relationship was not, however, such that he automatically subscribed to publications of Nancrede; thus he failed to acquire the Nancrede edition of Mallet du Pan, *History of the Destruction of the Helvetic Union* (1799). No information on James Bowdoin's dealings with Nancrede is available in the remnant of Nancrede's papers housed in the Public Archives of Canada.

40. James Bowdoin, who is said to have had "nearly everything in print" on the subjects of mineralogy and geology, purchased a collection of minerals from Haüy; see Benjamin B. Burbank, "James Bowdoin and Parker Cleaveland," *The Mineralogical Record* 19 (1988): 145, and Arthur M. Hussey II, "James Bowdoin and Geology at Bowdoin College," in this book.

41. Reel 21 of the Winthrop Papers, addressee not indicated. On the Naushon Island period of James Bowdoin's life, see Richard H. Saunders, "James Bowdoin III (1752-1811)," p. 23-25 in this book.

42. It is placed between those dates on reel 21 of the Winthrop Papers.

43. Letter to his father of November 1771, quoted in the biographical sketch in *Sibley's Harvard Graduates*, vol. 17 (Boston, 1975), 488.

44. *Sibley's Harvard Graduates*, 17:488.

45. For a discussion of types of private libraries, see Daniel Roche, "Noblesses et culture dans la France du XVIIIe: Les lectures de la Noblesse" in *Buch und Sammler, Private und öffentliche Bibliotheken im 18. Jahrhundert; Colloquium der Arbeitsstelle 18. Jahrhundert Gesamthochschule Wuppertal, Universität Münster, Düsseldorf vom 26.-28. September 1977* (Heidelberg, 1979), 9-27. The library of James Bowdoin most fits Roche's "grand administrateur" type, as exemplified by Turgot, though the term is not appropriate for this country.

46. Letter of Henry Dearborn to T. L. Winthrop, 31 March 1807, on reel 21 of the Winthrop papers.

47. For a list of about 300 such books, which includes about 100 histories and descriptions of America, plus 70 histories of other parts of the world and was prepared by James Madison for the Continental Congress in 1783, see Rutland, Robert A., *"Well Acquainted with Books," the Founding Framers of 1787, with James Madison's List of Books for Congress* (Washington, D.C., 1987).

48. Bowdoin did not acquire these books in order that they might provide assistance to him in mercantile pursuits. He did not see commerce as being beneath the dig-nity of a gentleman, as shown by the letter of 1799 to his nephew, quoted above, but he was not during the period of the formation of his library engaged in trade. He had been, though, even in privateering. See Kershaw, *James Bowdoin II*, 224, 226-28; and Saunders, p. 7, in this book.

49. Meyer Reinhold, *Classica Americana: The Greek and Roman Heritage in the United States* (Detroit: Wayne State University Press, 1984), 63. See Chapter 2, "The Quest for Useful Knowledge in Eighteenth-Century America," 50-93, for numerous instances of the use of the term.

50. Quoted in Alexandra Oleson, "Introduction: To Build a New Intellectual Order," in A. Oleson and Sanborn C. Brown, eds., *The Pursuit of Knowledge in the Early American Republic: American Scientific and Learned Societies from Colonial Times to the Civil War* (Baltimore and London: The Johns Hopkins University Press, 1976), xv.

51. Reinhold, 68.

52. Oleson, xvi; Reinhold, 79.

53. *Laws and Regulations of the Massachusetts Society for Promoting Agriculture* (Boston, 1793), 12, records Bowdoin as a trustee. In *Rules and Regulations of the Massachusetts Society for Promoting Agriculture* (Boston, 1796), Bowdoin is no longer recorded as a trustee, but he is noted, p. 75, as giving "interest of £.400 for 5 years." On p. 77 income of the society is noted, and under 1794 is recorded "By two years subscription of Hon. Mr. Bowdoin 160"; under 1796 is recorded "By Hon. Mr. Bowdoin's 3d year's subscription 80."

54. Robert L. Volz, *Governor Bowdoin & His Family: A Guide to an Exhibition and a Catalogue* (Brunswick, ME: Bowdoin College, 1969), 81-83.

55. The obituary notice is quoted from Thaddeus Mason Harris, *A Tribute of Respect, to the Memory of the Hon. James Bowdoin, Esq. in a Sermon, Preached at Dorchester, October 27, 1811* (Boston, 1811), where it appears on pp. [28]-32.

56. On the meaning of the word "literature," see René Wellek, "Literature and Its Cognates" in *Dictionary of the History of Ideas* (New York, 1973), 3:81-89.

57. Reinhold, 32.

58. Reinhold, 24. The classics also served, for many Americans, as a kind of laboratory in which one could test ideas about government. It has been said that in no country since antiquity did such a high proportion of the citizenry read the classics, and to the Founding Fathers they were sources to "ransack," "scour." See Reinhold, Chapter 3, "Classical Influences and Eighteenth-Century American Political Thought," 94-115. There is no evidence that Bowdoin used history in this fashion.

59. Cicero's *Select Orations* (1777), Horace's *Oeuvres* (1763) and *Works* (1790), the *Satires* of Juvenal (1802), Suetonius, *Lives* (1796) are no longer in the collection. The other kinds of books that have suffered some loss over the years, apart from pamphlets, are dictionaries and works of English literature, notably Gray, Pope, and Shakespeare.

60. Reinhold, esp. 30-32, 102.

61. Quoted in H. Trevor Colbourn, *The Lamp of Experience: Whig History and the Intellectual Origins of the American Revolution* (Chapel Hill: Published for the Institute of Early American History and Culture at Williamsburg, Virginia, by the University of North

Carolina Press), 5-6. See all of Chapter 1, "History and the Eighteenth-Century Colonist." See also Appendix II, which identifies historical works in a number of institutional and private libraries. Colbourn includes as historical some works that we would customarily call political, above all Algernon Sidney's *Discourses concerning Government,* a copy of which (1704), is the first book on the inventory of James Bowdoin's library.

62. Volz, 34.

63. Hoffer, 6.

64. Colbourn, 4-9; Hoffer, 14-22.

65. Hoffer, Chapter 2: "A History without Parallel," esp. pp. 50-56.

66. Quoted in Hoffer, 78.

67. James Bowdoin III seems to have followed a pattern of avoiding his father's footsteps. The father was first president of the American Academy of Arts and Sciences and a major donor; the son was a member but never contributed. The father was first president of the Humane Society of the Commonwealth of Massachusetts, founded in 1785, but the son, though a member, played no other role; see M. A. DeWolfe Howe, *The Humane Society of the Commonwealth of Massachusetts, an Historical Review, 1784-1916* (Boston, 1918). The father gave a telescope and orrery to Harvard and left a substantial bequest of £400; the son seems to have contributed no money. The father became in 1779 the first person other than a clergyman, professor, or tutor to serve as a fellow of the Harvard Corporation; the son did hold the same post, but he resigned it. The son did not, contrary to what one might customarily expect, become a member of the Massachusetts Historical Society when it was founded in 1794. In fact, it seems that he never visited the College named in honor of his father. One could perhaps attribute this pattern to what Henry Dearborn, in a letter to Thomas L. Winthrop of 31 March 1807, called Bowdoin's "rather retired manner in society." James Bowdoin III did, however, serve as a trustee of the Massachusetts Charitable Fire Society from its incorporation in 1794 to 1796; see Henry H. Sprague, *An Old Boston Institution: A Brief History of the Massachusetts Charitable Fire Society* (Boston: Little, Brown, and Co., 1893). Publications of the Massachusetts Society for Promoting Agriculture show that he also served as a trustee of that organization in the early 1790s. His manner may have kept him from top positions and from prolonged terms in office, but he clearly did participate in institutions unconnected with his father.

In the letterbooks (BCSC) is a poignant letter vis-à-vis his father that reveals the situation James Bowdoin III remained in all of his life. Dated 22 February 1809, it is addressed to James Temple Bowdoin, who had taken the name of Bowdoin, but, contrary to the terms spelled out, wished to live in England. The relevant portions of the letter read: "My original propositions to you were grounded upon no equivocal duties; nor on your part, did I suppose, that they rested on an equivocal acceptance, leaving to yourself a discretion upon the very point, which w.^d put it in your power to frustrate my father's wishes & my own expectations! . . . I will in all cases be sincere & do you justice, but I shall steadfastly adhere to the wishes & injunctions of my father in the

disposal of his & my own property. . . . It is certainly too late to explain away the most material motives to making you the proposition of succeeding to my father's name & estate." Three times he refers to his father's wishes, his name, even his "injunctions," and it seems that the condition of residence in the United States was the father's. That is also suggested, though not made explicit, in a letter of 11 September 1803 to James Temple Bowdoin (Sadik, 140), one that uses the terms "requirements & promises." James Bowdoin II, in extracting from the younger Bowdoin promises to carry out his "wishes," "requirements," "injunctions," did not necessarily know, on the basis of Sarah Bowdoin's age, that the marriage of his son and Sarah would remain childless. Sarah, born in 1761 (she had lived for some years in the Bowdoin household after she was orphaned), was, after all, in 1790, the year of the father's death, still of childbearing age. The marriage had, however, been childless for ten years, the wedding having taken place on 20 April 1780 (Sadik, 151). Although the elder Bowdoin did not necessarily know that the marriage would remain childless, a powerful piece of evidence suggests that he did. Just before the fifth anniversary of the marriage, on 1 March 1785, he withdrew from the Harvard College Library "Heath on Job," "Lowth on Prophets," and "Patricks Commentary." Two days later he took out "Paters on Job," "Scott's Job," and "Gray on Job." He was not a regular borrower, just a book or two a year only. This was an aberration, and very likely one stimulated by what he saw as a personal tragedy. In the Book of Job, the last tragedy to befall Job before he was himself covered with boils, was the death of his sons. Did James Bowdoin II learn for a certainty that from this marriage between cousins there would be no sons to carry on the family name?

68. Howard Mumford Jones, *America and French Culture, 1750-1848* (Chapel Hill, NC, 1927), 530-39, covers American views of the French Revolution from its start in 1789 up beyond the time of James Bowdoin's death.

69. William Bentley, *Diary of William Bentley, D.D.,* vol. 2, January 1793-December 1802 (Gloucester, MA: 1962), 3 (entry for 22 January).

70. Jeremy D. Popkin, "Journals: The New Face of News," in Robert Darnton and Daniel Roche, eds., *Revolution in Print: The Press in France, 1775-1800* (Berkeley and Los Angeles: University of California Press, 1989), 151.

71. Rutland, 25, 66.

72. *Thomas Jefferson's Library: A Catalog with the Entries in His Own Order,* ed. James Gilreath and Douglas L. Wilson (Washington, D.C.: Library of Congress, 1989), 127-31.

73. Appleton correspondence, BCSC. Vaughan must have been referring to Charles François Dupuis, *L'origine de tous les cultes, ou Religion universelle* (1795), 4v., in 4° or 12v. in 8°, a work that attempts to explain all religious beliefs by means of astronomy; see *Dictionnaire de biographie française* 12 (1970), 558. The work was not recorded in the inventory or catalog.

74. Bowdoin's lack of logical arrangement contrasts with Jefferson's, who arranged books broadly by subject, subdivided by size; see Gilreath and Wilson. There seems also to have been no subject order to the arrangement of

the books of James Bowdoin II, at least according to a partial inventory that gives indications of being in shelf order; see "The Bowdoin Library," *Proceedings of the Massachusetts Historical Society* 51 (1918): 362-68.

75. Gilreath and Wilson, 174.

76. Another portion of the inventory covered Naushon Island and the contents of the New Mansion House. It records "1 Secretary & Book case with books &c being locked could not be examined," the whole valued at $70. The inventory records no other books, certainly not a library, and refers to rooms as "room No. 1, on the right," etc. The inventory thus contrasts with a statement in Emerson, *Early History of Naushon Island*, 416, which is reprinted from *The Columbian Centinel* of 1825 and is dated 6 August 1825. The pertinent passage reads: "The drawing and sitting rooms appeared as though in a state of preparation for receiving company, and the library was well filled with books. In looking over them it is true that no production of a later date than 20 years was to be found to the utter exclusion of Scott and Byron, a leaf in a work upon chemistry turned down by the deceased owner [James Bowdoin III], and which he laid aside to open the pages of a future world, showed the bent of his genius. . . ." The above conveys that the house was left unmolested, and that agrees with a reminiscence printed in Emerson on pp. 409-10, which says that the family hurried to Boston after his death, in "a state almost of panic," and that the house remained precisely as left for seven or eight years. It is not possible to reconcile the inventory with the 1825 account.

77. After Jefferson approached Congress in 1814 about selling his library, he was asked to put a price on it. Unwilling to do so, he asked the Georgetown bookseller Joseph Milligan to suggest an average price. Milligan came up with $10 for a folio; $6 for a quarto; $3 for an octavo, and $1 for a duodecimo; see Gilreath and Wilson, 158. The appraisers of Bowdoin's library placed a value on each book. Duodecimos ranged from 50 cents to $1.50, with a very few lower or higher, and octavos ranged from 75 cents to $2.50, with a few at other prices. Quartos showed much wider variation, starting from $3 but going as high as $10 for the splendid 1780 Madrid (Ibarra) *Don Quixote* in Spanish as well as a few other works.

78. John Abbot sent a list of them to Thomas L. Winthrop in a letter of 21 December 1811, BCSC.

79. 12° = duodecimo; 8° = octavo; 4° = quarto; 2^O = folio. These refer to the number of leaves, a leaf being two pages, into which the sheet of paper is folded after printing. The fewer the number of folds, the larger the book. Folios generally are 30 cm. or somewhat taller; quartos 19 cm. or a bit more; octavos 15 cm. or so; and duodecimos are 12.5 cm. or more.

80. *Histoire des bibliothèques françaises: Les bibliothèques sous l'Ancien Régime 1530-1789, sous la direction de Claude Jolly* (Paris, 1988), 222. For an illustration of the usual arrangement, with the smallest books on the top shelves and the folios on the bottom shelves, see Gilreath and Wilson, [viii].

81. Letter of Thomas L. Winthrop to James Bowdoin, 28 July 1807, reel 21 of the Winthrop Papers.

82. Since the catalog prepared by Abbot begins with folios, apparently placed on a top shelf in the course of unpacking, could it be that the books noted as being in case 3 were also unpacked after being transported to the Beacon Street house from elsewhere, even from Naushon Island? The question presents itself, but the inventory of furnishings at Naushon records no such bookcases.

83. Kershaw, 98.

84. There is no indication that the resignation was prompted by ill will. In fact, a letter to George Erving of 2 November 1799 refers to purchasing a thermometer for Harvard.

85. The records of the Harvard Corporation record votes on book purchases.

86. See Harvard University Archives, UA III.50.15.70.2 (folder 2).

87. It was particularly appropriate that he should emulate Harvard in buying for the College in Maine, because it was seen as similar to that in Cambridge. The 1791 bill proposing to incorporate the College stated that it should enjoy "the advantages, privileges, immunities, franchises, and exemptions" granted to Harvard College. The General Court, in chartering the College, also established a system of governance similar to Harvard's. See Jurgen Herbst, *From Crisis to Crisis: American College Government 1636-1819* (Cambridge, MA: Harvard University Press, 1982), 215-16.

88. Benjamin Vaughan's copy is recorded on p. 107 of *Catalogue of the Library of Bowdoin College, in Brunswick, Maine* (Brunswick: 1821), under a section of "Books Deposited in the Library by a Friend of the College." The friend is known to be Benjamin Vaughan.

89. Gilreath and Wilson, 132-33.

90. In a letter in the Harvard University Archives, College Papers, 3:94, to Ebenezer Storer, Harvard's treasurer, dated 21 June 1796, Bowdoin notes that on 5 July he will be on his way to Hallowell. He could have been visiting Daniel Cony, but this may be a sign of contact with the great Hallowell collector, Benjamin Vaughan.

91. Appleton correspondence, BCSC.

Starred works are reproduced in color in this chapter. All books illustrated are from Special Collections, Hawthorne-Longfellow Library, Bowdoin College.

*1. Pierre Bulliard. *Herbier de la France, ou Collection complète des plantes indigènes de cet empire* (Paris, 1780–93), 3 text vols.; 6 plate vols. Plate vol. 1 (Plates 97–192): plate 100, *Champignon de la France.*

2. Bowdoin bookplate, inserted by the College in the volumes bequeathed by James Bowdoin III.

3. A Catalogue of Books of the late Hon. James Bowdoin Esq. together with his Cabinet of Minerals, & philosophical Instruments, left by will to the President & Trustees of Bowdoin College, p. 1. Compiled by John Abbot, the agent of the College. The catalogue of James Bowdoin's "Library of books, his Cabinet of minerals, and his philosophical instruments" is dated 3 December 1811. The last part of the bequest to be inventoried is the "Catalogue of Pictures," which is dated 5 February 1813.

4. The bookplate inserted in volumes acquired with the 1802 gift of Madam Elizabeth Bowdoin, mother of James Bowdoin III.

5. *Encyclopaedia Britannica* (Edinburgh, 1797). Vol. 1: frontispiece.

6. James Bowdoin to the Overseers and Corporation of Bowdoin College, 27 June 1794, announcing his intention to make a gift of money and lands. This copy is in the first volume of the Letter-books of outgoing correspondence.

*7. A selection of multi-volume sets belonging to James Bowdoin III.

*8. *Gazette nationale, ou le Moniteur universel,* 1789–1807. 36 vols.

9. *A Catalogue of Books in Various Branches of Literature, and in the Oriental, Greek, Latin, Saxon, French & English Languages: To be Sold on Thursday, May 27th, at Samuel Bradford's Auction-Room in Boston* (Salem, 1802). Title page.

10. Michael Symes. *An Account of an Embassy to the Kingdom of Ava* (London, 1800). Plate facing p. 298.

11. James Bowdoin to Jesse Putnam, 30 June 1802. P. 2.

*12. Alexander Wilson. *American Ornithology* (Philadelphia, 1808–14). Vols. 1–3 of 9 (1808–11). Vol. 1, plate 1.

13. Book label of the Parisian bookseller Théophile Barrois, ca. 1805.

14. *Catalogue of books belonging to Ja.^{s} Bowdoin taken at Paris Nov. 5.th, 1806.* P. 1.

15. *Debates, Resolutions and Other Proceedings of the Convention of the Commonwealth of Massachusetts* (Boston, 1788).

16. Louis Hennepin. *Nouvelle decouverte d'un tres grand pays situé dans l'Amerique entre le nouveau Mexique, et la mer glaciale* (Amsterdam, 1698). Engraved title page.

17. *The Federalist: A Collection of Essays, Written in Favour of the New Constitution* (New York, 1788). Vol. 1, p. 17.

18. Richard Rolt. *A New Dictionary of Trade and Commerce, Compiled from the Information of the most Eminent Merchants, and from the Works of the best Writers on Commercial Subjects, in all Languages* (London, 1756). Frontispiece.

19. [James Bowdoin III]. *Opinions Respecting the Commercial Intercourse between the United States of America, and the Dominions of Great-Britain, including Observations upon the Necessity and Importance of an American Navigation Act.* By a Citizen of Massachusetts (Boston, 1797). Title page.

20. *Collection complète des Tableaux historiques de la Révolution française* (Paris, 1802–04). Vol. 1: frontispiece.

21. Johann Joalchim Winckelmann. *Histoire de l'art chez les anciens* (Paris, 1794–95). Vol. 1: frontispiece and title page.

22. *Catalogue of the Library of Bowdoin College, in Brunswick, Maine* (Brunswick: Printed by Joseph Griffin, 1821). Title page.

FIG. 1 Specimens of hematite from the James Bowdoin III mineral collection.

JAMES BOWDOIN III AND GEOLOGY AT BOWDOIN COLLEGE

Arthur M. Hussey II

From approximately 1802 to 1806, James Bowdoin III (fig. 2) (color on p. 66) obtained all the books on mineralogy available at the time. Among his library, now housed in Bowdoin College's Special Collections, are *Traité élémentaire de minéralogie* by A. J. M. Brochant, *Tableau méthodique des Espèces Minérales,* by J. A. H. Lucas, *Traité Elémentaire de Minéralogie,* by Alexandre Brongniart, *Traité de Minéralogie,* by René-Just Haüy, and *System of Mineralogy and Metalurgy,* by Thomas Dodson.

Bowdoin's interest in mineralogy seems to have been motivated, at least in part, by his desire to establish economic mineral industries, particularly in his home state of Massachusetts. In 1809, Bowdoin wrote to William Maclure (1763-1840), eminent English mineral collector and geologist, requesting that Maclure purchase for him all the works of the distinguished English mineralogist Robert Jameson (1774-1854). He wrote to Maclure: "I observe that his mineralogical descriptions of the County of Dunfries suggest the method for searching for coal, which I suppose must make it interesting to be known in the U. S."[1] He also indicated his desire to establish a commercial salt works at his estate on Naushon Island, largest of the Elizabeth Islands, southwest of Falmouth, Massachusetts. He sought all the technical data for evaporating basin design and operation that was available to Maclure in England and France in order to design a similar facility at the family estate. No later correspondence indicates whether any success came of the venture.

In 1806, while living in France, James Bowdoin III purchased a collection of minerals and crystal models from the Reverend René-Just Haüy (1743-1822), professor and curator of minerals at the School of Mines in Paris. Reverend Haüy is regarded as the "father of geometrical crystallography" and was one of the leading mineralogists of his time (fig. 3). His *Traité de Minéralogie,* published in 1801, present-ed outstanding descriptions and illustrations of the geometric shapes of crystals. Haüy developed the idea that crystals are built up of countless small simple geometric units, an idea that greatly influenced modern crystallogic theory and has survived in our present-day concept of unit cells in the ionic configuration of crystal structure (fig. 4). He also formulated several significant laws of crystallography that still guide our reasoning today.

The collection purchased by James Bowdoin was assembled and catalogued from the extensive resources of the Haüy lab by J. A. Henry Lucas in 1806.[2] Mr. Lucas, the son of Jean-François Lucas, the "curator of the galleries" under Reverend Haüy, worked as Haüy's laboratory assistant, and was later to become a noted mineralogist in his own right (one of the books acquired by Bowdoin was his *Tableau methodique des Espèces Minérales).* According to Lucas's catalogue, the original collection consisted of 439 minerals and 58 ceramic crystal models, to which were later added an additional 300 or so crystal models illustrating most of the principal crystal forms pictured in Haüy's monumental five-volume *Traité de Minéralogie,* originally published in 1801 (fig. 5).

Specimens of the James Bowdoin Collection are generally small, averaging 2 x 3 x 3 cm (figs. 1 and 6). Most specimens are minerals, some with well-developed crystals or crystal groups. Some were rock specimens, a few were fossils, and some were:

curios, such as a calcified birds nest, an asphalt-saturated piece of linen from an Egyptian mummy, cast pieces of tin, lead, bismuth, antimony and chemicals made in the laboratory, such as salammoniac and blue vitriol. . . . One amusing example is specimen 249, classed under "substances metallic." It is a lump of melted and oxidized lead, the result of a bolt of lightning striking a lunatic asylum in Paris, France.[3]

The mineral specimens are mostly from localities in France but range over much of Europe and even into Siberia. Few, if any, are from the

F I G . 2 Gilbert Stuart, *Portrait of James Bowdoin III* (1752–1811).

United States. It is not likely that Haüy and his associates traveled overseas.

The crystal models average 3 x 2 x 2 cm, are made from baked clay and glazed with a brownish paint. Numbers scratched into them before firing correspond with those of crystals illustrated in the fifth volume of Haüy's treatise (figs. 7 and 10). Describing a visit he made to Bowdoin in 1975, the late Neil Yedlin, then curator of minerals at the Smithsonian Institution, observed of the crystal models:

Some of the mineral specimens of the Cleaveland Cabinet were very fine; some were good. Some were, well, historic. But those crystal models of baked clay were astounding! How was Haüy able to maintain accurate interfacial angles after they had been in a kiln for hardening? Or were they merely models to illustrate crystal habits to his students? We didn't measure them, nor, in the final analysis, do we care. There they are, evidence of the working of a great mind in the field of geology.[4]

In 1806, from William Maclure, Bowdoin acquired 119 specimens of rocks and minerals, mostly from localities in France, Switzerland, and England, but a few from the United States. Among those from the United States are garnet from Franconia Notch, New Hampshire; garnet and tremolite from Newbury, Massachusetts; epidote from Portsmouth, New Hampshire; garnet-bearing granite from Tyngsboro, New Hampshire, and Bedford, Massachusetts; and anthracite coal from Rhode Island.

The Haüy and Maclure materials constitute the James Bowdoin III collection, which was bequeathed to Bowdoin College on James Bowdoin's death in 1811. Unfortunately, over the years since their acquisiton, the identity of many of the Maclure specimens has been lost; they are probably among the numerous specimens for which labels are now missing. In the donor file only twelve specimens are positively identified as coming from Maclure to James Bowdoin. It appears that these specimens were acquired directly through Bowdoin's transactions with Maclure and had nothing to do with Haüy and his associates. After emigrating to and settling in the United States in 1796, Maclure began extensive geological mapping in this country, earning the title of "father of American geology."

In 1805 Parker Cleaveland (1780-1858) (fig. 8) was appointed to the newly created professorship of mathematics and natural and experimental philosophy at Bowdoin. It was not until the spring of 1808, however, that Cleaveland delivered his first lectures on chemistry and mineralogy. When he came to Bowdoin, he had no training in mineralogy or geology, but these subjects interested him. George Merrill describes the awakening of Cleaveland's interest in mineralogy:

His interest . . . was aroused more or less accidentally, his attention having been called to crystals of mica, quartz, and pyrite which were found by workmen engaged in blasting a ledge in the adjacent town of Topsham. On the not unnatural supposition that these might be of value, they were referred to the college professor who in this particular instance knew nothing specifically, and had only a faint idea where to look for information. After pursuing the mineral portion of Chaptal's *Mineralogy* and making provisional determinations, he packed a box of the specimens and sent them to Dr. Dexter, then professor of chemistry at Harvard, who verified the determinations, and sent a small collection of named minerals in return. Thus began the career of one who was to take front rank in forwarding the science of mineralogy in America.[5]

Cleaveland was also encouraged to become involved with mineralogy and geology by Benjamin Vaughan (1751-1835) of Hallowell, Maine.[6] Vaughan, who had moved to Maine just before the arrival of Cleaveland at Bowdoin, had resided for some time in England and France and had been educated in medicine and geology at the University of Edinburgh. There he must have been influenced directly by the founder of modern geology, James Hutton. Vaughan corresponded with Cleaveland over many years and sent him many specimens. In May of 1808, he wrote to Cleaveland: "I am glad that the work of a cabinet of minerals at Brunswick is begun. To him that hath, shall more be given. If I see anything which may be useful I will send it."[7] On 26 August 1808, Vaughan wrote again:

I shall send you a few specimens of minerals, but I expect many more. I am in hopes to persuade a friend to undertake to engage Mr. Bowdoin to make you a present of a collection of minerals bought very cheaply through Mr. Godon. . . . With your contributions to the college and others through Maine, added to the above, the college will begin to be noted for its collection, and these things always increase, where there is a beginning made, and active friends. I begin to think that Maine may be celebrated for its minerals in future times.[8]

In a letter dated 30 July 1810, Vaughan writes that he is sending Cleaveland more specimens, but he notes:

[it] is trifling to what you are likely soon to receive by the will of Mr. Bowdoin. He is very fast declining. But this from reasons of delicacy and interest, the friends of the college must keep to themselves. You will at the same time have his collection of minerals; and as I conjecture, something handsome in the way of funds.[9]

The James Bowdoin Collection came to the College upon the death of Bowdoin in 1811 at the age of fifty-nine. In addition to books, rock and mineral specimens, and crystal models, Bowdoin donated a modest amount of laboratory equipment for use in all fields of science, including a goniometer for crystallographic measurements. None of this equipment has survived in the inventory of the Department of Geology. There is no indication that the funds alluded to by Vaughan were included in the bequest.

FIG. 3 *Portrait of Réné-Just Haüy* (1743-1822), pioneer crystallographer and mineralogist.

Shortly after their arrival at the College, Parker Cleaveland prepared a handwritten catalogue of the mineral and rock specimens, and the crystal models (fig. 9). He identified the specimens with small yellow oval tabs and catalogue numbers in black (fig. 11).

The arrival of this collection and Haüy's mineralogical treatise was most opportune.[10] Cleaveland was preparing the manuscript for the first edition of his *Elementary Treatise on Mineralogy and Geology*, subsequently published in Boston in 1816 by Cummings and Hilliard. Cleaveland drew extensively on the work of Haüy, especially in the nomenclature of crystals and the classification of minerals by chemistry alone. Cleaveland does refer to Frederick Accum's *Elements of Crystallography, after the*

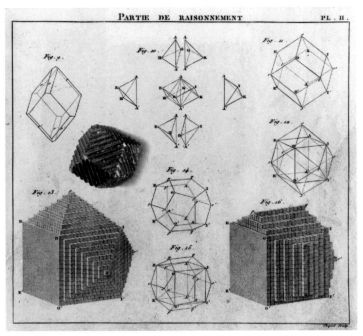

FIG. 4 Illustration from Haüy's *Traité de Minéralogie*, showing his concept of the makeup of crystals by small unit blocks, and a similar ceramic crystal model from the collection of the Department of Geology, part of the collection obtained by James Bowdoin III from the Réné-Just Haüy laboratory.

Method of Haüy, London, 1813,[11] but the College's acquisition of Haüy's book from James Bowdoin III preceded the publication of Accum's *Elements*. It is most likely that Haüy's treatise directly influenced Cleaveland's thinking and organization of his own work. Certainly the mineral specimens from different parts of Europe added significantly to the raw material Cleaveland needed to compile his work.

Cleaveland's treatise (fig. 12) was the first book on mineralogy published in the United States and immediately gained wide acceptance and esteem. George Merrill notes: "with the exception of Maclure's *Observations on the Geology of North America* undoubtedly the most important of the early publications was Parker Cleave--land's *Elementary Treatise on Mineralogy and Geology . . . .*"[12] A second edition in two volumes was published in 1819. Vaughan's influence on Cleaveland's work is clearly indicated by the fact that Cleaveland dedicated both editions to Vaughan. His dedication of the first edition states:

You will not, I trust, be displeased, and the Public, I am assured, will not be surprised, that I should embrace this favorable opportunity of addressing you, as the patron of general literature, and more especially of Natural Science.

It is indeed, an *elementary treatise only*, which is here offered to your notice. But it is no small encouragement to those, who are anxious to promote the progress of Mineralogy and Geology, to know, that these branches of knowledge receive the patronage and attention of such, as have, like yourself, devoted a large portion of life to the cultivation and improvement of deeper and more abstruse sciences.[13]

In the geology portion of both the first and second editions, Cleaveland was influenced by the Neptunist philosophy of the eminent German mineralogist Abraham Gotlob Werner, who believed that nearly all rocks were formed by water. Cleaveland classified rocks by their mode of creation as 1) volcanic, 2) aqueous, 3)

TRAITÉ

DE

MINÉRALOGIE,

PAR LE C^{EN}. HAÜY,

Membre de l'Institut National des Sciences et Arts, et Conservateur des Collections minéralogiques de l'École des Mines.

PUBLIÉ PAR LE CONSEIL DES MINES.

En cinq volumes, dont un contient 86 planches.

TOME PREMIER.

DE L'IMPRIMERIE DE DELANCE.

A PARIS,

CHEZ LOUIS, LIBRAIRE, RUE DE SAVOYE, N°. 12.

(X) 1801.

FIG. 5 Title page from Volume 1 of Réné-Just Haüy's *Traité de Minéralogie*.

FIG. 6 Specimens of calcite (right and center) and selenite (left) from the James Bowdoin III mineral collection.

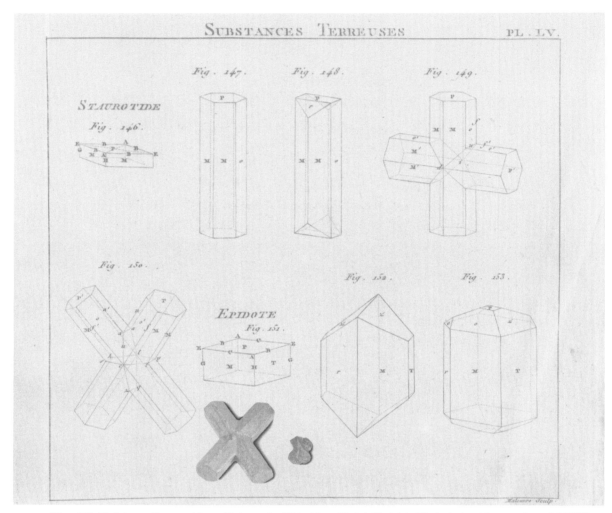

FIG. 7 Plate LV (*Substances Terreuses*) from Volume 5 of Réné-Just Haüy's *Traité de Minéralogie*, with crystal model 150T and a crystal of staurolite from the James Bowdoin III collection.

alluvial, 4) primative, or 5) transitional (the latter two being precipitates in the ocean). We have no record of discussions Vaughan might have had with Cleaveland to convince him to embrace the new ideas of James Hutton, particularly about the molten origin of granite, but if they happened they were of no avail. Cleaveland wrote a third edition of the book, but because of his refusal to give up Neptunism when all others were rejecting it, the book was not published.[14]

After Parker Cleaveland's death in 1858, his son-in-law, Peleg Chandler, financed the renovation of the top floor of Massachusetts Hall as a museum to house the College's and Cleaveland's extensive collections. At the dedication of the museum in 1873, Nehemiah Cleaveland, Parker's nephew, proposed the name "Cleaveland Cabinet" for these collections, and this is the name still used today for the College's mineral, rock, and fossil collections:

The Cabinet contained the James Bowdoin Collection in two large showcases on the north wall; in other cases around the room were Cleaveland's private collection and the large college collection he had assembled. In the center of the floor was the Shattuck Shell Collection in glass-topped cases. For many years following, the James Bowdoin Collection was often referred to as the Haüy Collection.[15]

The subsequent fate of the Cleaveland Cabinet (fig. 13) and with it the James Bowdoin Collection is described by Benjamin B. Burbank

132

'26 in large part from his own experiences as a Bowdoin College student, serious mineral collector, and longtime resident of Brunswick:

The college was expanding quite rapidly and therefore space for classrooms and offices became a problem. It first resulted in selling the Shattuck Shell Collection to clear the main floor, and next moving some minerals and display cabinets to the Searles Science Building where classes in mineralogy were being held. When more space was required, during the teens and early twenties, it was decided to cull the remaining specimens in Massachusetts Hall, eliminating what appeared to be the least spectacular material. Well over a thousand specimens were destined for the dump, including a considerable portion of the James Bowdoin Collection. Samuel Furbish, then treasurer of the college, asked for and was given the entire lot of culls which he placed in storage in a shed back of his brother's hardware store in Brunswick where it remained well into the 1930's. In the spring of 1938 the brother, Benjamin Furbish, contacted me, knowing my interest in minerals, and offered the entire lot because he needed the space they occupied. Again space problems were hounding the Cleaveland Cabinet of Minerals. Needless to say

FIG. 8 *Portrait of Professor Parker Cleaveland* (1780-1858).

the boxes and barrels of specimens were accepted and placed in dry storage for examination at leisure. What may have appeared dull and uninteresting to those doing the culling, was often historically valuable. The years in the shed back of the hardware store resulted in many of the labels falling off, rotting or otherwise becoming lost so that tracing back to the original collection is very difficult, involving much detective work and ingenuity. However, some of the specimens have been identified and returned to the collection at the college.

Even after the Cleaveland Cabinet had been rigorously culled it occupied too much space and finally it was boxed and placed in the basement of the college chapel, a humid and often wet place where labels molded, fell off and rotted. Some specimens were stolen.[16]

In 1956 a separate Department of Geology was established for the first time in the history of the College, and the late Marc W. Bodine, Jr., was appointed assistant professor and chairman. He recognized the historical significance of the collection and began a systematic recataloging. He, too, became aware of the decrepit condition of the boxed collections in the basement of the

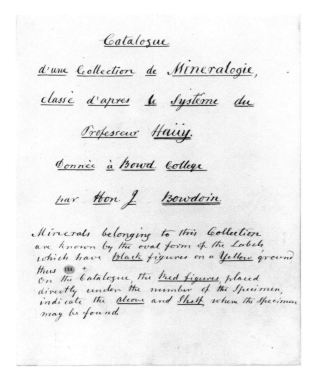

FIG. 9 *Catalogue d'une Collection de Mineralogie, classè d'apres le Systême du Professor Haüy. Donnèe à Bowd. College par Hon. J. Bowdoin.* Title page from the catalogue of the James Bowdoin III collection (ca. 1811), in Parker Cleaveland's handwriting.

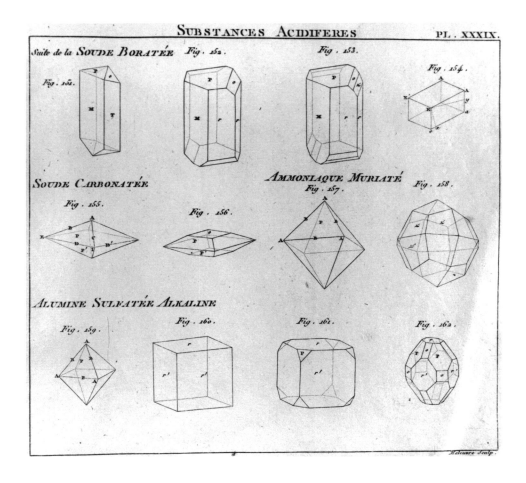

FIG. 10 Plate XXXIX *(Substances Acidiferes)* from Volume 5 of Réné-Just Haüy's *Traité de Minéralogie*, and five corresponding Haüy crystal models from the James Bowdoin III collection.

FIG. 11 Specimens of different varieties of quartz from the James Bowdoin III mineral collection, showing the oval black-on-yellow label that identifies this collection.

Chapel and in the storage space beneath the large lecture room in the biology side of Searles Science Building. As time and space allowed he moved the collections to the geology labs, then in Cleaveland Hall, and commenced the tedious chore of identifying specimens, correlating them to the different collections through the use of Cleaveland's original catalogues. Many specimens without documentation or catalogue number were merely added to the accession catalogue by mineral name, with hopes that future study would bring about correlation with the Cleaveland catalogues. I continued these efforts after I was appointed in 1961 to fill the position vacated by Professor Bodine. Large wooden cabinets with three tiers of drawers were constructed for the collection by the F. O. Bailey Company of Portland, Maine. Rock specimens and fossils were housed in metal storage cabinets and in wooden trays in steel shelving in the steam room of Cleaveland. Lack of space still hindered the proper care of these collections.

When the Department of Geology was moved in 1966 to newly renovated quarters in the basement of Hubbard Hall, more space was available and additional cabinets were built. Shortly after the move to Hubbard Hall, Benjamin B. Burbank

'26 volunteered his services to continue the recataloguing of the mineral collections and to devise public displays of the more significant materials. He prepared the display of the James Bowdoin Mineral Collection that can be seen in the first floor foyer of Hubbard Hall, along with other significant parts of the Cleaveland Cabinet. He also wrote the two most detailed studies of the history of the collection, one published in *Maine Geology* in 1982, and one published posthumously in the *Mineralogical Record* in 1988.

During the course of recataloguing, I made available to Mr. Burbank a drawer full of ceramic crystal models, not realizing their significance. Were they merely teaching materials used in mineralogy courses and laboratories? Searching the archives of the College, Burbank discovered a catalogue describing the crystal models that had been purchased by James Bowdoin. More research revealed that the catalogue pertained to the ceramic crystal models that had been shunted from box to drawer over the decades. A part of the James Bowdoin Collection long considered lost was found.

Inquiries of other institutions that might have acquired similar material revealed that these crystal models constitute a unique collection in

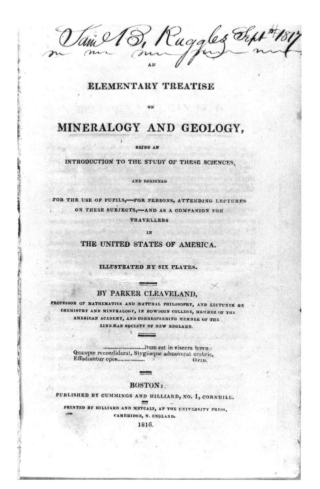

FIG.12 Title page of the first edition (1816) of Parker Cleaveland's *Elementary Treatise on Mineralogy and Geology.*

North America. No other institution has similar material from the laboratory of Haüy. For a large representative selection of these models, Mr. Burbank prepared the display that occupies a cabinet at the rear of the main teaching laboratory in the basement of Hubbard Hall.

Because of the importance of any collections that might contain mineral specimens and crystal models obtained from Reverend Haüy, considerable interest in the Bowdoin College holdings emerged in the 1970s. Apparently the only other collection of Haüy minerals is the collection of 429 small specimens given to Laval University, Quebec City, Province of Quebec, in 1816 by the Reverend Jean-Louis Desjardins, a friend of Reverend Haüy. The collection is reported in

correspondence as having been prepared by Henry Lucas under the supervision of Reverend Haüy.[17] Correspondence between René Bureau, curator of Laval University's Department of Geology, and officials in France at the Ecole Nationale Superieure des Mines and at the Museum National d'Histoire Naturelle, with which Haüy was associated until his death, indicate that, although Haüy's personal collection is kept at the National Museum, specimens selected and catalogued by Henry Lucas were from materials in Haüy's lab. The librarian at the Ecole Nationale Superieure des Mines assured M. Bureau that: "The collection of minerals which was given to Le Seminaire de Quebec in 1816 and classified by Henry Lucas, is perfectly authentic and precious, as Lucas was always working under the supervision and guidance of Haüy."[18] We can with reasonable confidence regard the Haüy materials of the Bowdoin Collection as equally authentic.

James Bowdoin III contributed to the development of mineralogy and geology at Bowdoin in another very significant way. Shortly after the signing of the Charter of the College by John Adams, governor of Massachusetts, in 1794, James Bowdoin III made a gift of "eight hundred and twenty three pounds, four shillings . . . and requested that it be used for the endowment of a chair of mathematics and natural and experimental philosophy."[19] This was in addition to his initial gift of 1,000 acres in the township of Bowdoin, Maine, and 300 pounds (roughly $1,000). It was through this endowment that Parker Cleaveland was elected to the faculty of Bowdoin College on 23 October 1805 and became the first professor of mathematics and natural and experimental philosophy. He offered the first courses in mineralogy shortly thereafter, holding classes and labs in the president's laundry in what is now Massachusetts Hall until appropriate space was made available.

Those of us who constitute the Department of Geology (Professor Hussey, Associate Professor Laine, and Assistant Professor Lea) are indebted to the scientific insight and generosity of James Bowdoin III, and to Parker Cleaveland, who

FIG. 13 The Cleaveland Cabinet in Massachusetts Hall, ca. 1890s.

began geological instruction at the College approximately 190 years ago. We honor these people in Bowdoin's history by offering a geology major and encouraging interdisciplinary studies between geology and the other science disciplines, as well as environmental studies. We recognize the importance and the uniqueness of the Haüy mineralogy and crystallography collection by providing public display of part of the material, and care of all of the material. Haüy's crystal models are now too precious to commit to instructional use in mineralogy laboratories; modern, mass-produced crystal models are used instead.

NOTES

BCSC is Special Collections, Hawthorne-Longfellow Library, Bowdoin College.

1. James Bowdoin III to William Maclure, 26 January 1809, BCSC.
2. Benjamin B. Burbank, "James Bowdoin and Parker Cleaveland" in *Mineralogical Record* 19 (1988): 145.
3. Ibid., 147.
4. Neil Yedlin, "Yedlin on Micromounting," *Mineralogical Record* 7: 31.
5. George P. Merrill, *The First Hundred Years of American Geology* (New Haven, CT: Yale University Press, 1924), 45.
6. Vandall King, personal communication, 1992. For more on Benjamin Vaughan, see Kenneth E. Carpenter, "James Bowdoin III as Library Builder," in this book, 85.
7. Benjamin Vaughan to Parker Cleaveland, Hallowell, 26 May 1808. BCSC.
8. Benjamin Vaughan to Parker Cleaveland, Hallowell, 26 August 1808. BCSC.
9. Benjamin Vaughan to Parker Cleaveland, Hallowell, 30 July 1810. BCSC.
10. Much of the material for this section comes from Benjamin B. Burbank, "The James Bowdoin Mineral Collection," *Maine Geology,* bulletin no. 2, 1982: 71-79.
11. On page 27.
12. Merrill, p. 42.
13. Parker Cleaveland, *Elementary Treatise on Mineralogy and Geology* (Boston: Cummings and Hilliard, 1816), dedication.
14. The third edition, part galley proofs and part manuscript, is in BCSC.
15. Burbank, 1982, 146.
16. Ibid.
17. Private communication, René Bureau, curator of Laval University's Department of Geology, to Benjamin Burbank, 1976. Copy of letter in Department of Geology files, Hubbard Hall, Bowdoin College.
18. B. Gauthier, librarian, Ecole Nationale Superieure des Mines, to René Bureau, curator of Laval University's Department of Geology Museum, 1976. Copy of letter in Department of Geology files, Hubbard Hall, Bowdoin College.
19. Lewis C. Hatch, *The History of Bowdoin College* (Portland, ME: Loring, Short, and Harmon, 1927), 8.

Starred works are printed in color in this chapter. All books photographed for this chapter except nos. 9 and 12 are in Special Collections, Hawthorne-Longfellow Library, Bowdoin College. The minerals are in the collection of the Department of Geology, Bowdoin College.

FIG. 1 Anonymous, *Venus and Adonis*

COPIES AND EDUCATION

James Bowdoin's Painting Collection in the Life of the College

Susan E. Wegner

Visitors to the Walker Art Building most often encounter James Bowdoin III's gift of art to the College in Gilbert Stuart's two noble portraits of Thomas Jefferson (fig. 2) and James Madison (fig. 3) (color pp. 14 and 15).[1] These two "stars" of the collection, which appear on postcards and slides, are well known outside of Brunswick. They have traveled on loan to other museums and have illustrated countless retellings of our nation's early history. In stark contrast to these familiar faces are the other sixty-eight oil paintings and eleven prints that comprised the rest of Bowdoin's great gift. Bequeathed to the nascent College at his death in 1811, these works, mentioned in Bowdoin's will as "all my pictures excepting family pictures," remain for the most part unseen and unmentioned, described most recently as "largely copies after old masters" in the *Handbook of the Collections*.[2] While Bowdoin's drawings collection and the family portraits have both been the subjects of major catalogues and exhibitions,[3] his collection of European works has never been treated as a whole, nor has even a full handlist been prepared.

The happy occasion of the College's Bicentennial provides an opportunity to examine this unseen majority of paintings and to ask why, at nearly two centuries' remove from the original bequest, we display only a fragment of Bowdoin's collection. Was Bowdoin's gift of art not as valuable as he believed? Are those copies unworthy of display in a serious museum in twentieth-century America?

This essay will trace the changing fortunes of copies after Old Master works and how these fortunes affected the perception of James Bowdoin's painting collection over time. We shall see how during their first century here the works, especially the copies after Old Masters, were lauded and displayed. At mid-century they were pruned of objectionable subject matter,

and later augmented by other monumental copies after ancient and Renaissance masters. During their second century at Bowdoin College, we see some of them dispersed and others relegated to storerooms as the presence of "copies" becomes an increasing embarrassment to a culture that privileges "originality."[4] Finally, the uneasy place Bowdoin's paintings—both copies and originals—hold today as objects of substantial historic, but limited aesthetic, interest highlights our own current assumptions about art's value within a liberal arts education.

GENESIS OF JAMES BOWDOIN III'S PAINTING COLLECTION

The seventy paintings and eleven prints that concern us here were amassed from several sources. Many of them probably belonged at one time to Bowdoin's father, Governor James Bowdoin II (1726-1790). We know from an inventory of his goods in 1774 that he had an extensive collection of pictures,[5] although it cannot be determined exactly what these were. The inventory mentions "pictures" without giving subject, author, dimensions, or even medium. Thus, it is possible that family portraits, mezzotints, and perhaps even drawings are included along with European oil paintings under the label "pictures." Still, it seems likely that a portion of James Bowdoin III's paintings came from his father's estate, in particular, the "eight large ps painted in Italy" mentioned in the 1774 inventory.

It has long been thought that some of Bowdoin's paintings were at one time owned by or had even been painted by the Scottish-born American artist John Smibert (1688-1751). Several of the copies after Old Masters among Bowdoin's seventy paintings have been attributed to Smibert or connected with his studio.[6] These include the copies after Titian's *Education* of *Cupid* (no. 2), after Poussin's *Continence of Scipio* (no. 3) (fig. 26), after Titian's *Danaë and the Shower of Gold* (no. 4) (fig. 8), after van Dyck's *Jean de Montfort* (no. 33), after Raphael's *Virgin and Child with St. Elizabeth and St. John* (no. 44), after Tintoretto's *Luigi Cornaro* (no. 48), after Titian's *Venus and Adonis* (no. 51) (fig. 1) (Nos. correspond to the handlist on p. 172). The only attributions to Smibert himself that seem plausible are the portrait copies after van Dyck and Tintoretto. There is strong circumstantial evidence that others, such as the Poussin copy, were seen in Smibert's possession.

It has been suggested that Smibert's copies after Old Masters would have been valuable as teaching tools in Bishop George Berkeley's Bermuda College. Berkeley had envisioned a utopian college in America that would, among other things, inhibit the spread of Catholicism in the New World while contributing to the conversion of the indigenous peoples to Christianity. Berkeley had enlisted Smibert as his professor of fine arts for the projected college, and the artist set sail for America with Berkeley's Bermuda group in 1728, bringing along at least part of his art collection. Copies of Old Masters would not

FIG. 2 Gilbert Stuart, *Portrait of Thomas Jefferson*

only have instructed students in the fine arts, but religious themes or didactic histories such as Poussin's *Scipio* could well have provided moral instruction. Perhaps some of the dozen religious pictures that found their way into James Bowdoin III's collection were originally intended to help in "converting the Savage Americans to Christianity," (as Berkeley advertised in his 1724/25 pamphlet advocating the project).[7] Since we now know with certainty that part of Bowdoin's drawing collection was at one time owned by Smibert,[8] it is quite possible that some paintings came from this source.

Another source for Bowdoin's collection was France. Letters from Paris during James Bowdoin III's stint as minister plenipotentiary to Spain (1805-1808) tell us that he purchased and sent home at least thirty-four paintings of unknown subject and size.[9] French themes, French artists, and French printed matter used in framing identify over a dozen works as probably stemming from those Paris years.[10] These include *Sleeping Cupid* (no. 13); Courtois' *Landscape* (no. 16); *Infant St. John* (no. 17); Vouet's(?) *Entombment* (no. 25); Patel's *Landscape* (no. 26); Jouillain's three *Landscapes*

FIG. 3 Gilbert Stuart, *Portrait of James Madison*

FIG. 4 Anonymous, *Ariadne*

(nos. 27, 28, 29); after Boze and LeFèvre, *Mirabeau* (fig. 11); *Portrait of a Clergyman*(?) (no. 49); after LeBrun, *Head of a Woman* (no. 55); Manglard's *Sea Fight* (no. 67), and LaCroix's *Seaport* (no. 68). [11]

Finally, the two distinguished portraits by Stuart, the Jefferson and Madison, were specifically commissioned by Bowdoin before he left for Spain and may have been intended for his embassy residence there. These works were never sent abroad, since Bowdoin quickly moved to Paris to negotiate with the French overlords of Spain.

To shed light on Bowdoin's attitude toward his painting collection, we need to examine the state of collecting and display in America and France during the late eighteenth century and to compare his acquisitions to other private collections of the day.

THE STATUS OF COPIES IN JAMES BOWDOIN III'S DAY

For this essay we define copy as a version or facsimile created after a pre-existing work of art, aiming to record part or all of that work faithfully. There are "autograph copies" like the Stuart Jefferson and Madison portraits, second versions of an artist's work prepared by that same artist. Most of the copies in the Bowdoin group are not of this type, but are copies by later artists after designs invented by Old Masters such as Raphael, Titian, Rubens, and Poussin.

Copies of great works were produced in abundance from antiquity onwards. And the copying of great works made by admired masters had been a standard part of artistic education since the Renaissance.[12] To understand the role that copies played in the art world at the end of the eighteenth century, we have James Bowdoin's own pronouncements to guide us. Bowdoin prided himself on being able to distinguish copies from originals and high-quality copies of masterworks from those of lesser quality. His letters reveal his own judgment on his level of discernment. To President Thomas Jefferson, he writes on 22 March 1805:

Will you permit me to make a tender of my services in procuring for you any specimens of ye Arts, either in sculpture or painting: & although I am no adept, yet from having been in Italy & having viewed the works of ye best Masters, if you would entrust me with your Commissions, I would execute them in the best manner in my power. Accident having thrown in my way a handsome piece of Modern Sculpture, a Cleopatra copied & reduced from the ancient one now at Paris, which for many years lay at the Palace of Belvidere at Rome: as I think it for the fineness of its Marble & the Neatness of its workmanship & finishing, among the best of ye Modern pieces of Sculpture, you will do me the favour to accept it & to place it in a Corner of your hall at Monticello: for which purpose I shall take the liberty of shipping it to you by ye first convenient opportunity. I was told it was purchased of a french Commissary in Italy, who wanted money: & that it had been taken from the apartments in ye Vatican, which were built by Pope Ganganelli Clement ye 14th, who was liberal as a Pope, & distinguished as a man of Taste & Learning.[13]

Bowdoin offers Jefferson a fine copy after a famous antique *Cleopatra* (fig. 4) (now known to

FIG. 6 Anonymous, *A Sculptor's Studio*

FIG. 5 Anonymous, *A Painter's Studio*

be *Ariadne*), one of the canon of revered ancient sculptures that Bowdoin had seen during his grand tour in 1774.[14] His comments on the little copy of the Cleopatra show that he is sensitive to the nature of modern versions after old masterpieces. He is alive to the nuances of workmanship and material and takes pains to establish the sculpture's provenance in the collections of men of taste and learning.

Jefferson seems not to have taken Bowdoin up on his offer to find art for him, but was pleased with the *Cleopatra*, saying, in a letter of 27 April 1805, that he would deposit it with "the memorials of those worthies, whose remembrance I feel a pride and comfort in consecrating there."[15] Part of the cachet of the sculpture for both men is the perceived theme—Cleopatra.[16] Bowdoin had owned the statue since 1802[17] and at the time of his death had an image of the tragic monarch in his painting collection (fig. 15). And it matters little that his gift to Jefferson was a scaled-down copy since it transmits the information of importance—the theme and the shape of the well-regarded antique work—in a pleasing, well-worked material.

A second comment by Bowdoin regarding copies in his own collection is found in his instructions regarding the shipping of paintings he had acquired in France. The letter, dated 13

FIG. 7 Frans Francken, the Younger, *Esther before Ahasueras*

May 1806, reads in part: "they are good pictures, original except in one or two instances and have been bought at small price."[18] Bowdoin believed himself capable of distinguishing good quality in both copies and originals and demonstrates no prejudice against acquiring the former. A survey of Bowdoin's seventy paintings reveals that at least a quarter of them are copies. It is impossible to state which works Bowdoin knew to be copies, but in the handlist prepared in 1813,[19] five are listed as copies after, or works in the style of, Old Masters.

Copies play a large role in a collection contemporary with Bowdoin's—that of Thomas Jefferson. As early as 1771, Jefferson records his plan to ornament Monticello with casts of antique statues and copies of Old Master paintings.[20] All of the statues he desired would have had to have been plaster casts or replicas. Paintings to be acquired are thought of in terms of famous works "copied by a good hand."[21] Jefferson's inventory of 1809 lists scores of copies in his possession after Guido Reni,

Raphael, and others.[22] These works were valued for their moralizing content[23] as emblems of virtue or warnings against vice, more than for their "originality" as works of art, as we would define it today. That images could educate and instruct the viewer in moral values is explained by several influential eighteenth-century writers on art, notably Jonathan Richardson in his *Essay on the Theory of Painting* (1715) and Joshua Reynolds in his *Discourses* (1797).[24]

Richardson recognizes two major purposes of painting, to impart pleasure and to improve, with improvement being the more noble aim. This, of course, is a restatement of the ancient notion of painting's ability to instruct and delight, articulated in Renaissance and Baroque art theory, which surely informed Richardson's views. For Richardson, "a painting which conveys an edifying or instructive thought is better than one which is merely attractive."[25] History painting was deemed most likely to improve the mind, with portraiture ranking nearly as high. More pleasure-giving than instructive were still-life and landscape.

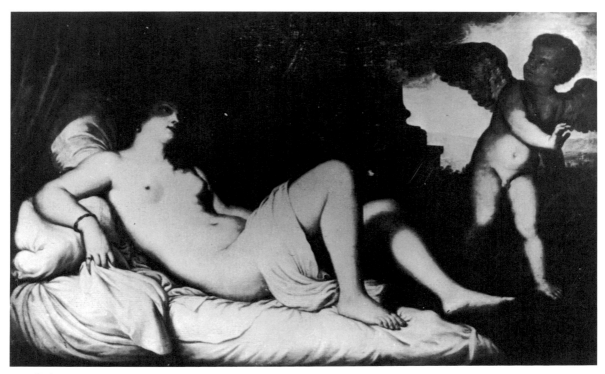

FIG. 8 Anonymous, *Danaë and the Shower of Gold*

It is clear that Richardson sees painting as fulfilling many of the same purposes as poetry, history, philosophy, and theology. Art, through its instructive powers, can reform manners and improve people.[26] Knowledge of many paintings can furnish the memory with beautiful images that then come to mind when reading history and literature. Richardson's restating of the Horatian dictum *Ut Pictura Poesis*, As is Painting, so is Poetry, sets painting very much within the context of modern education.

To serve such didactic functions, paintings need not be originals. They need only be of good quality and represent noble themes. Richardson states:

A copy of a very good picture is preferable to an indifferent original; for there the invention is seen almost entire, and a great deal of the expression and disposition and many times good hints of the colouring, drawing, and other qualities. An indifferent original hath nothing that is excellent, nothing that touches which such a copy I am speaking of hath.[27]

Indeed, within Richardson's rational science of connoisseurship, an interested viewer can be more certain of being able to perceive levels of quality than of being able to discern authorship or originality. Thus it is the perception of quality that is deemed most important.

This sense of placing good quality above originality is echoed in James Bowdoin III's statements cited above, and by many European and American collectors. The nineteenth-century French collector Charles de Brosses proclaimed his preference for copies: "I do not fret over acquiring originals by the great masters. For certain reasons of my own, I make no case for having originals by minor masters; I prefer beautiful copies of famous paintings, available at a price I can afford."[28] Jefferson's plan for the adornment of Monticello follows this same line of reasoning. Plaster casts of antiquities and copies "if copied by a good hand" far outnumber originals both in Jefferson's plan for his collection and in the final ornamenting of his home. Inventories of art sales in the British Isles around 1800 show that this attitude was widely shared. Hundreds of copies of Titians, Raphaels, and others were sold for substantial prices.[29]

DISPLAY OF ART IN COLLECTIONS AND MUSEUMS IN EIGHTEENTH-CENTURY FRANCE

James Bowdoin III's experience in Europe, particularly in Paris at the turn of the century, set him into a culture that was turbulent with debates on the functions and proper display of art. Foremost among these discussions in France was the accent on pedagogical purposes in the display of art. The period from 1750 to 1800 had seen the rise of the public museum in France, which greatly fostered this idea. The simple decorative motives that had characterized the hanging of private collections gave way to more reasoned and thoughtful arrangements. When the Museum National du Louvre opened in August 1793, the paintings were hung as in most private collections, that is, as a mixture of schools to show off contrasts between different types of painting. This mode followed the advice of earlier theorists like Félibien and Roger de Piles, who stressed knowledge of the excellence of the parts of painting. The ability to perceive quality in drawing, coloring, and other parts of painting was not limited to experts. All—amateurs, students of painting,

FIG. 9 Anonymous, *Adoration of the Magi*

artists—could participate. The eye would often travel in a zigzag over the wall of double- or triple-hung paintings, playing a Van Dyck off a Titian or a landscape against a still life. Indeed the great collector Mariette claimed to have learned immensely from the art and discussions held in collections like that of Crozat, the Duke of Orleans, and the 1750-1778 Luxembourg palace installation.[30]

However, at the opening of the Louvre in 1793, critics attacked this mixed-school mode of picture hanging, while the first museum commission defended its hanging strongly. Both sides argued for their point of view on the grounds of instruction. The commission defended the old model as a sure and rapid way of forming the taste and developing the genius of students.

The dealer Jean-Baptiste-Pierre LeBrun, who had helped form some important French collections of the 1780s, was one of the most vocal critics of the Louvre hanging:

It seems to me that a student's genius will develop far more quickly and his taste far more surely when he is able to contemplate a series of fine pictures together and follow the progress of a great painter, than when he has to look at landscape hanging next to a history painting, or a bambochade next to a Raphael.

He called the mixed hanging "as ridiculous as a cabinet *d'histoire naturelle* arranged without regard to genus, class, or family."[31]

The 1790s administration was criticized for not doing enough for the "pupils, copyists, and a large public eager for instruction in the history of art." The painter David wrote that "the Museum is by no means a frivolous assemblage of luxury objects which serves only to satisfy the collector. It needs to become an important school."[32]

Both defenders and critics of the first Louvre hanging agreed that students of art needed to learn by copying the best examples of Old Masters. This instructional purpose was their shared goal. Finally, LeBrun and David's point of view held sway. The didactic purpose was to be in future served by a far more "scientific" hanging of the pictures, according to school, master, and chronology. This followed very much the increasing trend toward a scientific and rational ordering of all knowledge.[33]

FIG. 10 John Faber the Elder, *Homer*

This highly politicized art debate was not the only event in the art world of late eighteenth-century Paris. Napoléon was flooding the city with art treasures brought back as booty from freshly conquered parts of Europe. In addition to the Louvre, the new Musée des Monuments Français was opened in 1795. This museum stated its didactic purposes for artists and the general public on the first page of its catalogue: "Cultivation of the arts enlarges a people's commerce and prosperity, purifies its morals, makes it more gentle and more ready to follow the laws by which it is governed. . ."[34]

Thus, James Bowdoin III, already familiar with the ideas expressed by English and American writers on the ability of art to instruct as well as delight,[35] stepped into this passionate debate when he arrived in Paris in 1805 as Jefferson's minister plenipotentiary to Spain. Bowdoin's intent to acquire art for himself and others is plain before his departure, and his desire to endow a college in honor of his father was also already fixed, the matter having been raised as

early as 1792.[36] In that year Bowdoin turned forty and he and his wife, Sarah, had had no children of their own. The childless couple would make the scholars of Bowdoin their intellectual heirs, endowing the College with lands and monies, but also a library and a collection of art.

ORGANIZATION OF THE
COLLECTION IN
JAMES BOWDOIN'S HOME

We do not know the precise arrangement James Bowdoin III made of his collection in his own home. Still, there are some general points that come clear from the catalogue of 1813. Like his French contemporaries, Bowdoin purchased and arranged a number of his paintings as pendants and pairs. There were at least ten pendants in Bowdoin's gift: pairs of paintings often by the same artist, of similar scale and subject matter. The Madison and Jefferson portraits are the most striking, having been commissioned as a pair from the start (figs. 2 and 3). There are also pairs of still life (1813.33 and 34), genre (1813.45 and 46) (figs. 5 and 6), animal pictures (no. 59 and no. 60 in 1813 inventory) (fig. 28), Biblical themes (1813.39 and no. 62) (figs. 7 and 9), and copies after Titian's *poesie* of *Venus and Adonis* (1813.21) and *Danaë* (no. 4) (figs. 1 and 8).[37]

James Bowdoin also followed a longstanding taste for a collection of "worthies," portraits of ancient and modern poets, philosophers, and statesmen. The Jefferson and Madison portraits are the most impressive of this type. A modest copy of a portrait of Mirabeau (fig. 11), said to be a favorite of Mr. Bowdoin's,[38] expands this category. Worthies from antiquity were represented by ten mezzotints showing sculpted busts of ancient poets, orators, and philosophers such as Homer and Demosthenes (figs. 10 and 12) after designs by Peter Paul Rubens. These were kept in Bowdoin's drawing room, somewhat incongruously along with a print of a modern governor of St. Martin.[39]

Jefferson had a fuller collection of such portraits, including sculpted busts of Turgot, Voltaire, Hamilton, and others.[40] Bowdoin apparently was to have received a sculpted bust of Apollo in 1802.[41] He had also attempted to procure some marble busts of unnamed subjects for himself while in France. Letters from 1807 reveal his desire to acquire marble busts from Florence or Livorno to place in his "Hall in Boston." He wanted busts to ornament his library,[42] perhaps with an effect in mind like that in Gullager's tiny portrait of James Bowdoin II in his study, where a portrait bust protrudes from a niche as if in conversation with Governor Bowdoin (fig. 13).

Such galleries of worthies had been a staple of collections since the Renaissance,[43] and a visitor to Bowdoin College in 1820 shows his expectation for such a grouping when he expresses some disappointment that the collection of presidents of the United States was limited to two, lacking effigies of "Washington, Adams and Munroe."[44]

To some extent Bowdoin's history paintings continued this theme of the worthies. Famous men and women of pagan and sacred history ornamented his walls—the exploits of young Achilles disguised as a girl (fig. 14), the courage of Esther (fig. 7), the moment of death for Queen Cleopatra (fig. 15). Examples of humankind's weakness, viciousness, and excess were also present in *Salome with the Head of John the Baptist* (fig. 17), *Lot and His Daughters*, and *The Discovery of Callisto's Pregnancy*.

FIG. 11 Anonymous, *Bust Portrait of Mirabeau*

APPRECIATION OF THE PAINTINGS AT BOWDOIN COLLEGE

The purported South Carolinian (actually Henry Putnam of Brunswick) whose remarks in 1820 are recorded above gives us one of the first glimpses of public reaction to Bowdoin's gift to the College. In 1820 the paintings are described as being hung in the philosophy chamber in Massachusetts Hall:

The philosophy chamber is capacious and handsome. It is dressed throughout with exquisite paintings, presented by Bowdoin. They are from the pencils of the first masters in Europe. The worthies, the patriarchs, and the martyrs of antiquity seem to have risen from the tomb. Here Homer, Anacreon, and Ovid seem to have stood to draw their heathen deities, that look down upon you in all the grandeur of fabled majesty. You can hardly realize, that you are not in a group of real life. Ulysses, in boyhood clad in the dress of a female, selects a sword from the trinkets presented him, and develops his character. You at once recognize the siege and taking of Troy. The wild beasts are bounding the forest; the trees are animated with all the beauty of the feathered tribe. The timid are winging their flight from the vulture; the hawk is perched, plucking the feathers from his victim.[45]

Impressed by the large mythological paintings, the writer recalls his ancient poets. When he does describe a particular painting, he confuses his Ovid, naming Ulysses rather than the young Achilles as the hero in drag among the daughters of Lycomedes (fig. 14 and cover). The wily Ulysses is present on the right, having hidden the sword to smoke out the young man. Our visitor interprets this rather unheroic scene as a vignette of developing character (probably meant in a positive sense rather than as a sign of Achilles' future rash and impulsive nature). The only remarks we hear are on subject matter—no care is given to whether the works are copies or originals or even whether they are beautiful. They are remarkable only for their content— heroic stories, lifelike realism, images of inspiring worthies. They are read for their stories just like the poets our visitor mentions—Homer, Anacreon, Ovid. The viewer is strongly oriented toward experiencing art in moral terms.

FIG. 12 John Faber the Elder, *Demosthenes*

The first decades of the painting collection's presence on campus passed with very few recorded reactions. By mid-century, however, increasing concern was voiced about caring for the collection and housing it in a proper gallery. With the leadership of President Leonard Woods (1807-1878) and the generosity of his cousin Theophilus Wheeler Walker (1813-1890), an art gallery became a fixed part of the new chapel planned by architect Richard Upjohn. Cleaning of the paintings was underway by 1850, with a clear sense of disposing of works that the Governing Boards felt could not be publicly exhibited. Eventually, four works were separated from the Bowdoin collection: no. 4, a copy after Titian's *Danaë and the Shower of Gold* (fig. 8); no. 47, *Diana and Endymion* (or *Venus and Adonis*) by an unknown painter; no. 52, *Lot and His Daughters*, artist unknown; and no. 61, listed as *Diana and Nymphs Bathing*, but identified as a *Callisto*, i.e. *The Discovery of Callisto's Pregnancy*, in recently discovered documents. These letters concerning the *Callisto* recount the Governing Boards' efforts to sell the work, just as they had sought to sell the *Danaë*. Although a buyer was identified—Mr. Thompson, who offered $100 for it—later writers assume the work, along with the *Diana* and the *Lot* went as payment to the restorer, George Howarth. We learn that the *Callisto* was attributed to Jacob Jordaens, a Flemish contemporary of Rubens, but whether this attribution offered by "Mr. Franquinet one of the best judges of Old Masters in the country" was correct, we cannot judge, since the work's current whereabouts are unknown.[46]

Why were these four works judged by the Boards to be unsuitable for the "private inspection of the young of either sex"? The Boards retained two other paintings of Venus and Adonis (1813.21 and 1813.50) (figs. 1 and 16), and one of nymphs bathing (1813.27). What may have disturbed them was the blatantly sexual subject matter of the scenes. The *Callisto* story turns around the stripping of the pregnant nymph Callisto by her outraged companions. *Danaë* is shown as she is "embraced by Jupiter in a Shower of Gold." The copyist of the *Danaë* followed Titian's highly erotic Naples version of the work, which also includes a little Cupid whose full frontal nudity only augments Danaë's pose of abandonment. The *Lot and His Daughters* by theme alone would have been problematic, since it depicts an incestuous seduction outside the burning city of Sodom. The Visiting Committee of 1852 described it as "a picture of no merit of any kind and only fit for a brothel."[47] Ironically, the Bowdoin College Museum of Art currently displays a work of this theme, which it acquired in 1970. The final work, a *Venus and Adonis*, we can only speculate had some comparably objectionable feature.

The expulsion of these works is justified in a statement of the Visiting Committee of 1850. "Some sections of our country and most foreigners may think this idea to be founded on a false delicacy but the purity of morals should in our opinion be allowed to hazard no contamination from spectacles thought among us to be in bad taste, however they may be considered by others differently educated."[48]

The Visiting Committee of 1852 echoed these sentiments. While the *Danaë* and *Callisto* are deemed to have considerable merit as works of art, they are just not suitable for the College Gallery:

In Europe where the eye has been long familiar to the exhibition of naked statues little hesitation would be made to admitting them into respectable galleries, but the *Danaë* is certainly designed to excite improper ideas, and objects which might be viewed with impunity by persons of mature age might have bad effects upon youth by exciting life passions yet dormant.[49]

Clearly the paintings soon to be cleaned and made ever more accessible to the public in the new Upjohn Chapel were deemed capable of influencing moral character. Presumably their power for ill effects was matched by a power for good effect.[50]

At no time during the deliberations over cleaning, selling, or housing the paintings is mention made of the difference between copies and originals. Indeed, the Titian copy of the *Danaë* is estimated by Howarth to be worth $1500, almost twice the yearly salary of $800 earned in 1848 by Professor Boody, professor of elocution and the instruction of rhetoric.[51] The stress is on content and on the effect on the viewers, especially the young.

THE PLACE OF ART IN THE CHAPEL:
The Sophia Walker Gallery and the Chapel Murals

With the construction of the Upjohn Chapel, the Bowdoin paintings found a new display location. This new Sophia Walker Gallery, named in honor of Theophilus Wheeler Walker's mother, on the second floor behind the organ, displayed not only Bowdoin's original bequest, but also the Bowdoin family portraits, which had come in 1826, and the Boyd collection, which had arrived in 1852. Art also was to figure prominently in the decoration of the interior of the Chapel proper, with twelve monumental copies of esteemed sacred paintings.

Leonard Woods, who became Bowdoin's fourth president in 1839, immediately undertook the challenge of financing and designing the new chapel. Woods was already strongly attuned to the aesthetic power of medieval church architecture, and a visit to Europe in 1840 with stops at Oxford, Paris, and the Vatican only reinforced that inclination. The power of Woods's admira-

tion for past art is cited in an encomium delivered at Bowdoin shortly after his death:

He painted the glory of these earlier ages of faith. Especially did he pay to the mediaeval church the honor so often withheld from it. He spoke of the singular perfection the fine arts obtained under its influence,—the cathedrals, solemn and magnificent, the music of the old composers, and the paintings of the old masters.[52]

Woods believed in the power of art to affect profoundly the quality of education. We hear him after his visit to Oxford in August of 1840:

I have passed [here], he writes, one of the happiest weeks of my life. All my pre-possessions in favor of the English system of education have been justified after the most minute inspection. The studies are not more extensive or more thorough than with us; but there is here a magnificence of architecture, an assemblage of paintings, statues, gardens, and walks; above all a solemnity and grandeur of religious worship which does more to elevate the taste and purify the character than the whole encyclopaedia of knowledge.[53]

Discussions between President Woods and artists such as Gervase Wheeler and advisers like William J. Hoppin on decoration for the Chapel began early. Already in 1847 Wheeler had sug-

FIG. 13 Christian Gullager, *Portrait of Governor James Bowdoin II*

151

FIG. 14 Attributed to Frans Francken III, *Achilles among the Daughters of Lycomedes*

gested decorations on the texts *Blessed are the Poor in Spirit* (Matthew 5:3) and *Search the Scriptures; for in them ye think ye have eternal life* (John 5:39),[54] although William J. Hoppin's letter to President Woods of 10 April 1847 tells us that Wheeler would not take up the figural work himself. Hoppin recounts of Wheeler:

He observed with much propriety that this falls within the province of the historical painters. . . . These pictures may be executed upon zinc plates in the studios of the artists and afterwards attached to the walls. I propose that they should be entrusted to our most distinguished men—say Huntington [a history and figure painter], Durand and others. One or two of them may be executed first and the rest follow as means of the Institution may permit.[55]

Later that summer, on 4 August 1847,[56] Hoppin reported to Woods that he had already spoken to Huntington and will speak to a Mr. Gray, but suggested postponing any more talks with prospective artists until the subjects had been decided. It seems that it had already been established that figural subjects were to fill the twelve bays on the long walls of the Chapel. Artists applied for the execution of this plan, and one, Mr. Ertle, even made two rough lists of

twelve Biblical subjects on the envelope of his calling card.[57]

A third list of proposed subjects prepared by another, presumably not an artist, includes secondary themes, perhaps for the lunettes. This anonymous list not only gives themes, but also names artists—Raphael, Michelangelo, Allston, Rubens—indicating that the works are to be monumental copies made after already existing images. Hoppin, on 4 August 1847, spoke of the difficulty of getting modern day artists to work at the high level of past art. He warned Woods:

We cannot hope to obtain pictures which will be perfectly satisfactory. There is much ignorance, I am sorry to say, even among the artists themselves as to the true objects of art. Too many of them consider it as a means by which nature may be servilely copied instead of a noble language by which to express lofty ideas. They seem not to know that the representation of lower truths must sometimes be neglected or omitted, in order to make that of higher ones more striking—that the painting of backgrounds and of the texture of draperies, is of less importance in works of the class we are considering than the *exhibition of character and feeling* [my emphasis].[58]

To Hoppin a forceful representation of character and feeling is needed in this Romanesque revival style chapel. The paintings should coordinate with this revival-style building and display a simplicity and majesty, conveying the solemnity of the purer, more primitive state of religion in past ages. The models, Hoppin implies, can be found in the past. Old Master paintings like those in Bowdoin's collection will set the level of ideas and expression that is sought after in the yet-to-be-commissioned murals for the Chapel.

The actual execution of the murals was very slow, the first two being completed only in 1856. It seems that President Woods had very definite ideas about the decoration and oversaw at least the first four subjects. His preferences were still influencing the choice of theme as late as 1915.[59] The first works executed were by Daniel Müller, a German artist from Canada. The first was paid for by Mrs. Jared Sparks, widow of Woods's friend, the former president of Harvard. The subjects chosen were *Paul Preaching on Mars Hill in Athens* (fig. 18) and *Peter Healing the Lame Man at the Beautiful Gate* (fig. 20) copied from Raphael's tapestry cartoons, at the time some of the most famous works of Western art in the world.[60] Both of Ertle's lists had included *St. Paul at Athens*, and the anonymous list had mentioned Raphael's version specifically along with his *Leper Cleansed at the Beautiful Gate*. Copies of these works stand in the first two bays of the north side—the latest New Testament events to be included in the cycle. The nice connection of St. Paul preaching with the lectern at the head of the Chapel probably accounts for its inclusion. Müller most likely worked from prints after Raphael's cartoons, greatly simplifying the compositions. It is said that the donor of monies for the *Lame Man*, Bellamy Storer, Esq., of Boston, an honorary graduate of the College, furnished the model. The colors of the murals show that Müller followed the original cartoons' color scheme well. Much of both scenes is cropped off to fit into the eccentric shape of Gervase Wheeler's ornamental polychrome frames, however, and the final effect is that of a rather large tarot card.

The *Daily Tribune* of Bath commented on the progress of Müller's work on 29 October 1855, praising his ability to adapt Raphael's master-

works to this new setting. Speaking of the St. Paul, it says:

The painting is not an original; but is an abridged copy from one of the celebrated cartoons of Raphael. . . . It was indeed difficult to abridge such a painting without injury to it; a process much like an abridgement of the *Odyssa* [sic] or *Aeneid*, which could not fail to be beautiful, but which would give but a very imperfect idea of the original. But difficult as such a work must always be, it must be acknowledged that it has been done in this case with so much skill, that it is a great ornament to the Chapel, and is creditable to the taste and genius of the copyist.[61]

The stress on excellence over originality and the comparison of painting to poetry were standard views of the day.

Few other connections are maintained with the anonymous list save the division of the walls into Old and New Testament scenes and the inclusion of *Adam and Eve* and *Moses Giving the Law*. The anonymous list had included an image of the Crucifixion to be copied after Rubens, but no such work was ever executed. Although the reputation of the Flemish master was very high, such strongly "Catholic" subject matter might not have suited potential donors' taste.[62] James Bowdoin's collection was believed to contain several Rubens originals and copies, the *Venus and Ceres* (so-called) (1813.12) (fig. 21), *Achilles among the Daughters of Lycomedes*, (1813.2) (fig. 14), attributed to Rubens by Gilbert Stuart(see Appendix I), and the *St. Simeon* (1813.11) (fig. 25) a copy after a portion of Rubens's great Antwerp altarpiece plundered by Napoléon's troops and displayed in the Louvre during James Bowdoin III's sojourn in Paris. Perhaps the idea to include a Rubens image reflected the state of understanding of the Bowdoin collection in the 1850s.[63]

The decoration of the rest of the bays of the Chapel continued unevenly throughout the next decades. Müller tried his hand at copying more modern artists' styles, the *Adoration of the Magi* (1858) after Peter Cornelius (1783-1867) the Nazarene painter who initiated the revival of mural painting in Germany;[64] and the *Annunciation* (1860) after Charles François Jalabert's (1819-1901) work on the wall of the chapel of Louis Napoléon at the Tuileries.

Raphael became the model once again for Charles Otto's copy of *St. Michael Vanquishing the Devil* (1866). Francis Lathrop (1849-1909) completed *Moses Giving the Law* in 1877, believed by many commentators to be designed after Raphael, but more likely modeled on a northern Italian image, perhaps a Tintoretto or Bassano.

Lathrop did use Raphael's *Transfiguration* as the model for his version of the same theme on the north wall (1877), which Mrs. William Perry gave in memory of her husband. Eighth in the series was Lathrop's *Baptism of Christ* (1877-1878), based on Carlo Marrati's work. Not until 1886 did work resume with Frederic Vinton's (1846-1911) *Adam and Eve* after Hippolyte Flandrin's (1809-1864) work for the church of

Saint-Germain-des-Prés done in 1856-1863. Twenty-two years later came Joseph B. Kahill's *David's First Triumph* after J. Tissot (1836-1902), given by Dr. Frederick H. Gerrish 1866, professor at the Medical School of Maine.

Dr. Gerrish also endowed the last two bays to be filled, the end two on the south side. These murals are the work of Miss Edna T. Marrett of Brunswick (1887-1968). Her *Prophet Isaiah* (1913) and *Delphic Sibyl* (1915) (fig. 19) after Michelangelo's figures from the Sistine Chapel ceiling are memorials to Professor Henry Leland Chapman and to Gerrish's brother, William Little Gerrish '64, a soldier in the Union Army who died at Petersburg, Virginia, in 1865. Marrett went on to paint the monumental musical angels (1917) after Fra Angelico that stand at the head of the Chapel.

The final effect of this group of copies after old and modern masters is somewhat difficult to gauge. Did they provide that solemnity and grandeur in religious worship that President Woods believed could "elevate the taste and purify the character"? We have few recorded reactions of viewers. An undated comment by a Visiting Committee claimed that students were "often seen gazing with earnest attention and apparent heartfelt interest upon the scenes so warmly portrayed to the eye deriving impressions both more vivid and durable than is *(sic)* likely to be obtained in any other mode."[65]

In 1880, when eight of the dozen were in place, Varney ranked these copies among Bowdoin College's art treasures.[66] A 1911 *Architectural Record* account described the mural decoration of the Chapel as "probably without any parallel" in mid-nineteenth century America. It identified as the "safest solution," the decision to make the decoration "chiefly of copies, as good as might be, of works already standard and classical."[67] Hatch, Helmreich, and Anderson each give brief accounts of the murals, but a full history and an assessment of the murals' significance has yet to be written.[68]

FIG. 15
(lower right) Anonymous, *Cleopatra,* (far left) Michael Carré, *Cattle ,* (top right) Anonymous, *Peasants and Cattle,* in the Sophia Walker Gallery, Chapel, before 1894

FIG. 16 Anonymous, *Venus and Adonis*

At this writing there is not even a complete set of documentary photographs of the works. Plans for their conservation have continually been delayed. Despite eloquent pleas for their care from John R. Ward '83 and architectural historian William Pierson, the Chapel and its paintings, as architect Christopher Glass, visiting lecturer in studio art, has recently observed, "have no constituency."

The murals' current state of oblivion is owed partly to the demise of the community practice of religion at Bowdoin, partly to the increasingly lower status of "copies" as the twentieth century unfolded, and partly to a shift of the artistic center of Bowdoin from the Chapel to the Walker Art Building, dedicated in 1894.

There had been high hopes for the Chapel as an artistic mecca. Many on the campus were optimistic about the effect Bowdoin's paintings would have once they were cleaned and rehung in the new Chapel's gallery. One board member proclaimed that the Sophia Walker Gallery would become "the most elegant resort of youth and beauty and taste our state affords."[69] Roswell D. Hitchcock, Collins Professor of Natural and Revealed Religion, who delivered the sermon on 7 June 1855 at the dedication of the new Chapel, spoke of the building as serving Art, Science, and Religion. We must remember that in 1855 none of the mural copies had yet been executed, although their themes and masters may have already been chosen. Thus Hitchcock's remarks must have been understood in terms of Bowdoin's collection of paintings as well as the projected murals.

According to Hitchcock, Art, Science, and Religion must all be studied if the College is to take the whole of human nature and make the most of it. Hitchcock sees three parts to humanity's spiritual constitution: "That by which we apprehend the Beautiful, which we call Taste; that by which we apprehend the True, which we call Intellect, and that by which we apprehend the Good which we call the Moral Sense." These three require development and culture if they are to bear their fruit of refinement, intelligence, and virtue.

In deference to our sense of Beauty, it must honor Art. In deference to our hunger for Truth, it must honor Science. In deference to our apprehension of a Divine Presence, it must honor Religion. And neither of these by itself alone, but all in harmony. Exclusive addiction to either one of them breeds mischief. Art unbalanced, becomes voluptuous; learning, arrogant, and religion, fanatical. While in a just blending of the three, there appears the fullness and symmetry of a perfect discipline. Lowest in rank as most mixed up with material forms, stands Art. Next above it is Science, perpetually gazing and struggling upwards from facts to principles, from phenomena to laws. Highest of all is Religion, as concerning itself supremely with the infinite and the eternal. This is the order of consciousness. It is the order also of history.[70]

The Chapel speaks to this tripartite whole. "In its Gallery of Painting it proclaims the legitimacy of Art." Even though art may occupy a lower rung in Hitchcock's platonic ordering of knowledge, yet it is honored. And in this scheme it would have been the *ideas* that art carried, more than its forms, or the names of its makers, that were of foremost importance. What the paintings meant to the students or to the community at large is revealed by scant evidence. An effort at cataloguing James Bowdoin's European paintings was evidently made by the painter Gilbert Stuart when he came to Brunswick to copy his own portraits of Jefferson and Madison in 1821 (see Appendix I). This "catalogue" was already lost in 1839, although we have reminiscences of it mentioned down into the twentieth century. Stuart seems to have esteemed the collection highly, evidently pronouncing as originals works he attributed to Rubens, Poussin, and Van Dyke.[71]

We first hear of a student concerned with the paintings on 23 July 1839.[72] John Rutherford Shepley '39 writes to Professor Parker Cleaveland expressing his worry over the state of preservation of the paintings. He also laments that Stuart's list has been lost and that so little has been recorded or discovered about their authorship and suggests that they be evaluated by a picture dealer, Mr. M. Hayward, who was exhibiting his own collection of Old Master paintings at the Athenaeum in Boston at the time. No reply is recorded from Cleaveland, who, along with President Allen, had been appointed by the Trustees as a committee to oversee the preservation of the pictures. Perhaps the demands of exhibition space and cleaning overshadowed all other considerations.

Once the paintings were housed in their new home, students were authorized by the Trustees to take charge of the gallery and open it for visitors.[73] These guardians, who were to be paid not more than $20 per year for this work, seem to have left no record of their impressions of the collection.

Later students' appreciation of the value of James Bowdoin III's paintings, whether aesthetic or monetary, seems to have been prompted by outside forces. A sensitive young detective—identified only as S—recounts in the *Bowdoin Orient* of 6 June 1877 his understanding of the sale of the copy of Titian's *Danaë* (fig. 8).[74] He traced the then-owner of the work, George Henry Hall of New York, who showed it with pride as a "first-rate" Titian copy and who could not be persuaded to part with it even for the sum of $2500. S concludes his letter with a plea (to this day unheeded) that efforts be made to restore the copy to the College.

In his account of the College's art treasures in 1880, Varney also lauds this "first-rate" copy of Titian's *Danaë*, which he believes displays the virtues of the Italian school of painting. Being able to distinguish different schools of painting was (and still is) one of the principal goals of refined art criticism, and the Bowdoin collection afforded a viewer a chance to learn just such skills.[75]

In assessing the value and significance of the works owned by the College in 1880, Varney directly confronts the question of copies. In his enumeration of the most noteworthy paintings he lists or discusses only seventeen works, at least

FIG. 17 Anonymous, *Salome with the Head of John the Baptist*

six of which he thinks may be copies after Titian, Poussin, Van Dyck, Rubens, and Paul Potter. In almost every case Varney judges the work either to be a "superior," "first-rate," or "fine" copy, or an original. Later in his essay, Varney addresses the claim of originality.

It is evident that several paintings of the Bowdoin collection are among the best works of art; but can we credit the statement of the catalogue in respect to those claimed to be originals? Of Mr. Bowdoin's veracity there is no question; but was he not deceived? Had he the means to purchase originals? And how did it happen that they could be purchased at all?[76]

Varney convinces us that a combination of Bowdoin's wealth, the valuable assistance he received from learned adepts, and the circumstance of the historical moment—Napoleon's plunder of the whole of European art—came together to favor Bowdoin's acquisition of originals. It is clear, however, that to Varney originali-

ty is not so much a concern as is excellence of execution. A copy or duplicate may easily rank among the best works of art.

A final student response from the 1883 *Orient* illustrates the growing tension between Art and Science, far from the ideal of balance among Art, Science, and Religion that Professor Hitchcock had outlined in his dedicatory sermon in 1855:

It seems decidedly foolish to stow away in a room seldom visited a collection of paintings worth thousands of dollars, and at the same time be suffering for the common necessities of life. . . . If these pictures are worth as much as claimed, they ought to be exchanged for a decent telescope and observatory. A gymnasium ought to be built with the proceeds of a 'Vandyke,' and better salaries paid the professors, so that the best of them need not be snatched away by richer colleges when they get a reputation here. There are lots of things we need, and we don't need that fossilized, antiquated collection of brown paint.[77]

157

COPIES AND CASTS IN THE WALKER ART BUILDING

In 1894 James Bowdoin's painting collection received its present home, the newly constructed Walker Art Building. The architectural program of the Walker made a point of enshrining art styles and masters from the past in its design, which reflects Renaissance villas, in its inscriptions listing the Vasarian cavalcade of great artists (with some modern additions, principally in the northerners), in its mural program (which lauds Athens, Venice, Rome, and Florence), and in its decoration, which employs monumental bronze and stone copies of antique statues.

The copies after antique sculpture are perhaps the most significant indicators of the enduringly high status of copies as educationally important. The current sculptural program of the Walker facade (fig. 27) includes two lions after the ancient and Renaissance examples now displayed in Florence at the Loggia dei Lanzi, full-standing bronze casts of the orator Demosthenes and the poet Sophocles copying revered ancient models, and copies of busts of the Hermes of Praxiteles, the bearded Dionysos, and the blind Homer. Originally, copies of a large Greek vase rested on cement reproductions of a classical altar set on the museum's parapet. All of these copies were meticulously treated in the descriptive catalogues of the Bowdoin College Art Collections from 1895 through 1930.[78] They are expunged from the 1950 catalogue and thereafter, as if the facade decoration had no bearing on the content or aims of the museum.

Of equal value with the Walker Art Building's facade copies after ancient masters was the large collection of plaster casts after antique masterworks once housed there. This collection was created between 1881 and 1922, and actually started before the Walker building was planned. The presence of these large casts in the cramped gallery space of the Chapel (fig. 24) may have contributed to the desire for a larger space devoted to the display of art.

In the early 1880s, with the encouragement of Curator and Professor Henry Johnson, friends of the College underwrote the purchase of several large-scale plaster casts of famous antique sculpture. They ordered the *Laocoön*, the *Dying Gaul*, the *Primaporta Augustus*, the *Marble Faun of Praxiteles*, the *Niobe and Her Daughter*, the *Artemis of Versailles*, and the *Apollo Belvedere*, among others, many of them through a London broker who ordered directly from Italy. The Honorable William W. Thomas 1860 presented five of the monumental casts, and a vote of the Boards on 12 July 1882 officially declared that: "the thanks of the College be presented to him for this repeated valuable addition to the art collection of the College." Judge Thomas stressed the educational importance of these casts in his letter of presentation: "I have had in mind the refining and educative power that masterpieces of art are certain to exert on students of recent as well as ancient times." These casts and other gifts of their kind graced the crowded rooms on the ground floor of the Chapel.[79]

The continuing high status of these plaster casts after antiquities is demonstrated by the Walker Art Building itself and by the catalogues of the collections up to 1930. The Sculpture Hall was the name given to the central rotunda of the Walker Art Building (fig. 22). At first it housed only the plaster casts, which were the very first objects to greet visitors to the museum after the welcoming facade copies. In contrast to these plaster copies, the Assyrian stone reliefs donated to the College in 1857 and now exhibited in the rotunda were housed in the basement of the building from 1895 to 1937.

The catalogues of the collection until 1930 provide detailed information about the original sculptures from which the casts had been made, and it was assumed that the virtues of the originals would be visible in the copies. In addition, donors of the casts were duly acknowledged, and several objects, like the paintings being done in the Chapel at the same time, carried special meaning as memorials. These casts were seen as an important addition to classical instruction at Bowdoin[80] and they included the very best of the canon of antique works accepted in the nineteenth century. In fact, most of the originals recorded in casts at Bowdoin had been gathered by Napoléon for his museums and may well have been on view when James Bowdoin III was in Paris. Henry Johnson's appreciation of the didactic value of copies after antique masterworks paralleled Bowdoin's own, and the canon of revered masterworks had changed remarkably little from 1805 to 1880.[81] However, by 1916 Johnson was looking forward to a time when only original works of art would be exhibited. This was probably in response to an overflow of copies which had been given as gifts to the museum.[82]

Around 1937 a major transformation took place in the College's attitude toward the cast collection. With the approval of President

FIG. 19 Edna T. Marrett, *The Prophet Isaiah* (left) and *The Delphic Sibyl* (right)

Kenneth C. M. Sills and of Director Henry Andrews, the industrious young assistant director, Professor Philip C. Beam, initiated the removal of the begrimed casts. The pieces were removed from view and lent to private preparatory schools in the state: Oak Grove School in Vassalboro and Fryeburg Academy in Fryeburg. All mention of the plaster cast copies was expunged from the 1950s handbook, and no description was included of the copies on the facade. The once-prized sculptural copies had become invisible.[83]

Bowdoin was following a process that had taken place earlier in larger public museums like the Boston Museum of Fine Arts. Collections of casts lovingly amassed in the name of education were ruthlessly purged when the tide of taste turned against them. Once seen as true mirrors of the most excellent works of pagan antiquity, plaster casts came to be denounced as the "Pianola of the Arts."[84] Two Bowdoin publications sharply underline this shift in attitude toward copies. From the 1930 catalogue's Prefatory Note by Director Henry E. Andrews, we have this excerpt from Ralph Waldo Emerson on the virtue of copies and their instructional value. Chosen by Professor Henry Johnson for his last catalogue, it summarizes the late nineteenth-century esteem in which copies were held.

I do not undervalue the fine instruction which statues and pictures give. But I think the public museum in each town will one day relieve the private house of

FIG. 20 Daniel Müller, *Peter Healing the Lame Man at the Beautiful Gate*

FIG. 21 Cornelis Schut I, *Allegory of Fruitfulness,* formerly *Venus and Ceres*

this charge of owning and exhibiting them. I go to Rome and see on the walls of the Vatican the Transfiguration, painted by Raphael, reckoned the first picture in the world; or in the Sistine Chapel I see the grand sibyl and prophets painted in a fresco by Michael Angelo—which have every day now for three hundred years inflamed the imagination and exalted the piety of what vast multitudes of men of all nations! I wish to bring home to my children and my friends copies of these admirable forms, which I can find in the shops of the engravers; but I do not wish the vexation of owning them. I wish to find in my own town a library and a museum which is the property of the town, where I can deposit this precious treasure, where I and my children can see it from time to time, and where it has its proper place among hundreds of such donations from other citizens who have brought thither whatever articles they have judged to be in their nature rather a public than a private property. A collection of this kind, the property of each town, would dignify the town, and we should love and respect our neighbors more. Obviously, it would be easy for every town to discharge this truly municipal duty. Every one of us would gladly contribute his share; and the more gladly, the more considerable the institution has become.[85]

In direct contrast to this, is the derisive and dismissive tone taken by Kevin Herbert in his laudable *Ancient Art in Bowdoin College* in 1964. Speaking of early donations to the College's collection, Herbert states:

Yet not everything received was worthy of the name of art. For example, in the early years of the museum plaster casts of sculpture and reduced bronze reproductions represented Greek and Roman art in the galleries. If to the contemporary eye viewing old photographs these versions appear worse than useless for purposes of instruction or appreciation, it must be remembered that in the years prior to the first World War almost every American museum depended upon such pallid devices to convey some idea of classical art.[86]

160

FIG. 22 View of the Rotunda of the Walker Art Building showing the plaster casts, before 1937

The day of the didactic copy had surely come to an end.

In his address delivered at the opening of the Walker Art Building on 7 June 1894, Martin Brimmer, founder and first president of the Boston Museum of Fine Arts, praised good reproductions as a worthy means of educating Americans. He felt that all the originals were already housed in European museums, but that through copies the *idea* of great art could be transmitted to Americans unable to acquire originals. Those unable to travel, as he and his good friend Leonard Woods had done in 1840, could still gain the benefit of great art through copies: "Plaster casts of all the best statues and bas-reliefs are to be had. Photographs of the famous pictures now give truthfully the gradations of light and shade. The rare coin is hardly distinguishable from the electrotype reproduction."[87]

Brimmer admitted that copies had some limitations, but expressed faith in the progress of technology that would continually narrow the gap between copy and original:

The plaster cast gives perfectly the form of the statue, but fails to give the texture of the marble, on which the play of light brings out the delicacy of the sculptor's modeling. The photograph of the picture offers no hint of its color. Yet, even in these respects much is to be hoped for at no distant day. The plaster will surely receive an artificial polished surface. Recent experiments show the probability that photographs correctly reproducing the color of the original picture will be made.[88]

Brimmer did not anticipate the arrival of a substantive collection of original Greek antiquities, which came to the College with the generous gift of Edward Perry Warren starting in 1912. Nor did he envision the wholesale repudiation of copies as a permanent part of the

FIG. 23 Anonymous, *Descent from the Cross*

museum's exhibitions. Copies in the gallery spaces were to become anathema at Bowdoin by 1937 as they had become at Boston in 1909. Copies, under the name of reproductions, continued to flourish as educational tools but only in perishable educational materials for sale or loan to students. As early as 1895 a series of heliotype reproductions after Blake, Dürer, and Raphael were made available to students as supplements to the library of art books donated by the Misses Walker. A collection of negatives reproducing the College's works of art was continually augmented from the late nineteenth century onward. By 1903 sixty different prints produced by Professor C. C. Hutchins from these negatives were being offered for sale. A few hundred lantern slides had also been added to the museum's library.[89]

By 1930 the museum owned 4,200 slides and 2,000 photographs, with 75 prints of the collection now offered for sale. Professor Johnson had seen to the complete documentation of the Old Master drawings in photographs in 1912-1913, and G. B. Webber made 279 small photographic prints of works of art in 1924. The negative file was enlarged in 1940-1941, and by 1949-1950 photographic postcards were made. By 1950, thousands of mounted photos and 1,500 slides, some in color, made up the museum's documentary holdings. A "Bowdoin Lending Gallery" established in 1935-1936 had 73 originals and reproductions by 1937-1938. By 1950 this student loan collection had 1,000 framed color reproductions, and its catalogue proclaimed, "In this and other ways the Museum is an integral part of the College's educational program." Art instruction had started with formal classes in 1913, but became separated from museum functions when the Visual Arts Center was completed in 1975. Art history and studio art became separate divisions within the academic Department of Art and received separate spaces in which to operate.[90]

Today the didactic function of copies is all but forgotten within the Bowdoin College Museum of Art. Visiting artists who come to make oil and watercolor copies of works in the collection are no longer featured in the museum's yearly Report to the President.[91] The Student Loan Program is defunct, and the sole surviving monumental plaster cast on view on the campus is the armless Venus de Milo, who stands disconsolately with other props in a corner of the third-floor painting studio of the Visual Arts Center. Reproductions in the form of slides, postcards, posters, and jewelry are available in the Museum Shop, but the expectations for their instructional potential are as modest as their scale.

CONCLUSION

When James Bowdoin III created a collection of art that included copies after esteemed Old Master paintings and ancient statuary, he embraced attitudes towards art's function that had been articulated by Renaissance theorists: that painting and sculpture could, like literature, instruct and delight; that the idea of a great work, therefore, could and should be transmitted to many viewers by way of copies; that copies, if of

FIG. 24 View of the north aisle of the Bowdoin College Chapel crowded with plaster casts and paintings, before 1894

good quality, could partake of many of the same virtues, especially the narrative and moral content, of the original. Underlying these views toward art was the assumption that there existed a kind of master list, a canon, of the greatest works of art, which could be agreed upon by all educated people (that is, by Europeans and cultured individuals in European colonies abroad).

This canon of masterpieces held sway well into the nineteenth and in some places the twentieth century. The two men who did most to protect, make visible, and build upon James Bowdoin's gift of art—President Leonard Woods and Professor Henry Johnson—shared to a large extent Bowdoin's belief in this canon as a standard of excellence against which all else could be measured. They also shared the belief that monumental copies of great works in paint and plaster could serve to instruct the young, not only to elevate those ineffable qualities called taste and refinement, but also to educate the young in the shared cultural heritage of the West—the great stories of the Bible and the myths and histories of antiquity with their consequent moral content.

Such ideas went beyond the walls of colleges and museums, filtering well into the fabric of middle-class American life. For example, cleverly marketed plaster casts available by catalogue became a standard decorative accessory in late nineteenth-century middle-class homes. C. Hennecke and Company of Milwaukee, Wisconsin, stresses in its 1887 retail catalogue of plaster copies after Florentine statuary the great purposes their wares served. Copies of great masterpieces could "elevate and refine our natures, and lift us out of the dull, sensual world." Reproduced images of heroes, ancient and modern, could instruct young children. From Hercules they could learn persistence and determination. Diana stood for chastity, Benjamin Franklin, thrift and inventiveness. A group of such copies served as a "visual textbook" promulgating accepted social values—female chastity, the value of industry, etc. Even the idea of "worthies" found in both Bowdoin's and Jefferson's collections was transmitted through such commercial conduits. Children could be taught painlessly by these mute models; the 1887 catalogue enjoins us to "raise the ideal of our children, let heroes, patriots, the noble in science, in art, in poetry, and in all the different avocations of life be with them and teach them silently and surely—that noble men and women may be the result of the unconscious

FIG. 25 Anonymous, *St. Simeon Holding the Infant Christ*

FIG. 26 Anonymous, *The Continence of Scipio*

education."[92] At Bowdoin, the belief in the possibility of such "silent instruction" through copies was largely extinguished by the late 1930s.

Ironically, the easy availability of such objects accelerated the decline of the status of copies, and by extension the status of the masterworks they copied, down to the level of outworn cliché and kitsch. The democratization of copying processes—photography, for example—pushed fine art copies out of the museum galleries and into museum shops.

As the twentieth century wore on, beliefs cherished by Bowdoin, Woods, and Johnson were gradually eroded and even came under attack. The rise of modernism in the arts, which opened Western art to primitive, Eastern, and other non-Greco-Roman traditions, challenged maintenance of a strict canon of masterworks. Neither the canon nor the moral values it embodied was to remain as the single guidepost for the twenti-

eth century. The idea of art as a means of conveying moral verities fell away to be replaced by the cult of the new.

This cult of "originality" elevated a supposedly unique, individual artistic expression above all else. Such a premium put on an original creation was strongly linked to a sense of private ownership. The work of art was exclusively the artist's own, often deliberately rejecting or overturning the canon of the past. It could be counterfeited, forged, or parodied, but there was no room for a legitimate emulation or copy. Any copying was somehow a reduction or loss, also pointing to a lack of "originality" in the copyist. These supposed original works could become the exclusive property of an individual collector or museum. This cult of originality grew hand-in-hand with an emphasis on art's monetary value that has come to be the primary definition even of Old Masters. Van Gogh's *Irises* now instructs

165

FIG. 27 Facade of the Walker Art Building

us first in the value of art as investment, not in some realm of morality or taste. Such an attitude hopelessly obscures our view of Old Master copies.

If we are to make sense of James Bowdoin III's legacy to us in the visual arts, we must make a conscious mental effort to understand his cherished copies in their full significance. They represent a rich cultural heritage of shared myth, faith, and moral ideal now so desperately longed for and sought out in the confusion of late twentieth century America.[93] We need not embrace such values blindly, but can reexamine them and retrieve what is useful to us.

As an example of how one might use a copy today, we could select the copy after Nicolas Poussin's *Continence of Scipio* (fig. 26). It depicts a story now no more familiar to us than biblical parables or Ovidian tales, one taken from Livy's *History of Rome*,[94] a text illustrating all types of moral conduct, both good and bad. The painting presents an interpretation of Scipio Africanus Major's (c.234–c.183 B.C.) clemency during his campaigns in Spain against the Carthaginians. Scipio received as part of the victor's booty a lovely young woman, whom he returned safely to her fiancé. We may critique the work as perpetuating a view of women as objects and possessions. We might also read Scipio's action as an exercise of choice that puts self-control or abnegation before the press of cultural norms toward instant gratification. Countless other readings are possible, but only if we get beyond the cash-register mentality that dismisses a copy as unoriginal and therefore unworthy of notice, of conservation or of display. If we open our minds to the way Jefferson, Bowdoin, and others thought about art, we may discover something of tremendous value for our own time and our own lives.

NOTES

I am indebted to many people whose contributions have informed this essay. I wish to thank Katharine J. Watson, Suzanne K. Bergeron, Helen S. Dubé, Lorena A. Coffin, Henrietta M. Tye, Mattie Kelley, and José L. Ribas '76 of the Bowdoin College Museum of Art; docent Sheila Rideout; Special Collections librarians Susan B. Ravdin '80 and Dianne M. Gutscher; librarians of the Maine Historical Society; Bowdoin graduates John R. Ward '83, Cecile M. Green '88, Marie E. Bengtsson '81, Jennifer S. Edwards '89, Anita L. Kimball '90, Ann E. Robertson '90, and Elizabeth H. Humphreys '93; colleagues Shelley R. Langdale '85, Julie L. McGee '82, Linda J. Docherty, Charles C. Calhoun, Clifton C. Olds, Paula Volent, Philip C. Beam, Gertrude Wilmers, Janet Marstine, Kathleen Curran; and Jo Anne Calderwood, who patiently and professionally word-processed this paper.

BCSC is Special Collections, Hawthorne-Longfellow Library, Bowdoin College.

1. The most recent work on these portraits is the soon-to-be-published study by Linda J. Docherty, "Public Portraits, Private Lives: Gilbert Stuart's Portraits of Thomas Jefferson and James Madison for James Bowdoin III." See also Marvin S. Sadik, *Colonial and Federal Portraits at Bowdoin College* (Brunswick, ME: Bowdoin College Museum of Art, 1966), 155-166.

2. *Bowdoin College Museum of Art, Handbook of the Collections*, ed. Margaret R. Burke (Brunswick, ME: Bowdoin College Museum of Art, 1981), xvii, and 35, "Many of these are copies, now confined to storage, rather than the originals James Bowdoin may have thought he was buying."

3. For the drawings, see David P. Becker, *Old Master Drawings at Bowdoin College* (Brunswick, ME: Bowdoin College Museum of Art, 1985). For the portraits, see Sadik.

4. On the relatively recent rise of the concept of originality see Susan Lambert, *The Image Multiplied, Five Centuries of Printed Reproductions of Paintings and Drawings* (New York: Abaris, 1987), 13.

5. "An Inventory of Goods at Present in the House of James Bowdoin Esqr....Done at His Request This 15th September 1774," Bowdoin and Temple Papers, Massachusetts Historical Society, Boston. Sheila Rideout has recently discovered a letter from Elizabeth Temple on 4 April 1774 to her brother, James Bowdoin III, regarding export of his pictures from Europe. Bowdoin and Temple Papers, Massachusetts Historical Society, Boston.

6. On Smibert and James Bowdoin II's collection see Becker, xiv-xv; Richard H. Saunders, "John Smibert's Italian Sojourn—Once Again," *Art Bulletin* 66, no. 2 (June 1984), 312-18; Miles Chappell, "A Note on John Smibert's Italian Sojourn," *Art Bulletin* 64, no. 1 (March 1982), 132-38; Sadik, 208-222.

7. For a diverting short history on American attitudes toward and moral expectations for the arts from seventeenth-century New England to today, see Robert Hughes, "Art, Morals, and Politics," *New York Review of Books*, 23 April 1992, 21-27.

Sacred pictures in Bowdoin's collection included *The Life of Christ: Adoration of the Magi* (nos. 38, 62), *Mary, St. Elizabeth, St. John and Christ* (no. 44), *St. Simeon Holding the Infant Christ* (no. 46), *Portrait of Christ* (no. 36), *Descent from the Cross* (no. 39), *Entombment* (no. 25). Some Old Testament scenes and events from the life of St. John the Baptist and St. Peter were also included: *Translation of Elijah* (no. 45), *Lot and His Daughters* (no. 52), *Esther Before Ahasuerus* (no. 63), *Infant St. John* (no. 17), *St. John Preaching* (no. 40), *Salome with the Head of St. John* (no. 35), *St. Peter Delivered from Prison* (no. 56).

On Smibert's participation in Berkeley's project and the artist's collection of Old Master copies see Henry Wilder Foote, *John Smibert Painter* (Cambridge, MA: Harvard University Press, 1950), 29, 229-231, and Richard H. Saunders, *John Smibert (1688-1751): Anglo-American Portrait Painter*, 2 vols. Diss. Yale, 1979 (Ann Arbor: UMI, 1982), 95-96, 107, 138.

Katharine Watson has suggested that some of the works from Smibert's studio originally intended for educational purposes in Bermuda were purchased specifically by James Bowdoin III with a similar educational aim in mind—the endowing of Bowdoin College in Maine, see Becker, xv.

8. Unpublished documents, London. I thank Paula Volent for this information.

9. James Bowdoin III Letterbooks, 13 May 1806, and undated invoice between letters of 13 and 15 October 1807, BCSC; see Sadik, 210.

10. A complete survey of the types of frames in the Bowdoin collection has yet to be done. This might give further information regarding the works' provenance.

11. A Flemish work, van Bloemen's *Farmyard Scene* (no. 9), has an eighteenth-century French printed text incorporated into its frame. A distinctive type of frame with mustard yellow paint on its upper edge is shared by several of the French works and some Dutch and Flemish paintings as well (nos. 7, 12, 20, 24, 26, 43, 66, and 67, for example). More research into eighteenth-century French frame construction may help to identify these works as some of those purchased by Bowdoin in Paris.

12. See, for example, Phyllis Pray Bober and Ruth Rubinstein, *Renaissance Artists and Antique Sculpture: A Handbook of Sources* (Oxford: Oxford University Press, 1986).

13. James Bowdoin III Letterbooks, 22 March 1805, BCSC, and Sadik, 208.

14. See Francis Haskell and Nicholas Penny, *Taste and the Antique: The Lure of Classical Sculpture*, 1500-1900 (New Haven: Yale University Press, 1981) on the most esteemed ancient sculpture. Bowdoin had seen the antique Ariadne himself on 29 March 1774 in the Vatican, where it had recently been installed as part of Clement XIV's museum. See note 35 below.

15. Jefferson Papers, Massachusetts Historical Society; Jefferson's (polygraph?) copy, Library of Congress; also James Bowdoin III Letterbooks, BCSC; as cited in Sadik, 208-209, 219, notes 2 and 3.

16. On the fame and infamy of Cleopatra in popular culture, see Lucy Hughes-Hallett, *Cleopatra: Histories, Dreams and Distortions* (New York: Harper & Row, 1990), also Haskell and Penny, 184-187.

17. James Bowdoin III Letterbooks, 12 July 1802, BCSC. I thank Linda Docherty and Jennifer Edwards for this reference.

18. James Bowdoin III Letterbooks, BCSC; and Sadik, 210.

FIG. 28 Photograph of James Bowdoin III bequest paintings in the College Chapel, including : (left) Anonymous, *John the Baptist Preaching to the Multitudes;* (center) Anonymous, *Combat of Hyena and Dogs;* (right) Anonymous, *Fox Devouring a Pheasant*

19. Historical files, BCMA.

20. Seymour Howard, "Thomas Jefferson's Art Gallery for Monticello," *Art Bulletin* 59 (Dec. 1977), 583.

21. Fiske Kimball, "Jefferson and the Arts," *Proceedings of the American Philosophical Society* 87, no. 3 (July 1943), 242 citing a note from 1782.

22. Howard, 597-600.

23. Kimball, 242.

24. Carol E. Hevner, "Rembrandt Peale's Dream and Experience of Italy," in *The Italian Presence in American Art 1760-1860,* ed. Irma B. Jaffe (New York: Fordham University Press, 1989), 18, on the availability of such works.

25. Jonathan Richardson [senior], *Two Discourses. I. An Essay on the Whole Art of Criticism as it relates to painting shewing how to judge. I. Of the Goodness of a Picture; II. Of the Hand of the Master; and III. Whether 'tis an Original or a Copy. II. An Argument in Behalf of the Science of a Connoisseur; Wherein Is Shewn the Dignity, Certainty, Pleasure, and Advantage of It* (1719), I, 105.

26. Carol Gibson-Wood, *Studies in the Theory of Connoisseurship from Vasari to Morelli* (New York: Garland Press, 1988), 122.

27. Richardson, I, 179, Gibson-Wood, 116; Richard Spear in *Retaining the Original, Multiple Originals, Copies and Reproductions.* Vol. 20, *Studies in the History of Art* (Washington, D.C.: National Gallery, 1989), 97. For more on Richardson, see Carol Gibson-Wood, "Jonathan Richardson and the Rationalization of Connoisseurship," *Art History* 7 (1984), 38-56.

28. Cited in Germain Bazin, *The Museum Age,* trans. Jane van Nuis Cahill (New York: Universe Books, Inc., 1967), 116.

29. See *The Index of Paintings Sold in the British Isles During the Nineteenth Century,* ed. Burton B. Fredericksen (Santa Barbara, CA: ABCCLIO, ca. 1988-), vol. 1, 1801-1805, vol. 2, 1806-1810. Compare comments on copies by the American artist John Vanderlyn (1775-1852) cited by Marius Schoonmaker, *John Vanderlyn* [Kingston, NY,

1950], 44, quoted by David Alan Brown, *Raphael and America* (National Gallery of Art, Washington, D.C., 1983), 22.

30. Andrew L. McClellan, "The Politics and Aesthetics of Display: Museums in Paris 1750-1800," *Art History* 7 (1984), 455, citing in note 90, p. 463, *Catalogue des objets contenus dans la galerie du Muséum français,* 1793, 'avertissement.' Also McClellan "Art Theory and Modes of Pictorial Display in Early Modern France," CAA 1992, Chicago. Colin B. Bailey, "Conventions of the Eighteenth-Century *Cabinet de Tableau:* Blondel d'Azincourt's *La première idée de la curiosité,"* *Art Bulletin* 69 (1987), 431-447.

31. J. B. P. Lebrun, "Observations sur le Museum National par le Citoyen Lebrun, peintre et marchand de tableaux, pour servir de suite aux réflexions qu'il a déjà publiée's sur le même objet," Paris, 1793, 15 (Bibliothèque Nationale, Vp. 19787), cited in Bailey, 445.

32. Bibliothèque Nationale, Le 653, "Convention Nationale: Second Rapport sur la nécessité de la suppression de la Commission du Museum fait au nom des Comité d'Instruction Publique et des Finances par David," 27. Nivose an II (16 Jan. 1794), n.p., cited in Bailey, 446.

33. McClellan, 456.

34. Cited in Michael Greenhalgh, *The Classical Tradition in Art. From the Fall of the Roman Empire to the Time of Ingres* (New York: Harper and Row, 1978), 220.

35. While Bowdoin's library contains no copy of Richardson's works, it is likely that he knew of Richardson's ideas. Bowdoin had a friendship with Ward Nicholas Boylston, with whom he traveled through Italy in 1773-74 visiting famous sites, including art collections. From Boylston's diary of the trip, an unpublished manuscript in the Massachusetts Historical Society, it is clear that Boylston had a cultivated appreciation of art. Bowdoin surely learned something from him. I thank Sheila Rideout for this information.

Bowdoin's library includes a few volumes on art, several of them acquired during his stay in France. *Les monumens religieux: tableaux, statues etc. par Madame de Genlis; Vies des Premier Peintures de Roi, B. Lepicier,* Paris, 1752; *Dictionnaire portatif des Beaux Arts par M. Lacombe,* Paris, 1759; *Anecdotes des Beaux Arts,* Paris, 1776-80, are listed among Bowdoin's catalogue of books taken at Paris, 5 Nov. 1806, at the end of James Bowdoin III Letterbook II, BCSC. Further, Bowdoin possessed some pamphlets of drawing exhibitions at the Musée Napoléon and Musée Central des Arts; a cyclopaedia of arts and sciences, Titi's *Nuovo Studio di Roma,* 1708; and a French edition of Winckelmann's *History of Art,* 1794-1803. This was not an extensive art library. Basic sources such as Vasari's *Lives of the Artists* are lacking, indicating that Bowdoin's interest in art was less passionate than some of his other pursuits. See Kenneth Carpenter's essay in this volume for a more thorough characterization of Bowdoin's library.

36. Louis C. Hatch, *The History of Bowdoin College* (Portland, ME: Loring, Short and Harmon, 1947), 4.

37. Pendants in Bowdoin's paintings include:

1813.17	Jouillain
1813.27	Jouillain
1813.48	Jouillain
1813.24	Boudwyns and Bout
1813.29	Boudwyns and Bout
1813.33	Fyt
1813.34	Fyt
1813.32	van Bloemen
1813.38	van Bloemen
1813.45	Anon., *Sculptor's Studio*
1813.46	Anon., *Painter's Studio*
1813.54	Stuart
1813.55	Stuart
No. 59	*Fox and Pheasant*
No. 60	*Hyena and Dogs*
No. 69	*Peasants and Cattle*
No. 70	*Peasants and Cattle*
1813.39	Franco, attrib.
No. 62	Franco, attrib.
No. 4	after Titian
1813.21	after Titian

See Bailey, 437-443, on pendants and pairs in eighteenth-century French contexts.

38. Henry Johnson, *Descriptive Catalogue of the Bowdoin College Art Collections* (Brunswick, ME: Bowdoin College, 1895), 41.

39. MS, 1813 Inventory prepared by John Abbott, BCMA.

40. Howard, 598.

41. James Bowdoin III Letterbooks, 12 July 1802, BCSC. I thank Linda Docherty and Jennifer Edwards for this information.

42. James Bowdoin III Letterbooks, 1 May, 18 June, 28 Oct. 1807, BCSC; Sadik, 209. James Bowdoin II owned busts of Addison and Shakespeare in plaster of Paris. See Gordon E. Kershaw, *James Bowdoin, Patriot and Man of the Enlightenment* (Brunswick, ME: Bowdoin College Museum of Art, 1976), 13.

43. On the Renaissance tradition of the worthies or famous men, see Randolph Starn, "Reinventing Heroes in Renaissance Italy," in *Art and History, Images and Their Meaning,* eds. Robert I. Rotberg and Theodore K. Rabb (Cambridge: Cambridge University Press, 1988), 74-77

with bibliography. Creighton Gilbert, "On Castagno's Nine Famous Men and Women: Sword and Book as the Basis for Public Service," in *Life and Death in Fifteenth-Century Florence,* eds. Marcel Tetel, Ronald G. Witt, and Rona Goffen (Durham and London: Duke University Press, 1989), 174-192. C. L. Joost-Gaugier, "Poggio and Visual Tradition: *Uomini Famosi* in Classical Literary Description," *Artibus et historiae* 12, (1985), 57-74.

44. *A Description of Brunswick, (Maine;) in Letters By a Gentleman from South Carolina, to a Friend in that State* (Brunswick, ME: Joseph Griffin, 1820), 21. Charles Calhoun has kindly brought to my attention that the gentleman was actually Henry Putnam, a Brunswick resident.

45. *A Description,* 20-21.

46. Howarth to Woods, 12 January 1852, BCSC, Museum of Art files. Materials were not yet filed in 1992.

47. Ernst Helmreich, *Religion at Bowdoin College: A History* (Brunswick, ME: Bowdoin College, 1982), 85.

48. BCSC, cited in Sadik, 220, note 25.

49. Helmreich, 85.

50. On the power of art see David Freedberg, *The Power of Images, Studies in the History and Theory of Response* (Chicago: University of Chicago Press, 1989), especially Chapter 13. The Senses and Censorship. On the effect of lascivious pictures like *Jupiter and Danaë,* see Lope de Vega, *The Case for Painting as a Liberal Art,* in Vincencio Carducho, *Diálogos de la pintura* (Madrid, 1633). Translated from edition of D. G. Cruzada Villaamil (Madrid, 1865), 371-378, by Robert Enggass and Jonathan Brown, *Italy and Spain, 1600-1750, Sources and Documents* (Englewood Cliffs, NJ: Prentice-Hall, Inc., 1970), 170; St. Augustine, *Confessions,* trans. J. G. Pilkington (Ipswich: W. S. Cowell, Ltd., 1962), I, 15, where he recounts Terence's description of a youth incited to lust by looking at a picture of *Danaë and the Golden Shower.*

51. Howarth to Woods, "My Report respecting Paintings," Feb. 1850, BCSC, Museum of Art, not yet filed in 1992.

52. Charles Carroll Everett, *Leonard Woods, A Discourse* (9 July 1977), 12.

53. Warren L. Draper, *The Life and Character of Leonard Woods, D.D., L.L.D.* (Andover, 1880), 44.

54. Wheeler to Woods, 1847, BCSC, Chapel Papers.

55. Hoppin to Woods, 10 April 1847, BCSC, Chapel Papers. Asher B. Durand, whom Hoppin names in his letter, proclaimed the high purpose of art: "It is only through the religious integrity of motive by which all real artists have been activated," cited in Roger B. Stein, *John Ruskin and Aesthetic Thought in America, 1840-1900* (Cambridge, MA, 1967), 217.

56. Hoppin to Woods, 4 August 1847, BCSC, Chapel Papers.

57. BCSC, Chapel Papers, Miscellaneous.

58. Hoppin to Woods, 4 August 1847, BCSC, Chapel Papers. In this same letter Hoppin quotes a passage from Count Raczynski, author of *Histoire de l'art moderne en Allemagne* and great admirer of the Nazarene painters' revival of fresco painting in Germany. Perhaps Hoppin helped focus ideas for the Chapel's mural decoration on a combination of Old Master works and Nazarene compositions, such as Cornelius's *Adoration of the Magi.*

59. Roger B. Ray, "Edna Marrett and Her Chapel Murals," *Bowdoin Alumnus* (Fall 1982), 20.

60. On the fame of Raphael's tapestry cartoons see Lambert, 105, 112. In 1858 Raphael's cartoons were photographed by Charles Thompson Thurston before their transfer from Hampton Court to the South Kensington Museum. A very popular set of prints after the Raphael cartoons was published by George Baxter around 1860. The choice of two Raphael cartoons as models for the Chapel murals predates both these events.

On reproductive prints after Raphael, see R. M. Mason and M. Natale, *Raphael et la seconde main* (Geneva: Musée d'art et d'histoire, 1984); Kimball, 242. On Raphael's high reputation in America, see Brown and Marjorie B. Cohn, *Francis Calley Gray and Art Collecting for America* (Cambridge: Harvard University Press, 1986), 123-132. James Bowdoin III's collection of drawings included a print by Ugo da Carpi after Raphael's cartoon of the *Death of Ananias* (1811.72). Bowdoin also owned a copy after a Raphael *Holy Family* (1813.9).

61. *Daily Tribune*, Bath, 29 October 1855, BCSC, Chapel Papers.

62. On Americans' distaste for certain Catholic images, see Lillian B. Miller, "'An Influence in the Air,' Italian Art and American Taste in the Mid-Nineteenth Century," in Irma B. Jaffe, ed., *The Italian Presence in American Art, 1760-1860* (New York: Fordham University Press, 1989), 45.

63. The status of Rubens's Antwerp altarpiece was very high in America, particularly since it was so well known through reproductive prints. In 1830 the Boston Athenaeum had displayed a highly praised copy of Rubens's *Descent from the Cross*, the central image from the altarpiece. It had been copied by F. de Brackelaer, a Flemish painter. See Alexander Everett, "Exhibition of Pictures at the Athenaeum Gallery," *North American Review* 31 (October 1830), 323-324, cited in Cohn, 112. Henry Wadsworth Longfellow made a point of visiting Antwerp to view Rubens's famous work, which impressed him greatly. See Longfellow letters of 5, 8, and 21 June 1842. *The Letters of Henry Wadsworth Longfellow*, Andrew Hilen, ed. (Cambridge, MA: Belknap Press of Harvard University Press), vol. 2, 411, 414, 421.

64. On the Nazarenes, see Keith Andrews, *The Nazarenes: A Brotherhood of German Painters in Rome* (New York: Hacker Art Books, 1988).

65. Hatch, 423.

66. George J. Varney, "The Art-Treasures of Bowdoin College," *Art Journal* (1880), 376.

67. Montgomery, "Architecture of American Colleges, VII—Brown, Bowdoin, Trinity, Wesleyan," *Architectural Record* (February 1911), 152.

68. For lists of painters, subjects, donors, and honorees, see Varney, 376. Two versions of an anonymous, undated pamphlet on the murals contain some errors (BCSC, Chapel Papers). Hatch, 421-424; *Descriptive Catalogue of the Art Collections of Bowdoin College*, Fourth Edition (Brunswick, ME, 1930), 110-111. Helmreich, 86-87; Ray, 20-21; and Patricia McGraw Anderson, *The Architecture of Bowdoin College* (Brunswick, ME: Bowdoin College Museum of Art, 1988), 28, give modern accounts with Helmreich's being the most complete and accurate.

Dr. Kathleen Curran is currently preparing a book on the *Rundbogenstil* in Germany and its influence in America, with the Upjohn Chapel as a premier example. She has spoken on the Bowdoin murals at the Meeting of the Society of Architectural Historians in Cincinatti, 1991, "New Thoughts on the Introduction of Polychromy in America."

69. Cited in Hatch, 453.

70. Roswell D. Hitchcock, Sermon, [7 June 1855], Dedication of the Chapel, n.p., BCSC, Chapel Papers. In 1870 Hitchcock published a new analysis of the Holy Bible with original engravings. Hitchcock's sentiments are echoed by many American ministers around mid-century. On religion's need of art in nineteenth-century America see Lawrence W. Levine, *Highbrow/Lowbrow, The Emergence of Cultural Hierarchy in America* (Cambridge: Harvard University Press, 1988), 150.

71. See Appendix I for a summary of Stuart's observations as recorded in later sources.

72. Shepley to Cleaveland, 23 July 1839, BCSC, Chapel Papers.

73. Bowdoin College Governing Boards Votes, 4 August 1857, BCSC.

74. "The Picture 'Sold by Order of the Boards,'" *Bowdoin Orient* 7, no. 4, 6 June 1877, 43-44.

75. Varney, 377. George Thomas Little, "Historical Sketch," in *General Catalogue of Bowdoin College and the Medical School of Maine 1794-1894* (Brunswick, ME: Bowdoin College, 1894), 29, also considered the Titian copies remaining in the collection to be adequate representations of the Italian school of painting. An anonymous, undated list of the "choicest pieces" in the Bowdoin collection presumably made right before the works were to be exhibited in the Chapel for the first time, lists no. 4, *Danaë and the Golden Shower*, among the twenty-six best. Presumably this one individual thought the painting worthy of display at Bowdoin (BCSC, Chapel Papers, Miscellaneous).

76. Varney, 377.

77. Cited in Hatch, 453.

78. Johnson, 12-13; *Descriptive Catalogue of the Bowdoin College Art Collections*, rev. ed. (Brunswick, ME: Bowdoin College, 1903), 11-12; Henry Johnson, *Descriptive Catalogue of the Art Collections of Bowdoin College*, third rev. ed. (Brunswick, ME: Bowdoin College, 1906), 11-12; *Descriptive Catalogue* (1930), 14-15. One possible "reading" of the Walker Art Building's facade might be: This temple to the three visual arts—painting, architecture, and sculpture—invokes the great art of the Western tradition, beginning with the Greeks and continuing up through the seventeenth-century masters Murillo and Rembrandt. Art finds its natural place among the liberal arts, and these artists named here match the power of the ancient orators and poets—Sophocles, Demosthenes, and Homer—whose images frame the entrance. That power is a power to delight and to instruct.

79. On the purchase orders for the plaster casts, see BCMA file, Plaster Casts. Vote of the Boards, 12 July 1882, BCSC, where Thomas's letter is also preserved; cited in Hatch, 452. Undated photographs of the Chapel show what appears to be the north aisle of the building with seven of the casts displayed among the paintings.

Another shows the Laocoön and Augustus gracing the portals of the library.

80. Johnson (1895), 8, and Henry Johnson, Pamphlet for 1881 Commencement, Works of Art in the College Chapel, North Wing (BCSC), where casts are listed and described as purchased with money from friends of the College "who are specially interested in Bowdoin as a college of the times." The needs of the department still require further monies, and Johnson asks for help from anyone who wants "to help Bowdoin College in her endeavors to impart a generous classical education." The Boston Museum of Fine Arts had a comparable educational purpose behind its large collection of plaster casts. See Levine, 151-154.

81. Bowdoin had sought to acquire a bust of Apollo, perhaps the Apollo Belvedere, see note 41.

82. Cited in Hatch, 456.

83. Philip C. Beam, *Personal Recollections of the Museum of Art and the Department of Art at Bowdoin College* (Brunswick, ME: Bowdoin College Museum of Art, 1991), 16. Beam recounts the Herculean effort to refurbish the galleries after forty years of neglect and the subsequent disposal of the grimy plaster casts around 1939.

84. Matthew Stewart Prichard, assistant director of the Boston Museum of Fine Arts, 1903-1906, quoted in Levine, 154.

85. From Emerson's "Domestic Life" in *The Complete Works of Ralph Waldo Emerson*, vol. 7 (Boston and New York: Houghton Mifflin Company, 1904), 130-132; quoted in *Descriptive Catalogue* (1930), 6-7.

86. Kevin Herbert, *Ancient Art in Bowdoin College* (Cambridge: Harvard University Press, 1964), 2.

87. Martin Brimmer, *An Address Delivered at Bowdoin College Upon the Opening of the Walker Art Building* (Boston and NY: Houghton Mifflin and Co., 1894), 26. On Brimmer's trip with Woods, see Everett, 16.

88. Brimmer, 26-27.

89. On the transformation of the work of art in the face of multiple copies, see Walter Benjamin, "The Work of Art in the Age of Mechanical Reproduction," in *Illuminations*, 217-251. Heliotype reproductions at the museum, Johnson (1895), 10. Hutchins's photos, *Descriptive Catalogue* (1903).

90. On the documentary photographic collections and lending gallery, see *Descriptive Catalogue* (1930), 11-12; *An Illustrated Handbook of the Bowdoin College Museum of Fine Arts in the Walker Art Building, Brunswick, Maine*, fifth ed. (Brunswick, ME: Bowdoin College, 1950), 10-11; Beam, 12, 19. On art instruction at Bowdoin, see Hatch, 202, and Beam 12, 17, 21-22.

91. In *Bowdoin College Bulletin*, no. 197, May 1930, President's Report, 1930-1931, "Report of the Director of the Museum of Fine Arts," the Stuart *Jefferson* had been copied; in 1933-34, the James Bowdoin portrait by Feke was being copied. George Swift made several copies after the LaCroix *Seaport* (1813.31) and one after the Raphael copy (1813.9).

92. Deborah Anne Federhen, et al., *Accumulation and Display, Mass Marketing Household Goods in America 1880-1920* (The Henry Francis du Pont Winterthur Museum, 1986), 98, 101.

93. On late twentieth-century art and the search for something more than modernism's outworn notion of "perpetual innovation and the creation of new styles," see Suzi Gablik, *The Reenchantment of Art* (New York: Thames and Hudson, 1991).

94. Livy, *History of Rome*, 26:50. The story is retold by the Renaissance writer Petrarch in his poem *Africa* 4:375-88, which praises Scipio's virtue. An eighteenth-century understanding of the picture is published by Sadik, 213. It is Dr. Alexander Hamilton's description of a *Scipio* he saw in Smibert's studio on 24 July 1744: "I went this night to visit Mr. Smibert, the limner, where I saw a collection of fine pictures, among the rest that part of Scipio's history in Spain where he delivers the lady to the prince to whom she had been betrothed. The passions are all well touched in the severall faces. Scipio's face expresses a majestic generosity, that of the young prince in gratitude, the young lady's gratitude and modest love, and some Roman souldiers standing under a row of pillars apart in seeming discourse, have admiration delineated in their faces. But what I admired most of the painter's fancy in this piece is an image or phantome of chastity behind the solium upon which Scipio sits, standing on tip-toe to crown him and yet appears as if she could not reach his head which expresses a good emblem of the virtue of this action." See also Foote, 89-90, who comments on the work's appeal to the moral sentiment of eighteenth-century viewers.

The numbers used here correspond to the numbering used in the 1813 Abbott Inventory preserved in manuscript in BCSC. Included in this list are works that are no longer at Bowdoin College, but which made up part of the original bequest of the Honorable James Bowdoin III. Measurements of deaccessioned works are taken from a variety of documentary sources.

1. Anonymous (seventeenth-century Italian?)
Fish Shambles
oil on canvas
38 x 52 5/8 inches (96.5 x 133.8 cm)
1813.13

2. Anonymous, after Titian, Italian (1477-1576)
Education of Cupid
oil on canvas
47 x 66 inches
1813.23

3. Anonymous, after Nicholas Poussin, French (1594-1665) (fig. 26)
The Continence of Scipio
oil on canvas
46 x 62 inches (116.8 x 157.5 cm)
1813.10

4. Anonymous, after Titian, Italian (1477-1576) (fig. 8)
Danaë and the Shower of Gold
oil on canvas
ca. 3 feet 8 inches x 5 feet 8 inches
Whereabouts unknown. Formerly C. Klackner, 7 West 28th St., New York, NY (1915); Miss Jennie Brownscombe; Mr. George Hall, 10th St. Studio, NY, NY (1863?); Mr. Nathan Cummings, Bowdoin Class of 1817, Portland, ME (ca. 1860?)

5. Anonymous (fig. 5)
A Painter's Studio
oil on canvas
26 3/4 x 33 inches (67.8 x 83.9 cm)
1813.46

6. Anonymous (fig. 6)
A Sculptor's Studio
oil on canvas
26 1/2 x 33 1/8 inches (67.3 x 84.2 cm)
1813.45

7. Gaspar de Witte, Flemish (1624-1681)
Still Life with Dead Birds
oil on canvas
27 x 33 inches
1813.30

8. Bernaert de Bridt, Flemish (active 1688-1722)
Still Life with Hare, Fruit and Bird
oil on canvas
32 1/2 x 22 1/2 inches
1813.37

9. Jan Frans van Bloemen, Flemish (1622-1740)?
Farmyard Scene
oil on canvas
22 1/2 x 32 1/2 inches
1813.38

10. Anonymous, Flemish School? (fig. 29)
Sacking of a Town
here retitled *Massacre of Protestants*
oil on canvas
(59 x 70 cm)
Whereabouts unknown. Formerly Mr. Emery Booker, Brunswick, ME (1941). Last recorded at Bowdoin, 1930; recorded as no longer present, 1941.

11. Jan Frans van Bloemen, Flemish (1662-1740)?
Farmyard Scene
oil on canvas
22 1/2 x 32 1/2 inches
1813.32

12. David Ryckaert the Younger, Flemish (1612-1661)
Surgeon and Patient
oil on canvas
21 1/2 x 33 inches
1813.36

13. Anonymous, after Nicolas Mignard, French (1605/1608-1668)?
School of Guido Reni, Italian (1575-1642)
Sleeping Cupid
oil on canvas
23 1/2 x 28 1/4 inches
1813.35

14. Anonymous
Landscape with Aged Herdsman and Cattle
oil on canvas
28 3/4 x 38 1/2 inches (73 x 98 cm)
1813.1

15. Anonymous, formerly attributed to Nicolaas
P. Berchem, Dutch (1620-1683)
Landscape with Travelers
oil on canvas
22 1/2 x 27 1/2 inches
1813.41

16. Attributed to Jacques Courtois, French
(1621-1676)
Landscape with Figures
oil on canvas
20 x 25 inches
1813.14

17. Anonymous, formerly attributed to Jacques
Stella (1595-1657)
Infant St. John the Baptist
oil on canvas
27 1/2 x 23 inches (72.5 x 58.5 cm)
1813.42

18. Anonymous, manner of Adriaen Van
Ostade, Dutch (1610-1685)
Dairy Woman of Holland
oil on canvas
26 x 21 inches
1813.47

19. Attributed to Hendrik van Steenwyck the
Younger, Dutch (?-before 1649) (fig. 30)
formerly *Church Interior with Meal by
Candlelight*
here retitled as *Babylonians Consuming
Offerings Made to the Idol Bel*
18 1/8 x 15 5/8 inches (46 x 40 cm)
Last recorded at Bowdoin, 1930; recorded
as no longer present, 1941. Presumed
destroyed; corresp. 16 March 1948, curator
Albert S. Roe
Wadsworth Atheneum, Hartford,
Connecticut, Ella Gallup Sumner and Mary
Callin Sumner Collection
1940.196
Provenance: [Victor D. Spark, New York],
ca. 1940

20. Jacques Fouquières, French (1600-1659)
Landscape with Dancing Peasants
oil on canvas
17 x 23 inches
1813.25

21. Anonymous, after? Melchior Hondecoeter,
Dutch (1636-1695)
Poultry
oil on canvas
13 x 18 1/4 inches
1813.18

22. Anonymous
The Several Stages of Human Life
(45 x 57 cm)
Whereabouts unknown. Last recorded at
Bowdoin, 1930; recorded as no longer
present, 1941.

23. Adriaen Frans Boudewyns, Flemish
(1644-1711)
Peeter Bout, Flemish (1658-1719)
Landscape with Ruins and Figures
oil on canvas
11 x 16 inches
1813.24

24. Adriaen Frans Boudewyns, Flemish
(1644-1711)
Peeter Bout, Flemish (1658-1719)
Landscape with Ruins and Figures
oil on canvas
10 1/2 x 16 inches
1813.29

25. Attributed to Simon Vouet, French
(1590-1649)
Entombment of Christ (?) or *Maries at the Tomb (?)*
oil on copper
(29 x 42 cm)
Whereabouts unknown. Last recorded at
Bowdoin, 1930; recorded as no longer
present, 1941.

26. Pierre Patel, French (1605?-1676)
Landscape with Ruins
oil on canvas
14 x 17 1/2 inches (35.6 x 44.5 cm)
1813.19

27. François Jouillain, French (1697-1778)
Landscape with Nymphs Bathing
oil on panel
9 3/4 x 12 7/8 inches
1813.27

28. François Jouillain, French (1697-1778)
Torre dei Schiavi
oil on panel
9 7/16 x 12 3/4 inches (24 x 32.4 cm)
1813.48

29. François Jouillain, French (1697-1778)
Landscape with Hunters
oil on panel
10 1/2 x 12 3/4 inches
1813.17

30. Gilbert Stuart, American (1755-1828)
(fig. 3)
Portrait of James Madison, 1805-07
oil on canvas
48 1/4 x 39 3/4 inches (122.9 x 101.0 cm)
1813.54

31. Gilbert Stuart, American (1755-1828)
(fig. 2)
Portrait of Thomas Jefferson, 1805-07
48 3/8 x 39 3/4 inches (122.9 x 101.0 cm)
1813.55

32. After Philips Wouwerman, Dutch
(1614/1619-1668)
by Wilhelm Fischbein (1751-1829)
Artillery
oil on panel
9 1/4 x 13 1/2 inches
1813.28

33. After Anthony van Dyck, Flemish
(1599-1641)
by John Smibert, American (1688-1751)
Jean de Montfort
oil on canvas
28 1/2 x 22 inches
1813.5

34. Attributed to Nathaniel Smibert, American
(1735-1756)
The Reverend Samson Occom (?)ca. 1756 (?)
oil on canvas
30 1/4 x 24 3/4 inches
1813.4

35. Anonymous, after Guido Reni?, Italian
(1575-1642) (fig. 17)
Salome with the Head of St. John the Baptist
oil on canvas
23 x 30 inches
1813.3

36. Anonymous
Bust Portrait of Christ
oil on canvas
30 x 24 inches
1813.7

37. Anonymous, after Joseph Boze, French
(ca. 1746-1826), and Robert Lefèvre,
French (1756-1830) (fig. 11)
Bust Portrait of Mirabeau
oil on canvas
19 1/2 x 14 inches
1813.16

38. After Paolo Veronese, Italian (1528-1588)
by Hendrik van Balen, Flemish (1560-1638)
Adoration of the Magi
oil on panel
19 1/2 x 25 1/2 inches
1813.43

39. Anonymous (fig. 23)
Descent from the Cross
oil on canvas?
(71 x 58 cm)
[1813.49]
Whereabouts unknown. Last recorded at
Bowdoin, 1930; recorded as no longer
present, 1941.

40. Anonymous (fig. 28)
John the Baptist Preaching to the Multitudes
oil on canvas?
(47 x 65 cm)
[1813.51]
Whereabouts unknown. Last recorded at
Bowdoin, 1930; recorded as no longer
present, 1941.

41. Anonymous
Portrait of a Man in a Ruff
"Aetatis Suae 62 Anno 1647"
oil on canvas
42 x 36 inches
1813.53

42. Attributed to Jan Fyt, Flemish (1609-1661)
Still Life with Dead Birds
oil on canvas
26 x 19 1/2 inches (66 x 49.5 cm)
1813.33

43. Attributed to Jan Fyt, Flemish (1609-1661)
Still Life with Dead Birds and Hare
oil on canvas
26 x 19 1/2 inches (59.8 x 49.5 cm)
1813.34

44. Anonymous, after Raphael, Italian
(1483-1520)
Virgin and Child with St. Elizabeth and St. John
43 1/4 x 39 3/4 inches (109.5 x 101 cm)
1813.9

45. Anonymous
Translation of Elijah
oil on canvas
28 x 23 inches
1813.6

46. Anonymous, after Peter Paul Rubens,
Flemish (1577-1640) (fig. 25)
St. Simeon Holding the Infant Christ
oil on canvas
34 x 45 inches
1813.11

47. Anonymous
Venus and Adonis
probably oil on canvas
small
Whereabouts unknown. Deaccessioned ca.
1850s. Formerly in collection of Mr. George
Howarth, Boston (1853?)

48. After Jacopo Tintoretto, Italian
(1518-1594)
by John Smibert, American (1688-1751)
Luigi Cornaro
oil on canvas
30 x 25 inches
1813.8

49. Anonymous, French?
Portrait of a Clergyman
oil on canvas
30 x 25 inches
1813.20

50. Anonymous, Flemish?
Torture Scene from the Inquisition, 1644
(48 x 34 cm)
Whereabouts unknown. Last recorded at
Bowdoin, 1930; recorded as no longer
present, 1941.

51. Anonymous, after Titian, Italian
(1477-1576) (fig. 1)
Venus and Adonis
oil on canvas
52 x 71 inches
1813.21

52. Anonymous
Lot and His Daughters
medium unknown
small
Whereabouts unknown. Deaccessioned ca.
1850s. Formerly in collection of Mr. George
Howarth, Boston (1853?)

53. Anonymous, after an Italian work? (fig. 15)
Cleopatra
oil on panel
(66 x 52 cm)
[1813.52]
Whereabouts unknown. Last recorded at
Bowdoin, 1930; recorded as no longer
present, 1941.

54. Anonymous
String of Perch
(33 x 29 cm)
Whereabouts unknown. Last recorded at
Bowdoin, 1930; recorded as no longer
present, 1941.

55. Anonymous, after Charles LeBrun, French
(1619-1690), eighteenth-century artist?
Head of a Woman (Fear?)
oil on panel
9 1/2 x 7 1/2 inches
1813.15

56. Attributed to Antonio Balestra, Italian
(1666-1740)
St. Peter Delivered from Prison by an Angel
oil on canvas
58 x 44 inches (147.3 x 111.8 cm)
1813.22

57. Anonymous, eighteenth-century Flemish?
    (fig. 16)
    Venus and Adonis (formerly *Diana and
    Endymion*)
    oil on canvas
    41 3/4 x 54 3/4 inches
    1813.50

58. Cornelis Schut I, Flemish (1597-1655)
    (fig. 21)
    Allegory of Fruitfulness (formerly *Venus and
    Ceres*)
    oil on canvas
    44 1/2 x 58 1/2 inches
    1813.12

59. Anonymous, Flemish School? (fig. 28)
    Fox Devouring a Pheasant
    oil on canvas?
    (57 x 49 cm)
    Whereabouts unknown. Last recorded at
    Bowdoin, 1930; recorded as no longer
    present, 1941.

60. Anonymous, Flemish School? (fig. 28)
    Combat of Hyena and Dogs
    oil on canvas?
    (57 x 49 cm)
    Whereabouts unknown. Last recorded at
    Bowdoin, 1930; recorded as no longer
    present, 1941.

61. Attributed to Jacob Jordaens, Flemish
    (1593-1678)
    Discovery of Callisto (Formerly *Diana and
    Nymphs Bathing*)
    oil on canvas?
    2 feet 6 inches x 3 feet 6 inches
    Whereabouts unknown. Deaccessioned ca.
    1850s. Formerly in the collection of Mr.
    George Howarth, Boston (1853?)

62. Anonymous, Italian? (fig. 9)
    Adoration of the Magi
    oil on canvas?
    (63 x 49 cm)
    Whereabouts unknown. Last recorded at
    Bowdoin, 1930; recorded as no longer pre-
    sent, 1941.

63. Frans Francken, the Younger, Flemish
    (1581-1642?) (fig. 7)
    Esther before Ahasueras
    oil on panel

20 13/16 x 31 1/2 inches (52.8 x 80.1 cm)
1813.39

64. Adam? Willaerts, Dutch (1577-1664)
    Ships on a Stormy Coast
    oil on panel
    14 x 25 inches (35.6 x 63.5 cm)
    1813.26

65. Attributed to Frans Francken III, Flemish
    (1607-1655) (fig. 14)
    Achilles among the Daughters of Lycomedes
    oil on panel
    20 1/16 x 31 11/16 inches
    (51.9 x 80.5 cm)
    1813.2

66. Attributed to Bartholomeus Breenberg,
    Dutch (ca. 1620–after 1663)
    Landscape with Herd and Flock
    oil on canvas
    19 1/2 x 26 1/2 inches
    1813.44

67. Adrien Manglard, French (1695-1760)
    Sea Fight
    oil on canvas
    21 1/2 x 34 1/2 inches
    1813.40

68. Charles F. LaCroix, French (?-1784)
    Seaport with Fortress, 1754
    oil on canvas
    13 9/16 x 25 3/16 inches (34.5 x 64.0 cm)
    1813.31

69. Anonymous (fig. 15)
    Peasants and Cattle
    oil on canvas?
    (38 x 54 cm)
    Whereabouts unknown. Last recorded at
    Bowdoin, 1930; recorded as no longer
    present, 1941.

70. After Paulus Potter, Dutch (1625-1654)
    by Michael Carré, Dutch (1657-1727 or 47)
    (fig. 15)
    Cattle
    oil on canvas?
    (40 x 48 cm)
    Whereabouts unknown. Last recorded at
    Bowdoin, 1930; recorded as no longer
    present, 1941.

APPENDIX I
GILBERT STUART'S LOST
"CATALOGUE" OF THE PAINTINGS
OF JAMES BOWDOIN III

This so-called catalogue is first mentioned in a letter of 23 July 1839 as lost already during the time when J. R. Shepley worked as a librarian (BCSC, Parker Cleaveland papers). Stuart presumably visited Bowdoin College around 1821 to make copies of his Madison and Jefferson portraits, and made his comments on the other works then. They can be summarized as follows:

No. 3. *Continence of Scipio*
Gilbert Stuart thought it an original or a first-rate copy from Nicolas Poussin (1870 catalogue, no. 3; 1880 catalogue, no. 3, p. 377; 1895 Catalogue, no. 132, p. 40).

Nos. 30 and 31. Stuart's own *Madison and Jefferson*
"Stuart declared in 1821 that he regarded them as good as originals, A. S. P." (ca. 1855 ms. catalogue, with notes by Alpheus Spring Packard '16, member of the Bowdoin faculty, 1816-1884; Sadik, p. 159).

No. 33. *Jean de Montfort*
"I heard Stuart say that he recognized it as an original by Vandyke, having seen it forty years before in Europe—This was said in 1821 or about that time. A. S. P." (ca. 1855 ms. catalogue, with notes by Packard; Sadik, p. 160).

No. 46. *St. Simeon*
Thought by Stuart to be an original by Rubens (1870 catalogue). "This noble picture, the most remarkable of the collection, is in the style of Rubens and was thought by Stuart to be an original. It is either a duplicate or a fine copy of *St. Simeon with the Child Jesus* by Rubens, in the Cathedral at Antwerp" (1880 catalogue, p. 377).

No. 65. *Achilles*
Attributed by Stuart to Rubens (1870 catalogue) Previous to and independent of the judgment of Stuart [ca. 1821] a record accompanying the painting describes it as an imitation of Rubens by Teniers (1895 catalogue, no. 147, p. 42).

FIG. 29 Anonymous, *Sacking of a Town*, retitled *Massacre of Protestants*

An undated ms. in BCSC, Chapel papers, misc., describes the paintings "some which Stuart and other competent judges have pronounced originals by Titian, Rubens, Poussin, Teniers and Van Dyke."

The 1950 catalogue inflates Stuart's pronouncements a bit, claiming that "Stuart on a visit to Brunswick in 1821 pronounced them original paintings by Raphael [no evidence], Titian [no evidence], Tintoretto [no evidence], Van Dyck and Poussin" (p. 24).

APPENDIX II
NOTES ON SOME LOST PAINTINGS

The So-Called *Sacking of a Town*
(no. 10) (fig. 29)

This painting, known to me only from photographs, shows not the sack of a town, but a massacre in a northern town. The view encompasses an impressive harbor with two towers flanking the entrance into the town. Comparison with sixteenth-century documentary prints suggests that this may be an episode from the fierce Catholic-Protestant conflicts of that century and the next.

I believe that the work shows a massacre of Protestants, an event that occurred with

FIG. 30 Attributed to Hendrick van Steenwyck the Younger, *Church Interior with Meal by Candlelight*, retitled *Babylonians Consuming Offerings Made to the Idol Bel*

appalling frequency. Such massacre or persecution pictures were abundant in sixteenth-century France, and a good number of engravings record specific events with general patterns: Catholic troops armed with harquebuses, swords, and halberds massacre defenseless men and women. These horrors are seen from an elevated vantage point looking down a principle street. Sometimes a river or body of water marks the foreground.

The Bowdoin family may have acquired this painting as a kind of record of their ancestors' history in France. Pierre Baudouin had fled the French city La Rochelle, site of two important sieges in the Catholic-Protestant conflict, 1572/73 and 1627/8. While it cannot be said with certainty that this work shows the persecutions of the Huguenots at La Rochelle, the general similarity of the massive towers to that of the

port of La Rochelle may have been enough for the Bowdoins.

Two other Bowdoin pictures may have had links to the theme of Catholic persecution of Protestants: a *Torture Scene from the Inquisition* (no. 50) and the *Church Interior with a Meal by Candlelight* (no. 19), here identified as *Babylonians Consuming Offerings Made to the Idol Bel* (fig. 30). Professor Henry Johnson described the former and the *Sacking* in unpublished notes found in his desk, now in BCSC:

50—A scene in the inquisition, a picture from the Flemish School 1644, an interior at night, a young man over whose head is held a staff(?) perpendicularly by an old man, the principal figure. The latter holds in his right hand [unreadable] is dressed in full robes, chains and medals hanging about his neck. In the center and left are five figures seated at a table into whose heads bits are being driven by two servants standing. The fifth figure is of a gentleman dressed in black holding a drinking horn full of blood.

48 x 34 cm

10—*Sacking of a Town*, Flemish School

"Flamaind anagram P.S." on back of frame not of picture. no. 187 on back of picture. Conflagration of large building on the left between which and the spectator is outlined a high pier on which is built a lofty tower surmounted by 3 spires. In the foreground several boats full of combatants, several swimming. The center of the picture shows a view down a street on each side of which are lofty continuous rows of buildings. On the right and nearest the water is a round tower in the [unreadable] are slaughtered bodies and scenes of murder depicted. In the middle distance is a lurid flame, on the extreme right the full moon is just rising showing the outline of a distant windmill.

59 x 70 cm

The third work is described in the early nineteenth-century anonymous manuscript "Catalogue of Paintings in the Picture Gallery of Bowdoin College" in the files at the Walker Art Building:

No. 19. *Funeral Obsequies*
Painter unknown.

Scene in the interior of a church(?)
In the background is the altar while in the foreground apparently is a "Paddy Wake." The picture is one of the gems of the collection.

The painting is now in the Wadsworth Atheneum (Sumner Collection, 1940.196), oil on canvas, 18 1/8" x 15 5/8" (46 x 40 cm). Attributed to Hendrick van Steenwyck the Younger, the painting has been identified as showing Babylonians consuming offerings made to the idol Bel, a theme from the apocryphal book of Bel and the Dragon. Verses 1-22 recount Daniel's refusal to worship the idol Bel and his exposure of the priests' fraud in consuming the food offerings supposedly devoured by the living god. This anti-idolatry theme could have had an anti-Catholic reading in the Protestant Netherlands in the seventeenth century. It is ironic that the nineteenth-century catalogue compiler understood it in just the opposite way, as a scene of a Catholic wake.

These three works may well have held special place in the Bowdoin family history. The works connected them to their Huguenot ancestors, chronicling the persecution that Pierre Baudouin had successfully escaped in the late 1680s. This aspect of the family's personal mythology could be celebrated in paintings as well as in the eulogies and biographies that have survived down to the present. James Bowdoin III proudly wrote "I am the eldest descendant from one of the unfortunate families which was obliged to fly their native country on account of religion; a family, which, as I understand, lived in affluence, perhaps elegance, upon a handsome estate in the neighborhood of Rochelle, which at that time (1685) yielded the considerable income of 700 louis d'ors per annum" (Winthrop, 3).

References:

[Perrissin, Jean, ca. 1536-ca. 1611] *Premier volume, contenant Quarante tableaux ou Histoires diverses qui sont memorables touchant les guerres, massacres, and troubles advenus en France en ces dernieres anees* [Geneva, J. de Laon? ca. 1570].

Robert C. Winthrop. *The Life and Services of James Bowdoin,* 2nd ed. [An Address Delivered Before the Maine Historical Society, at Bowdoin College, on the Afternoon of the Annual Commencement, September 5, 1849] (Boston: Press of John Wilson and Son, 1876), 2-5, 46.

Wadsworth Atheneum Paintings, Catalogue I, *The Netherlands and the German-speaking Countries, Fifteenth-Nineteenth Centuries,* ed. Egbert Haverkamp-Begemann (Hartford, 1978), 41, 190-191.

COPY AFTER TITIAN
Danaë and the Shower of Gold (no. 4) (fig. 8)

This painting seems finally to have been sold after much discussion to Mr. Nathan Cummings 1818, for the sum of $250 around 1860. Cummings sold the work in 1863 to Mr. George Henry Hall of New York, an artist and collector in whose 10th Street studio it was seen in 1877. Mr. Hall bequeathed it to Miss Jennie Brownscombe, the illustrator, around 1915. It was advertised for sale by C. Klackner, 7 West 285th Street, in New York, in 1915 (BCMA files).

The *Danaë* is the most famous and infamous of the Bowdoin paintings separated from the collection since 1813. Titian's first pair of *Danaë* and *Venus and Adonis* was made for Cardinal Alessandro Farnese, the *Danaë* now in Naples, Museo di Capodimonte and the *Venus and Adonis* lost, but represented in close replicas like those in Washington, The National Gallery, and New York, The Metropolitan Museum of Art (49.7.16). These works were immensely famous during Titian's lifetime, and he made second versions after them on the occasion of Philip II of Spain's betrothal. This pair of works in a variety of variants and copies had an extensive afterlife well into the seventeenth, eighteenth, and nineteenth centuries.

James Bowdoin III's *Danaë* was a copy after Titian's Naples version with a little Cupid in the foreground. The *Venus and Adonis* copy paired with it (no. 51) follows closely the version now in the Metropolitan Museum of Art. Bowdoin's pictures thus reflected Titian's earliest ideas set down in the pair he made for Cardinal Farnese.

One index of the fame of Titian's pair of *poesie* is the sale of numerous copies of them in England around 1801. Burton B. Frederickson, ed., *The Index of Paintings Sold in the British Isles During the 19th Century, 1801-1805*, vol. 1, lists among the Titian pictures ten sales of versions of *Venus and Adonis* and eleven of *Danaë*, either copies or purported originals. The pair in James Bowdoin III's collection fit right in with British taste at the time.

The American outrage against Titian's nudes is not limited to the *Danaë*, whose power to incite lust might well have been linked with the passage in the classic comedy *The Eunuch* of Terence (act 3, scene 5), where a picture of a *Danaë* inspires a young man. St. Augustine, Johannes Molanus (1570), and the Dominican writer Ambrogio Catarino Politi (1542) all comment on Terence's *Danaë* and its effects. Mark Twain, in *A Tramp Abroad* (1880), describes Titian's *Venus of Urbino* as "the foulest, the vilest, the obscenest picture the world possesses." This passage is cited and discussed by Leo Steinberg, "Art and Science: Do They Need to be Yoked?" *Daedalus* (Summer 1986), 11; and by David Freedberg, *The Power of Images, Studies in the History and Theory of Response* (Chicago: University of Chicago Press, 1989), 345-6. Jane Clapp, *Art Censorship, A Chronology of Proscribed and Prescribed Art* (Metuchen, NJ: Scarecrow Press, Inc., 1972), 101, records a 1794 notice of Wertmuller's painting of a nude *Danaë* that caused a scandal when exhibited in Philadelphia. See also Wayne Craven, *Sculpture in America* (New York: Crowell, 1968), 23, and Edgar P. Richardson, *Painting in America* (New York: Crowell, 1965).

A Bowdoin alumnus, Nathaniel Hawthorne 1825, comments not on *Danaë* specifically but on the female nude in sculpture. In his *Marble Faun* of around 1859 he has his artist, Miriam, a painter in Rome, say: "Every young sculptor seems to think that he must give the world some specimen of undecorous woman-hood, and call it Eve, a Venus, a Nymph, or any other name that may apologize for the lack of decent clothing. I am weary, even more ashamed, of seeing such things"(See Craven, 122).

References:

Frederick Rudolph, *Curriculum: A History of the American Undergraduate Course and Study Since 1636* (San Francisco: Jossey-Bass Publishers, 1978), reports that the *Danaë* left the College in 1860.

"Picture Sold by Order of the Boards," *Bowdoin Orient*, 6 June 1877, reports the work to have been sold in the 1860s for $250, which subsequently funded the painting of the copy after Jalabert's *Annunciation* in the Chapel.

Sadik, 220, note 25, says disposed of around 1850 to help defray restoration expenses; Hatch, 449-450, says *Danaë* was sold in 1860; Helmreich, 86, implies 1860 or later; Burke, 35; *Descriptive Catalogue* (1930), 110.

CONCORDANCE

MODERN ACCESSION NUMBER	1813 ABBOTT INVENTORY	1895 CATALOGUE THROUGH 1930 CATALOGUE	MODERN ACCESSION NUMBER	1813 ABBOTT INVENTORY	1895 CATALOGUE THROUGH 1930 CATALOGUE
1813.1	14	127	1813.36	12	152
1813.2	65	147	1813.37	8	168
1813.3	35	124	1813.38	9	157
1813.4	34	194	1813.39	63	150
1813.5	33	151	1813.40	67	136
1813.6	45	196	1813.41	15	172
1813.7	36	195	1813.42	17	133
1813.8	48	197	1813.43	38	160
1813.9	44	126	1813.44	66	170
1813.10	3	132	1813.45	6	162
1813.11	46	148	1813.46	5	161
1813.12	58	146	1813.47	18	175
1813.13	1	144	1813.48	28	138
1813.14	16	135	[1813.49]	39	128
1813.15	55	200	1813.50	57	165
1813.16	37	143	[1813.51]	40	129
1813.17	29	139	[1813.52]	53	130
1813.18	21	174	1813.53	41	177
1813.19	26	134	1813.54	30	184
1813.20	49	198	1813.55	31	183
1813.21	51	123	——	25	131
1313.22	56	142	——	19	145
1813.23	2	122	——	62	149
1813.24	23	155	——	50	156
1813.25	20	141	——	10	159
1813.26	64	169	——	59	163
1813.27	27	137	——	60	164
1813.28	32	171	——	70	173
1813.29	24	154	——	22	176
1813.30	7	153	——	69	201
1813.31	68	140	——	54	199
1813.32	11	158	——	4	——
1813.33	42	167	——	47	——
1813.34	43	166	——	52	——
1813.35	13	125	——	61	

S tarred works appear in color in this chapter. All works are the property of the Bowdoin College Museum of Art unless otherwise noted.

*1. Anonymous
after Titian
Italian, 1477–1576
Venus and Adonis
oil on canvas
52 x 71 inches
Bequest of the Honorable James
    Bowdoin III
1813.21

2. Gilbert Stuart
American, 1755–1828
Portrait of Thomas Jefferson, 1805–1807
oil on canvas
48 3/8 x 39 3/4 inches
Bequest of the Honorable James
    Bowdoin III
1813.55

3. Gilbert Stuart
American, 1755–1828
Portrait of James Madison, 1805–1807
oil on canvas
48 1/4 x 39 3/4 inches
Bequest of the Honorable James
    Bowdoin III
1813.54

4. Anonymous
Ariadne
marble
27 x 37 1/2 x 13 1/2 inches
Monticello, Thomas Jefferson Memorial
    Foundation
© 1992 Thomas Jefferson Memorial
    Foundation, Inc.
Photographer: Edward Owen

5. Anonymous
German?
A Painter's Studio
oil on canvas
26 3/4 x 33 inches
Bequest of the Honorable James
    Bowdoin III
1813.46

6. Anonymous
German?
A Sculptor's Studio
oil on canvas
26 1/2 x 33 1/8 inches
Bequest of the Honorable James
    Bowdoin III
1813.45

7. Frans Francken, the Younger
Flemish, 1581–1642
Esther before Ahasueras
oil on panel
20 13/16 x 31 1/2 inches
Bequest of the Honorable James
    Bowdoin III
1813.39

8. Anonymous
after Titian
Italian, 1477–1576
Danaë and the Shower of Gold
oil on canvas
ca. 48 x 68 inches
Bequest of the Honorable James
    Bowdoin III
1813 Abbott Inventory No.4

9. Anonymous
Italian?
Adoration of the Magi
oil on canvas?
63 x 49 cm.
Bequest of the Honorable James
    Bowdoin III
1813 Abbott Inventory No. 62

10. John Faber the Elder
    Dutch, ca. 1660–1721
    Formerly thought to be after Peter Paul
        Rubens
    Flemish, 1577–1640
    Homer
    mezzotint
    14 x 10 1/16 inches
    Bequest of the Honorable James
        Bowdoin III
    1813.58

11. Anonymous
    after Joseph Boze
    French, 1756–1830
    and Robert Lefèvre
    French, ca. 1746–1826
    Bust Portrait of Mirabeau
    oil on canvas
    14 x 19 1/2 inches
    Bequest of the Honorable James
        Bowdoin III
    1813.16

12. John Faber the Elder
    Dutch, ca. 1660–1721
    after Peter Paul Rubens
    Flemish 1577–1640
    Demosthenes
    mezzotint
    13 15/16 x 10 inches
    Bequest of the Honorable James
        Bowdoin III
    1813.61

13. Christian Gullager
    Danish, 1759–1826
    Portrait of Governor James Bowdoin II
    oil on wooden panel
    11 x 8 5/8 inches
    Bequest of Mrs. Sarah Bowdoin Dearborn
    1894.2

*14. Attributed to Frans Francken III
    Flemish 1607–1667
    Achilles among the Daughters of Lycomedes
    oil on panel
    20 1/16 x 31 11/16 inches
    Bequest of the Honorable James
        Bowdoin III
    1813.2

15. lower right:
    Anonymous
    copy after an Italian work?
    Cleopatra
    oil on panel
    66 x 52 cm.
    Bequest of the Honorable James
        Bowdoin III
    1813 Abbott Inventory No. 53

    far left:
    Michael Carré,
    Dutch, 1657–1727 or 1747?
    Copy after Paulus Potter
    Dutch, 1625–1654
    Cattle
    oil on canvas?
    40 x 48 cm.
    Bequest of the Honorable James
        Bowdoin III
    1813 Abbott Inventory No. 70

    top right:
    Anonymous
    Peasants and Cattle
    oil on canvas?
    38 x 54 cm.
    Bequest of the Honorable James
        Bowdoin III
    1813 Abbott Inventory No. 69

16. Anonymous
    Flemish, eighteenth century
    Venus and Adonis (formerly *Diana and
        Endymion*)
    oil on canvas
    41 3/4 x 54 3/4 inches
    Bequest of the Honorable James
        Bowdoin III
    1813.50

*17. Anonymous
    after Guido Reni
    Italian, 1575–1642
    Salome with the Head of John the Baptist
    oil on canvas
    23 x 30 inches
    Bequest of the Honorable James
        Bowdoin III
    1813.3

18. Daniel Müller
    German, active 1850s
    after Raphael
    Italian, 1483–1520
    Paul Preaching on Mars Hill in Athens, 1856
    mural, on support, affixed to the wall
    ca. 20 feet tall
    Chapel, Bowdoin College, Brunswick,
        Maine
    Photograph by Patrick L. Pinnell

19. Edna T. Marrett
    American, 1887–1968
    after Michelangelo
    Italian, 1475–1564
    The Delphic Sibyl (right)
    The Prophet Isaiah (left)
    mural, on support, affixed to the wall
    ca. 20 feet tall
    Chapel, Bowdoin College, Brunswick,
        Maine
    Photograph by Patrick L. Pinnell

20. Daniel Müller
    German, active 1850s
    after Raphael
    Italian, 1483–1520
    *Peter Healing the Lame Man at the Beautiful
        Gate*
    mural, on support, affixed to the wall
    ca. 20 feet tall
    Chapel, Bowdoin College, Brunswick,
        Maine
    Photograph by Patrick L. Pinnell

*21. Cornelis Schut I
    Flemish, 1597–1655
    Allegory of Fruitfulness (formerly *Venus and
        Ceres*)
    oil on canvas
    44 1/2 x 58 1/2 inches
    Bequest of the Honorable James
        Bowdoin III
    1813.12

*22. View of the rotunda of the Walker Art
    Building showing the plaster casts. Original
    glass slide in Visual Arts Center Slide
    Library, Bowdoin College.

23. Anonymous
    Descent from the Cross
    oil on canvas?
    71 x 58 cm.
    Bequest of the Honorable James
        Bowdoin III
    1813 Abbot Inventory No. 39

24. View of the north aisle of the Bowdoin
    College Chapel crowded with plaster casts
    and paintings, before 1894

*25. Anonymous
    After Peter Paul Rubens
    Flemish, 1577–1640
    St. Simeon Holding the Infant Christ
    oil on canvas
    34 x 45 inches
    Bequest of the Honorable James
        Bowdoin III
    1813.11

*26. Anonymous
    after Nicolas Poussin
    French, 1594–1665
    The Continence of Scipio
    oil on canvas
    46 x 62 inches
    Bequest of the Honorable James
        Bowdoin III
    1813.10

27. Facade of the Walker Art Building
    McKim, Mead & White, 1894

28. Photograph of James Bowdoin III bequest
    paintings in the College Chapel, including,

    on the left:
    Anonymous
    John the Baptist Preaching to the Multitudes
    oil on canvas?
    47 x 65 cm.
    Bequest of the Honorable James
        Bowdoin III
    1813 Abbott Inventory No. 40

    in the center:
    Anonymous,
    Flemish School?
    Combat of Hyena and Dogs
    oil on canvas?
    57 x 49 cm.
    Bequest of the Honorable James
        Bowdoin III
    1813 Abbott Inventory No. 60

    on the right:
    Anonymous
    Flemish School?
    Fox Devouring a Pheasant
    oil on canvas?
    57 x 49 cm.
    Bequest of the Honorable James
        Bowdoin III
    1813 Abbott Inventory No. 69

29. Anonymous
    Flemish School?
    Sacking of a Town
    here retitled *Massacre of Protestants*
    oil on canvas
    59 x 70 cm.
    Bequest of the Honorable James
        Bowdoin III
    1813 Abbott Inventory No. 10

30. Attributed to Hendrick van Steenwyck the
        Younger
    Dutch, before 1649
    Church Interior with Meal by Candlelight
    here retitled *Babylonians Consuming
        Offerings Made to the Idol Bel*
    oil on canvas
    18 1/8 x 15 5/8 inches
    Bequest of the Honorable James
        Bowdoin III
    1813 Abbott Inventory No. 19
    now in the Wadsworth Atheneum,
        Hartford, Connecticut
    Ella Gallup Sumner and Mary Callin
        Sumner Collection
    1940.196

FIG. 1 Robert Gordon Hardie, *Portrait of Harriet Sarah Walker*

THE LEGACY:
THE WALKER GIFT, 1894

Lillian B. Miller

The Walker Art Building (fig. 2) was formally presented to the President and Trustees of Bowdoin College in Brunswick, Maine, on Thursday, 7 June 1894. In the presence of a distinguished audience, the keynote speaker, Martin Brimmer, president of Boston's Museum of Fine Arts, affirmed "conspicuously and deliberately" the significance of art in humanistic studies.[1] The ceremonies celebrated achievements of the imagination as well as recognition of a highly generous gift to the College by Harriet Sarah Walker (1844–1898) (fig. 1) and Mary Sophia Walker (1839–1904) (fig. 3), who sought to honor the memory of their late uncle and the College's benefactor, Theophilus Wheeler Walker (1813-1890) (fig. 4).

Three years had elapsed between this June celebration and the day in April 1891 when Harriet Walker first wrote to William Dummer Northend 1843 of Salem, a member of the Board of Overseers, asking him to call to discuss her late uncle's interest in the College's Sophia Walker Picture Gallery.[2] Theophilus Walker, Harriet's bachelor uncle, had been fascinated since the 1840s by the "large and valuable" art collection that Bowdoin had received in the early part of the century from James Bowdoin III. Dismayed at finding the paintings crowded together in a badly ventilated room in the old wooden chapel, Walker had responded with a thousand-dollar gift to the campaign of his cousin, the Reverend Leonard Woods, Jr. (1807-1878), president of the College, to replace the old chapel with Richard Upjohn's impressive stone building in the German Romanesque style. Walker's gift was to provide improved gallery space for the College's paintings, which had come to the institution from its first patron and his widow in the early part of the century.[3] His gift helped make possible the inclusion of an art gallery in the new building. In gratitude, in 1850 the Governing Boards of the College voted to name the room after Walker's mother, Sophia Wheeler Walker.[4]

Theophilus Walker had grown up in rural South Danvers, Massachusetts, in an orthodox ministerial family. Rejecting theological studies at Dartmouth College, he came to Boston while still a boy and through hard work and thrifty habits rose in the business world. From a modest hardware shop in Boston, he expanded his business interests to investments in clipper ships sailing the California route and cotton and woolen mills in the Salem-Peabody area in Massachusetts and, by 1865, in Lewiston, Maine.[5] His milling interests brought Walker occasionally to Brunswick, where he would visit his cousin, of whom he was very fond. On such occasions, he would tour the College, devoting particular attention to the Sophia Walker Gallery. Now and then he came to the College incognito to study the art works and check on their condition.[6] Even after President Woods's resignation in 1866, Walker maintained his concern for the gallery, returning repeatedly to the Brunswick campus and the painting collection.[7]

The College authorities took notice of his interest. Throughout the years that followed President Woods's departure, Walker was courted by various officials and, in particular, during the late 1880s by Northend, who at the time was actively engaged in planning capital improvements in anticipation of the celebration of Bowdoin's centenary in 1894.[8] The library required more space, President William DeWitt Hyde wanted a modern science building, and Professor of Latin and Librarian George T. Little worried about the condition of the art collection.[9]

In 1889, Little and Northend seriously began to seek funds for a new library. In the belief that Walker's sentimental attachment to his mother would make him sympathetic to the idea of a memorial building, the two men included a top

FIG. 2 Facade of the Walker Art Building

floor art gallery in their plans as an invitation to Walker to fund the entire project.[10] However, Walker feared that such a combining of interests would lead to neglect of the paintings and opted, instead, for a separate building erected specifically for art. Possessing a fortune of at least three or four million dollars, according to Northend's calculations, Walker was not intimidated by the estimates of between forty and fifty thousand dollars for such a structure. Moreover, "the girls," Walker told Northend, referring to the two nieces who shared his Waltham mansion with him, "were rather in favor of the project."[11]

To encourage Walker's commitment to an art museum, Northend suggested that his son, architect William W. Northend (1857-1894), draft a preliminary design. Before the younger Northend could do so, however, Theophilus Walker suddenly died on 15 April 1890, leaving no will and therefore no gift to Bowdoin.

A year later, however, much to Northend's surprise, the project was resuscitated. Having settled claims to the estate from their uncle's other relatives, Theophilus's nieces, Harriet Sarah and Mary Sophia Walker, took charge of the remaining estate and announced their intention to carry out their uncle's interest "in the enlargement of the Sophia Walker Picture Gallery."[12]

Within three years, their decision was realized in an elegant Renaissance "temple of art" designed by Charles Follen McKim of the prestigious firm of McKim, Mead & White and presented to Bowdoin College in time for its centenary celebration.[13]

The story of the construction of the Walker Art Building has been detailed in an undergraduate honors paper, an M.A. thesis, and the museum's own publications.[14] This essay considers some implications of the Walker gift that relate to patronage of the arts and the relationship between taste and class in the northeastern United States at the turn of the century.

THE WALKER SISTERS

Having decided to fulfill their uncle's wish to provide a building for Bowdoin's art collection as a memorial to his mother and their grandmother, the Walker sisters, whom Northend described as intelligent and knowledgeable, entered actively into the project. "They don't want much advice until they ask for it," he noted after meeting Mary Sophia.[15] The sisters selected the building's architect, approved the design and decorations, oversaw the details of construction, and defined its purposes and use. They immersed themselves in aesthetic literature, traveled to Europe and met dealers and artists, bought a collection of art works designed to educate future generations of students, had their portraits painted, and participated in a small but enthusiastic and intelligent way in the delights of art patronage. Through their selection of McKim, their approval of the four muralists who decorated the building's rotunda, and their continuing gifts to the museum, the Walker sisters expressed their tastes and attitude toward art, which they shared with other members of their Boston social class.

Not much is known about the Walker sisters' lives prior to their uncle's death in 1890. According to Laura F. Sprague, the sisters grew to maturity on a farm in Groton, Massachusetts, and joined their uncle in Waltham sometime between 1866 and 1870.[16] They may have trav-

FIG. 3 Anna Elizabeth Klumpke, *Portrait of Mary Sophia Walker*

eled to Europe and visited art museums in France and Italy, for once having decided to provide a museum building for Bowdoin College, Harriet expressed clear opinions concerning museum architecture, pronouncing many such buildings "most unhappy in their treatment, not in the least in harmony with the treasures they contain."[17] Perhaps she had in mind Boston's Victorian Gothic museum on Copley Square (1872-1876) (fig. 5), which did not move to its new neoclassical building on the Fenway until 1906. The sisters surely must have paid occasional visits to nearby Boston, where the annual art exhibitions of the Boston Athenaeum would have attracted them.[18] In the spirit of the Aesthetic Movement, Harriet collected miniatures and textiles, including a fine sixteenth-century Flemish tapestry (fig. 8), which were appropriate objects for a genteel Boston woman to accumulate.[19] Along with ornamental looking glasses, antique furniture, and various objets d'art and small mementoes, the Walker household contained some nineteenth-century landscape and other oil paintings, a few family portraits by Joseph Ames, some decorative works, and Harriet's watercolor sketches and paintings on velvet and ceramic, most of which were willed to Bowdoin after Harriet's death.[20]

The Walker sisters emerged into Boston's cultural world after their uncle died and they had inherited his fortune. Only then—and particularly following their major act of philanthropy, the Walker Art Building—do their names appear in public documents. They are not listed in city directories before 1890, suggesting that it was not until after their uncle's death that they purchased their fashionable property at 53 Beacon Street in Boston. They did not participate in the cultural institutions of Boston's elite society until 1891, when Mary Sophia joined the Museum of Fine Arts, paying a subscription fee of ten dollars. Harriet did not become a member until 1896, although she gave her first gift—two tapestries—in 1893 and her second—a collection of over one hundred miniatures—in 1895.[21] In 1903, after Harriet's death, Mary subscribed $20 rather than the usual $10, and in her will, Mary

FIG. 4 Daniel Chester French, *Theophilus Wheeler Walker*

named the museum as one of her residuary legatees.[22] In 1893, both sisters bought their first share in the neighboring Boston Athenaeum, with Mary Sophia taking Harriet's share upon her death in 1898.[23]

It seems clear that up to the time of their uncle's death the Walker sisters were neither connoisseurs nor actively involved with the art world, although they did experience art as household furnishing and as leisure-time activity. The necessity or desire to pay tribute to their generous uncle, and their sudden possession of millions of dollars, opened up to the Walkers an intellectual and aesthetic world that would dominate their remaining years.

THE ARCHITECT AND THE BUILDING

Although Harriet and Mary Walker shared with their uncle his enthusiasm for Bowdoin's collection of paintings, the two women did not actually see the paintings and casts until they visited the College in 1891 in the company of Northend (since they never traveled "unattended").[24] The scattered works, "sadly in need of a lighted shelter," appealed to their imagination.[25] It was then that they indicated to Northend their willingness to underwrite a "building that will be elegant, a great attraction, and very useful for those who have any art genius."[26] They had also decided on their architect; before visiting Bowdoin, they had met Northend and his son William at the Essex County Courthouse in Salem, which the younger Northend had designed.[27] Perhaps they discussed an architect for the project at that time. A few days after their return from Brunswick, Harriet wrote to Charles McKim asking that he design "a Picture Gallery" for the College.[28]

In commissioning one of the country's foremost architects rather than young Northend,[29] the Walkers underscored the popularity of the new taste for the Classic Eclectic style that would soon dominate turn-of-the-century American building. The Chicago Columbian Exposition of 1893, which was heavily indebted to the designs of the McKim, Mead & White firm, and the Boston Public Library (1887-1895), which was totally McKim's, had dazzled the public and elevated their architect to the top of his profession.[30] The dark and forbidding appearance of Northend's courthouse, built in the Richardsonian Romanesque revival style and reminiscent of Richardson's famous Allegheny County Court House and Jail of 1884-1890 in Pittsburgh, would not have appealed to the Walkers, who, when they sought a plan from McKim, specified that they wished something light in color, functional, and refined.[31]

McKim's plan responded precisely to their specifications: a one-story fireproof building with at least two galleries—one for the "old pictures" in the Bowdoin collection and one for later acquisitions, with a space set aside for the Sophia Walker Gallery. Its Renaissance design expressed both physically and symbolically its aesthetic purpose, recalling the artistic creativity of the Florentine Renaissance and the great classical and medieval collection of another of its prototypes, the Villa Medici (1572-1579) in Rome.[32] Its light brick facade, symmetrical organization, Palladian entrance decorated with carvings, and elegant entrance portico, approached by a broad flight of stairs and guarded by a pair of lions (fig. 9), gave the building a grace and significance that was also monumental. Its historical references marked it as a museum,[33] while its simple yet refined design and fine craftsmanship established the ideal purpose of art. The building expressed its function also in high and long walls well suited to the exhibition of paintings and in the flow of the rooms which, while separating the two main collections owned by the College, was designed not to tire visitors. The building represented a meeting of tastes: McKim's attraction to the Italian Renaissance and the Walker sisters' Boston-conditioned taste for Federal and neo-classical architecture as interpreted in their two homes—in the elegant symmetry of Georgian Gore Place (1805-1806) in Waltham, the country estate built by the Federalist governor of Massachusetts, Christopher Gore, and his wife that Theophilus Walker had purchased for himself and his nieces; and the bow-front classicism of Charles Bulfinch's Beacon Hill row houses, one of which Harriet and Mary Sophia purchased after Theophilus's death.[34]

McKim's use of Italian Renaissance prototypes reflected in part the desire of people of his class and profession to bring beauty and order to the crowded and confused appearance of American cities—an early manifestation of what was to become during the first decade of the twentieth century a full-fledged City Beautiful movement. These Americans, as Leland Roth has pointed out, "returned from travels in Paris and Venice longing to create in their own country the architectural pleasures that had captivated them abroad." They wanted buildings that announced their class status, wealth, and good taste, while at the same time being functional, structurally solid, and handsome.[35] In turning to historic

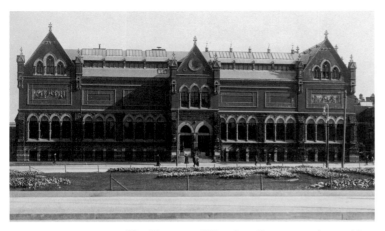

FIG. 5 The Museum of Fine Arts, Boston, was housed in this Victorian Gothic building on Copley Square before moving to its present site in 1906.

examples, they found these architectural values expressed in New England Georgian mansions, which, however, were "too diminutive," and thus "scarcely able to provide those qualities of scale and assuredness that were more and more desired in the exploding cities."[36] The many books illustrating Renaissance and classic architecture published at the time offered welcome solutions to the problem of combining a domestic tradition with European monumentality; they also provided an architectural authority that was symbolically as well as aesthetically satisfying. For McKim, these publications and the historic buildings he visited on his many trips abroad offered the opportunity to study the past, and to develop from the examples of classical architecture both principles and designs that allowed him to express "the things of the intellect and the imagination, and, above all, 'the ethical qualities of which the Renaissance was a consummate type.'"[37] It was with these principles in mind that he designed the Walker Art Building.

DEFINITION OF ART AND THE MUSEUM

Whatever its prototypes,[38] McKim's classical plan for the Walker Art Building was highly appropriate for a museum devoted to the visual arts, given the definitions assigned to art and museums at the time. For McKim and the clients

he influenced, Renaissance architecture best expressed the "ethical qualities" of "good order and proportion and balance, and those eternal verities that are the very essence of beauty."[39] These were the abstractions that peppered the rhetoric of nineteenth-century Americans interested in encouraging appreciation of art in their communities. Convinced that art was capable of inculcating morality, improving the mind, and refining manners—results beneficial to a republican society—they sought to match at home the artistic climate of Europe, where tradition, religion, and public art institutions seemed to have fostered a general appreciation of art and the artistic vocation. To Americans bent on reform of the national culture, museums and art galleries that would collect and present art to the people promised an antidote to American materialism and the concentration on business and technology that the rapid economic growth of the United States encouraged.[40]

The establishment in the 1870s of the two most important art museums in the country—the Metropolitan Museum of Art in New York and

FIG. 6 Historical photograph of Rotunda, Walker Art Building, showing dome, murals, lantern, and sculptures

the Museum of Fine Arts in Boston—gave further impetus to the movement to found museums in America's larger cities, a movement that was assisted by the growth of large individual fortunes and a tradition of cultural philanthropy and civic pride.[41] Apologists for big business and individual accumulation of wealth preempted the idea of the social significance of art to justify acquisitiveness and elevate the businessman. The man of wealth who patronized art "to please his taste and invest his money," as George William Sheldon wrote in 1888, was also contributing to society by introducing the "decorative" ideal into the everyday life of the common citizen. It was due to "the general goodwill of our wealthier classes toward the fostering of a national art," according to Sheldon, that museums such as the Metropolitan or Boston's owed their existence.[42]

Cultural philanthropists believed, as did such museum advocates as the Bostonian Charles Callahan Perkins, artist, composer, and art patron, that it was necessary for individuals as well as nations to develop "that degree of aesthetic culture which . . . will enable them to recognize and appreciate the beautiful in nature and art." The "humblest function" of the arts was to give enjoyment to all classes; the highest was "to elevate men by purifying the taste and acting upon the moral nature." Practically speaking, however, Perkins defined art's purpose as not only the education of the middle and lower classes in American traditional values, but also "the creation of a standard of taste" that would improve American manufactures.[43]

Perkins's museum plan was influenced by the South Kensington Museum in London (now the Victoria and Albert), which collected art for training workers in industrial design. "The designer needs a museum of art, as the man of letters needs a library, or the botanist a herbarium," wrote Martin Brimmer, the first president of Boston's museum and the keynote speaker at the dedication of the Walker Art Building.[44] Training in industrial design did not demand original works of art, which were beyond the budget of these institutions. Watercolor copies and photographic reproductions of important paintings, along with good casts of classical statu-

FIG. 7 Assyrian, *Winged Genius*

FIG. 8 Flanders, *The Conference Between Scipio and Hannibal before the Battle of Zama*

FIG. 9 *Lion sculpture,* Walker Art Building

ary, both Perkins and Brimmer argued, were "quite as useful for our purpose." Their purpose was nothing less than "the education of a nation in art, not . . . making collections."[45]

Perkins's campaign began at home, with an appeal to Harvard University and Yale College to establish professorships of art and "by aiding art projects . . . put into willing hands the lever with which to move the American world."[46] A quarter of a century later, Bowdoin College, with the help of the Walker sisters, began to move toward the kind of art education that Perkins envisioned.

In their emphasis on the museum as a useful educational institution, museum personnel began to stress the importance of historical representativeness in their collections. It was a principle of organization that evolved naturally from their mission as well as from an effort to bring order out of the hodgepodge of disparate collections.

Large archaeological expeditions funded by universities and museums were sending home collections of Egyptian, Assyrian, and Mediterranean artifacts, making possible a concentration on history. As early as 1860, an alumnus of the Medical School of Maine at Bowdoin had recognized the educational value of such ancient relics when he procured for the College five large Assyrian mural reliefs from the ninth century B.C.E. palace of Assurnasirpal II (fig. 7).[47] By the 1870s, museums in Boston, New York, and at the universities of Pennsylvania and Chicago were receiving similar collections for similar academic purposes.

By the turn of the century, it became generally accepted that if a museum was to achieve greatness, as Roger Fry, curator for a brief time at the Metropolitan Museum, contended in 1905, it had to acquire the best examples of the art of different civilizations, from the ancient Assyrians to the

Oriental, to the Italian thirteenth and fourteenth centuries. Historical art promised new artistic experiences rather than a constraint on them.[48] It was a "blessing" for Americans to be able to select from historical periods, wrote Henry James in 1867, for it enabled them to "deal freely with forms of civilization not only [their] own, . . . [to] pick and choose and assimilate and in short (aesthetically and culturally) claim [their] property wherever [they] find it."[49] Decades later, the artist John La Farge (1835-1910), whose mural *Athens* in the Walker Art Building attempted to evoke the spirit of that ancient city, expressed similar sentiments: "We are not," he said, ". . . fixed in some tradition; and we can go where we choose—to the greatest influences, if we wish, and still be free for our future."[50]

Travel and affluence spurred the transit of original examples of classical, Japanese, and Mediterranean art to American museums, with the result that the previously acceptable casts and copies were soon regarded as inappropriate. As American aesthetic thought gradually moved out of the orbit of Ruskinian morality during the 1880s and 1890s and toward a new conception of art as experience and important for its pictorial qualities alone, critics began to talk more about color and design than subject matter; increasingly, the original work of art that revealed the creator's hand appeared as more emotionally valid than the copy. By the first decade of the twentieth century, "joy not knowledge" determined the programs of museums, and the museum's stated function began to include the acquisition of objects important for their aesthetic qualities, "qualities which give a thing worth simply as an object for our perceptive faculties."[51]

The Walker gift occurred during a time that bridged these two points of view. The sisters had grown to maturity during the mid-nineteenth century, when Boston taste was still dominated by an aesthetic—partly Ruskinian in source and partly Unitarian—that asserted a relationship between art, religion, and nature. That the Walkers were committed to all three interrelated domains is evinced by Mary's will, which left the country estate and the greater part of her inherited fortune to the Episcopal Diocese. Should the

FIG. 10 Elihu Vedder, *In the Beginning*

diocese decline the bequest, it was left to the public for enjoyment of its natural beauties. The will also made provision for continued support of the Bowdoin College museum and its art collection. The gift of the building acknowledged their commitment to the didactic, or educational, purpose of art and, in the very style of the building, murals, works of art, and time-honored casts, to the importance they placed on tradition and the classical past. Harriet's collections of eighteenth-century English and French miniatures, American and Barbizon paintings, objets d'art from Spain and Japan, and antiquities from Cyprus, many of which were obtained from Boston dealers, were intended to educate students and visitors in the history of art, provide aesthetic information, meet the demands of the spirit as well as of the mind, and aid in "the diffusion of culture."[52] Such was the prevailing rationale of conservative Bostonians, who were nurtured on idealism and convinced that Beauty was akin to Virtue, who sought an art characterized by truth to nature, spirituality, and morality, and who were devoted to Italy, the classical past, and the traditions of Renaissance painting.[53]

SAPIENZA · PENSIERO · ANIMA · VITA · NATVRA · ARMONIA · AMORE · COLORE · FORMA

FIG. 11 Elihu Vedder, *Rome*

FIG. 12 Abbott H. Thayer, *Florence*

MURALS

One of the first important decisions the sisters made, even while the museum building was being constructed, was its interior decoration. In this decision, they were undoubtedly advised by McKim who, in recreating the Renaissance in America, sought to achieve architectural grandeur by enlisting the cooperation of painters and sculptors including Augustus Saint-Gaudens, Kenyon Cox, and Elihu Vedder. McKim's design of a high dome in the rotunda of the Walker Art Building was intended to set off a sculpture gallery consisting primarily of casts; it also called for murals (fig. 6). Although at first only one was contemplated—Elihu Vedder's *The Art Idea*—the design created four lunettes that were envisioned as surrounding the entrance with splendid color while symbolically conveying the building's meaning.[54]

McKim may have suggested the four artists to paint the lunettes, since he knew them all personally, but the Walker sisters were surely acquainted with their work, for all were connected with Boston in some way, either through patronage or exhibitions. Their art encapsulated the very essence of the American Renaissance movement, and, in its intellectual content, spoke to what the artist and writer Charles Herbert Moore called "the spirit of Boston."[55]

Elihu Vedder (1836-1923) had enjoyed a long relationship with Boston art dealers and collectors from the time he left Richmond, Virginia, for Boston soon after the Civil War. His membership in the Allston Art Club in the 1860s, in which he established a friendship with such Boston artists as William Morris Hunt and John La Farge, his illustrations for Edward Fitzgerald's translation of *The Rubáiyát of Omar Khayyám* (1884) (fig. 10), and his business relationships with art dealers Doll and Richards and, later, Williams and Everett, guaranteed that his work would find its way into Boston collections.[56] Decorative, literary, and symbolic, Vedder's figures displayed such technical skills as color harmonies, strong draftsmanship, and chiaroscuro, features that appeared to Boston collectors as imaginative manifestations of the spiritual. His

FIG. 13 Abbott H. Thayer, *Virgin Enthroned*

long residence in Rome and skill in adapting Italian Old Masters into a highly individual expression also appealed to Bostonians as well as to McKim, who was creating similar adaptations in architecture.[57] Originally called *The Art Idea*, Vedder's mural (fig. 11) was transformed into *Rome Representative of the Arts* when the decision was made to have the murals symbolize the four major sources of western art—Athens, Rome, Florence, and Venice. The ease with which Vedder made the conversion underlines the close relationship between the historical sense and classical idealism.

Abbott Handerson Thayer (1849-1921) was very much a Bostonian both by birth and artistic tastes. Growing up in Boston during a period that witnessed the peak of Emersonian influence, Thayer, according to his biographer, Nelson C. White, "showed the influence of this aspect of his youthful environment throughout his life."[58] Three years of study in the Paris studio of Jean-Léon Gérôme provided Thayer with the French academic training so congenial to Boston tastes, a training especially notable in

FIG. 14 Kenyon Cox, *The Arts*

his "close values, truth of color in the neutrals, and simplicity of conception."[59] By 1883 and 1884, Thayer's reputation had spread, and his portrait commissions increased. Bostonians admired his portrait of the president of Wellesley College, Alice Freeman Palmer (1889-1890), while his double portrait of his children, Mary and Gerald (1889-1890: National Museum of American Art), "excited much interest" when it was exhibited in the city and led to more portrait commissions. However, it was probably the highly successful exhibition at the Museum of Fine Arts in the spring of 1893 of his *Virgin Enthroned* (fig. 13), an evocation of a fifteenth-century Venetian madonna designed to express spiritual or moral values through the symbolism of wings, haloes, and classical dress, that brought him to the Walkers' notice.[60] Thayer had had no previous experience with mural painting, and the Bowdoin mural—*Florence* (fig. 12)—was to be his only effort in this medium.[61]

By 1893, Kenyon Cox (1856-1919) had earned a favorable reputation as a popular illustrator, art critic, and successful teacher. He was one of the artists selected by McKim to create a mural decoration for the Chicago Columbian Exposition and would later be asked to participate in the mural project at the new Library of Congress (fig. 14). Since the days of Washington Allston, Bostonians interested in art had shared Cox's enthusiasm for the color of sixteenth-century Venetian painters; they approved Cox's enthusiasm for classical and Renaissance art, which he quite deliberately studied in the belief that their "guiding principles" would stimulate him to "invent new forms."[62] Presented with Venice as his subject, Cox traveled to that city to make studies for his mural (fig. 17), selecting as sources Veronese's ceiling panel in the Doge's palace, *Venice Enthroned* or *Venice Triumphant*, Bellini's altarpieces, Titian's *Sacred and Profane Love* (ca. 1515), and Giorgione's *Madonna Enthroned with SS. Liberalis and Francis* (1504).[63]

John La Farge, the last of the artists to deliver his mural, *Athens* (fig. 18), was Boston's own artist.[64] Although born in New York, he placed himself squarely in Boston's orbit from the time of his Newport studies with William Morris Hunt and his illustrations of Alfred Tennyson's novel *Enoch Arden* in 1865 for Boston publishers Ticknor and Fields, as with his later work as designer of the splendid windows for H. H. Richardson's Trinity Church (1877-1902).[65] His decorative windows could also be found in Harvard University's Memorial Hall in Cambridge (1878-1891) and in such homes as the William Watts Sherman house in Newport, R. I. (1878) or the Washington B. Thomas (later

Henry P. Kidder) house in Beverly, Massachusetts (1884). In 1878, Peirce and Company in Boston held one of the earliest auctions of his paintings, which was followed the next year by an auction at Leonard's Gallery. Doll and Richards exhibited and sold his paintings in 1890, 1892, and 1893, and it was from this well-known Boston gallery that the Walker sisters purchased his watercolors painted in Japan, *Meditation of Kuwannon* (1886) (fig. 15) and *Tokio Geisha Dancing in the House of Our Neighbor, Nikko* (fig. 16).[66]

Although the art philosophy and styles of the four artists differed in many particulars, they shared a common training in French academic studios that their murals reflect.[67] By their very prescription as allegories of the historic sources of Western art, all four paintings evoke the academic tradition of figure painting and are modeled upon, or resonate, the art of the Italian Renaissance. They all feature ennobled women in various states of dress and undress, flanked by lesser figures and objects that serve iconographic purposes: Painting with her palette, Commerce as winged Mercury, Venice with crown and scepter,

FIG. 15 John La Farge, *Meditation of Kuwannon*

Minerva with helmet, shield, and lance, the laurel wreath of glory, the Tree of Life, the lyre of harmony, the celestial globe of knowledge and exploration, and the owl of wisdom. All the murals refer either symbolically or through the inclusion of an actual landmark to the city being represented. Purposefully decorative, the female figures share the classicized features, flowing draperies, and symbolism to be found in both easel and mural paintings of the 1880s and 1890s. As students of Gérôme, Cox and Thayer had specialized in drawing the nude female figure, idealizing it in both indoor and outdoor locales according to the allegorical requirements. Vedder had become thoroughly acquainted with the fresco work of Michelangelo and Raphael during his long residence in Rome, while La Farge, "the most learned painter of our times," according to the art critic Frank Jewett Mather, Jr., had been exposed to a variety of classical sources, from archaic Greek to Augustan Roman.[68]

Neither McKim, nor the Walker sisters, nor the Bowdoin authorities objected to the presence of nude female figures. So accustomed were they and their contemporaries to such allegorical depictions that the possible effect of

FIG. 16 John La Farge, *Tokio Geisha Dancing in the House of Our Neighbor, Nikko*

FIG. 17 Kenyon Cox, *Venice*

FIG. 18 John La Farge, *Athens*

FIG. 19 Augustus Saint-Gaudens, *Robert Louis Stevenson*

these apparitions on vulnerable college men never figured in discussions concerning the mural designs. As Bailey Van Hook has noted, the idealized features and passivity of such female figures, the generalized settings, their two-dimensionality and obviously decorative, rather than illustrative, purpose had so long "personified a host of abstract virtues and values" that their appearance was taken for granted. A student's response to the semi-nude nymph in La Farge's *Athens* suggests this easy acceptance of the female nude in art. Dismissing both the "jumbled" symbolism in the painting and "the beautiful contour of [the nymph's] limbs," he reserved his praise instead for La Farge's coloring, which was, he concluded, the picture's "greatest beauty."[69] It was regarded as appropriate that poetry and painting in art should be personified by the female figure, for such cultural pursuits were seen as woman's domain, while Commerce, Labor, or Industry—the basic, active concerns of society—were man's responsibility. The president of Bowdoin College, William DeWitt Hyde, defined the separate spheres of men and women when he lectured to the senior class at Smith College a few weeks after the Walker Art Building was dedicated: "it is the province of men to subdue the wilderness; that

of women, to make it blossom as the rose. It is man's province to make life materially and politically possible; it is women's province to make it aesthetically and socially worth living."[70]

Classical and idealized, the Bowdoin murals were designed to convey a cultural ideal. Their message of peace and harmony attained through the arts must have appeared in ironic contrast to the frightening accounts of riots accompanying railroad strikes, the march of Coxey's army of unemployed veterans from Ohio to Washington, D.C., and the violent protests of anarchists and socialists that were filling the newspapers throughout the weeks preceding the dedication of the Walker Art Building. At the College's commencement exercises celebrating the institution's centennial a few weeks later, the symbolic message of the murals was further heightened by U. S. Supreme Court Chief Justice Melville Weston Fuller's dire warnings to the crowd of visiting alumni and guests of the threat to traditional American ideals from labor forces, foreigners, and "foreign ideologies." Reminding his audience that popular government could only be preserved through the power of the law and the constitutional protection of private property, Fuller, Class of 1853, called on Bowdoin's graduates, educated "in the cultivation of the humanities or of the phenomena and laws of nature or of economy," to provide the leadership essential to the preservation of American institutions.[71]

FIG. 20 Constant Troyon, *Goat and Sheep*

201

FIG. 21 Winslow Homer, *The End of the Hunt*

FURTHER CONTRIBUTIONS OF THE WALKER SISTERS

What role could that shining new Renaissance palace and its ideal art play in providing Bowdoin students with the qualities of leadership required to meet the threats to traditional American society? How could exposure to the classical allegories projected on the walls of a classicized building influence young men, and eventually young women, so that they might reconcile an artistic ideal with the realities of life's experiences? These were the questions asked by a student in 1902 in an article in *The Bowdoin Quill* called "A Dream of Beauty," and they were the questions facing the Walker sisters even while they listened to Martin Brimmer expound on the "essential elements of a more perfected life, Righteousness, Truth, and Beauty."[72] The student wondered how "a university cherished by a people so prone to realism and so seldom appealed to through idealism" could "establish an ideal society within its precincts," a society that would be, in the words of the Swiss philosopher Amiel, "a form of poetry." The student's answer was "to fashion some spot which, by its 'ineffable charm', keeps ever calling us near to the true goal of all of us, to the ideal, to perfection,—to beauty in a word, which is only truth seen from another side."[73] The Walkers' museum provided such a "spot," while their purpose in its establishment expressed his "dream of beauty." Convinced that art was, in Brimmer's words, "a great, even an indispensable instrument in the complete education of men and women . . . worthy of careful and appreciative study, entitled to a place in every sound scheme of liberal training," the Walker sisters envisioned their gift as the first step in a comprehensive college program involving the visual arts. Through education in the arts—through exposure to art's harmonious view of Nature, to its moral and spiritual truths, to the importance of Love as symbolized by idealized women and children, and to nobility of purpose as conveyed by the artists' dedication to Beauty and Tradition—students would develop that "conservatism which secures that which is best in the past . . . united to the progress which is essential to any future."[74]

The sisters' first effort to reach their goal, after the building's dedication, was to ask Martin Brimmer to recommend books about artists for a museum library. Brimmer took the Walker sisters' request with him to London, where he enlisted the help of Charles Locke Eastlake (1836-1906), keeper of the National Gallery and writer on art. Most of the books Brimmer recommended were traditional histories of Italian art and biographies of artists, reference works extending from Vasari's sixteenth-century *Lives* to Michael Bryan's eighteenth-century *Dictionary of Artists*.[75] Of most interest in the list of books Eastlake suggested to Brimmer were the writings on Italian paintings of Giovanni Morelli, the only author on the list who was in the vanguard of aesthetic criticism. In attempting to establish more scientific measurements for Italian paintings, Morelli influenced such connoisseurs as

FIG. 22 Rosa Bonheur, *Lion Cubs*

Bernard Berenson, Roger Fry, Herbert Horne, and Langston Douglas, whose scholarly approach to early art was significant in influencing the taste of such a collector as Isabella Stewart Gardner who, at the time that the Walker sisters were celebrating the completion of their "Temple of Art" at Bowdoin, was contemplating the purchase of her first Botticelli, a painting that would launch her in the creation of Fenway Court.[76] The Walker sisters were not committed to this kind of connoisseurship; their artistic interests and limited financial means ruled out a collection such as Mrs. Gardner was assembling.[77] On the other hand, the books the Walkers purchased for a museum library would eventually introduce students to the new methods of art analysis as well as traditional art-historical scholarship.

In deciding to present to the museum art that would advance the education of Bowdoin students while contributing to their spiritual development, the Walkers were constrained to select contemporary works for the most part, with an occasional foray into the past. Their choices reflect conservative Boston taste: sculptures by the Beaux-Arts trained Daniel Chester French (fig. 4) and Augustus Saint-Gaudens (fig. 19), reproductions of classical sculptures, ancient glass from Thomas B. Clarke's collection "for educa-

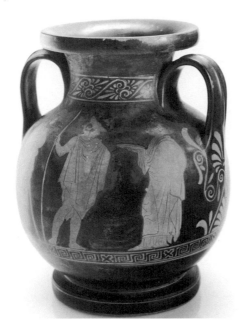

FIG. 23 The Dinos Painter, *Red-Figure Pelike*

FIG. 24 Hermanus Willem Koekkoek, *Council of War*

tional purposes,"[78] and paintings by members of the French and American Barbizon schools.[79]

The Walkers' choice for the building's facade of bronze copies of Demosthenes from the marble copy of Polyeuktos of Athens (80 B.C.E.) and Sophocles from a Greek marble of the late fourth century B.C.E. instead of the *Great Hermes* and *Samothrace Victory*, which were Saint-Gaudens's recommendation, asserted the educational rather than the aesthetic purpose of their gift. Symbolically, the sober statues of the orator Demosthenes and dramatist Sophocles must have seemed more important for a men's college than the glorious winged Victory or fleet-footed Mercury.[80] Saint-Gaudens's bas-relief of the bedridden British poet Robert Louis Stevenson (fig. 19) reflected literary Boston's Anglophilia, while the Barbizon works (some of which later turned out to be copies)—Millet's *Peasant Woman Seated*, Corot's *Near Ville d'Avray*, Troyon's *Goat and Sheep* (fig. 20), and Daubigny's *Vallée de la Marne*—and those of the

American landscapists whose art was linked to the Barbizons either through style or actual residence in France—J. Foxcroft Cole, F. Hopkinson Smith, W. T. Richards, Winslow Homer (fig. 21), John La Farge—expressed Boston's remedy for dirty streets, factories, immigrant workers, and the threat of industrial violence—and even the despoiling of Maine's glorious forests by lumber and textile factories.[81] The Barbizon works, both French and American, with their emphasis on repose and sentiment, communicated refined tastes and traditional aesthetic values in the face of social and environmental upheaval.

The Walkers' brief encounter with the French *animalier* painter Rosa Bonheur illustrates the importance they assigned to Barbizon art in their educational program. When they visited France in 1895, the sisters were invited by Rosa Bonheur's companion, the American portraitist Anna Klumpke, who had recently painted Mary Sophia's portrait in Boston, to visit Bonheur's studio. Here they ordered a copy of one of the artist's horse studies.[82] Over four years later, their order remained uncompleted.[83] In 1898 Harriet Walker died, and Rosa Bonheur the following year. Persistent, Mary Walker urged Anna Klumpke, who had inherited Rosa Bonheur's estate, to select for Bowdoin a painting from the sale and exhibition of Bonheur's works that Klumpke was organizing in Paris. A few months later, the *Lion Cubs* (fig. 22) arrived in Boston together with a portrait drawing of Rosa Bonheur by Anna Klumpke.[84]

Rosa Bonheur is not a popular artist today. At the time the Walkers visited her studio she was very famous, in America as well as in her native land. Her popularity as an animal painter had reached its zenith in mid-century,[85] but in 1895 she was still fulfilling commissions and had become a legendary figure, partly as a result of her unconventional life style.[86] Her art was not as unconventional as her persona. In picturesque scenes of farm life, she glorified Nature and the common laborer, emphasized realism and "scientific" detail, and expressed the ideals of democracy and the natural life. The new middle-class patrons of art in France, England, and America responded to "the deep feeling" she manifested for "the poetry of nature" and her "intense love . . . for the beings and the things pertaining to that nature."[87] Tranquil landscapes, sentimental but highly naturalistic renderings of animals, and a spiritual approach to the animal kingdom constituted a non-threatening art for societies undergoing social change— France in the 1840s and 50s, the United States at the turn of the century.[88] The Walkers' insistence upon including an example of Rosa Bonheur's work in a museum intended for undergraduate education in the arts helps to explain in general their choice of objects for the Sophia Walker Gallery and their motives in donating a Renaissance museum building to Bowdoin College.

The Walkers made a bolder artistic decision when they ordered from the expatriate Bostonian Edward Perry Warren h '26 (1860-1928), an eccentric but scholarly collector of Greek antiquities, a classical amphora, "of the type known as a pelikè . . . of Attic make and belong[ing] to

the best period of the fine red-figured style," dated circa 430-420 B.C.E. (fig. 23). Interest in original Greek artifacts, despite their "pagan" message, was increasing in Boston as a result of Warren's extensive and important purchases on behalf of the Museum of Fine Arts, Boston. The Walkers' desire to obtain an example of this kind of art was dictated, however, more from their sense of the educational and historical value of the classical ideal than from a realization of the actual meaning of the pictures on the vase. They were impressed by the explanation that the drawings resembled so closely "those upon the frieze of the Parthenon as to illustrate in the most interesting manner the influence of the great masters of the period upon those of the smaller arts."[89] Perhaps they were also aware of the beauty of the original Greek objects coming to the Boston museum from Warren.

In any case, their gift turned out to be "bread upon the waters": it brought Bowdoin's gallery into Warren's purview, reminding him of the special relationship he had with Maine. The Warren family fortune originated in great part from the family's S. D. Warren paper mill at Westbrook on the Presumpscot River about thirty miles from Brunswick. The realization that

FIG. 25 Sarah Goodridge, *Daniel Webster*

FIG. 26 John Rollin Tilton, *Temple, Aegina*

Bowdoin College possessed a fireproof and well-monitored building dedicated to the classical ideal influenced Warren to make an initial gift to the museum in 1916, which he followed by larger donations totaling six hundred objects.[90] Warren was committed thereafter to "provide exceptional opportunities for the exceptional among Bowdoin men." "A coin, a gem, a vase, a statuette," Warren's Oxford colleague J. D. Beazley wrote in explaining Warren's philosophy, "would speak of Greece in the heart of Maine; and sooner or later there would be a student whose spirit would recognize them. There was no hurry; an acorn in the forest."[91]

THE INFLUENCE OF THE WALKER GIFT

Inexperienced in art patronage and lacking the advice of connoisseurs or artists, the Walker sisters could only be guided by the tastes and philosophy of art prevailing in Boston during their years of residence in the city. They assimilated the rationale underlying the founding of the Museum of Fine Arts that art exerted an uplifting influence, that good taste was an important element in maintaining the quality of both social and personal life, and that it was through artistic knowledge and experience that good taste developed. Committed to the support of institutions that, they believed, were essential for the preservation of cultural and social tradi-

tions, Boston's social and economic leaders had since the mid-eighteenth century assumed the duties and obligations of cultural as well as economic stewardship. The Walker sisters' gift to Bowdoin College was an expression of this pattern of stewardship.

The Walkers shared, too, the tastes of many of their Boston contemporaries. They responded to art of different historical times and places, idealized allegories, decorative objets d'art, nineteenth-century French landscape painting, and similar works by local artists. Theirs was an eclectic taste that extended to paintings as far apart in feeling and subject matter as Hermanus Willem Koekkoek's *Council of War* (fig. 24) and John Rollin Tilton's *Temple, Aegina* (fig. 26). Koekkoek (1867-1929) was a third-generation member of a famous Netherlander family of marine and landscape painters, who had achieved some fame in London for his newspaper and journal illustrations. He was particularly famous for his military scenes. Tilton (1828-1888) was an expatriate American artist who resided in Rome and sent home picturesque renditions of Italian and Greek landscape.[92]

The Walkers purchased individual works of art that caught their fancy or possessed didactic value rather than constituting important elements in a collecting plan. For instance, when Mary Sophia saw William Morris Hunt's charcoal studies for his Albany mural *Discoverer* (fig. 27) at the sale of his works in 1897, she purchased them through Doll and Richards for Bowdoin in the belief that they would be "an interesting addition to our group of drawings by Modern Painters." Harriet sent the museum a miniature of Daniel Webster by Sarah Goodrich that contained a lock of the statesman's hair, which she had purchased from a Goodrich relative with the expectation that both the artist and the subject would add to the educational value of the museum's collection (fig. 25).[93]

The Walkers ignored certain artistic schools, either because they did not come into their purview or were beyond their budget, such as Dutch and Italian Old Masters. They seemed unaware of the work of the French Impressionists, whose paintings were introduced to Boston

in the Foreign Exhibition of 1883 and at the St. Botolph Club in 1892. Some Bostonians with long experience in art collecting, like Denman Waldo Ross and Desmond Fitzgerald, had begun to collect Impressionist works in the 1880s, but for most Bostonians, and certainly those who were active in the Museum of Fine Arts, Impressionism seemed a passing fad, not worthy of notice. It was not until 1906 that the first Monet came into the Boston Museum's collection, and not until the opening of the Evans Wing in 1915 that the museum began to receive gifts of Impressionist works in any notable way.[94] The Walker sisters probably never saw paintings of this school, and, given their relative inexperience with art, it would have been unusual, indeed, for them to have demonstrated such avant-garde taste.

The Walkers' major legacy to Bowdoin College was the art building itself. Once established, institutions assume a life of their own. So did the Walker Art Building. Offering a prestigious setting, an attentive audience, and the promise of future development, it invited dona-

tions from collectors and art-oriented alumni. Such collections that followed the Walkers'— a group of Native American pottery and stone axes in 1893 from Virginia Dox; 143 classical coins from its first director, Henry Johnson, in 1919; Overseer James Phinney Baxter's collection of 36 watches in 1921; a collection of etchings from Charles A. Coffin h '22 in 1923; Dana Estes's collection of 143 Cypriote and Egyptian objects in 1902 and 1911; Edward Perry Warren's gifts of classical antiquities; and George Hamlin's bequest in 1961 of an important collection of John Sloan paintings, along with other gifts of individual paintings, pieces of sculpture, and examples of various decorative arts—contributed to a college museum outstanding among similar institutions in the country. The Walker Art Building was truly "an acorn in the forest," the seed of studies in art that would transcend its genteel origins and become a force for aesthetic pleasure and knowledge in the lives of the thousands of students who have wandered through its halls, absorbed its lessons, and been influenced by its vision.

NOTES

BCSC is Special Collections, Hawthorne-Longfellow Library, Bowdoin College. All correspondence is in BCSC unless otherwise noted. BCMA is Bowdoin College Museum of Art.

I am indebted to Laura F. Sprague, consulting curator of decorative arts for the Bowdoin College Museum of Art, for sharing her extensive researches into the Walker family genealogy, residences, and art collection; to Susan L. Ransom for her careful editing; and to scholars Eileen Sinnott Pols and Ann Elaine Robertson for their informed studies of the architecture of the Walker Art Building.

1. Martin Brimmer, *Address delivered at Bowdoin College Upon the Opening of the Walker Art Building, June VII. MDC-CCXCIV* (Boston and New York: Houghton Mifflin and Co., 1894), 2.

2. Harriet Sarah Walker to William D. Northend, 6 April 1891; Misses Walker to Northend, 4 June 1891, Walker correspondence.

3. Report of Robert Hallowell Gardiner, chairman of Chapel Committee, November 1839, Chapel file, BCSC.

4. Leonard Woods, Jr., to Theophilus W. Walker, Brunswick, 9 September 1850. In 1852, Walker was asked to select the room in the building that should be set aside as the Sophia Wheeler Walker Gallery. See Leonard Woods, Jr., to "My dear Cousin," Brunswick, 24 August 1852. For Woods, see *Dictionary of American Biography*.

5. See Obituary, "Theophilus W. Walker," in "Recent Deaths," *Boston Evening Transcript*, 16 April 1890, 5; Eileen Sinnott Pols, "The Walker Art Building, 1894. Charles F. McKim's First Museum Design," M. A. thesis, University of Texas at Austin, 1985, 37-38. Pols's thesis provides valuable and extensive documentary materials concerning the planning and construction of the Walker Art Building and the commissioning of its murals.

6. See W. D. Northend to George T. Little, 16 July 1889, Northend biographical files.

7. President Woods had opposed the effort of some members of the Board to rescind the degree awarded to Confederate president Jefferson Davis by Bowdoin College in 1858. The controversy engendered by the president's unpopular stance upset Walker, who shared his cousin's politics, but his concern for the paintings and interest in the College remained unabated. When the paintings began to show signs of deterioration as a result of faulty heating and lack of care, Walker called their condition to the attention of the college authorities, and during the 1860s, he protested the preemption of the gallery by the Maine Historical Society that resulted in the dispersal of the paintings to other college buildings. See Pols, 39, 40; Ann Elaine Robertson, "The Facade of the Walker Art Building. Indicator of the Architect's and Patrons' Intentions." Honors paper for the Department of Art History, Bowdoin College, 1990. Copy in files of BCMA, 21-22; W. D. Northend to George T. Little, 16 July 1889, Northend biographical files.

8. Northend's interest in the College's art collection began as early as January 1881, when he sought contributions from alumni for the conservation of two portraits. See copy of W. D. Northend to alumni, January 1881, Northend biographical files.

9. George T. Little served also as curator of the art collection between 1887 and 1892; in 1892, he became head of the library and Henry Johnson, professor of modern languages, assumed his curatorial duties.

10. W. D. Northend to George T. Little, 16 July 1889, Northend biographical files; see also Pols, 40.

11. W. D. Northend to George T. Little, 25 November 1889, Northend biographical files.

12. W. D. Northend to George T. Little, 22 June 1890, 6 April 1891, Northend biographical files; Misses Walker to W. D. Northend, 5 June 1891, Walker correspondence.

13. William D. Northend, dedication speech at the Walker Art Gallery, reported in the student newspaper, *The Bowdoin Orient*, 20 June 1894, 51; quoted in Robertson, 6.

14. See Pols, 40; Robertson, 6; Richard V. West, *The Walker Art Building Murals*, Occasional Papers I, (Brunswick, ME: Bowdoin College Museum of Art, 1972); David S. Berreth, *Nineteenth-Century American Paintings at Bowdoin College* (Brunswick, ME: Bowdoin College Museum of Art, 1974).

15. W. D. Northend to George T. Little, 21 April 1891, Northend biographical files.

16. See Appendix, p. 217.

17. Harriet S. Walker to Charles F. McKim, 6 July 1891, Walker correspondence.

18. The sisters may also have given art special study. Not only was Harriet an amateur artist, but an intriguing entry in the list of exhibitors at the Paris Salon for both 1879 and 1880 names a possible relative, a Mlle. Sophia A. Walker, "née aux États-Unis d'Amérique," as a pupil of G. Boulanger and Lefebvre, and indicates that she was exhibiting a portrait drawing of a "Mlle H. . . ." Lois Marie Fink, *American Art at the Nineteenth-Century Paris Salons* (New York and Cambridge: Cambridge University Press, 1990), 402. According to Fink, the portrait drawing may have been either a miniature or watercolor since all works that were not oils were categorized under "D" for drawings.

19. The Flemish tapestry was left to the Museum of Fine Arts, Boston, by Mary Sophia in 1904, as a gift from Harriet. Mary also presented a portion of Harriet's collection of miniatures (fifty-seven of them) and a Brussels tapestry of the sixteenth or seventeenth century to Bowdoin College after Harriet's death. See Bowdoin Museum of Fine Arts. Walker Art Building, *Descriptive Catalogue of the Paintings, Sculpture, and Drawings and of the Walker Collection*, 4th ed. (Brunswick, ME: Bowdoin College, 1930), 26, 39-41, 47; Last Will and Testament of Mary Sophia Walker, filed 18 February 1904. #64003, Middlesex County Courthouse, Cambridge, MA. Copy in BCSC, Misses Walker Papers. Also see Adolph S. Cavallo, *Tapestries of Europe and of Colonial Peru in the Museum of Fine Arts, Boston*, 2 vols. (Boston: Museum of Fine Arts, 1967), 1:109-15, 2: plate 31. I am grateful to Laura F. Sprague for calling this last reference to my attention.

20. These were the kinds of artistic objects encouraged by the writers of the Aesthetic Movement, whose influence was particularly strong from the 1870s through the 1880s. See the Metropolitan Museum of Art, *In Pursuit of Beauty: Americans and the Aesthetic Movement* (New York,

1986), especially chapter 3. For a listing of the Walker Collection, see *Descriptive Catalogue*, nos. 911-21, 926-54, 1183-1389. Nos. 1183-1389, which were probably owned by either Mary alone or both sisters, were bequeathed to Bowdoin in Mary's will (see note 19) in 1904. Of approximately the 464 objects listed here, 202 came from the Walkers' Gore Place in Waltham, Massachusetts. I am indebted to Laura F. Sprague for this information.

21. See Museum of Fine Arts, Boston, *Annual Report of the Trustees of the Museum of Fine Arts*, vols. 14-21 (1889-1896), Boston, Mass., 1890-1897. Each annual volume lists subscribers for the year as well as donors. For Harriet's gifts, see *Annual Report*, 1893, 66; *Annual Report*, 1895, 17, 51, 67. Members of the family did precede the sisters as subscribers; Mrs. Nathaniel Walker (Susan Seaver Walker), an aunt and wife of Theophilus's business partner, subscribed annually beginning in 1889, and the sisters' cousin, Grant Walker, son of the Nathaniel Walkers, became a subscriber in 1890.

22. See Museum of Fine Arts, Boston, *Annual Report* 27 (1903). The Boston Museum of Fine Arts was named residuary legatee in the event that neither the Convention of the Protestant Episcopal Church, to which the major part of the Walker estate was left, nor the Trustees of Public Reservations, second in line to inherit, accepted the provisions of Mary's will within ten years of its probate. See "Last Will and Testament of Mary Sophia Walker," n. 19.

23. See *The Athenaeum Centenary: The Influence and History of the Boston Athenaeum from 1807 to 1907 with a Record of its Officers and Benefactors and a Complete List of Proprietors* (Boston, 1907), 168, 171. I am indebted to Laura F. Sprague for this citation.

24. W. D. Northend to George T. Little, 21 April 1891, Northend biographical files; Harriet S. Walker to Charles F. McKim, 6 July 1891, Walker correspondence.

25. Harriet S. Walker to C. F. McKim, 6 July 1891, Walker correspondence.

26. W. D. Northend to George T. Little, 1 July 1891, Northend biographical files.

27. W. D. Northend to George T. Little, 21 April 1891, Northend biographical files.

28. Harriet S. Walker to Charles F. McKim, 6 July 1891, Walker correspondence.

29. William W. Northend (1857-1894) is not listed in any of the published histories of architecture in America. Only one reference to him has been located: Bryant F. Tolles, Jr., and Carolyn K. Tolles, *Architecture in Salem: An Illustrated Guide* (Salem, MA: Essex Institute with the cooperation of Historic Salem, 1983), 119-20. His Essex County Courthouse building is illustrated on p. 119. Further information about Northend has been obtained from an obituary in the files of the Essex Institute Library, for which I am grateful to Mary Fabisvewski. Perhaps Northend's precarious health—he died soon after completing the courthouse—prevented him from taking on the Bowdoin commission.

30. At the time of the construction of the Walker Art Building, McKim was also planning the American Academy in Rome (1894-1905), which probably also heightened his interest in Renaissance Roman architecture.

31. See Harriet S. Walker to C. F. McKim, 6 July 1891, Walker correspondence.

32. Many classical buildings have been suggested as models for the Walker, along with the Villa Medici: the Pazzi Chapel of the Florentine Filippo Brunelleschi, the Villa Giulia and the Pantheon in Rome, and the Loggia dei Lanzi in Florence. See Robertson, 10-17, 51-67; H. Barbara Weinberg, "American 'High' Renaissance: Bowdoin's Walker Art Building and Its Murals," *The Italian Presence in American Art, 1860-1920*, ed. Irma B. Jaffe (New York: Fordham University Press, and Rome: Istituto della Enciclopedia Italiana, 1992), 121.

33. From 1803 on, the Villa Medici had been home to the French Academy. Robertson (p. 7) suggests that McKim "wanted to transfer the fame of the building and the prestige of the Academy to the architecture of the Walker."

34. See Leland Roth, *McKim, Mead and White Architects* (New York: Fordham University Press, 1983), especially 115, 130-38, 144, 154, 166-67.

35. Leland Roth, "McKim, Mead & White Reappraised," in *Monograph of the Works of McKim Mead & White 1879-1915* (1914, rev. ed., New York: B. Blom, 1973), 11.

36. Ibid.

37. Charles Herbert Moore, *The Life and Times of Charles Follen McKim* (Boston, 1929), 308.

38. See Robertson, 7; Patricia Anderson, *The Architecture of Bowdoin College* (Brunswick, ME: Bowdoin College Museum of Art, 1988). McKim's biographer, the artist Charles Herbert Moore, cited as one of McKim's favorite buildings the Villa Medici, which he used as his model for the New York State building of the Chicago World's Fair in 1892. The Villa Medici has also been called the model for the Walker Art Building.

39. Moore, 308.

40. See Lillian B. Miller, *Patrons and Patriotism: The Encouragement of the Fine Arts in the United States, 1790-1860* (Chicago: University of Chicago Press, 1966).

41. In his account of the construction of the Boston Public Library, for instance, Charles Herbert Moore, chairman of the National Commission of Fine Arts, noted that when Samuel A. B. Abbott of the BPL Board of Trustees called on McKim to design a building for the organization, Abbott advised that it "should be not merely a storage place for books, but also an expression of the civic consciousness of an ancient city justly proud of its historic past, its present culture, and imbued with a sense of future greatness." ("Charles Follen McKim," in *More Books. The Bulletin of the Boston Public Library* 6, 3 [March 1931]: 91.)

42. George William Sheldon, *Recent Ideals of American Art* (New York and London: Garland Publishers, 1888, repr. 1977), 2.

43. Charles C. Perkins, "Museums of Art," *Journal of the American Social Science Association*, 2; quoted in Walter Muir Whitehill, *Museum of Fine Arts Boston: A Centennial History*, 2 vols. (Cambridge, MA: Belknap Press of Harvard University Press, 1970), 1: 9.

44. Martin Brimmer, "The Museum of Fine Arts Boston," *The American Architect and Building News* (30

October 1880); quoted in Whitehill, *Museum of Fine Arts, Boston*, 1: 13.

45. Perkins and Brimmer are quoted in Whitehill 1: 10, 13. The acceptance of copies in the form of prints, photographic reproductions, and casts of antique statuary was widespread in university museums and institutions in small cities throughout the country. In their speeches at the dedication of the Walker Art Building, both Northend and Brimmer indicated that the study of art at Bowdoin could proceed on the basis of such copies. Brimmer, 26; *Orient*, 20 June 1894; Robertson, 6. Also see Charles C. Perkins, "American Art Museums," *North American Review* 111 (July 1870): 1-29.

46. Perkins, 27.

47. The gift came from Dr. Henri B. Haskell, an 1855 alumnus of the Medical School of Maine. See Margaret R. Burke, ed., *Handbook of the Collections* (Brunswick, ME: Bowdoin College Museum of Art, 1981), 2-5, and Barbara N. Porter, "Assyrian Bas-Reliefs at the Bowdoin College Museum of Art" (brochure) (Brunswick, ME: Bowdoin College Museum of Art, 1989).

48. Denys Sutton, ed., *The Letters of Roger Fry*, 2 vols. (New York, 1972), 1:233. Literary historians have been critical of the period's interest in history. Van Wyck Brooks (*New England: Indian Summer, 1865-1915* [New York]: E. P. Dutton, [1940], 424), for example, called the historical interests of Boston in the 1890s "a mood of retrospection": "it was closely allied to the moods of regret and defeat," he wrote, and was responsible for the lack of vigor in Boston's culture at that time. His criticism of Boston's concentration on history has been echoed in more recent years by T. Jackson Lears in his *No Place of Grace: Antimodernism and the Transformation of American Culture, 1880-1920* (New York: Pantheon Books, 1981). In art, the historical sense provided a positive source of training and stylistic development and exerted different influences. See, for example, Lois Marie Fink, "The Innovation of Tradition in Late Nineteenth-Century American Art," *The American Art Review* X, 2 (November 1978): 63-71.

49. Henry James to Thomas Sergeant Perry, 20 September [1867], in Leon Edel, *Henry James, 1843-1870: The Untried Years* (Philadelphia: Lippincott, 1953), 264. The entire letter appears in Leon Edel, ed., *Henry James Letters* (Cambridge, MA: Belknap Press of Harvard University Press, 1974), 1:74-79.

50. John La Farge, "The American Academy at Rome, The Field of Art," *Scribner's Magazine* 28 (August 1900), 254.

51. Benjamin Ives Gilman, *Museum Ideals of Purpose and Method* (Cambridge, MA: Harvard University Press, 1923), 91. For the reaction against the aesthetic ideas of John Ruskin, which had dominated American thought about art from the mid-nineteenth century to the 1890s, see Roger Stein, *John Ruskin and Aesthetic Thought in America, 1840-1900* (Cambridge, MA: Harvard University Press, 1967), 198-223. For more on the role of casts and copies at Bowdoin, see Susan Wegner's essay in this book.

52. Kenyon Cox, "Museums of Art and Teachers of Art," in *Art Museums and Schools: Four Lectures by G. Stanley Hall, Kenyon Cox, Stockton Axson, and Oliver S. Tonks* (New York: Charles Scribner's & Sons, 1913), 56.

53. For the Walker bequest, see Mary Sophia Walker's will, note 19. During the earlier half of the nineteenth century, Bostonians generally held to the idea expounded by Francis Hutchinson in the early eighteenth century (*An Inquiry into the original of our ideas of beauty and virtue . . .* [London, 1726]) that beauty when allied with virtue became "a force for good." Recognition of the beautiful accompanied the development of "a moral taste" and the enjoyment of beauty was made possible by the development of "sentiment." The emphasis on beauty allied with morality continued to dominate Boston aesthetics through the Victorian period. See Janice Simon, "The Crayon, 1855-1861: The Voice of Nature in Criticism, Poetry, and the Fine Arts," 2 vols. Ph.d. diss., University of Michigan, 1990, 1: 344-46. For changing viewpoints, see Metropolitan Museum of Art, *In Pursuit of Beauty*, n. 20.

54. For a history of the murals at Bowdoin College, see West.

55. Moore, *Charles Follen McKim*, 92.

56. See Elihu Vedder, *The Digressions of V. Written for his own Fun and that of his Friends* (Boston and New York: Houghton Mifflin Company, 1910), 255-79, 403-08. For Boston purchasers of Vedder's paintings, see Vedder, Appendix, 459-501, especially, 478-81. Also see "Speculations and Contemplations on a Sale in Boston," 505-07; Regina Soria, *Elihu Vedder: American Visionary Artist in Rome (1836-1923)* (Cranbury, NJ: Fairleigh Dickinson University Press, 1970), 41-45, 183-97. The Williams and Everett sale is described by Soria on 143-45. See also William Howe Downes, "Boston Painters and Paintings," *Atlantic Monthly* 62 (1888). Vedder's work was exhibited from 1866-68 and in 1874 at the Boston Athenaeum; later, his works were given or purchased for the new Museum of Fine Arts. See Mabel M. Swan, *The Athenaeum Gallery, 1827-1873* (Boston: Boston Athenaeum, 1940), 282.

57. It was Vedder's "sense of history and tradition concerning art" that first suggested to McKim that Vedder be invited to participate in the "first public mural decoration in America"—the Manufacturers and Liberal Arts Building of the Chicago Columbian Exposition—and in the decoration of the Walker Art Building. See Soria, 208-09.

58. Nelson C. White, *Abbott H. Thayer, Painter and Naturalist* (Hartford, CT: William L. Bauhan, 1951), 12, 37, 38.

59. Metropolitan Museum of Art, *Memorial Exhibition of the Work of Abbott Handerson Thayer* (New York, 1922), xv. See also White, 17, 24-29. Thayer's study at the Ecole des Beaux-Arts emphasized composition, the human figure, and drawing. Thayer "could always draw like an angel, if he chose to do so," commented the art critic Royal Cortissoz (*Memorial Exhibition*, xv).

60. White, 55, 61-62. The prominent Boston collector J. Montgomery Sears purchased *Virgin Enthroned* for $8,000. Publicity concerning Sears's purchase, laudatory reviews of the painting in Boston newspapers, and the enthusiasm its exhibition generated in the "crowds" of visitors greatly enhanced Thayer's reputation in that city during the spring of 1893. The Walkers could not have avoided hearing about him.

61. For details concerning Thayer's difficulties with this commission, see Pols, 102-105, and West, 22-25.

62. "Whenever he took up his palette," according to Cox's friend and fellow-muralist Edwin Blashfield, "he thought first and last of the Venetians." Edwin Howland Blashfield, *Commemorative Tribute to Kenyon Cox* (New York, 1922), 2. For quote, see Kenyon Cox, *The Classic Point of View: Six Lectures on Painting Delivered on the Scammon Foundation at the Art Institute of Chicago in the Year 1911* (New York: C. Scribner's Sons, 1911), 87.

63. See Pols, 99, and West, 6-13.

64. La Farge did not deliver his mural until 13 September 1898. Work on it was delayed as a result of the artist's illness and the necessity to finish prior commitments of at least twenty-five stained glass windows. See H. Barbara Weinberg, *The Decorative Work of John La Farge* (New York: Garland Publishers, 1977), 284-85.

65. La Farge's work in stained glass windows was universally appreciated. In 1887, McKim commissioned La Farge to design a window for Trinity Church as a memorial to his wife, who had recently died. See Phillips Brooks to C. F. McKim, 22 February 1887, 31 March 1887, New York Public Library, Maloney-Garrison Collection.

66. For sales and exhibitions of La Farge's work in Boston, see Henry Adams, et al., *John La Farge* (exh. cat.) (New York: Abbeville Press for the Carnegie Museum of Art, Pittsburgh, and the National Museum of American Art, Smithsonian Institution, Washington, D.C., 1987), 246-47. The *Meditation of Kuwannon* is illustrated on p. 53.

67. See Weinberg, note 32, 124-30.

68. See West, 18; Soria, *Vedder*, 214; Frank Jewett Mather, Jr., "John La Farge—An Appreciation," *The World's Work* 21, 5 (March 1911), 14086; quoted in West, 28.

69. Bailey Van Hook, "From the Lyrical to the Epic. Images of Women in American Murals at the Turn of the Century," *Winterthur Portfolio* 26, 1 (Spring 1991): 63-80, quote on 67; Freeman Milliken Short, "John LaFarge and His Painting 'Athens.'" *Bowdoin Quill* 3, 6 (June 1900): 161-64. For the origin and meaning of female personifications in such allegories, see Marina Warner, *Monuments and Maidens: The Allegory of the Female Form* (New York: Atheneum, 1985). For the passivity assigned to women in nineteenth-century discourses, see Griselda Pollock, *Vision and Difference: Femininity, Feminism and Histories of Art* (London and New York: Routledge, 1988), 96.

70. William DeWitt Hyde, "The Social Function of the Scholar: Address to the Senior Class at Smith College, June 19, 1894." (Northampton, MA, 1894), 21. BCSC, Hyde, Collection of Addresses, 1883-1904.

71. "Bowdoin's Centennial Oration by Chief Justice Fuller and Poem by Arlo Bates," *Boston Evening Transcript*, 28 June 1894. Fuller's address is given in full.

72. Brimmer, 31.

73. "H," "A Dream of Beauty," *Bowdoin Quill* 6 (1902): 44-50.

74. Brimmer, 24; Fuller, note 71.

75. The books Brimmer listed as Eastlake's recommendations included: Franz Theodor Kugler (1808-1858), *Handbook of Painting: The Italian Schools of Painting. Based on the Handbook of Kugler*, ed. and rev. by Austen Henry Layard (1817-1894); Joseph Archer Crowe (1825-1896) and G. B. Cavalcaselle (1820-1897), *A History of Painting in Italy, Umbria, Florence, and Siena from the Second to the Sixteenth Century*, 1864, ed. Langston Douglas (London and New York: Scribner's, 1903-14); Crowe and Cavalcaselle, *The Early Flemish Painters* (London, 1857); Michael Bryan (1757-1821), *A Biographical and Critical Dictionary of Painters and Engravers, from the revival of the art under Cimabue to the present time* (London: G. Bell, 1816, and many revised and enlarged editions through the 1930s, under name of *Bryan's Dictionary of Painters and Engravers*); Giorgio Vasari (1511-1574), *Lives of the Eminent Painters, Sculptors and Architects* (Florence, 1550) (transl. by Mrs. Jonathan Foster [London, 1850-1907, 6 vols., many editions]); Giovanni Morelli (1816-1891), *Italian Painters: Critical Studies of Their Works* (London: J. Murray, 1892-93, transl. from the German); Morelli, *Italian Masters in German Galleries* (transl. by Mrs. Louis M. Richter, London, 1883). See Martin Brimmer to Miss Walker, London, 9 July 1894.

76. See Ernest Samuels, *Bernard Berenson: The Making of a Connoisseur* (Cambridge, MA, and London, England: Belknap Press of Harvard University Press, 1979), 207-208. Mrs. Gardner saw Botticelli's *Death of Lucretia* in London during the summer of 1894 and purchased it in December of that year.

77. The Italian paintings that Mrs. Gardner assembled for Fenway Court were generally unavailable until a decade or so after the Walkers' gift. The greater part of the Gardner Collection was acquired in the early twentieth century through the efforts of such connoisseurs as Bernard Berenson. In 1894, these kinds of Old Master works were not only out of the economic range of the sisters, but out of the range of their experience.

78. See M. S. Walker to Professor Johnson, 20 February 1894.

79. The Barbizon painters and their American followers were particularly prominent in Boston collections of the mid-nineteenth century. The Walkers purchased their Millet, Mauve, Von Bremen, and Troyon from John F. Hooper of Boston, who had been left the paintings by his aunt, Mrs. Nathaniel Hooper, member of a family famous in Boston for its important art collections. Works by Millet, Von Bremen, Mauve, Troyon, and Daubigny were important pieces in the collections of Martin Brimmer, H. P. Kidder, Thomas Wigglesworth, and Quincy Shaw among many Boston collectors; they also were to be found in such Providence collections as those of John A. Brown and Robert C. Taft. See Edward Strahan, ed., *The Art Treasures of America: Being the Choicest Works of Art in the Public and Private Collections of North America*, 3 vols. (1879-1882, reprint ed., New York & London: Garland Publishing, 1977), 3: 93-94. Also see Peter Bermingham, *American Art in the Barbizon Mood* (Washington, D.C.: Smithsonian Institute Press, 1975), 35-38 and passim. Unfortunately, some of the Barbizon paintings acquired by the Walkers turned out to be copies.

80. In *The Future in America* (New York: St. Martin's Press, 1906), H. G. Wells described Boston as a city of plaster casts, in particular the *Nike of Samothrace*: "It is incredible," he wrote, "how many people in Boston have selected her for their aesthetic symbol and expression.

Always that lady was in evidence about me, unobtrusively persistent, until at last her frozen stride pursued me into my dreams. That frozen stride became the visible spirit of Boston in my imagination" (225).

81. The taste for the Barbizons was not limited to Boston; at the World's Columbian Exposition of 1893, the most popular and "fashionable" display in the American painting section was the loan exhibition "Foreign Masterpieces Owned by Americans," which featured a large percentage of paintings by Millet and Corot as well as the other members of the original Barbizon group. See Bermingham, 87-88.

82. Anna E. Klumpke to Miss Walker, Paris, 8 October 1895. Object file, 1901.6, BCMA.

83. See Anna E. Klumpke to Miss [Mary] Walker, Paris, 29 October 1895. Object file, 1901.6, BCMA.

84. Anna E. Klumpke to Miss [Mary] Walker, Paris, 6 March 1900. Object file, 1901.6, BCMA. Bonheur had known that the drawing was going to Bowdoin, and "was pleased over it" (Klumpke to Miss Walker, by 1 October 1900, Object file, 1901.6, BCMA).

85. See Dore Ashton and Denise Browne Hare, *Rosa Bonheur: A Life and a Legend* (New York: Viking Press, 1981), 3, 49, 63-64, 69, 88-89, 90-103.

86. Ashton and Hare, 81.

87. Ashton and Hare, 70, 80.

88. For a discussion of the meaning of animals in Barbizon and American Barbizon works, see Bermingham, 74-86.

89. *Descriptive Catalogue*, 1930, 38.

90. See Kevin Herbert, *Ancient Art in Bowdoin College* (Cambridge, MA: Harvard University Press, 1964).

91. Ibid., 8-9; see also Martin Green, *The Mount Vernon Street Warrens* (New York: Charles Scribner's & Sons, 1989), 216-17. For more on Edward Perry Warren, see Charles C. Calhoun, "An Acorn in the Forest" in *Bowdoin* 61, 1 (September 1987), 2-12.

92. Carol Troyen and Pamela S. Tabbas, *The Great Boston Collectors* (Boston: Museum of Fine Arts, 1984), 11-14. The Tilton and Koekkoek were purchased by the sisters for their own collection and willed to Bowdoin. The Bowdoin College Museum of Art's *Descriptive Catalogue* (1930) and its *Handbook of the Collections* (1981) name the artist of *Council of War* as Hermanus Koekkoek (1815-1882), Hermanus Willem's uncle. It is highly unlikely that the older man would have painted this scene, since his oeuvre consisted primarily of romantic marine and landscape paintings, while his nephew specialized in military scenes. See Marius, *Dutch Painters of the Nineteenth Century*, ed. Geraldine Norman (1903; reprint ed., Woodbridge, Suffolk, England, 1973), 89, 268, 269. For exhibition of the paintings of members of the Koekkoek family of artists in America up to 1876, see James L. Yarnell and William H. Gerdts, comps., *The National Museum of American Art's Index to American Art Exhibition Catalogues* (Boston, MA: G.K. Hall, 1986); for Tilton, see E. P. Richardson, *Painting in America: From 1502 to the Present* (New York: Thomas Y. Crowell, 1956, 1965), 231.

93. See Mary Walker to Henry Johnson, 28 March 1897; Harriet S. Walker to Henry Johnson, 10 August 1897.

94. Troyen and Tabbas, 28.

S tarred works are reproduced in color in this chapter. All works are the property of the Bowdoin College Museum of Art unless otherwise noted.

*1. Robert Gordon Hardie
     American, 1854–1904
     Portrait of Harriet Sarah Walker
     oil on canvas
     33 x 42 inches
     Bequest of Miss Mary Sophia Walker
     1904.4

 2. Facade of the Walker Art Building
     McKim, Mead & White, 1894
     historic photograph
     Special Collections, Bowdoin College
       Library

*3. Anna Elizabeth Klumpke
     American, 1856–1942
     Portrait of Mary Sophia Walker
     oil on canvas
     22 x 26 inches
     Bequest of Miss Mary Sophia Walker
     1904.3

 4. Daniel Chester French
     American, 1850–1931
     Theophilus Wheeler Walker
     bronze bas relief
     52 1/2 x 28 1/2 inches
     Gift of the Misses Harriet Sarah and Mary
       Sophia Walker
     1894.148

 5. Facade of the Copley Square Building
     May 12, 1902
     William Morris Hunt Memorial
       Library
     Photograph by T.E. Marr
     Photo courtesy of the Museum of Fine Arts,
       Boston

 6. Rotunda, Walker Art Building
     ca. 1900

 7. Assyrian
     Winged Genius, ca. 885–860 B.C.
     gypsum
     90 9/16 x 58 13/16 x 6 7/16 inches
     Gift of Dr. Henri B. Haskell m 1855
     1860.2

 8. Flanders, Brussels, second half of the
       16th century or first quarter of the
       17th century
     The Conference Between Scipio and Hannibal
       before the Battle of Zama
     wool and silk: tapestry
     147 x 180 inches
     Gift of Miss Harriet Sarah Walker
     Courtesy of the Museum of Fine Arts,
       Boston

 9. Lion sculpture, Walker Art Building

10. Elihu Vedder
     American, 1836–1923
     In the Beginning, 1883–84
     (Illustration for *The Rubáiyat of Omar*
       Khayyám)
     Chalk, pencil, and watercolor on paper
     17 11/16 x 13 5/16 inches
     Museum Purchase and gift from Elizabeth
       W. Henderson in Memory of Her
       Husband, Francis Tracy Henderson
     National Museum of American Art,
       Smithsonian Institution

*11. Elihu Vedder
      American, 1836–1923
      Rome
      oil on canvas
      144 x 288 inches
      Gift of the Misses Harriet Sarah and
        Mary Sophia Walker
      1893.37

*12. Abbott H. Thayer
American, 1849–1921
Florence
oil on canvas
144 x 288 inches
Gift of the Misses Harriet Sarah and
  Mary Sophia Walker
1893.36

13. Abbott H. Thayer
American, 1849–1921
Virgin Enthroned, 1891
oil on canvas
72 5/8 x 52 1/2 inches
Gift of John Gellatly
National Museum of American Art,
  Smithsonian Institution

14. Kenyon Cox
American, 1856–1919
The Arts
oil on canvas, adhered to wall with white
  lead adhesive
114 x 408 inches
Courtesy, Library of Congress

15. John La Farge
American, 1835–1910
Meditation of Kuwannon, 1886
watercolor on paper
14 5/16 x 10 3/4 inches
Gift of the Misses Harriet Sarah and
  Mary Sophia Walker
1904.18

16. John La Farge
American, 1835–1910
*Tokio Geisha Dancing in the House of Our
  Neighbor, Nikko,* 1886
watercolor and gouache over graphite
13 1/8 x 8 3/4 inches
Gift of the Misses Harriet Sarah and
  Mary Sophia Walker
1904.19

*17. Kenyon Cox
American, 1856–1919
Venice
oil on canvas
144 x 288 inches
Gift of the Misses Harriet Sarah and
  Mary Sophia Walker
1893.38

*18. John La Farge
American, 1835–1910
Athens
oil on canvas
108 x 240 inches (lunette shape)
Gift of the Misses Harriet Sarah and
  Mary Sophia Walker
1893.35

19. Augustus Saint-Gaudens
American, 1848–1907
Robert Louis Stevenson, 1889
bronze medallion
17 3/4 inches (diameter)
Gift of the Misses Harriet Sarah and
  Mary Sophia Walker
1904.29

20. Constant Troyon
French, 1810–1865
Goat and Sheep
oil on canvas
29 1/4 x 41 11/16 inches
Gift of the Misses Harriet Sarah and
  Mary Sophia Walker
1894.5

21. Winslow Homer
American, 1836–1910
*The End of the Hun*t
watercolor
15 1/8 x 21 3/8 inches
Gift of the Misses Harriet Sarah and
  Mary Sophia Walker
1894.11

22. Rosa Bonheur
French, 1822–1899
Lion Cubs
oil on canvas
25 x 31 1/4 inches
Gift of the Misses Harriet Sarah and
   Mary Sophia Walker
1901.6

23. The Dinos Painter
Greek, ca. 425–400 B.C.
Red-Figure Pelike
terra cotta
14 13/16 x 11 7/16 (diameter) inches
Gift of the Misses Harriet Sarah and
   Mary Sophia Walker
1895.2

24. Hermanus Willem Koekkoek
Dutch, 1867–1929
Council of War
oil on canvas
34 1/4 x 49 5/8 inches
Gift of the Misses Harriet Sarah and
   Mary Sophia Walker
1904.8

25. Sarah Goodridge
American, 1788–1853
Portrait of Daniel Webster
watercolor on ivory
4 1/2 x 3 7/8 inches
Gift of the Misses Harriet Sarah and
   Mary Sophia Walker
1897.13

26. John Rollin Tilton
American, 1828–1888
Temple, Aegina
oil on canvas
30 3/4 x 48 inches
Gift of the Misses Harriet Sarah and
   Mary Sophia Walker
1904.15

27. William Morris Hunt
American, 1824–1879
Compositional Study for Discoverer *Mural*
crayon on board
12 3/4 x 19 3/4 inches
Gift of the Misses Harriet Sarah and
   Mary Sophia Walker
1897.7

FIG. 1 Gore Place, a great federal-period country seat in Waltham, Massachusetts, was built in 1805-1806 by Governor Christopher and Rebecca Gore. Theophilus Walker was lauded for his preservation of the house and its magnificent grounds. He and his nieces occupied the estate longer than any other family, from 1856 until the death of Mary Sophia Walker in 1904.

THEOPHILUS WHEELER WALKER AND GORE PLACE

Laura Fecych Sprague

Theophilus Wheeler Walker (1813-1890), a talented entrepreneur whose investments in New England's emerging textile industry brought him great wealth, maintained a life-long interest in the art collection of James Bowdoin III. Unlike many benefactors of the College, Walker was not an alumnus. Had he based his philanthrophy on familial loyalty, his gift would have gone to Dartmouth College, the alma mater of both his father, the Reverend Samuel Walker (1799-1826) (Class of 1802), and his brother-in-law, the Reverend Charles Walker (1795–1847) (Class of 1823), the father of Mary Sophia Walker (1839–1904) and Harriet Sarah Walker (1844–1898) (Miller figs. 1 and 3). Instead of obtaining a college degree, however, Theophilus Walker entered the world of commerce and industry. His successes made his philanthropy possible; he chose to become a patron of Bowdoin College for reasons that revolved around both his family and his businesses.[1]

Walker and his cousin, the Reverend Leonard Woods, Jr. (1807–1878), president of Bowdoin from 1839 to 1866, were close friends, and Walker assisted Woods in his tireless efforts to complete the Chapel. Bowdoin College was just a short walk from the Brunswick station of the Maine Central Railroad, where Walker would have changed trains on his visits to two of his textile factories, the Androscoggin Mills in Lewiston and the North Vassalboro Woolen Mills, north of Augusta. Walker could easily have walked up from the station to visit Woods or to roam the campus "incognito."[2]

Despite the establishment of the Walker Gallery in the Chapel, Bowdoin College did not provide for the exhibition and study of the paintings in a manner Walker thought appropriate, thus his "unfavorable opinion in regard to the *pictures*. He could not seem to find out much about them." Walker revealed his frustrations to both his nieces and his friend William

D. Northend 1843, a Bowdoin College Overseer, that he "could find no nucleus of the gallery." His conviction that the pictures needed better care was combined with the persistence of Northend, who pursued the possibility of an art building with Walker over many years.[3]

Unmarried, Walker concentrated on his businesses, family, and special interests, and enjoyed his privacy. Many of these traits he shared with his cousin, Leonard Woods, whose father, the Reverend Leonard Woods, Sr., had been appointed Theophilus's guardian in 1826. The beloved president and scholar, Woods enjoyed "the luxurious retirement of his study"; he disliked public appearances to the point of being labeled a recluse. So, too, did Walker establish a retreat at his home, Gore Place, in Waltham, Massachusetts; when Walker returned to Waltham from the bustling Boston waterfront, he passed through "a dense belt of forest trees, shutting out the commonplace world."[4]

THEOPHILUS WALKER AND "CHASTE AND TASTEFUL ARCHITECTURE"

Without Walker's personal papers, much about him remains unknown. However, the buildings he owned, preserved, and maintained, or whose construction he supported, reveal his interest in architecture. The earliest building in whose construction he is known to have been involved was the 1847 Danvers Bleachery in South Danvers (now Peabody), Massachusetts. The factory, which provided critical processes in the manufacture of cloth, was housed in a three-story gable-roofed stone building. Its clerestory dormers, slate roof, and wooden cornice added to the structure's stylish Gothic appearance.[5]

Theophilus involved himself in the construction of a building again in 1850 at Bowdoin by

FIG. 2 The Androscoggin Mills, built in 1860 in Lewiston, Maine, up the Androscoggin River from Brunswick, is seen in its earliest known view of 1874–1876. Walker served as its president from 1865 to 1890; the mill's success accounted for much of Walker's wealth.

supporting President Woods's effort to complete Richard Upjohn's ambitious chapel. "In order that the aid promised by me," be paid, Walker required assurances that the sums subscribed "shall be judged sufficient by Mr. Upjohn to finish the Chapel according to his designs, and . . . that the work will be prosecuted uninteruptedly [sic] to its completion." The 1845 German romanesque revival design was almost unprecedented in America at the time, making it a most avant-garde structure.[6]

A very different building, the North Vassalboro Woolen Manufacturing Company near Waterville, Maine, was hailed during its construction in 1851 as "one of the most beautiful and substantial buildings in New England." The two-story brick structure with a "circular" roof had many windows which were "great facilities for light and ventilation. . . .The entire building presents a rare sample of chaste and tasteful architecture."[7]

Amos D. Lockwood, a pioneering mill engineer, conceived a Second Empire design for the new and massive Androscoggin Mills of 1860. (Walker's close associate at the mill, Lockwood joined Bowdoin's Board of Overseers in 1869 and served as a Trustee from 1870 until 1884). The mansard roof crowning five stories, and two towers with round-arched belfries punctuating the facade, gave the mill a symmetry and monu-

mentality that had been unknown in Lewiston (fig. 2). In 1871 a colleague observed that "the Androscoggin Mills have such an imposing French [mansard] roof building, surrounded with well laid out grounds, that an English mill man, when he first saw it, supposed it must be some public museum." In 1865 Walker, in his role as president of the Androscoggin Mills, supported the construction of two churches in Lewiston designed by Boston architects John Stevens and Thomas Silloway.[8]

At home at Gore Place, Walker inhabited one of this country's finest examples of federal-period domestic architecture. The building is noted for its architectural simplicity, harmonious proportions, and the brillant use of interior light. And the Walker Art Building, "*the architectural feature of the college grounds,*" was one of the first examples of classical revival architecture in America. In choosing Charles F. McKim for this "*balanced and symmetrical design,*" Mary Sophia and Harriet Sarah Walker paid Theophilus a great honor.[9]

Walker's successful enterprises provided the resources for his philanthropy. Beginning as a hardware and commission merchant in Boston, Theophilus established Walker & Brother in 1842, and from 1854 operated from 17 Merchants Row (fig. 3) until his death in 1890. He founded the Danvers Bleachery in 1847; his investments in Maine's textile industry drew Walker closer to Bowdoin College. Overseer William D. Northend reported in 1889 that Walker's "plant at Vassalboro cost him $1,200,000."

The Vassalboro Woolen Manufacturing Company was "the largest woolen mill in New England," and its "finest broadcloths, cassimeres, doeskins and beavers" were recognized for their quality in Boston, New York, and London.[10] Beginning with the construction of its first mill in Lewiston in 1860, the Androscoggin Mills excelled in the production of sheeting, shirtings, and drillings, a heavy twilled cloth. Demand for their tenting fabrics during the Civil War propelled the construction of a second mill building in 1862. Theophilus had joined the board in 1860, serving as president from 1865 until his death in 1890.[11]

After having lived at various addresses in Boston and Danvers between 1835 and 1855, Walker purchased Gore Place in Waltham, Massachusetts, in April 1856 for $40,000. The grandness of this country seat and its historical significance must have influenced Walker's move. Here he combined interests in architecture, landscape architecture, and agriculture, following ideas established fifty years earlier when the Gores developed the property.[12]

A philosophy of preservation (also evidenced in the scrupulous precision and neatness with which his mills were kept) accounts for Walker's meticulous attention to all aspects of Gore Place, ranging from the appearance of the mansion house to the cultivation of 140 acres of farmlands, woodlands, and orchards.[13] In 1889 landscape architect Charles Eliot praised Gore Place:

This strikingly peaceful and lovely scene, so religiously preserved by its present owner that he can say that only the gales have harmed it since he came into possession more than thirty years ago, impresses the most casual passer-by, and teaches owners of country-seats a lesson of first importance. Here is not one rare tree . . . only common trees, grass, water, smooth ground, and a plain building. The scene is interesting, impressive, and lovable, and it is this solely by reason of the simplicity, breadth, and harmony of its composition. This is real landscape architecture of the purest type.[14]

Here, nieces Mary and Harriet came to live with him after the death of their mother, Theo-philus's sister, Hannah Walker Walker. Theophilus had also cared for his younger and only surviving brother after the death of their mother in 1831, making Nathaniel his partner in 1842. Nathaniel's children, Annie (1848–1895), Grant (1851–1922), and Amelia (b. 1858), were heirs-in-law with Mary and Harriet to Theophilus's estate.[15]

CHRISTOPHER GORE AND GORE PLACE

Like his friend and neighbor James Bowdoin III, Christopher Gore held prominent positions in Massachusetts society. Gore served with James Bowdoin at the 1788 state convention, and in 1789 he purchased a fashionable residence on Bowdoin Square, opposite the Bowdoin mansion near the State House. In 1793 Gore built Gore Place, the "farm in Waltham," which provided not only a retreat from urban Boston, but also a place for Gore to conduct agricultural experiments. After this house was damaged by fire, the Gores began to plan a new country seat.[16]

Keen observers of architecture, Christopher and Rebecca Gore were particularly taken by the neoclassical style they had seen in both London and Paris, where Christopher served as a diplomat. The work of architects Etienne-Louis Boullée and Claude-Nicolas Ledoux drew attention to the innovative neoclassical styles in France. Jacques-Guillaume Legrand was less well-known than Boullée and Ledoux in France and abroad, but he was highly regarded in Paris. The Gores met Legrand in 1801, and on one occasion Christopher reported: "Mrs. G. is now with Monsieur LeGrand in the adjoining parlour building houses." With Rufus King as their intermediary, the Gores corresponded with Legrand, who is believed to have drawn plans from Rebecca Gore's sketches.[17]

On its completion in 1806, Gore Place, "built and fitted up in patrician style, [was] the most elegant mansion in New England." The main brick dwelling of two stories is flanked by hyphen arcades. Both arcades terminate in Greek temple-form pavilions. The love of geo-

FIG. 3 Theophilus Walker ran his businesses from the Walker & Brother Counting Room at 17 Merchants Row in Boston from 1854 until 1890. This rare view of a nineteenth-century commercial interior, commissioned in 1893 by the Walker sisters, depicts portraits of his sailing vessels and standard office furniture. Stylish during the 1830s, the Boston Empire armchairs were revered by Walker throughout his life; one survives in the Walker collection, BCMA.

metric shapes is evident throughout the house. In the main block, the great two-story hall with marble floor features an interior elliptical wall. Behind it is the two-story oval parlor whose exterior wall creates the curved garden facade (fig. 1).[18] The mansion house stood in the middle of the estate, and:

a straight avenue, shaded by double rows of trees, conducted the visitor to this stately abode. Shady walks radiated from the house to the east and west, secluding it upon all sides, except that one opening permitted a view of the [Charles] river a half-mile across the lawn, and of the fields beyond it. The trees which bordered the avenues and walks and ornamented the grounds were tastefully grouped, occasionally converting the walks into Gothic aisles, one of which formed a vista opposite the east window of the library.[19]

Following a visit in 1856 the Massachusetts Horticultural Society reported that:

much of it was under tillage, and the rest in grass, grain and woodland; and the manor lot consisted of shade grounds, lawn, large fruit and flower gardens, greenhouses, a vegetable department, and walks, driveways, and outbuildings.

Inside and out, Gore Place served as an American model of a *ferme ornée*, an estate where the aesthetics of architecture and landscape design shared equal importance with agricultural reform. These ideals were espoused by the Massachusetts Society for Promoting Agriculture, which both Gore and James Bowdoin helped to found in 1791.[20]

THE WALKERS AT GORE PLACE

Theophilus Walker occupied Gore Place alone from 1856 until 1866. After their mother died, Harriet Sarah and Mary Sophia sold their family's Groton, Massachusetts, farm and moved in with their uncle at Gore Place. The 1870 federal census recorded Mary, age thirty-one, as "keeping house," with Harriet, age twenty-six, "at home." Three or four servants lived at the main house. The estate foreman, who resided on the grounds, was assisted by gardeners and farm hands living in Waltham and Watertown.[21]

Theophilus's successful shipping business offered many opportunities for the two sisters. Voyages of his ships to the Mediterranean Sea and southern American cities made distant ports accessible, and there is some evidence that family members traveled in this country and abroad. In 1848 the ship *Sophia Walker* sailed to Malaga, Spain, and Palermo, Sicily. A contemporary account mentions that a "Mr. Gore" (possibly Samuel, a cousin of Susan Grant Walker, wife of Theophilus's younger brother, Nathaniel), met the captain and others on board the vessel in Palermo. A photograph, probably from the 1870s, documents a visit by at least Mary Sophia Walker to Naples, Italy. In 1852 Theophilus spent the month of August at "the White Hills of Newport," Rhode Island. His nieces may have retreated with him to that fashionable seaside resort. Among their Newport friends was Eliza Henley Luce, daughter of U. S. Naval Commodore John Dandridge Henley, a nephew of Martha Dandridge Custis Washington.[22]

Some evidence sheds light on how the Walkers lived at Gore Place for nearly half a century. The spacious interior had rooms set aside for special functions. The first floor included two entrance halls, the great marble hall, the spacious oval parlor, a library, a billiard room, a drawing room, and a family dining room, in addition to the service areas in the west wing. While Theophilus Walker updated some rooms with sophisticated French wallpapers in the Gothic revival and fresco styles, Gore-period features were preserved in other rooms. The great oval parlor and drawing room retained early nineteenth-century French wallpapers. Perhaps Nathaniel Walker's father-in-law, Moses Grant, Jr. (1785–1862), a prominent wallpaper manufacturer and importer in Boston, commented on their extraordinary nature, thereby contributing to their preservation.[23]

The oval parlor is one of the most impressive spaces. Two stories high and measuring 29 by 21 feet, it served as the "picture gallery." Both its shape and harmonious proportions are reminiscent of the Walker Art Building's Sophia Walker Gallery. Harriet's magnificent Flemish tapestry, *Conference between Scipio and Hannibal before the Battle of Zama,* would have dominated even this ample space (see Miller fig. 6). The family's collection of large historical and landscape oil canvases, works on paper, and sculpture by American and European artists may have been exhibited here.[24]

On Mary Sophia's death in February 1904, Gore Place was offered as a site for an Episcopal cathedral for the eastern Massachusetts diocese. With an endowment for maintenance, the furnished mansion could have been "used for a Bishop's residence, church school, or some other church work."[25] In June, four months after Mary Walker's death, Marian Lawrence Peabody, the daughter of Bishop William Lawrence:

drove to Waltham to see the 'Bishop's Palace.' It was quite like a fairy tale and the day being of the misty Corot sort heightened the unreal feeling. . . . The trees were superb, being so old and always having good care.[26]

Mary Walker's estate was valued at $1,150,000, with the cash value set around $750,000 by the diocese. Within a month of Mary's death, the diocese observed that "the bequest is a good nest-egg. Whether it will build and endow a cathedral for Boston is another matter." Should the church decline to accept the terms of her bequest, the will provided that Gore Place be given to the Trustees of Public Reservations "to be kept forever. . . as a public reservation." She provided an endowment to keep the "estate as a whole in perfect order."[27]

Mary Walker wished that Gore Place be used for the benefit of the church, but she did not impose special restrictions. The diocese voted to accept the Walker bequest on 27 May 1907. In

1911 the church sold Gore Place to an automobile manufacturer who used the house as a showroom; Gore Place later served as the club house for the Waltham Country Club. In 1935 Mary Walker's goddaughter, Helen Bowditch Long Patterson, rallied forces to save the property from demolition. Since that time the Gore Place Society has operated the house and forty acres as a historic site. Because the society focuses on the Gore period to 1834, Theophilus Walker and his nieces play only a minor role in the interpretation of the property; the best memorial to them and their philanthrophy remains the Walker Art Building.[28]

NOTES

BCSC is Special Collections, Hawthorne-Longfellow Library, Bowdoin College. BCMA is Bowdoin College Museum of Art.

1. Obituary, *Boston Evening Transcript*, 16 April 1890, 5; "Dedication of Walker Art Building," *Orient*, 20 June 1894, 50-52. Laura Fecych Sprague, "A Life of Industry and Preservation: A Short History of Theophilus Wheeler Walker," and "The Reverend Samuel Walker and His Descendants," 1993, BCMA files.

2. Parker Cleaveland and Alpheus Spring Packard, *History of Bowdoin College* (Boston: James Ripley Osgood & Co., 1882), 120; *Time-Tables of the Maine Central Railroad*, 1 July 1878, Maine Historical Society; *Atlas of the State of Maine* (Houlton, ME: George N. Colby & Co., 1884), 39, 59, 68. Eileen S. Pols, "The Walker Art Building 1894: Charles F. McKim's First Museum Design" (M. A. thesis, University of Texas at Austin, 1985), 1, 39. William D. Northend to George T. Little, 16 July 1889, Northend biographical files, BCSC.

3. William D. Northend to George T. Little, 16 July and 25 November 1889, 10 April 1891, BCSC; Patricia M. Anderson, *The Architecture of Bowdoin College* (Brunswick, ME: Bowdoin College Museum of Art, 1988), 44; Pols, 39.

4. Guardianship, Essex County Registry of Probate, New Series, Book 45:118. Cleaveland and Packard, 120-124; [Charles W. Eliot], *Charles Eliot, Landscape Architect* (Boston: Houghton, Mifflin & Co., 1902), 239-243.

5. John A. Wells, *The Peabody Story: Events in Peabody's History, 1629-1972* (Salem, MA: Essex Institute, 1972), 244; "Barlow's Insurance Surveys for Danvers Bleachery," 1874 and 1889; Jessica Randolph, assistant librarian, Museum of American Textile History, North Andover, Massachusetts, kindly identified this source at the museum. A photograph of the bleachery (Peabody, Massachusetts, photograph file, Phillips Library, Peabody-Essex Museum), shows the stone building behind an 1885 addition.

6. Theophilus W. Walker to [Bowdoin College], n.d., Chapel financial papers, BCSC. Anderson, 26-28; Denys Peter Myers, *Maine Catalog: Historic American Buildings Survey* (Augusta: Maine State Museum, 1974), 114.

7. *The Eastern Mail* (Waterville, Maine), 16 October 1851. Jacqueline Field kindly brought this reference to my attention. It is not certain if Walker had a hand in the construction of the mill or simply invested in it afterwards.

8. Samuel B. Lincoln, *Lockwood Greene: The History of an Engineering Business, 1832-1958* (Brattleboro, VT: Stephen Greene Press, 1960), 65-73. I am grateful to Roger G. Reed, Maine Historic Preservation Commission, for sharing his research of and sources for these Lewiston buildings, including fig. 2. See also Roger G. Reed, "Amos D. Lockwood," *A Biographical Dictionary of Architects in Maine* (Augusta: Maine Historic Preservation Commission, forthcoming). *Memorial of the One Hundredth Anniversary of the Incorporation of Bowdoin College with the General Catalogue*, 1894, 5, 6, 10, of the general catalogue. Androscoggin Mills directors' records (1860-1928), Bates Manufacturing Co., Lewiston, Me., on deposit at Maine Historical Society, Portland.

9. Charles A. Hammond: "Where the Arts and Virtues Unite: Country Life Near Boston, 1637-1862" (Boston University, Ph.D. diss., 1982), 124. Anderson, 43-48.

10. Sprague, "A Life of Industry"; William D. Northend to George T. Little, 25 November 1889, BCSC. Henry D. Kingsbury and Simeon L. Deyo, eds.; *Illustrated History of Kennebec County, Maine*, 2 vols. (New York: H. W. Blake & Co., 1892), 2:1104-1105; Samuel Boardman, *The Agriculture and Industry of the County of Kennebec, Maine, with Notes upon Its History and Natural History* (Augusta: Kennebec Journal Office, 1867), 170-171. For descriptions of these fabrics, see Florence M. Montgomery, *Textiles in America, 1650-1870* (New York: W. W. Norton & Co., 1983), 160-161, 192-193, 222. *Official Catalogue of the New-York Exhibition of the Industry of All Nations*, revised edition (New York: G. P. Putnam & Co., 1853), 63. *The Eastern Mail* (Waterville, ME) 16 October and 13 November 1851.

11. *Maine Business Directory* (Boston: Briggs & Co., 1867), 268; Montgomery, 225; James S. Leamon, *Historic Lewiston: A Textile City in Transition* (Lewiston, ME: Lewiston Historical Commission, 1976), 12-13; Androscoggin Mills directors' records (1860-1928), Bates Manufacturing Co., on deposit at Maine Historical Society, Portland.

12. Boston city directories for the years 1835 to 1856; Eliza H. Sprague kindly verified his Danvers residency; Middlesex County Registry of Deeds, Book 740: 332-334; Helen R. Pinkney, *Christopher Gore: Federalist of Massachusetts, 1758-1817* (Waltham, MA: Gore Place Society, 1969), 49-50.

13. "Barlow's Insurance Surveys for Danvers Bleachery," 1874 and 1889, Museum of American Textile History; Albert Emerson Benson, *History of the Massachusetts Horticultural Society* (Boston: Massachusetts Horticultural Society, 1929), 115.

14. [Charles W. Eliot], 239-243.

15. Sprague, "The Reverend Samuel Walker and His Descendants"; Guardianship, Essex County Registry of Probate, New Series, Book 80:162; Theodore Woodman Gore, comp., "The Gore Family: John Gore of Roxbury and His Descendants to the Ninth Generation," (typescript, n.d., ca. 1989), 187, Gore Place Society (hereafter GPS); Theophilus Walker, docket 27910, Middlesex County Registry of Probate.

16. Pinkney, 48-50, 65-66, 82-83; Harold and James Kirker, *Bulfinch's Boston, 1787-1817* (New York: Oxford University Press, 1964, endpapers).

17. Pinkney, 84-87; Hammond, 121-124.

18. Edward Augustus Kendall, *Travels through the Northern Parts of the United States in the Years 1807 and 1808*, 3 vols. (New York: I. Riley, 1809), 3:10; Hammond, 120, 124; Pinkney, 86-87, floor plan illustrated in signature opposite 87.

19. Justin Winsor, *The Memorial History of Boston, 1630-1880*, 4 volumes (Boston: Ticknor & Fields, 1881), 4:634.

20. Hammond, 1, 120, 124; Benson, 115; Pinkney, 49-50.

21. Federal census for 1860, 1870, 1880, 1890, and 1900, National Archives and Records Administration, Waltham, MA; Middlesex County Registry of Deeds, Book 967:71-75; see Waltham and Watertown city directory extracts at GPS which Edythe Cederlund kindly noted.

22. "Journal of Manuel Fenollosa, Salem, Massachusetts, commencing February 7, 1848, on his tour to Europe in the Bark Sophia Walker, Capt. E. Wiswell," Phillips Library, Peabody-Essex Museum; W. H. Whitmore, comp., *The Genealogy of the Families of Payne and Gore* (Boston, 1875), 29-30. Mary Sophia's photograph at GPS is marked "Grillet & Cie, Photographes du Roi, Chiatamone, 6, Naples." Theophilus Walker to Leonard Woods, 30 August 1852 penned inside Leonard Woods to Theophilus Walker, 24 August 1852, Woods correspondence, BCSC. Martha F. McCourt and Thomas R. Luce, *The American Descendants of Henry Luce of Martha's Vineyard, 1640-1985*, 4 volumes (Vancouver, WA: Mrs. James McCourt, 1985), 2:531.

23. Richard C. Nylander, Elizabeth Redmond, and Penny J. Sander, *Wallpaper in New England: Selections from the Society for the Preservation of New England Antiquities* (Boston: Society for the Preservation of New England Antiquities, 1986), 12-13, 168-169, 194-195; Hammond, 125. Whitmore, 29-30. In a series of photographs by Frank Cousins (Phillips Library, Peabody-Essex Museum, and Society for the Preservation of New England Antiquities) taken around 1911, the furnishings had been removed, but many of the wallpapers are clearly depicted. GPS retains fragments of some of the mid-nineteenth-century papers; further study should help determine place and date of manufacture.

24. Katharine J. Watson observed the connection between Gore Place's oval parlor and the Sophia Walker Gallery during a 1990 visit to Gore Place. Adolph S. Cavallo, *Tapestries of Europe and of Colonial Peru in the Museum of Fine Arts, Boston*, 2 vols. (Boston: Museum of Fine Arts, 1967), 1:109-115; will and codicils of Mary Sophia Walker, Walker papers, BCSC.

25. Will and codicils of Mary Sophia Walker, Walker papers, BCSC.

26. Marian Lawrence Peabody, *To Be Young Was Very Heaven* (Boston: Houghton Mifflin, 1967), 305-306.

27. *The Church Militant* 7, no. 2 (Boston, March 1904); Nora Murphy, archivist for the Episcopal diocese, kindly provided a copy of the article on the Walker bequest. Copy of the diocese convention resolution in Mary Sophia Walker, docket 64003, Middlesex County Registry of Probate. Will and codicils of Mary Sophia Walker, Walker papers, BCSC.

28. Copy of the diocesan convention resolution in Mary Sophia Walker, docket 64003, Middlesex County Registry of Probate; a search of subsequent diocesan convention minutes may reveal the vote that approved the sale of Gore Place. Walter F. Starbuck, *Picturesque Features of the History of Waltham* (Waltham, MA: Waltham Publishing Co., 1917), 19-23; Lorette Treese, "The Gores of Gore Place," *Early American Life* 22, no. 2 (April 1991): 66.

LIST OF ILLUSTRATIONS

1. Gore Place, Waltham, Massachusetts,
   ca. 1890-1895
   Photograph by the Halliday Historic
      Photograph Company
   Courtesy of the Society for the Preservation
      of New England Antiquities

2. Androscoggin Mills, Lewiston, Maine,
   1874-1876
   Photograph by Drew & Worthing
   Courtesy of the Society for the Preservation
      of New England Antiquities

3. Harry Fenn
   English, 1845-1911
   The Interior of Walker and Bro. Counting Room
   (17 Merchants Row, Boston), 1893
   ink and wash heightened with white on
      paper
   14 x 21 inches
   Gift of the Misses Harriet Sarah and Mary
      Sophia Walker
   1904.34

AUTHORS

RICHARD H. SAUNDERS III, who contributed the introductory biography, "James Bowdoin III (1752-1811)," is a 1970 graduate of Bowdoin College and assistant professor of art and director of the Museum of Art at Middlebury College. One of his areas of scholarly specialization is American colonial portraiture. In 1987, he coauthored the exhibition catalogue *American Colonial Portraits, 1700-1776* with Ellen G. Miles for the National Portrait Gallery. His book *John Smibert (1688-1751): A Scottish Artist in Italy, England and America* will be published for the Barra Foundation and Yale University Press in 1994. Another area of research for Mr. Saunders is early patronage of the arts in America; his study with Helen Raye, *Daniel Wadsworth: Patron of the Arts*, accompanied an exhibition of the same title at the Wadsworth Atheneum in 1981.

CLIFTON C. OLDS, author of "The Intellectual Foundations of the College Museum," is Edith Cleaves Barry Professor of the History and Criticism of Art at Bowdoin College and former acting director of the Museum of Art. A scholar of European medieval and Renaissance art and society, specifically the art of Albrecht Dürer and the imagery of love and death, Professor Olds has most recently written on the philosophy of art and theory regarding the teaching of art history. His interest in the history of the American college museum began with his research on German *Wunderkammern*, from which the campus museum descends.

LINDA J. DOCHERTY, who wrote "Preserving Our Ancestors: The Bowdoin Portrait Collection," is associate professor of art history at Bowdoin and a specialist in American and nineteenth-century European art and criticism, focusing on problems of national identity in art, the relationship between art and science, and portraiture. She is currently writing a book, *Native Art/National Art: Art Criticism, Scientific Culture, and American Identity, 1876-1893*. Professor Docherty has also been a curatorial advisor on the portrait installation for the *Legacy* exhibition.

KENNETH E. CARPENTER, author of "James Bowdoin III as Library Builder" and a 1958 graduate of Bowdoin College, is assistant director for research resources, Harvard University Library, and editor of *The Harvard Library Bulletin* and *The Harvard University Library: A Documentary History*, a microfiche publication of 1990. He has lectured and published extensively on the bibliography of economic literature and the origin and history of early American libraries, including *The First 350 Years of the Harvard University Library* of 1986. Mr. Carpenter is also exhibition consultant for the display of the books.

ARTHUR M. HUSSEY II, professor of geology, has for years taught Bowdoin classes using mineralogical specimens and crystal models given by James Bowdoin III. He is a senior field geologist with the Maine Geological Survey, does field investigations in the southwestern region of the state, and has contributed numerous maps to the Geological Survey. Mr. Hussey bases his essay, "James Bowdoin III and Geology at Bowdoin College," on research begun by Benjamin B. Burbank, who first published the historic mineral collections in the 1980s.

SUSAN E. WEGNER, author of "Copies and Education: James Bowdoin's Painting Collection in the Life of the College," is associate professor of art history at Bowdoin College. In her earlier research and publications, many of which deal with Sienese art of the sixteenth and early seventeenth centuries, Professor Wegner concentrated on the doctrine of imitation in Italian art and the value of copies in sixteenth-century artistic education, concerns that inform her research on this project. At the 1991 meetings of the College Art Association, she presented a paper entitled "The Collection of James Bowdoin III (1752-1811)." Ms. Wegner also has acted as curatorial consultant for the installation of James Bowdoin III's European paintings and prints in the exhibition.

LILLIAN B. MILLER, advisor to *The Legacy of James Bowdoin III*, has written the concluding essay, "The Legacy: The Walker Gift, 1894." Ms. Miller is historian of American culture and editor of the Peale Family Papers at the National Portrait Gallery, Smithsonian Institution, and much of her scholarship relates to the Peale family of artists. She served as curator of the 1992-1993 exhibition *In Pursuit of Fame: Rembrandt Peale: 1778-1860* at the National Portrait Gallery and published a biography of Peale bearing the same title to accompany the exhibition (University of Washington Press, 1992). She is presently working on volume 4 of *Selected Papers of Charles Willson Peale and His Family* (Yale University Press) and *Rembrandt Peale: A Catalogue Raisonné*. Among her most important books is *Patrons and Patriotism: The Encouragement of the Fine Arts in the United States 1790-1860*, published in 1966 and 1974, which serves as background for *The Legacy of James Bowdoin III*. She has begun a sequel volume, *The Hereditary Tradition: Artistic Taste and Collections in the United States, 1860-1920*.

LAURA FECYCH SPRAGUE'S appendix essay documents the lives of the Walker family. Her research is one part of her responsibility as curator of the Walker Gallery section of the *Legacy* exhibition. Ms. Sprague is consulting curator of decorative arts at the Bowdoin College Museum of Art and is a scholar of American decorative arts and of the colonial and federal culture of Maine. She served as editor and contributing author for the 1987 catalogue *Agreeable Situations: Society, Commerce, and Art in Southern Maine, 1780-1830* for the Brick Store Museum.

BOWDOIN COLLEGE MUSEUM OF ART

STAFF
Katharine J. Watson, *Director*
Suzanne K. Bergeron, *Assistant Director for Operations*
Helen S. Dubé, *Coordinator of Education Programs*
Chaké K. Higgison '78, *Museum Shop Manager*
Mattie Kelley, *Registrar*
José L. Ribas '76, *Technician*
Victoria B. Wilson, *Administrative Secretary to the Director*
Justin P. Wolff '92, *Andrew W. Mellon Curatorial Intern*

SECURITY OFFICERS
Edmund L. Benjamin
Jaime R. Reatiraza
Edward D. Ruszczyk

CUSTODIAN
Roger L. Nadeau

STUDENT ASSISTANTS
Kate H. Cheney '96
Peter D. DeStaebler '93
Rebecca Kirsten Griffiths '94
Mark P. Kontulis '95
Christopher A. Row '94
Jonathan D. Stuhlman '96
Meg P. Succop '94
Julia W. Vicinus '93
Jennifer M. Vondrak '95
Tanya F. Weliky '94

FORMER STAFF MEMBERS
participating in *The Legacy of James Bowdoin III*

John W. Coffey, *Curator of Collections*
Lorena A. Coffin, *Administrative Secretary to the Director*
Marilyn H. Dwyer, *Museum Shop Manager*
Donald A. Rosenthal, *Associate Director and Curator of Collections*
Krista S. Sullivan, *Museum Shop Manager*
Isabel L. Taube '92, *Andrew W. Mellon Curatorial Intern*
Henrietta M. Tye, *Registrar*
Marion M. Winkelbauer, *Museum Shop Manager*
Roxlyn C. Yanok, *Assistant Director for Operations*

BIBLIOGRAPHY

SPECIAL COLLECTIONS, HAWTHORNE-LONGFELLOW LIBRARY

As of this writing (January 1994), the records of the College are being transferred from Special Collections to the new College Archives. Most, if not all, of the documents marked BCSC in endnotes to this book will be housed in the Archives section of the Hawthorne-Longfellow Library (next to Special Collections on the third floor) from now on. They include: Bowdoin family papers, records, and correspondence, James Bowdoin III's two letterbooks, Sarah Bowdoin's diary, Governing Boards votes, Chapel papers, and correspondence among President Woods, William Northend, and the Walker sisters.

BOWDOIN-TEMPLE PAPERS, MASSACHUSETTS HISTORICAL SOCIETY

Many of the Bowdoin family letters and papers are in the Winthrop Papers in the Massachusetts Historical Society, Boston. Excerpts from unpublished documents in the society's collections are quoted with permission. Of particular interest in several of the essays is "An Inventory of Goods at Present in the House of James Bowdoin Esqr . . Done at His Request This 15th September 1774."

PUBLISHED ABOUT OR BY BOWDOIN COLLEGE

These publications, many of which are cited in more than one essay, do not appear in the individual bibliographies that follow.

Anderson, Patricia McGraw. *The Architecture of Bowdoin College.* Brunswick, ME: Bowdoin College Museum of Art, 1988.

Beam, Philip C. *Personal Recollections of the Museum of Art and the Department of Art at Bowdoin College.* Brunswick, ME: Bowdoin College Museum of Art, 1991.

Becker, David P. *Old Master Drawings at Bowdoin College.* Brunswick, ME: Bowdoin College Museum of Art, 1985.

Berreth, David S. *Nineteenth-Century American Paintings at Bowdoin College* (exh. cat.). Brunswick, ME: Bowdoin College Museum of Art, 1974.

Bowdoin Museum of Fine Arts, Walker Art Building. *Descriptive Catalogue of the Paintings, Sculpture, and Drawings and of the Walker Collection.* 4th ed. Brunswick, ME, 1930.

Brimmer, Martin. *Address delivered at Bowdoin College Upon the Opening of the Walker Art Building, June VII. MDCCCXCIV.* Boston and New York: Houghton Mifflin and Co., 1894.

Calhoun, Charles C. "An Acorn in the Forest." *Bowdoin* 61, 1, September 1987.

Calhoun, Charles C. *A Small College in Maine: Two Hundred Years of Bowdoin.* Brunswick, ME: Bowdoin College, 1993.

Cleaveland, Nehemiah, and Alpheus Spring Packard. *History of Bowdoin College.* Boston: James Ripley Osgood & Company, 1882.

Hatch, Lewis C. *The History of Bowdoin College.* Portland, ME: Loring, Short, and Harmon, 1927.

Helmreich, Ernst. *Religion at Bowdoin College: A History.* Brunswick, ME: Bowdoin College, 1982.

Herbert, Kevin. *Ancient Art in Bowdoin College.* Cambridge, MA: Harvard University Press, 1964.

Johnson, Henry. *Descriptive Catalogue of the Bowdoin College Art Collections.* Brunswick, ME: Bowdoin College, 1895, and rev. ed., 1903, 1906.

Kershaw, Gordon E. *James Bowdoin: Patriot and Man of the Enlightenment* (exh. cat.). Brunswick, ME: Bowdoin College Museum of Art, 1976.

Kershaw, Gordon E. *James Bowdoin II: Patriot and Man of the Enlightenment.* Lanham, MD: University Press of America, 1991.

Little, George Thomas. "Historical Sketch." In *General Catalogue of Bowdoin College and the Medical School of Maine 1794-1894.* Brunswick, ME: Bowdoin College, 1894.

Northend, William D. Dedication speech at the Walker Art Gallery. *The Bowdoin Orient,* 20 June 1894, 51.

Pols, Eileen S. "The Walker Art Building 1894: Charles F. McKim's First Museum Design." Master's thesis, University of Texas at Austin, 1985.

Porter, Barbara N. "Assyrian Bas-Reliefs at the Bowdoin College Museum of Art" (brochure). Brunswick, ME: Bowdoin College Museum of Art, 1989.

[Putnam, Henry.] *A Description of Brunswick, (Maine;) in Letters By a Gentleman from South Carolina, to a Friend in that State.* Brunswick, ME: Joseph Griffin, 1820.

Ray, Roger B. "Edna Marrett and Her Chapel Murals." *Bowdoin Alumnus.* 56, no. 2, Fall 1982.

Sadik, Marvin S. *Colonial and Federal Portraits at Bowdoin College.* Brunswick, ME: Bowdoin College Museum of Art, 1966.

Short, Freeman Milliken. "John LaFarge and His Painting 'Athens.'" *Bowdoin Quill* 3, no. 6 (June 1900): 161-64.

"The Picture 'Sold by Order of the Boards,'" *Bowdoin Orient* 7, no. 4, 6 June 1877.

Volz, Robert L. *Governor Bowdoin & His Family: A Guide to an Exhibition and a Catalogue* (exh. cat.). Brunswick, ME: Bowdoin College, 1969.

West, Richard V. *The Walker Art Building Murals, Occasional Papers, I.* Brunswick, ME: Bowdoin College Museum of Art, 1972.

The Winslows: Pilgrims, Patrons and Portraits (exh. cat.). Brunswick, ME: Bowdoin College Museum of Art, 1974.

JAMES BOWDOIN III (1752–1811)
RICHARD H. SAUNDERS III

Akers, Charles W. *The Divine Politician,* 1982.

Boylston, Ward Nicholas. Travel diary, 1773-1775. Massachusetts Historical Society, Boston.

Emerson, Amelia. *Early History of Naushon Island,* 1935.

Extract from A Disclosure By The Rev. J. S. Buckminster, Preached In The Church In Brattle Square, Boston, October, 1811, The Sabbath After the Interment Of Hon. James Bowdoin, 1848.

Frederick, Rudolph. *The American College and University,* 1962.

Griswold, A. Whitney. *Farming and Democracy,* 1952.

Jaffe, Irma B. *John Trumbull: Patriot-Artist of the American Revolution,* 1975.

"James Bowdoin and His Collection of Drawings," *Connoisseur* (December 1947).

Jenks, William. *An Eulogy Illustrative of the Life and Commemorative of the Beneficence of the Late Hon. James Bowdoin Esquire,* 1812.

Jensen, Merrill, and Robert A. Becker, eds. *The Documentary History of the First Federal Elections 1788–1790.* Vol. 1.

Kirker, Harold. *The Architecture of Charles Bulfinch,* 1969.

Morrison, Samuel Eliot. *Harrison Gray Otis,* 1969.

"Names of Carriage Holders in Boston 1768." *Massachusetts Historical Society Proceedings.* 2nd series, vol. 1.

Prime, Temple. *Some Account of the Bowdoin Family,* 1894.

Redmond, Elizabeth. "The Codman Collection of Pictures." *Old-Time New England* 71, 1981.

Shipton, Clifford K. *Sibley's Harvard Graduates.* Vol. 17. Boston: Massachusetts Historical Society, 1975.

Sizer, Theodore, ed. *The Autobiography of Colonel John Trumbull,* 1953.

Smith, Page. *John Adams.* Vol. 2. 1962.

Teynac, Françoise, Pierre Nolot, and Jean-Denis Vivien. *Wallpaper: A History,* 1981.

Watson, F. J. B. "Americans and French Eighteenth-Century Furniture in the Age of Jefferson." In *Jefferson and the Arts: An Extended View,* 1979.

Winsor, Justin. *Memorial History of Boston.* Vol. 4, 1880.

THE INTELLECTUAL FOUNDATIONS OF THE COLLEGE MUSEUM
CLIFTON C. OLDS

Aagaard-Mogensen, Lars, ed. *The Idea of the Museum: Philosophical, Artistic, and Political Questions.* Vol. 6 of *Problems in Contemporary Philosophy.* Lewiston, NY: Edwin Mellen Press, 1988.

Adams, Charles Francis. *Familiar Letters of John Adams and His Wife, Abigail Adams, During the Revolution.* New York: Hurd and Houghton, 1876.

Alexander, Edward. *Museums in Motion: An Introduction to the History and Function of Museums.* Nashville: American Association for State and Local History, 1979.

Baas, Jacquelynn. "A History of the Dartmouth College Museum." In *Treasures of the Hood Museum of Art, Dartmouth College.* New York: Hudson Hills Press in association with the Hood Museum of Art, Dartmouth College, 1985.

Bacon, Francis. *Gesta Grayorum.* English Reprint Series 22. Liverpool: Liverpool University Press, 1968.

Bazin, Germain. *The Museum Age*. Translated by Jane van Nuis Cahill. New York: Universe Books, 1967.

Bowen, W. Wedgwood. *A Pioneer Museum in the Wilderness*. Hanover, NH: Dartmouth College Museum, 1958.

Chetham, Charles. "Why the College 'Should Have its Gallery of Art.'" *Smith Alumnae Quarterly,* February 1980.

Cohn, Marjorie. *Francis Calley Gray and Art Collecting for America*. Cambridge, MA: Harvard University Press, 1986.

Comfort, George Fisk. "Esthetics in Collegiate Education." *The Methodist Quarterly Review,* October 1867.

Comstock, Helen. "The Yale Collection of Italian Paintings." *The Connoisseur* 118 (September 1946).

Constable, W. G. *Art Collecting in the United States of America: An Outline of a History*. London: Thomas Nelson and Sons, 1964.

Egbert, Donald. *Princeton Portraits.* Princeton: Princeton University Press, 1947.

Emerson, Ralph Waldo. *The Complete Works of Ralph Waldo Emerson*. Edited by E. W. Emerson. Vol. 7, *Art*. Boston: Houghton, Mifflin, 1904.

Faison, S. Lane, Jr. *Handbook of the Collection: Williams College Museum of Art*. Williamstown, MA: Williams College Museum of Art, 1979.

Fielding, Mantel. *Dictionary of American Painters, Sculptors and Engravers*. Edited by Glenn B. Opitz. Philadelphia: Lancaster Press, 1926, or Poughkeepsie, NY: Apollo, 1983.

Findlen, Paula. "The Museum: Its Classical Etymology and Renaissance Genealogy." *Journal of the History of Collections* 1, no. 1, 1989.

Gilman, Benjamin. *Museum Ideals of Purpose and Method*. Boston: Boston Museum of Fine Arts, 1918.

Handbook of the Gallery of Fine Arts. New Haven: Associates in Fine Arts at Yale University, 1931.

Harris, Jean. *Collegiate Collections 1776-1886*. South Hadley, MA: Mount Holyoke College, 1976.

Howe, Winifred. *A History of the Metropolitan Museum of Art*. New York: Metropolitan Museum of Art, 1913.

Hunter, Michael. "The Cabinet Institutionalized: The Royal Society's 'Repository' and Its Background." In *Origins of Museums*, edited by Oliver Impey and Arthur MacGregor. Oxford: Clarendon Press, 1985.

Impey, Oliver, and Arthur MacGregor, eds. *The Origins of Museums*. Oxford: Clarendon Press, 1985.

Jarves, James J. "American Museums of Art." *Scribner's Monthly* (July 1879).

————. "On the Formation of Galleries of Art." *Atlantic Monthly* (July 1860).

————. *Art Hints: Architecture, Sculpture, and Painting*. New York: Harper & Bros., 1855.

Kenseth, Joy. *The Age of the Marvelous*. Hanover, NH: Hood Museum of Art, Dartmouth College, 1991.

Lee, Rensselaer. "Ut Pictura Poesis: The Humanistic Theory of Painting." *Art Bulletin* 22 (1940).

Levine, Lawrence W. *Highbrow/Lowbrow: The Emergence of Cultural Hierarchy in America*. Cambridge, MA: Harvard University Press, 1988.

MacGregor, Arthur. "The Cabinet of Curiosities in Seventeenth-Century Britain." In *Origins of Museums*, edited by Oliver Impey and Arthur MacGregor. Oxford: Clarendon Press, 1985.

Miller, Lillian. *Patrons and Patriotism: The Encouragement of the Fine Arts in the United States, 1790-1860*. Chicago: University of Chicago Press, 1966.

"Museums of Art as a Means of Instruction," *Appleton's Journal* 15 (January 1870).

Offner, Richard. *Italian Primitives at Yale University*. New Haven: Yale University Press, 1927.

Orosz, Joel. *Curators and Culture: The Museum Movement in America, 1740-1870*. Tuscaloosa: University of Alabama Press, 1990.

Osborne, Carol. *Museum Builders in the West: The Stanfords as Collectors and Patrons of Art, 1870-1906*. Palo Alto: Stanford University Museum of Art, 1986.

Parris, Nina G., comp. *Checklist of the Paintings, Prints and Drawings in the Collection of the Robert Hull Fleming Museum*. Burlington: University of Vermont, 1977.

Perkins, Charles. "American Art Museums." *North American Review* 111, no. 228 (July 1870).

Richardson, Edgar, Brooke Hindle, and Lillian B. Miller. *Charles Willson Peale and His World*. New York: Harry N. Abrams, 1983.

Schildt, Göran. "The Idea of the Museum." In *The Idea of the Museum: Philosophical, Artistic, and Political Questions,* edited by Lars Aagaard-Mogensen. Vol. 6 of *Problems in Contemporary Philosophy.* Lewiston, NY: Edwin Mellen Press, 1988.

Schupbach, William. "Some Cabinets of Curiosities in European Academic Institutions." In *The Origins of Museums,* edited by Oliver Impey and Arthur MacGregor. Oxford: Clarendon Press, 1985.

Small, Harold A. *Form and Function: Remarks on Art.* Berkeley: University of California Press, 1947.

Smith College. *Bulletin of Smith College Hillyer Art Gallery,* May 1920.

———. *The Smith College Museum of Art Catalogue.* Northampton, MA: Smith College, 1937.

Stearns, John, and Donald Hansen. *The Assyrian Reliefs at Dartmouth.* Hanover, NH: Dartmouth College Museum, 1953.

Steegmuller, Francis. "James Jackson Jarves: Thumb-nail Sketch of a Collector." *Magazine of Art* 41 (April 1948).

———. *The Two Lives of James Jackson Jarves.* New Haven: Yale University Press, 1951.

Thurman, M. "Museums and Education: The Role of the Art Object." In *Museums and Education,* edited by Eric Larabee. Washington, D.C.: Smithsonian Institution Press, 1968.

Vanderbilt, Kermit. *Charles Eliot Norton: Apostle of Culture in a Democracy.* Cambridge, MA: Belknap Press of Harvard University Press, 1959.

Vassar College Art Gallery Catalogue. Poughkeepsie, NY: Vassar College, 1939.

Vassar College Art Gallery: Selections from the Permanent Collection. Poughkeepsie, NY: Vassar College, 1967.

von Schlosser, Julius. *Die Kunst- und Wunderkammern der Spätrenaissance: Ein Beitrag zur Geschichte des Sammelwessens.* Leipzig, 1908.

PRESERVING OUR ANCESTORS:
THE BOWDOIN PORTRAIT
COLLECTION
LINDA J. DOCHERTY

Ariès, Philippe. *Centuries of Childhood: A Social History of Family Life.* Translated by Robert Baldick. New York: Vintage Books, 1962.

Belknap, Waldron Phoenix, Jr. *American Colonial Painting: Materials for a History.* Cambridge: Belknap Press of Harvard University Press, 1959.

Breen, T. H. "The Meaning of 'Likeness': American Portrait Painting in an Eighteenth-Century Consumer Society." *Word and Image* 6 (October–December 1990).

Brilliant, Richard. *Portraiture.* London: Reaktion Books, 1991.

Calvert, Karin. "Children in American Family Portraiture, 1670 to 1810." *William and Mary Quarterly* 39 (January 1982).

Canaday, John. "With Special Reference to Robert Feke." *New York Times.* Sunday, 18 September 1966.

DeLorme, Eleanor Pearson. "Gilbert Stuart: Portrait of an Artist." *Winterthur Portfolio* 14 (Winter 1979).

Dresser, Louisa. "Christian Gullager, an Introduction to His Life and Some Representative Examples of His Work." *Art in America* 37 (July 1949).

Duncan, Carol. "Happy Mothers and Other New Ideas in Eighteenth-Century French Art." In *Feminism and Art History: Questioning the Litany,* edited by Norma Broude and Mary D. Garrard. New York: Harper and Row, Icon Editions, 1982.

Fairbrother, Trevor J. "John Singleton Copley's Use of British Mezzotints for His American Portraits: A Reappraisal Prompted by New Discoveries." *Arts* 55 (March 1981).

Fleischer, Roland E. "Emblems and Colonial American Painting." *American Art Journal* 20 (1988).

Fortune, Brandon Brame. "Charles Willson Peale's Portrait Gallery: Persuasion and the Plain Style." *Word and Image* 6 (October–December 1990).

Gerdts, William H. "Natural Aristocrats in a Democracy, 1810–1870." *American Portraiture in the Grand Manner: 1720-1920,* by Michael Quick. (exh. cat.) Los Angeles: Los Angeles County Museum of Art, 1981.

Lester, Katherine Morris and Bess Viola Oerke. *Accessories of Dress.* Peoria, IL: Manual Arts Press, 1940.

Lovell, Margaretta M. "Reading Eighteenth-Century American Family Portraits." *Winterthur Portfolio* 22 (Winter 1987).

Mason, George C. *The Life and Works of Gilbert Stuart, 1820-1894*. New York: B. Franklin Reprints, 1972.

Meyer, Arlene. "Portraiture." Paper presented at an NEH Summer Seminar for College Teachers, Houghton Library, Harvard University, 1990.

Miles, Ellen G., ed. *The Portrait in Eighteenth-Century America*. Newark, DE: University of Delaware Press, 1993.

Oliver, Andrew. *Portraits of John and Abigail Adams*. Cambridge: Harvard University Press, 1967.

Panofsky, Erwin. *Idea: A Concept in Art Theory*. Translated by Joseph J. S. Peake. New York: Harper & Row, Icon Editions, 1968.

Prown, Jules. *John Singleton Copley*. 2 vols. Washington, D.C.: National Gallery of Art, 1966; Cambridge: Harvard University Press, 1966.

Reynolds, Sir Joshua. *Discourses on Art*. Edited by Robert W. Wark. New Haven: Yale University Press, 1975.

Saunders, Richard H., and Ellen G. Miles. *American Colonial Portraits, 1700–1776* (exh. cat.). Washington D.C.: Smithsonian Institution Press for the National Portrait Gallery, 1987.

Severens, Martha R. "Jeremiah Theus of Charleston: Plagiarist or Pundit?" *Southern Quarterly* 24 (Fall–Winter 1985).

Shipton, Clifford K. *Sibley's Harvard Graduates*. Vol. 17. Boston: Massachusetts Historical Society, 1975.

Simon, Robin. *The Portrait in Britain and America*. Oxford: Phaidon, 1987.

Witness to America's Past: Two Centuries of Collecting by the Massachusetts Historical Society. (exh. cat.) Boston: Massachusetts Historical Society and Museum of Fine Arts, Boston, 1991.

JAMES BOWDOIN III AS LIBRARY BUILDER
KENNETH E. CARPENTER

Bentley, William. *Diary*. Vol. 2, January 1793-December 1802. Gloucester, MA, 1962.

"The Bowdoin Library." *Proceedings of the Massachusetts Historical Society* 51 (1918).

Bulliard, Pierre. *Herbier de la France, ou Collection complète des plantes indigènes de cet empire*. Paris, 1780–93.

Burbank, Benjamin B. "James Bowdoin and Parker Cleaveland." *Mineralogical Record* 19 (1988).

Carpenter, Kenneth E. *The First Hundred Years of the Harvard University Library*. Cambridge, MA: Harvard University Library, 1986.

Chipley, Louise. "The Enlightenment Library of William Bentley." *Essex Institute Historical Collections* 122 (1986).

Colbourn, H. Trevor. *The Lamp of Experience: Whig History and the Intellectual Origins of the American Revolution*. Chapel Hill: Published for the Institute of Early American History and Culture at Williamsburg, Virginia, by the University of North Carolina Press.

Dearborn, Benjamin. *The Columbian Grammar: Or, an Essay for Reducing a Grammatical Knowledge of the English Language to a Degree of Simplicity*. Boston: Printed for the author, 1795.

Dupuis, Charles François. *L'origine de tous les cultes, ou Religion universelle*. 1795.

Emerson, Amelia Forbes. *Early History of Naushon Island*. 2d ed. Boston: Howland and Company, 1981.

Gilreath, James, and Douglas L. Wilson. *Thomas Jefferson's Library: A Catalog with the Entries in His Own Order*. Washington, D.C.: Library of Congress, 1989.

Harris, Thaddeus Mason. *A Tribute of Respect, to the Memory of the Hon. James Bowdoin, Esq. in a Sermon, Preached at Dorchester, October 27, 1811*. Boston, 1811.

Herbst, Jurgen. *From Crisis to Crisis: American College Government 1636–1819*. Cambridge, MA: Harvard University Press, 1982.

Histoire des bibliothèques françaises: Les bibliothèques sous l'Ancien Régime 1530–1789, sous la direction de Claude Jolly. Paris, 1988.

Hoffer, Peter Charles. *Revolution and Regeneration: Life Cycle and the Historical Vision of the Generation of 1776*. Athens: University of Georgia Press, 1983.

Howe, M. A. DeWolfe. *The Humane Society of the Commonwealth of Massachusetts, an Historical Review, 1784–1916*. Boston, 1918.

Jenks, Reverend William. *An Eulogy, Illustrative of the Life, and Commemorative of the Beneficence of the Late Hon. James Bowdoin, Esquire, with the Notices of his Family; Pronounced in Brunswick, (Maine) at the Request of the Trustees and Overseers of Bowdoin College, on the Annual Commencement, Sept. 2d, 1812*. Boston, 1812.

Jones, Howard Mumford. *America and French Culture, 1750–1848*. Chapel Hill, NC, 1927.

Kraus, Joe W. "The Book Collections of Early American College Libraries." *Library Quarterly* 43 (1973).

Massachusetts Historical Society. *Collections of the Massachusetts Historical Society*. 7th series, vol. 6 (1907).

Massachusetts Society for Promoting Agriculture. *Rules and Regulations of the Massachusetts Society for Promoting Agriculture*. Boston, 1796.

McKay, George L. *American Book Auction Catalogues from 1713 to 1934*. New York, 1937.

Michener, Roger. "The Bowdoin College Library: From Its Beginnings to the Present Day." Master's thesis, University of Chicago Graduate Library School, 1972.

Murray, Craig C. *Benjamin Vaughan (1751–1835): The Life of an Anglo-American Intellectual*. New York: Arno Press, 1982.

Nason, Emma Huntington. *Old Hallowell on the Kennebec*. Augusta, ME, 1909.

Oleson, Alexandra. "Introduction: To Build a New Intellectual Order." In *The Pursuit of Knowledge in the Early American Republic: American Scientific and Learned Societies from Colonial Times to the Civil War*, edited by A. Oleson and Sanborn C. Brown. Baltimore and London: Johns Hopkins University Press, 1976.

Peterson, Merrill D. "The American Scholar: Emerson and Jefferson." In *Thomas Jefferson and the World of Books: A Symposium Held at the Library of Congress September 21, 1976*. Washington, D.C.: Library of Congress, 1977.

Poivre. *Travels of a Philosopher*. Augusta, ME, 1797.

Popkin, Jeremy D. "Journals: The New Face of News." In *Revolution in Print: The Press in France, 1775–1800*, edited by Robert Darnton and Daniel Roche. Berkeley and Los Angeles: University of California Press, 1989.

Quincy, Josiah. *The History of Harvard University*. Cambridge: John Owen, 1840.

Rutland, Robert A. *"Well Acquainted with Books," the Founding Framers of 1787, with James Madison's List of Books for Congress*. Washington, D.C., 1987.

Reinhold, Meyer. *Classica Americana: The Greek and Roman Heritage in the United States*. Detroit: Wayne State University Press, 1984.

Roche, Daniel. "Noblesses et culture dans la France du XVIIIe: Les lectures de la Noblesse." In *Buch und Sammler, Private und öffentliche Bibliotheken im 18. Jahrhundert; Colloquium der Arbeitsstelle 18. Jahrhundert Gesamthochschule Wuppertal, Universität Münster, Düsseldorf vom 26.-28. September 1977*. Heidelberg, 1979.

Sprague, Henry H. *An Old Boston Institution: A Brief History of the Massachusetts Charitable Fire Society*. Boston, 1893.

Stern, Madeleine B. "Joseph Nancrede, Franco-American Bookseller-Publisher, 1761–1841." *Papers of the Bibliographical Society of America* 70 (1976).

Taylor, Earl R. "Thomas Wallcut, 1758–1840: Portrait of a Bibliophile." *The Book Collector* 32 (1983).

Wellek, René. "Literature and Its Cognates." In *Dictionary of the History of Ideas*. New York, 1973.

Wilson, Douglas L. "Jefferson's Library." In *Thomas Jefferson: A Reference Biography*, edited by Merrill D. Peterson. New York, 1986.

Winans, Robert. *A Descriptive Checklist of Book Catalogues Separately Printed in America 1693-1800*. Worcester, 1981.

Wolf, Edwin, 2nd. "Great American Book Collectors to 1800." *Gazette of the Grolier Club*, no. 16 (June 1971).

JAMES BOWDOIN III AND GEOLOGY AT BOWDOIN COLLEGE
ARTHUR M. HUSSEY II

Burbank, Benjamin B. "The James Bowdoin Mineral Collection." *Maine Geology*, bulletin no. 2 (1982).

————. "James Bowdoin and Parker Cleaveland." *Mineralogical Record* 19 (1988).

Cleaveland, Parker. *An Elementary Treatise on Mineralogy and Geology*. Boston, MA: Cummings and Hilliard, 1816.

Merrill, George P. *The First Hundred Years of American Geology*. New Haven, CT: Yale University Press, 1924.

Yedlin, Neil. "Yedlin on micromounting." *Mineralogical Record* 7 (1976).

COPIES AND EDUCATION:
JAMES BOWDOIN'S PAINTING
COLLECTION IN THE LIFE OF
THE COLLEGE
SUSAN E. WEGNER

Andrews, Keith. *The Nazarenes: A Brotherhood of German Painters in Rome.* New York: Hacker Art Books, 1988.

Bailey, Colin B. "Conventions of the Eighteenth-Century *Cabinet de Tableau:* Blondel d'Azincout's *La première idée de la curiosité."* *Art Bulletin.* 69 (1987).

Bazin, Germain. *The Museum Age.* Translated by Jane van Nuis Cahill. New York: Universe Books, 1967.

Benjamin, Walter. "The Work of Art in the Age of Mechanical Reproduction." *Illuminations.*

Bibliothèque Nationale, Le 653, "Convention Nationale: Second Rapport sur la nécessité de la suppression de la Commission du Museum fait au nom des Comité d'Instruction Publique et des Finances par David." Nivose an II (16 January 1794).

Bober, Phyllis Pray, and Ruth Rubinstein. *Renaissance Artists and Antique Sculpture: A Handbook of Sources.* Oxford: Oxford University Press, 1986.

Brown, David Alan. *Raphael and America.* National Gallery of Art, Washington, D.C., 1983.

Chappell, Miles. "A Note on John Smibert's Italian Sojourn." *Art Bulletin* 64, no. 1 (March 1982).

Cohn, Marjorie B. *Francis Calley Gray and Art Collecting for America.* Cambridge: Harvard University Press, 1986.

de Vega, Lope. *The Case for Painting as a Liberal Art.* In *Diálogos de la pintura,* edited by Vincencio Carducho. Madrid, 1633. Translated from edition of D. G. Cruzada Villaamil (Madrid, 1865).

Docherty, Linda J. "Public Portraits, Private Lives: Gilbert Stuart's Portraits of Thomas Jefferson and James Madison for James Bowdoin III," forthcoming.

Draper, Warren L. *The Life and Character of Leonard Woods, D.D., L.L.D.* Andover, 1880.

Enggass, Robert, and Jonathan Brown. *Italy and Spain, 1600–1750, Sources and Documents.* Englewood Cliffs, NJ: Prentice-Hall, Inc., 1970.

Everett, Alexander. "Exhibition of Pictures at the Athenaeum Gallery." *North American Review* 31 (October 1830).

Everett, Charles Carroll. *Leonard Woods, A Discourse.* 9 July 1977.

Federhen, Deborah Anne, et al. *Accumulation and Display: Mass Marketing Household Goods in America 1880–1920.* Henry Francis du Pont Winterthur Museum, 1986.

Foote, Henry Wilder. *John Smibert Painter.* Cambridge, MA: Harvard University Press, 1950.

Fredericksen, Burton B., ed. *The Index of Paintings Sold in the British Isles During the Nineteenth Century.* Vol. 1, *1801-1805,* and vol. 2, *1806-1810.* Santa Barbara, CA: ABC-CLIO, ca. 1988-.

Freedberg, David. *The Power of Images, Studies in the History and Theory of Response.* Chicago: University of Chicago Press, 1989.

Gablik, Suzi. *The Reenchantment of Art.* New York: Thames and Hudson, 1991.

Gibson-Wood, Carol. "Jonathan Richardson and the Rationalization of Connoisseurship." *Art History* 7 (1984).

———. *Studies in the Theory of Connoisseurship from Vasari to Morelli.* New York: Garland, 1988.

Gilbert, Creighton. "On Castagno's Nine Famous Men and Women: Sword and Book as the Basis for Public Service." In *Life and Death in Fifteenth-Century Florence,* edited by Marcel Tetel, Ronald G. Witt, and Rona Goffen. Durham and London: Duke University Press, 1989.

Greenhalgh, Michael. *The Classical Tradition in Art. From the Fall of the Roman Empire to the Time of Ingres.* New York: Harper and Row, 1978.

Haskell, Francis, and Nicholas Penny. *Taste and the Antique: The Lure of Classical Sculpture, 1500–1900.* New Haven: Yale University Press, 1981.

Hevner, Carol E. "Rembrandt Peale's Dream and Experience of Italy." In *The Italian Presence in American Art 1760–1860,* edited by Irma B. Jaffe. New York: Fordham University Press, 1989.

Hilen, Andrew, ed. *The Letters of Henry Wadsworth Longfellow.* Cambridge, MA: Belknap Press of Harvard University Press.

Howard, Seymour. "Thomas Jefferson's Art Gallery for Monticello." *Art Bulletin* 59 (Dec. 1977).

Hughes, Robert. "Art, Morals, and Politics." *New York Review of Books,* 23 April 1992.

Hughes-Hallett, Lucy. *Cleopatra: Histories, Dreams and Distortions.* New York: Harper & Row, 1990.

Joost-Gaugier, C. L. "Poggio and Visual Tradition: *Uomini Famosi* in Classical Literary Description." *Artibus et historiae* 12 (1985).

Kimball, Fiske. "Jefferson and the Arts." *Proceedings of the American Philosophical Society* 87, no. 3 (July 1943).

Lambert, Susan. *The Image Multiplied, Five Centuries of Printed Reproductions of Paintings and Drawings.* New York: Abaris, 1987.

Lebrun, J. B. P. "Observations sur le Museum National par le Citoyen Lebrun, peintre et marchand de tableaux, pour servir de suite aux réflexions qu'il a déjà publiées sur le même objet." Paris: Bibliothèque Nationale, 1793.

Levine, Lawrence W. *Highbrow/Lowbrow, The Emergence of Cultural Hierarchy in America.* Cambridge, MA: Harvard University Press, 1988.

Mason, R. M., and M. Natale. *Raphael et la seconde main.* Geneva: Musée d'art et d'histoire, 1984.

McClellan, Andrew L. "Art Theory and Modes of Pictorial Display in Early Modern France." Chicago: CAA, 1992.

McClellan, Andrew L. "The Politics and Aesthetics of Display: Museums in Paris 1750–1800." *Art History* 7 (1984).

Miller, Lillian B. "'An Influence in the Air,' Italian Art and American Taste in the Mid-Nineteenth Century." In *The Italian Presence in American Art, 1760–1860,* edited by Irma B. Jaffe. New York: Fordham University Press, 1989.

Richardson, Jonathan, Sr. *Two Discourses. I. An Essay on the Whole Art of Criticism as it relates to painting shewing how to judge. I. Of the Goodness of a Picture; II. Of the Hand of the Master; and III. Whether 'tis an Original or a Copy. II. An Argument in Behalf of the Science of a Connoisseur; Wherein Is Shewn the Dignity, Certainty, Pleasure, and Advantage of It.* (1719). Part 1.

Saunders, Richard H. "John Smibert's Italian Sojourn—Once Again." *Art Bulletin* 66, no. 2 (June 1984).

———. *John Smibert (1688–1751): Anglo-American Portrait Painter.* 2 vols. Ph. D. diss., Yale University, 1979. Ann Arbor: UMI, 1982.

Schoonmaker, Marius. *John Vanderlyn.* Kingston, NY, 1950.

Schuyler, Montgomery. "Architecture of American Colleges VII: Brown, Bowdoin, Trinity, Wesleyan." *Architectural Record* (February 1911).

Spear, Richard. *Retaining the Original, Multiple Originals, Copies and Reproductions.* Vol. 20, *Studies in the History of Art .* National Gallery, 1989.

St. Augustine. *Confessions.* Translated by J. G. Pilkington. Ipswich: W. S. Cowell, Ltd., 1962.

Starn, Randolph. "Reinventing Heroes in Renaissance Italy." In *Art and History, Images and Their Meaning,* edited by Robert I. Rotberg and Theodore K. Rabb. Cambridge: Cambridge University Press, 1988.

Stein, Roger B. *John Ruskin and Aesthetic Thought in America, 1840–1900.* Cambridge: Harvard University Press, 1967.

Varney, George J. "The Art-Treasures of Bowdoin College." *Art Journal* (1880).

THE LEGACY:
THE WALKER GIFT, 1894
LILLIAN B. MILLER

Adams, Henry, et al. *John La Farge* (exh. cat.). New York: Abbeville Press for the Carnegie Museum of Art, Pittsburgh, and the National Museum of American Art, Smithsonian Institution, Washington, D.C., 1987.

Ashton, Dore, and Denise Browne Hare. *Rosa Bonheur: A Life and a Legend.* New York: Viking Press, 1981.

The Athenaeum Centenary: The Influence and History of the Boston Athenaeum from 1807 to 1907 with a Record of its Officers and Benefactors and a Complete List of Proprietors. Boston, 1907.

Bermingham, Peter. *American Art in the Barbizon Mood.* Washington, D.C.: Smithsonian Institute Press, 1975.

Blashfield, Edwin Howland. *Commemorative Tribute to Kenyon Cox.* New York, 1922.

Brimmer, Martin. "The Museum of Fine Arts Boston." *The American Architect and Building News* (30 October 1880).

Brooks, Van Wyck. *New England: Indian Summer, 1865–1915.* New York: E. P. Dutton, [1940].

Bryan, Michael. *A Biographical and Critical Dictionary of Painters and Engravers, from the revival of the art under Cimabue to the present time.* London: G. Bell, 1816.

Cavallo, Adolph S. *Tapestries of Europe and of Colonial Peru in the Museum of Fine Arts, Boston.* 2 vols. Boston: Museum of Fine Arts, 1967.

"Charles Follen McKim." *More Books. The Bulletin of the Boston Public Library* [March 1931].

Cox, Kenyon. "Museums of Art and Teachers of Art." In *Art Museums and Schools: Four Lectures by G. Stanley Hall, Kenyon Cox, Stockton Axson, and Oliver S. Tonks.* New York: Charles Scribner's Sons, 1913.

———. *The Classic Point of View. Six Lectures on Painting Delivered on the Scammon Foundation at the Art Institute of Chicago in the Year 1911.* New York: C. Scribner's Sons, 1911.

Crowe, Joseph Archer, and G. B. Cavalcaselle. *A History of Painting in Italy, Umbria, Florence, and Siena from the Second to the Sixteenth Century.* 1864. Edited by Langston Douglas. New York: Scribner's, 1903–14.

———. *The Early Flemish Painters.* London, 1857.

Downes, William Howe. "Boston Painters and Paintings." *Atlantic Monthly* 62 (1888).

Fink, Lois Marie. "The Innovation of Tradition in Late Nineteenth-Century American Art." *The American Art Review* 10, 2 (November 1978).

———. *American Art at the Nineteenth-Century Paris Salons.* New York and Cambridge: Cambridge University Press, 1990.

Gilman, Benjamin Ives. *Museum Ideals of Purpose and Method.* Cambridge: Harvard University Press, 1923.

Green, Martin. *The Mount Vernon Street Warrens.* New York, 1989.

Hyde, William DeWitt. *Practical Idealism.* New York, 1897, 1899, 1905, 1908.

Kugler, Franz Theodor. *Handbook of Painting: The Italian Schools of Painting. Based on the Handbook of Kugler.* Edited and revised by Austen Henry Layard.

La Farge, John. "The American Academy at Rome, The Field of Art." *Scribner's Magazine* 28 (August 1900).

Lears, T. Jackson. *No Place of Grace: Antimodernism and the Transformation of American Culture, 1880–1920.* New York: Pantheon Books, 1981.

Marius. *Dutch Painters of the Nineteenth Century.* Edited by Geraldine Norman. Reprint ed. Woodbridge: Suffolk, England, 1973.

Mather, Frank Jewett, Jr. "John La Farge—An Appreciation." *The World's Work* 21, no. 5 (March 1911).

Metropolitan Museum of Art. *In Pursuit of Beauty: Americans and the Aesthetic Movement.* New York, 1986.

Miller, Lillian B. *Patrons and Patriotism: The Encouragement of the Fine Arts in the United States, 1790–1860.* Chicago: University of Chicago Press, 1966.

Moore, Charles Herbert. *The Life and Times of Charles Follen McKim.* Boston, 1929.

Morelli, Giovanni (1816–1891). *Italian Painters: Critical Studies of Their Works.* Translated by J. Murray. London.

———. *Italian Masters in German Galleries.* Translated by Mrs. Louis M. Richter, London, 1883.

Museum of Fine Arts, Boston. *Annual Report of the Trustees of the Museum of Fine Arts.* Vols. 14–21 (1889–1896). Boston, MA, 1890–1897.

Perkins, Charles C. "American Art Museums." *North American Review* 111 (July 1870).

———. "Museums of Art." *Journal of the American Social Science Association.*

Pollock, Griselda. *Vision and Difference: Femininity, Feminism and Histories of Art.* London and New York: Routledge, 1988.

Richardson, E. P. *Painting in America: From 1502 to the Present.* New York, 1956, 1965.

Roth, Leland. "McKim, Mead & White Reappraised." In *Monograph of the Works of McKim Mead & White 1879–1915.* New York: B. Blom, 1973.

———. *McKim, Mead and White Architects.* New York: Fordham University Press, 1983.

Samuels, Ernest. *Bernard Berenson: The Making of a Connoisseur.* Cambridge, MA, and London, England: Belknap Press of Harvard University Press, 1979.

Sheldon, George William. *Recent Ideals of American Art.* New York and London: Garland Publishers, 1888, repr. 1977.

Simon, Janice. "*The Crayon,* 1855–1861: The Voice of Nature in Criticism, Poetry, and the Fine Arts." 2 vols. Ph.d. diss., University of Michigan, 1990.

Soria, Regina. *Elihu Vedder: American Visionary Artist in Rome (1836–1923).* Cranbury, NJ: Fairleigh Dickinson University Press, 1970.

Stein, Roger. *John Ruskin and Aesthetic Thought in America, 1840–1900.* Cambridge, MA: Harvard University Press, 1967.

Strahan, Edward, ed. *The Art Treasures of America: Being the Choicest Works of Art in the Public and Private Collections of North America.* 3 vols., 1879–1882. Reprint ed., New York and London, 1977.

Sutton, Denys, ed. *The Letters of Roger Fry.* 2 vols. New York, 1972.

Swan, Mabel M. *The Athenaeum Gallery, 1827-1873.* Boston: Boston Athenaeum, 1940.

Tolles, Bryant F., Jr. and Carolyn K. Tolles. *Architecture in Salem: An Illustrated Guide.* Salem, MA: Essex Institute with the cooperation of Historic Salem, 1983.

Troyen, Carol, and Pamela S. Tabbas. *The Great Boston Collectors.* Boston: Museum of Fine Arts, 1984.

Van Hook, Bailey. "From the Lyrical to the Epic. Images of Women in American Murals at the Turn of the Century." *Winterthur Portfolio* 26, 1 (Spring 1991).

Vasari, Giorgio. *Lives of the Eminent Painters, Sculptors and Architects.* Florence, 1550. Translated by Mrs. Jonathan Foster. 6 vols. London, 1850–1907, many editions.

Vedder, Elihu. *The Digressions of V. Written for his own Fun and that of his Friends.* Boston and New York: Houghton Mifflin Company, 1910.

Warner, Marina. *Monuments and Maidens: The Allegory of the Female Form.* New York: Atheneum, 1985.

Weinberg, H. Barbara. "American 'High' Renaissance: Bowdoin's Walker Art Building and Its Murals." In *The Italian Presence in American Art, 1860-1920*, edited by Irma B. Jaffe. New York: Fordham University Press, and Rome: Istituto della Enciclopedia Italiana, 1992.

———. *The Decorative Work of John La Farge.* New York: Garland Publishers, 1977.

Wells, H. G. *The Future in America.* New York: St. Martin's Press, 1906.

White, Nelson C. *Abbott H. Thayer, Painter and Naturalist.* Hartford, CT: William L. Bauhan, 1951.

Whitehill, Walter Muir. *Museum of Fine Arts Boston: A Centennial History.* 2 vols. Cambridge: Belknap Press of Harvard University Press, 1970.

Yarnell, James L., and William H. Gerdts, comps. *The National Museum of American Art's Index to American Art Exhibition Catalogues.* Boston, MA, 1986.

THEOPHILUS WHEELER WALKER AND GORE PLACE
LAURA FECYCH SPRAGUE

Androscoggin Mills directors' records (1860–1928), on deposit by Bates Manufacturing Co., Lewiston, ME, at Maine Historical Society, Portland.

"Barlow's Insurance Surveys for Danvers Bleachery." 1874 and 1889.

Benson, Albert Emerson. *History of the Massachusetts Horticultural Society.* Boston: Massachusetts Horticultural Society, 1929.

Boardman, Samuel. *The Agriculture and Industry of the County of Kennebec, Maine, with Notes upon Its History and Natural History.* Augusta, ME: Kennebec Journal Office, 1867.

Cavallo, Adolph S. *Tapestries of Europe and of Colonial Peru in the Museum of Fine Arts, Boston,* 2 vols. Boston: Museum of Fine Arts, 1967.

The Church Militant 7, no. 2. Boston, March 1904.

[Eliot, Charles W.], *Charles Eliot, Landscape Architect.* Boston: Houghton, Mifflin & Co., 1902.

Federal census for 1870, 1880, 1890, and 1900. National Archives and Records Administration, Waltham, MA.

Fenellosa, Manuel. "Journal of Manuel Fenollosa, Salem, Massachusetts, commencing February 7, 1848, on his tour to Europe in the Bark Sophia Walker, Capt. E. Wiswell." Phillips Library, Peabody-Essex Museum, Salem, MA.

Gore, Theodore Woodman, comp. "The Gore Family: John Gore of Roxbury and His Descendants to the Ninth Generation." Typescript, n.d., ca. 1989. Gore Place Society, Waltham, MA.

Hammond, Charles A. "Where the Arts and Virtues Unite: Country Life Near Boston, 1637–1862." Ph.D. diss., Boston University, 1982.

Kendall, Edward Augustus. *Travels through the Northern Parts of the United States in the Years 1807 and 1808.* 3 vols. New York: I. Riley, 1809.

Kingsbury, Henry D., and Simeon L. Deyo, eds. *Illustrated History of Kennebec County, Maine.* 2 vols. New York: H. W. Blake & Co., 1892.

Kirker, Harold and James. *Bulfinch's Boston, 1787–1817.* New York: Oxford University Press, 1964.

Leamon, James S. *Historic Lewiston: A Textile City in Transition*. Lewiston, ME: Lewiston Historical Commission, 1976.

Lincoln, Samuel B. *Lockwood Greene: The History of an Engineering Business, 1832–1958*. Brattleboro, VT: Stephen Greene Press, 1960.

McCourt, Martha F., and Thomas R. Luce. *The American Descendants of Henry Luce of Martha's Vineyard, 1640–1985), 4 vols. Vancouver, WA: Mrs. James McCourt, 1985.

Montgomery, Florence M. *Textiles in America, 1650–1870*. New York: W. W. Norton & Co., 1983.

Myers, Denys Peter. *Maine Catalog: Historic American Buildings Survey*. Augusta: Maine State Museum, 1974.

Nylander, Richard C., Elizabeth Redmond, and Penny J. Sander. *Wallpaper in New England: Selections from the Society for the Preservation of New England Antiquities*. Boston: Society for the Preservation of New England Antiquities, 1986.

Official Catalogue of the New-York Exhibition of the Industry of All Nations. Rev. ed. New York: G. P. Putnam & Co., 1853.

Peabody, Marian Lawrence. *To Be Young Was Very Heaven*. Boston: Houghton Mifflin, 1967.

Reed, Roger G. "Amos D. Lockwood." *A Biographical Dictionary of Architects in Maine*. Augusta: Maine Historic Preservation Commission, forthcoming.

Sprague, Laura Fecych. "A Life of Industry and Preservation: A Short History of Theophilus Wheeler Walker," and "The Reverend Samuel Walker and His Descendants," unpublished reports, 1993, BCMA.

Starbuck, Walter F. *Picturesque Features of the History of Waltham*. Waltham, MA: Waltham Publishing Co., 1917.

Treese, Lorette. "The Gores of Gore Place." *Early American Life* 22, no. 2, April 1991.

Wells, John A. *The Peabody Story: Events in Peabody's History, 1629–1972*. Salem, MA: Essex Institute, 1972.

Whitmore, W. H., comp. *The Genealogy of the Families of Payne and Gore*. Boston, 1875.

Winsor, Justin. *The Memorial History of Boston, 1630–1880*, 4 vols. Boston: Ticknor & Fields, 1881.

INDEX

Italic page numbers refer to illustrations or captions.

A

Abbot, John, 113-15, 118n.1, 123n.78
Abbott, Samuel A. B., 209n.38
Académie Royale des Sciences, 38
Accum, Frederick, 129-30
Achilles Among the Daughters of Lycomedes (attr. to Francken), 149, *152*, 153, 177
Adam and Eve (Vinton, after Flandrin), 153, 154
Adams, Abigail, 5, 13, 59
Adams, John, 13, 27n.83, 46, *67*, 67, 109, 119n.6, 136
Adams, Samuel, 109
Adoration of the Magi (after Cornelius), *147*, 153
Aesthetic Movement, 190, 208n.20
Aesthetics, 195, 210n.51. *See also* Ruskin, John
Africa (Petrarch), 171n.94
Agriculture societies, 13, 107, 121n.53, 220
Albrecht V, Duke of Bavaria, 37, 44
Alchemy, 36
Aldrovandi, Ulisse, 37, 38
Alexandria, Egypt, library of, 49n.8
Alexandria, cargo vessel, 7
Allegheny County Courthouse and Jail (Richardson), 191
Allegory of Fruitfulness, formerly *Venus and Ceres* (Schut), 153, *160*
Allston Art Club, 197
Amerbach, Bonifacius, 38
American Academy, Rome (McKim), 209n.30
American Academy of Arts and Sciences, 16, 85, 91, 107, 119n.16, 120n.23, 122n.67
American Journal of Science and Art, 40
American Ornithology (Wilson), 97
American Philosophical Society, 50n.24
Amherst College, acquires Assyrian bas-reliefs, 52n.67
Ancient Art in Bowdoin College (Herbert), 160
Anderson, Patricia McGraw, 154
Andrews, Henry E., 159
Androscoggin Mills, Lewiston (ME), 217, *218*, 218
Ann, Princess of Denmark, portraits of, *62*, 63
Annunciation (after Jalabert), 153
Anthropology, 36
Antwerp altarpiece (Rubens), 153, 170n.63
Apollo Belvedere, plaster cast of, 158
Appleton, Jesse, 85, 119n.7
Archaeological Institute of America, 53n.78
Architecture, 191-92, 209nn.29-30, 209n.32, 209n.41, 217-19
Ariadne (anon.), gift of JB III to Jefferson, *16*, 17-18, 22, *143*, 144, 167n.14
Armstrong, Gen. John, *16*, 18, 19-20
Art: auctions of, 199; canon of masterworks, 165; copies (*see* Copies of art); display of, in 18th-c. France, 147-48; as experience, 195; fine versus useful, 42-3; framing, 167n.11; God's, 45; as history, 41-42; JB II's books on, 112-13; JB III's books on, 168-69n.35; as material culture, 195, 210n.53; modernism in, 165; moral value of, 44-46, 145, 149, 150-51, 163, 166, 170n.78, 171n.94, 195, 210n.53; and nature, 195; nudes, 150-51, 180, 199, 201, 211n.69; originality in, 141, 157, 165; place of, and museums, 192-95; and religion, 195; sacred, in JB III's collection, 167n.7 (*see also* Bowdoin College: Chapel); and science, 39-41, 157; as surrogate for religion, 52n.65

Art collections: Boston Museum of Fine Arts (*see* Boston Museum of Fine Arts); JB II's, 141; JB III's, 5, 8-9, 20, 21-22, 25, 55-79, 141-43, 148-49, 167n.7, *168*, 170n.60, 187; Bowdoin College, 33, 85-86, 149-57 (*see also* Walker Art Building); Martin Brimmer's, 211n.79; John A. Brown's, 211n.79; Charleston Museum, 49n.7; Chicago Art Institute, 47; Corcoran Gallery, 47; Dartmouth College, 33, 52n.67 (*see also* Hood Museum of Art); Harvard University, 33, 43-44, 47, 48, 50n.28; Hooper family, 211n.79; H. P. Kidder's, 211n.79; Thomas Jefferson's, *16*, 17-18, 22, 52n.70, 144, 145, 146, 148; Metropolitan Museum of Art, New York, 43, 47, 192; Mount Holyoke College, 34, 39, 40; Notre Dame, 34; Oberlin College, 48; Pennsylvania Academy of Fine Arts, 50n.24; Philadelphia Museum of Art, 47; of portraits, 41, 51n.34; Princeton University, 34, 41, 48; Quincy Shaw's, 211n.79; Smith College, 34, 47; Stanford University, 34; Robert C. Taft's, 211n.79; University of Michigan, 43; University of Vermont, 34, 43, 52n.67; Vassar College, 34, 40, 43, 44, 45; Walker sisters', 188; Thomas Wigglesworth's, 211n.79; Yale University, 33, 34, 39, 40-42, 43, 47, 51n.29, 52n.67
Art dealers, 197, 199, 206
Art Idea, the (Vedder), see *Rome Representative of the Arts* (Vedder)
Arts, the (Cox), 198
Ashmole, Elias, 26n.21, 38
Ashmolean Museum, Oxford, 26n.21, 37, 38, 46
Assurnasirpal II, relief carvings of, 33, 45-46, 52n.67, 159, *193*, 194, 210n.47
Astronomy, 36
Athens (La Farge), 195, 198, *200*
Auctions: art, 199; book, 95-96, 120n.32
Augustine of Hippo, Saint, 180

B

Babylonians Consuming Offerings Made to the Idol Bel, formerly *Church Interior with a Meal by Candlelight* (attr. to Steenwyck), *178*, 178-79
Bacon, Francis, 37-38
Badger, Joseph, portrait of JB I by, *58*, 61, 78n.28
Baptism of Christ (Lathrop), 154
Barbizon painters, 204, 211n.79, 212n.81
Barnet, William, 88
Barrois, Théophile, 101
Basel, university museum at, 38
Baudouin, Pierre, 60, 178, 179
Baxter, James Phinney, 207
Bayard, Mary Bowdoin, 78n.31
Bazin, Germain, 41, 42
Beacon Hill, Boston: Bulfinch row houses on, 191; Bowdoin house on, 13, 120n.25
Beam, Philip C., 159, 171n.83
Beauty, 34, 156, 202, 210n.53; utility of, 46-48
Beazley, J. D., 206
Benjamin, Walter, 76
Benson, Eugene, 41, 45, 46
Bentley, William, 85, 111
Berenson, Bernard, 203, 211n.77
Berkeley, Bishop George, 39, 60, 142

245

Scientific instruments, *see* "Philosophical apparatus"

Scipio Africanus Major, Publius Cornelius, 166, 171n.94

Scott, George, 2

Sculptor's Studio, a (anon.), 144

Sculpture: Assyrian (see Assurnasirpal II, relief carvings of); copies and casts of, 120n.27, 148-49, 158-62, 171n.80, 171n.83, 193, 203, 210.45

S. D. Warren paper mill, Westbrook (ME), 205

Sea Fight (Manglard), 143

Seaport (LaCroix), 143, 171n.91

Sears, J. Montgomery, 210n.60

Seelye, L. Clarke, 47

Séminaire de Québec, mineral collection at, 136

Shattuck Shell Collection, Bowdoin College, 132

Shaw, Quincy, 211n.79

Sheaff(e), William, Susannah, and Ann, 8

Sheldon, George William, 193

Shepley, John Rutherford, 156

Sherman, William Watts, La Farge's window designs for home of, 198

Silliman, Benjamin, 51n.29

Sills, Kenneth C. M., 159

Sketches of History (Lord Kames), 52n.70

Sleeping Cupid (after Mignard), 142

Sloan, John, 207

Smibert, John, 8, 60, 61, 78n.28; JB III's art purchases from, 167n.7, 171n.94; as copyist, 8, 9, 141-42, *165*, 166, 177; *Portrait of James Bowdoin II, 54,* 60-61

Smith, F. Hopkinson, 204

Smith, John, portrait of Princess Ann by, 62

Smith College art collection, 34, 47

Smithsonian Institution, 48

Sonne, Dr. Neils, 103

Sophia Walker, merchant ship, 221

Sophia Walker Gallery, Bowdoin College, 151, *154,* 155, 187, 205, 208n.4, 223n.24

Sophocles, bronze copy of statue of, 158, 170n.78, 204

South Kensington Museum, London (Victoria and Albert), 193

Sparks, Mrs. Jared, 153

Sprague, Eliza H., 222n.12

Sprague, Laura F., 188, 208, 209n.20

Stained glass windows, 198-99, 211nn.64-65

Stanford University Museum of Art, 34, 48

Stanford, Leland, 48

Steinberg, Leo, 180

Stevenson, Robert Louis, Saint-Gaudens's sculpture of, *201,* 204

Stewart, Duncan, 2, *3*

Storer, Bellamy, 153

Storer, Ebenezer, 123n.90

Stuart, Gilbert, 59; catalogue of JB III's art collection by, 153, 156, 177; *Portrait of Elizabeth Temple Winthrop,* 69, *70; Portrait of Elizabeth, Lady Temple,* 59, 70, 75, 76; *Portrait of James Bowdoin III, 12,* 17, 59, *66; Portrait of James Madison, 15,* 22, 68, *68,* 141, *142,* 143, 148, 156, 177; *Portrait of John Temple,* 70, 75; *Portrait of Sarah Bowdoin, 12,* 17, 59, 69, *71; Portrait of Sarah Winthrop Sullivan,* 59, 76, *76; Portrait of Thomas Jefferson, 14,* 22, 69, *141, 142,* 143, 148, 156, 171n.91, 177

Sullivan, George, 24, 72, 73, 79n.49

Sullivan, George R., *see* Bowdoin, George R. J.

Sullivan, James (great-nephew of JB III), *see* Bowdoin, James

Sullivan, James (judge), 10

Sullivan, Sarah Winthrop, 20, 24, 59, 64, 70, 72, 74, 75, 76, 79n.49

Swan, James, 12, 27n.83

Swift, George, 171n.91

Syracuse University, copies of fine art at, 43

System of Mineralogy and Metalurgy (Dodson), 127

T

Tableau Méthodique des Espèces Minérales (Lucas), 127

Taft, Robert C., 211n.79

Talleyrand-Périgord, Charles Maurice de, 19

Tammany American Museum, New York, 40

Tapestry: *Conference between Scipio and Hannibal before the Battle of Zama, 193,* 208n.19, 221; Raphael's cartoons for, 153, 170n.60

Tappan, Elizabeth Winthrop, 79n.59

"Tarpaulin Turnips," 28n.91

Taste, 44, 108, 156, 193, 206

Temple, Augusta, *see* Palmer, Augusta Temple

Temple, Elizabeth Bowdoin, 4, 10, 27n.49, 64, 68, 69-70, 79n.49, 86, 167n.5; Blackburn's portrait of, *3,* 26n.8, 59, 63, 64-65; Copley's portrait of, *6,* 70, *73,* 79n.55; Malbone's portrait of, 59, 69, 72; Stuart's portrait of, 59, 70, 75; Trumbull's portrait of, *9,* 59, 70, *74*

Temple, Grenville, 69, 70, *74,* 100

Temple, James Bowdoin, *see* James Temple Bowdoin

Temple, John, 4, *6,* 8, *9,* 10, 69, 70, *74,* 75, 79n.57

Temple, Aegina (Tilton), *206, 206,* 212n.92

Thacher, George, 119n.7

Thayer, Abbott H., *196, 197,* 197-98, 199, 210nn.59-60

Thayer, Mary and Gerald, 198

Theology, books on, 112, 119n.21

Thomas, Washington B., La Farge's window designs for home of, 198-99

Thomas, William W., 158

Tilton, John Rollin, 206

Titian (Tiziano Vercelli), 180; copies after, *140,* 142, *146,* 148, 150, *155,* 156, 170n.75, 179-80

Tokio Geisha Dancing in the House of Our Neighbor, Nikko (La Farge), 199, *199*

Tradescant, John, 38

Traité de Minéralogie (Haüy), 115, 127, *130, 132, 134*

Traité élementaire de minéralogie (Brochant), 127

Traité Elementaire de Minéralogie (Brongniart), 127

Tramp Abroad, a (Twain), 180

Transcendentalism, 34, 40

Transfiguration, the (Raphael), 154

Travel books, 111-12

Trinity Church, Boston (Richardson), 198, 211n.65

Trollope, Thomas Adolphus, 46

Troyon, Constant, *201*

Trumbull, John, 8, *9,* 10, 27n.49, 39, 70, *74*

Trumbull Gallery, Yale, 33, 39, 40, 51n.29

Truth, 156, 202; and art, 34-44

Twain, Mark (S. L. Clemens), 180

U

Union College, acquires Assyrian reliefs, 52n.67

Unitarian aesthetics, 195

Universal knowledge, 35, 39; ordering of, 147

University of Michigan, museum of art at, 43

University of Vermont: art collections, 34, 43, 52n.67; scientific collection, 39

Universo teatro, Quiccheberg's, 44

Upjohn, Richard, 150, 187, 218